THE **BUSINESS** OF **ADVICE**

How to manage and develop a successful financial advice business

Second edition

David Shelton

taxbriefs
financial publishing

The Business of Advice

Taxbriefs Limited
Centaur Media plc
St Giles House
50 Poland Street
London W1F 7AX

Telephone 020 7970 6471
Facsimile 020 7970 6485
info@taxbriefs.co.uk
www.taxbriefs.co.uk

ISBN 978-1-905482-52-8

British Library Cataloguing in Publication Data. A catalogue record for this book is available from the British Library.

Printed and bound in Great Britain by CPI Antony Rowe Ltd, Chippenham.

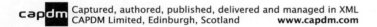 Captured, authored, published, delivered and managed in XML
CAPDM Limited, Edinburgh, Scotland   www.capdm.com

Author

David Shelton is an independent consultant with over 20 years of working in marketing and business development in the financial sector. For the last 12 years he has worked with a wide variety of IFAs specifically helping them deal with a range of business issues. These include strategic planning, designing service, effective marketing, managing people and implementing projects for change.

With unparalleled experience of running over 500 consultancy exercises across a range of advisory businesses, all the tools and techniques David sets out have proven effective and time efficient.

David has written many articles and speaks at conferences on the development of the financial advice market, with particular regard to distribution, service design, and business planning. He is a Fellow of the Chartered Institute of Marketing and is married with two grown up children.

Foreword

Fay Goddard,
Chief Executive of the Personal Finance
Society

Welcome to the second edition of *The Business of Advice*. The mission of the Personal Finance Society is far more than qualifications and technical updating. The Society is concerned with every member's professional development in its widest sense, and that means assisting members with their business planning and practice.

For this reason, we are pleased to support Taxbriefs in bringing you this revised publication, which includes updated sections on adviser charging and service design, as well as new case studies and examples. In addition, the associated website has brand new tools and templates along with additional modelling spreadsheets to help you determine the cost of your service and pricing policy.

The Business of Advice is well-named: providing financial advice is a business and we should make no apology for that. Delivering a professional and sustainable client service requires advisers to run well-managed and efficient businesses that also need to be profitable. In the new post Retail Distribution Review world, the challenge for advisory businesses will be even greater.

In summary, *The Business of Advice* provides a fully comprehensive toolkit which can be used in its entirety or selectively — it is not a text book but a unique manual and route map for enhancing every aspect of managing an advice business.

The author of *The Business of Advice*, David Shelton, is a widely acclaimed expert in the strategy and management of financial advisory businesses. He built his knowledge and skill advising hundreds of firms of advisers. So it is good to see all his experience and wisdom brought together in this invaluable publication.

Fay Goddard
May 2011

Skandia UK

Launched in 1979, Skandia UK is a leader in the new model of long-term investments, offering flexible and tax-efficient solutions. Skandia continues to lead the platform market with funds under management of £33.9 billion*, making it the largest investment platform operator in the UK market today.

Skandia is part of the wealth management business of Old Mutual plc, a leading international long-term savings group. Old Mutual plc has £303.1 billion* of funds under management and approximately 57,000 employees.

The Skandia platform is focused on meeting the needs of the end investor and is aimed exclusively at financial advisers who provide high quality, customer focused investment solutions. The platform offers the flexibility to tailor a service proposition and remuneration structure to meet the needs of each individual client or segment of clients. The platform also gives clients and advisers greater control over the process of investing from risk profiling and asset allocation through to the review and ongoing management of portfolios. Unlike many other platforms, it also creates an online audit trail for advisers to evidence their investment process and recommendations.

The platform has a consistent fund range across all tax wrappers offering a wide variety of investment strategies. These include:

- A wide range of mutual funds from which advisers can construct bespoke portfolios;
- A fully packaged range of risk rated funds for advisers that want to focus purely on their clients' financial planning goals and outsource both fund manager selection and asset allocation decisions;
- The first platform based protected fund, managed to perform in line with a specified risk target.

Skandia is well known for using innovation to unlock new opportunities for customers. Skandia's managed fund analyser enables advisers to work out whether a customer's current managed fund holding matches their attitude to risk. This demonstrates Skandia's commitment to challenging the status quo in order to improve customer outcomes.

*as at 31.12.2010

Add to this Skandia's straightforward, consistent and competitive charging structure and its award winning service levels and you have the most compelling platform proposition in the market.

Over the past year Skandia has continued to lead the platform market as it prepares for the Retail Distribution Review. Our partnership with financial advisers over the last 30 years has been fundamental to our success and remains the cornerstone of our business model. By ensuring financial advisers are fully prepared to prosper in a post-RDR world, we hope we are also ensuring our continued long-term and mutually beneficial relationship. We hope that the sponsorship of this comprehensive resource has a positive impact on your business.

Contact details

Derek Bryden
Area Sales Manager, Scotland and Northern Ireland
07809 756713
derek.bryden@skandia.co.uk

Mike Steggles
Area Sales Manager, North
07970 088331
mike.steggles@skandia.co.uk

Nick Webb
Area Sales Manager, Midlands
07970 088253
nick.webb@skandia.co.uk

Nigel Jeffries
Area Sales Manager, South West
07872 636448
nigel.jeffries@skandia.co.uk

Lee Keeper
Area Sales Manager, South
07970 088115
lee.keeper@skandia.co.uk

Nick Jones
Area Sales Manager, London
07970 088264
nick.jones1@skandia.co.uk

Robin Barrow
Head of Adviser Direct, UK
023 8072 9864 / 07841 496715
robin.barrow@skandia.co.uk

skandia :

RDR Readiness Centre

helping you find your way to a better business

Skandia are committed to helping you prepare for the RDR - a successful adviser business means a successful Skandia. Our new online resource is designed to help those advisers looking to transition their business to a post-RDR world. The first module of the RDR Readiness Centre is 'How to design a new service proposition' and is split into three key areas:

1. Business costs
2. Investment process
3. Services and charges

In addition to in-house views, we've signposted some really useful insights from the likes of AIFA FFWD, The Business of Advice handbook, JPMorgan and the FSA.

Would your business make it through the Lions' Lair?

Watch the Lions' Lair - providing a light-hearted and interesting perspective on designing a new service proposition. (▶)

The RDR Readiness Centre will grow over time and the following modules will be added throughout 2011:

- How to introduce a new service proposition to a client
- How to drive profitability in your business

Please visit www.skandia.co.uk/areyouready to find out more.

A Member of the 🔶 OLD MUTUAL Group

Contents

Introduction

If over 90% of advice businesses do not have a strategic plan, just think of the scale of the opportunity for the 10% that do!

We all know that having a plan is no guarantee to success and that many advice businesses survive without one. But think about your car. It could run for years and years without you looking under the bonnet, but what state would it be in when you finally took it to the scrapyard?

You have to think about your business in the same way. In fact, you are not just trying to maintain it — you should be actively increasing its value. There are no substitutes for creativity and entrepreneurial flair, but if they are applied with superb management practice and a clear vision, their potential will be maximised.

This book offers no certainty of success; that is down to you. But it does give you tried and tested tools and techniques that work in the advice sector. We will avoid theory and jargon, and deal in practicalities and approaches that save you time.

To make sure that you run your business well and build a plan that is achievable, we deal with every aspect of managing and growing your business. The book is split into the following seven parts:

- Practical strategic planning techniques.
- Designing service that will attract the right clients.
- Marketing your business cost effectively.
- Controlling your finances and managing growth.
- Running your business efficiently.
- Finding and keeping the best people.
- Fine tuning your business to keep it on track.

The following chart shows how the seven parts fit together.

1. Part 1 on **strategic planning** provides a framework and range of tools to analyse your business and the market. It goes on to help you decide on business direction and how you are going to achieve your business ambitions. The approach is practical, and you will develop a plan that is realistic and achievable. This part is not designed to produce a long list of actions and projects that lack of time will defeat; it is about

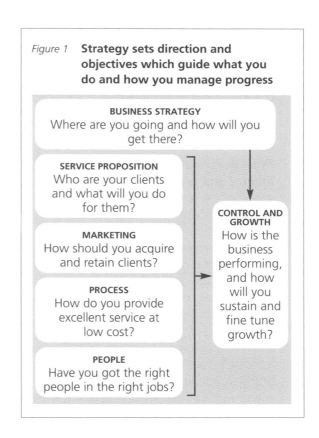

Figure 1 **Strategy sets direction and objectives which guide what you do and how you manage progress**

BUSINESS STRATEGY
Where are you going and how will you get there?

SERVICE PROPOSITION
Who are your clients and what will you do for them?

MARKETING
How should you acquire and retain clients?

PROCESS
How do you provide excellent service at low cost?

PEOPLE
Have you got the right people in the right jobs?

CONTROL AND GROWTH
How is the business performing, and how will you sustain and fine tune growth?

prioritising and concentrating on the most important issues.

2. **Service design** is essential for all advice businesses, and part 2 covers this in detail. It deals with what you are offering, who it is for and how you will deliver it. We begin with target market definition and profiling your client base to help design service that is attractive to them and for which they will pay. We analyse market position to make sure that you are competing in the best place in the market, and that you have an offering that is consistent with your business strengths and operating model. We look at the differences between employed and self-employed advisers, and how you can develop a service and pricing proposition that is manageable and cost effective to deliver. The final chapter in this part deals with the essential issue of pricing and making sure that your advice charges are profitable and credible with your clients.

3. When you are satisfied that service is robust, you can move on to part 3, **marketing**. The marketing process is split into three distinct and manageable chapters, with a fourth

dealing with marketing planning. The process covers brand profile, client acquisition and client retention, and concentrates on maximising the value of the resources and effort that are devoted to marketing. The widest range of techniques is covered, with clear guidance on which techniques you should use for different marketing tasks. The chapter on planning provides a streamlined and proven process to help you organise your marketing activity as efficiently as possible.

4. Part 4 deals with the very different issues of **finance and growth**. There is a detailed review of the construction and use of financial accounts, with an emphasis on the insight they provide into the health and effectiveness of the business. You will also cover best practice approaches to budgeting and cash flow management, which are critical in the financial advice sector. Too many sound businesses suffer due to liquidity problems or the failure to budget properly and track progress. There is a detailed chapter on business value, which sets the traditional multipliers into context and provides a clear set of criteria for valuing businesses and preparing them for sale. This chapter is designed for buyers and sellers, and will give you a broad perspective on where to concentrate if you are intending to sell and what questions to ask if you are intending to buy. The final chapter in this part deals with the detail of the acquisition process, succession planning and the best legal structure for your business.

5. The **efficiency** with which you run your business is the subject of part 5. The goal of this part is service delivery, ensuring that you provide the service designed in Part 2 as consistently and cost effectively as possible. There is a detailed analysis of the main processes, from initial client contact through to review meetings for established clients. This is supplemented by a chapter on information technology to help you decide if you have the right back office software and how to go about changing if necessary. Outsourcing is an important feature of the advice market and has a direct bearing on business efficiency. You will review when outsourcing makes sound business sense and how to make sure you get the right supplier. Finally, we deal with project management, which is an essential capability that you need to implement your plans and make changes

in the business. This has many applications and links with other parts of the book.

6. **People** are one of the most important assets of advice businesses, and all the people issues and processes are covered in part 6. The central part of this is the job description, and we deal with job design and provide several examples that cover the majority of jobs in advice businesses. This is the foundation for performance management, and you will find all the pro-formas and templates you need to undertake this objectively. The chapter on reward covers all employee types, and employed and self-employed advisers. The approach to profit-related reward is also covered, and you will find examples of generic bonus frameworks that you can use. We then deal with every aspect of the recruitment process, which is one of the most difficult things you have to do. The aim is to take as much risk out of this as possible. We cover everything from drawing up a recruitment specification to advertising the job, developing selection criteria and providing effective induction. The final chapter in this part deals with internal communication and change management. It is hard to achieve consistently high standards in this area, so our aim is to give you a range of best practice techniques.

7. Part 7 is about **fine tuning** your business. There will often be times when you are satisfied that your overall strategy and direction are right but the business is losing its efficiency or competitiveness. This may be more pronounced during a recession, but fine tuning your business is as important as keeping fit and should be done regularly. You will get to your destination more quickly and use fewer resources.

You will find plenty of case studies and examples to show good practice, as well as checklists and 'killer questions' for you to benchmark where you stand. We also give specific guidance to help you put the contents of this book into practice, including agendas and content for meetings, and templates for completion.

You can use this book from start to finish, or just take individual chapters if you need to concentrate on a single issue. There are plenty of cross references, so you can choose the order that suits you best.

Finally, for many of the management challenges that you deal with, there are no 'right answers'. In fact, the right answers are those which are relevant and practical for your business. In practice, it is hard to achieve perfection in all areas, and you have to judge where the priorities lie. This book will help you do that and make changes in your business which have a lasting and positive effect.

THE WEBSITE

The Business of Advice is not just a book but a whole programme to help you develop your business. To maximise its value, we have created a website which contains the text which you can access in online format or as PDFs, plus all the templates that you will need to construct your business plan and put many of the tools and techniques into practice. You can download the templates as PDFs or Word documents to amend them to suit your business. In addition you will find Powerpoint presentations and Excel spreadsheets as extra tools to use in developing your own plans.

The aim is to give you complete flexibility in how you apply the content of the book to your business. The templates are exactly the same as those in the book which means you can work on them while referring to the text and examples, or print them off to use in meetings with colleagues.

The website will also contain business planning tips and examples as well specific applications of business planning tools.

You can access the website by going to **www.businessofadvice.co.uk** and access subscriber-only information.

Part 1: Strategic planning

How to plan the development of your business over the next three to five years

"Vision without action is a daydream. Action without vision is a nightmare."

Japanese proverb

Introduction: Take control of your business

When you have completed this Part, you will be able to:

✔ Apply a range of strategic planning tools and techniques.
✔ Analyse the competitive position of your business.
✔ Identify how changes in the market will influence your business.
✔ Confirm the key issues that your plan must include.
✔ Develop a realistic three year vision.
✔ Specify the main strategic actions that you will need to take.
✔ Develop a detailed implementation plan.
✔ Identify and manage planning risks.
✔ Monitor and control progress of your plan.

How many advisers do you know who have sold their business for less than they thought it was worth? The answer will be many and, with the combined effect of the retail review and the post banking crisis trading conditions, there will be many more. This should give you a compelling reason to plan to maximise value and ensure you can secure the best exit route. The only way to achieve this is by planning how you will do it.

Whether your planned exit is in two or 20 years, you need to develop your business in a way that maximises its value and gives you as many exit options as possible. Of course, there are many other reasons for practical planning, but there is no denying that well planned and managed businesses are likely to be valued higher than others.

This Part concentrates on the strategic planning process, and will provide you with a framework and all the tools and techniques that you will need to develop a robust plan. The processes in this Part have been used extensively with advice businesses and directly support analysis and action planning. This means that you can adopt a highly practical approach to planning your business.

If you are confident that your business plan is in good shape, you can move on to the next parts of the book. They deal with the detail of business management and operation, where you can concentrate on specific aspects of your business. If you do not need to develop a brand new plan, the final section is about fine tuning to make sure that you maintain a flexible and open-minded approach to the growth and development of your business.

The strategic planning process has a direct parallel with the planning work you undertake for your clients. You have to build up a detailed picture of their current position, understand what is really important to them and where they want to get to. Finally, you need to work out how they are going to make the journey and then monitor progress along the way. This is exactly what you will be doing for your business as you apply the content of this Part.

Blue and White Financial Services Limited will be used as a case study throughout this Part, so you will see how the business plan is constructed. All the main planning templates can be downloaded from the 'Business of Advice' website at www.businessofadvice.co.uk

We will cover:

- Strengths and weaknesses.
- Opportunities and threats.
- Key issues.
- Vision and strategy.
- Implementation planning.
- Managing risk.
- Monitoring progress.

How effective is your strategic planning?

The Table below asks Ten Killer Questions about strategic planning. These questions also summarise what is 'good' in the operation of an effective planning process in advice businesses.

For each question, give your business an objective score (1 is poor, and 10 is excellent) and ask others what they think. Circulate the questionnaire using **Template 1.1 from Part 1 – Strategic Planning** on the website

If you have scored over 50%, you will be ahead of the market. Most advice businesses do not undertake formal long term planning, although many can articulate very clearly what they are trying to achieve. It is also the case that the majority of firms will have achieved their key financial targets in most years and have concluded

that a formal planning process is not necessary.

The reasons why advice businesses do not undertake formal planning are well known:

- Perceived lack of time.
- Satisfied with recent and current performance.
- Uncertain of process for planning.
- Unfamiliar with some of the planning tools.
- Concerned that rapid market change will render the plan obsolete well before three years have passed.

You may well recognise this list, so the challenge for this chapter is to give you tools that work and a planning process that is very time-efficient. We will cover these in Chapter 3.

Finally, there are significant benefits from effective strategic planning. It:

- Provides the business with direction and exit opportunities.
- Enables different views on the future to be expressed and debated.
- Provides opportunity to prioritise and test ideas.
- Facilitates strategic thinking in contrast to the day to day operation of the business.
- Supports teambuilding with an agreed direction and plan.

STRATEGIC PLANNING: Ten killer questions

Score: 1 = poor, and 10 = excellent

To what extent:

1. Do you have a written down strategic plan?

2. Is the plan referred to regularly to check progress and direction?

3. Have you presented your plan to the advisers and support staff?

4. Have you devoted at least two days to strategic planning in the past year?

5. Can you describe the scale and scope of the business in three to five years?

6. Do you know what actions you will take to develop the business in the longer term?

7. Have you achieved your turnover and profit targets in at least seven of the last ten years?

8. Are your planning meetings well organised and do you stick to the agenda?

9. Do you use management information and reporting to monitor progress against your plan?

10. Do you make sure that your one year operational plans contribute to achieving your long term aims?

Chapter 1

Context, analysis and key issues

By the end of this chapter, your business will benefit from:

✔ Management understanding of how the business compares to others.
✔ Identification of competitive position: strengths and weaknesses.
✔ Evaluation of how external changes could affect the business and what should be done.
✔ Identification of the most important issues that the business must deal with in a three year time period.

In order to develop a robust long term plan, it is important that the initial analysis is objective and thorough. Where possible, comparisons with other businesses should be made and the full implications of any major issues identified and recognised as 'key issues'. Start by creating a brief business profile, a snapshot of where you are now — use **Template 1.2 from the Strategic Planning section** of the website.

1 How advice businesses work

Many advisers find benchmarking extremely helpful when undertaking strategic planning. They want to know where their business stands in the market and if their clients, advisers, back office and management are better or worse than other similar businesses.

If you think about your business, you will know that these activities and functions have to work together. You will also know that if a major part fails, the entire business suffers. The following figure makes the point.

As Figure 1.1 shows, four major areas have to interrelate. These are:

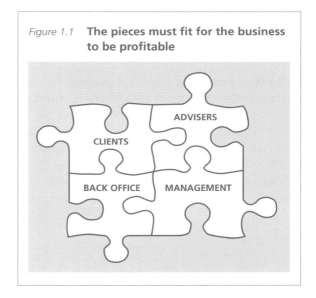

Figure 1.1 **The pieces must fit for the business to be profitable**

- Clients: their number and value.
- Advisers: their productivity and ability.
- Back office: processes, IT and what people do.
- Management: style and leadership, operations and planning.

The parts of the jigsaw have to work together and be effective on their own. It is common to find two advice businesses that have similar propositions, specialisations, services and adviser numbers, but vastly different productivity and profit. The high level explanation for this is that parts of the jigsaw are not working or are not joined up.

Client productivity is determined by a combination of the number and value of clients. There is a clear trend for advice businesses to reduce client numbers and concentrate on those who are more profitable. The days of cross-subsidisation between clients have long passed, and such an approach is unsustainable. You should periodically review your clients and segment them by value to the business. In particular, avoid the maintenance of a long and unproductive list, which will distract you from the more important and lucrative clients.

Principals will often claim that their **advisers** fail to fully identify all the needs of clients, and that the product and fund solutions they propose are incomplete. There is a tendency to deal with the immediate issue and fail to identify and plan how additional issues will be covered.

This argument is often used to support the development of ongoing service that makes sure all client needs are dealt with over time. This is not to suggest that every solution has to be implemented at the outset, but a plan is agreed with the client to phase implementation over a reasonable time period. If you fail to do this, you will not maximise adviser and client productivity.

Back office processes and what **people** do determine the efficiency of your business. A poor back office will lose you clients through bad service, and will draw you into administration and day to day issues. This means that your productivity will fall, along with that of your fellow advisers. Businesses that have advisers who advise and administrators who administrate tend to be more

productive and profitable. Everyone concentrates on their strengths, efficiency and revenues rise and costs fall.

The final part of the jigsaw is **management**. For many advisers, this presents a real challenge: you have to write the business, run the business and develop the business. But do you? Management is about leadership and delegation, and there is often a failure to identify all the management tasks that have to be undertaken. If you can achieve this, then delegation becomes easier and the business is better managed.

All of the issues raised here may well feature as strengths or weaknesses for your business. If you need to deal with any of them, the subsequent chapters will guide you through the process and give examples of good practice.

1.1 The shape of advice businesses

The optimum size and shape of advice businesses is almost impossible to define. This is because the mix of clients, advisers, infrastructure and management varies in infinite combinations. However, if we take the vast majority of the market with turnover up to £5m pa, we can produce a framework that provides a benchmark against which you can test your business. This is not perfect, but if your structure and financials differ greatly, then at least you can ask why. There may be very good explanations, but use of a benchmark is a good way to play devil's advocate.

The example that follows is based on a business that employs its advisers and turns over £875,000 pa. It has six advisers (including directors) and five

BUSINESS SUCCESS requires all the individual parts of the business to work efficiently and together. If any single part fails, the business will not achieve its potential.

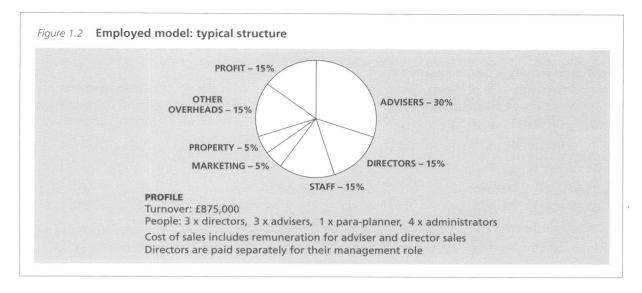

Figure 1.2 **Employed model: typical structure**

PROFIT – 15%

OTHER OVERHEADS – 15%

ADVISERS – 30%

PROPERTY – 5%

MARKETING – 5%

DIRECTORS – 15%

STAFF – 15%

PROFILE
Turnover: £875,000
People: 3 x directors, 3 x advisers, 1 x para-planner, 4 x administrators
Cost of sales includes remuneration for adviser and director sales
Directors are paid separately for their management role

support staff. The cost profile is typical of many businesses that adopt the employed model and, as suggested above, provides an indication of the cost structure for businesses with up to £5m turnover.

The **employed model** will tend to have around 30% of its costs accounted for by advisers, including remuneration for the director-advisers for their sales. However, you should always pay yourself and other directors separately for your management roles, particularly as any purchaser would need to consider the cost of employing people to undertake the management tasks should you decide to leave.

Almost 50% of costs will be accounted for by staff and other overhead costs, leaving around 15% operating profit for the typical employed model.

This means that if your profit exceeds this amount, you are above market average, but you have to make sure that you are calculating profit in the same way and correctly allowing for your remuneration. This will be covered in detail in Part 4.

By comparison, the **self-employed model** will look very different. In this example, the turnover is the same as the employed model above, but everything else is different. There are eight advisers (including two directors) and three administrators. As with the employed example, this cost structure will be typical for businesses with up to £5m turnover.

The typical self-employed model will generate profit between 5% and 10%, so if you are above this, you are ahead of the market average. As you can see, advisers account for a large part of the cost, and the 60% here takes account of any fixed

'desk charge' and regulatory costs that advisers are required to meet. In this model, marketing costs will be lower and the need for space will be less. In addition, the number of administrative staff tends to be lower, and any para-planner support that is needed is often funded by the advisers directly from their remuneration.

Both models have their merits and there tends to be a polarised view in the market where principals support one model or the other, but rarely both. The advantages of the employed model are:

- More control over advisers with process and compliance benefits.
- Greater consistency in client targeting and service.
- Opportunity to tie in advisers through bonus and profit share schemes (not entirely ruled out for self-employed firms but generally less likely).
- Likely to secure a more equitable balance of reward between advisers and owners.

The main disadvantages include:

- Higher cost of recruitment with a need to support adviser income in the first few months, and therefore with implications for capital and rate of expansion.
- Potentially more difficult to disengage people.
- Less flexibility to increase or reduce adviser numbers in short time periods.

In part, the analysis of the self-employed model will be the opposite of the employed model but the perspective is slightly different. Self-employed firms have the following advantages:

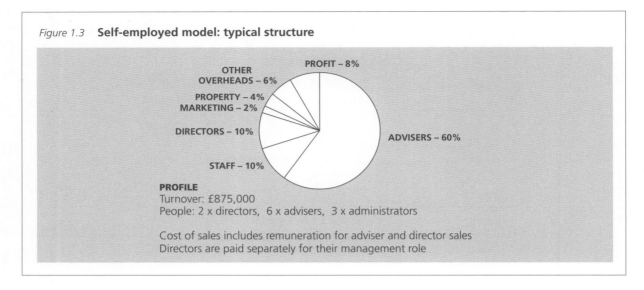

Figure 1.3 **Self-employed model: typical structure**

PROFILE
Turnover: £875,000
People: 2 x directors, 6 x advisers, 3 x administrators

Cost of sales includes remuneration for adviser and director sales
Directors are paid separately for their management role

- Flexibility with regard to expansion and contraction.
- Lower risk related to recruitment with capital less of a constraint to growth.
- Less financial exposure to poor performers.
- Lower back office costs (because typically more of the support work is undertaken by advisers or their own support staff (paid for by them).

The disadvantages include:

- Difficult to apply consistent corporate service standards because different advisers will tend to run their own different client banks – this is an important issue in the context of adviser charging and service definitions.
- Difficult to run marketing and client acquisition campaigns across the business because of the adviser and client bank differences.
- Clients unlikely to perceive as much value in the brand as with the employed model – mainly because the advisers will operate and sometimes present themselves as a 'business within the business'.
- Profit is lower because self-employed advisers have the power to leave – and that is reflected in the balance of reward between owners and advisers.
- Less value built into the business because much of the revenue is transferred to the advisers, including any recurring revenue.

All of the above issues tend to make the self-employed firms more difficult to manage because of the inherent differences and tendency to fragment, but this does not necessarily make one model better or worse than the other. As with all sectors, the main difference between success

and failure depends on the principals and how they run the business. Indeed, there are many successful firms in both camps – and many unsuccessful ones as well.

The important issue at this stage is for you to use these examples and comparisons as context for the business planning that is to follow. If you can manage your business so that advisers, clients and back office all integrate and achieve a balance close to the models above, then you will make a profit. The harder you work at this, the greater the profit and the success of the business for all its stakeholders.

An additional approach to benchmarking is to think about the performance of other firms in other sectors and rate how you stand against them. Indeed, it is often what firms do in other markets that provides examples that could transfer to your business. Make a specific point of recognising good and bad practice in other firms. For example, if you work with professional introducers, they will provide an excellent source of good and bad practice; if you operate on the high street, look at what the best and worst retailers do. Thinking about firms that you admire and the reasons why is often a good basis to judge how good you are and whether or not you can apply their good practices.

1.2 How should you prepare a strategic plan?

You need to undertake strategic planning within a defined framework. The different elements of planning must be dealt with in a specific sequence to make sure that everything that is important is covered, and that you analyse the business and the

Figure 1.4 **Strategic planning process**

OPPORTUNITY ANALYSIS

Strengths & weaknesses   Opportunities & Threats

KEY ISSUES
- - - - - - - - - - - - - - - -

DIRECTION

PRACTICAL BUSINESS VISION
- - - - - - - - - - - - - - - -

ACTION

IMPLEMENTATION PLAN

MONITORING PROGRESS

market before you specify direction and actions.

Figure 1.4 summarises the framework.

As the chart shows, the process is broad and wide ranging at the start and becomes much more specific and detailed at the end. This is because at each stage there is prioritisation of what is important and what needs to be dealt with. As you would expect, a wide range of issues will emerge under the '**opportunity analysis**' section, but only a few of them will have a direct bearing on the business. These are identified at the '**key issues**' stage and will normally form part of the implementation plan.

The middle section on **direction** is designed to summarise where the business is headed and what it will look like in between three and five years. As you will see further on, this can be quite detailed and helps prioritise the **implementation plan**, manage risks and monitor progress in the final section.

We will work through each of the sections in detail and introduce tools that you can use to undertake an objective analysis at each stage. The model is outlined in Table 1.1.

The following is a list of times or circumstances when business planning is a good idea:

- When you say to yourself, "This market is changing so fast that we really need to sort out what we do".

- When colleagues ask, "How are we going to get through the next few years?"
- If you feel that the business is running you instead of you running the business.
- If you have no targets or plans for the following year, or they are just an incremental increase on the previous year.
- When you amalgamate with other businesses.

Table 1.1 **Strategic plan**

STRENGTHS–WEAKNESSES ANALYSIS
Analysis of competitive capability

↓

OPPORTUNITIES AND THREATS
Identification of changes in the
market that will affect your business

↓

KEY ISSUES
Confirmation of what is important for the future

↓

VISION AND STRATEGIES
A high level view of your business
and how it is going to move ahead

↓

IMPLEMENTATION
The actions to achieve the 'vision'

↓

MONITORING PROGRESS
Plan to keep the business on track,
manage risk and monitor performance

CASE STUDY

'What's the point in planning when there is so much change in the market? We cannot see three months ahead, let alone three years.'

Blue and White Financial Services was established in 1982 and is based in Brighton. It has one office and seven advisers supported by seven staff. This includes a compliance manager and office manager, who deals with the IT set-up and ad hoc projects as they arise.

The business has around 2,000 clients and has recently completed a segmentation exercise based on client value. Blue and White is 'whole of market' and works on fees and commissions. It will operate adviser charging from the Retail Distribution Review (RDR) deadline.

Brian Marshall and Lucy Smith have joint ownership of the business and are both advisers, producing around 40% of the revenue between them. Current turnover is around £1.2m and recurring income accounts for about 50% of the total.

The monthly management meeting is in full swing, and the debate turns to changes in the market and how the Retail Review is likely to affect Blue and White in the longer term. "I think we need to sort out a decent business plan to get ourselves well positioned for these changes," said Lucy. "We are too incremental in our approach and don't really drive the business forward. We must think past the RDR towards 2015".

Brian disagreed. "We have done well over the years without much of a plan and, with all this change, the plan will be out of date before the ink is dry!" Den Alderson, one of the advisers who had been with Brian and Lucy from the start, agreed: "These always end up as a talking shop, an academic exercise; the strategy looks great and then nothing happens — remember the last time: we had loads of ideas, but when we got back to the office the phone started to ring and that was it!"

Lucy was not one to back down. "I hear what you're saying, but that is no excuse: I just don't like feeling out of control; at least if we had a plan we would be able to react better to changes and opportunities. If we had an idea of what we were trying to achieve we could deal with things like acquisition enquiries a whole lot better." Brian agreed: "You are right on acquisition; remember how we agonised about Ray Pinnock's business and whether or not it would fit with Blue and White?"

"Why don't we ask Siobhan Martin to run the planning process for us, so we can take part properly? Let's give it a day of our time, out of the office, and see if we get something out of it — if it works, it is a day well spent."

Siobhan Martin was the competent office manager, who knew how to deal with the principals and had a good working relationship with them. Brian and Den warmed to the idea, and it was suggested that Patrick Fuller, the senior administrator, join them to get a good set of perspectives. Brian said, "We'll use the Goldstone Hotel, because it is quiet and we won't be interrupted. That way we can give it our best shot, plus the Sussex Bitter is very good as well!"

CASE STUDY KEY POINT

You need to secure acceptance from the senior team that it is worth running the planning process. You also need to use the skills of someone who understands your business and the market to manage the process so you can play a full part. Finally, there is never a good or bad time to start planning, but those in favour of planning will argue that it is better for you to decide on business direction rather than let external events take over.

2 Identify your business strengths and weaknesses

You should start the planning process with a detailed analysis of the strengths and weaknesses of the business. Along with the review of the marketplace, this provides the foundations for the plan that follows. The more thorough and objective you can be, the more realistic your plan.

2.1 How to undertake your strengths and weaknesses analysis

You should use the main business functions to provide a structure:

- Treating Customers Fairly.
- Strategic planning.
- Financial performance and management.
- Marketing.
- Client service and relationships.
- People processes.
- Data management.
- Business processes and IT.

To organise this, you need a framework to make sure that nothing is missed. Table 1.2 contains two columns of statements that relate to each of the above headings. One column is positive and the other is negative.

You should work through this Table, using the statements to make your assessment and come to a view on where your business stands. Remember to make comparisons with competitors as well as firms in other sectors.

This framework is very effective, and you can either use it in the planning meeting or circulate it in advance and collate the responses to use in the meeting. If more than six people are involved, analysis in advance will save time and enable you to home in on the more important issues. The practical management of this will be covered in Chapter 3 on implementing planning processes in your business. Use **Template 1.3 in Part 1 — Strategic Planning** on the website to complete your strengths and weaknesses analysis.

An alternative 'Business Scorecard' approach is contained in **Template 1.4** on the website. It is a short questionnaire that picks up the same issues as Table 1.2 and, as with the Table, is designed to stimulate discussion. Table 1.2 is more thorough, but you should select the tools that will work best in your business.

2.2 Assessing the impact of strengths and weaknesses

There is often a debate about the relative importance and impact of particular strengths or weaknesses. This is normal, because we all hold different opinions, and the model shown in Figure 1.5 can help facilitate the discussion. The chart looks at two dimensions: the importance of the issue (strength or weakness) and where the business stands. It also summarises the generic action that should be taken.

The case study shows how you can use this model and how it will help you concentrate on the more important areas. Use **Template 1.5 in Part 1 — Strategic Planning** on the website to complete your analysis.

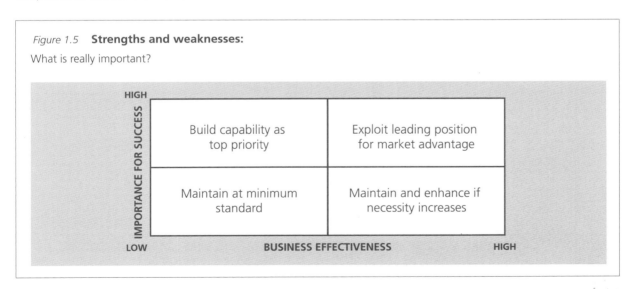

Figure 1.5 **Strengths and weaknesses:**
What is really important?

	BUSINESS EFFECTIVENESS	
HIGH (IMPORTANCE FOR SUCCESS)	Build capability as top priority	Exploit leading position for market advantage
	Maintain at minimum standard	Maintain and enhance if necessity increases
	LOW	**HIGH**

Table 1.2

FUNCTION	NEGATIVE	POSITIVE
TREATING CUSTOMERS FAIRLY	• No strategy: top team not engaged with TCF. • TCF not on 'radar' or a regular agenda item. • No ongoing monitoring of TCF KPIs. • Inconsistent or ad hoc service and pricing. • Client surveys not part of the 'way we do business'. • No desire to respond to further FSA initiatives on TCF.	• TCF planned and communicated. • Key issues identified and dealt with. • Advisers adopt and follow consistent company standards. • Clients have choice and structured ongoing service. • TCF routine 'agenda' item, supported by RPI data. • Client surveys are routine.
STRATEGIC PLANNING	• No written down plans. • Plans not reviewed and updated. • Plans not communicated to rest of staff. • Uncertain vision for business in the next three to five years. • Driven by short term pressures.	• Written down plan which is referred to regularly. • Top team agree on direction. • Plan updated on a regular basis (every 12–18 months). • Clear direction and implementation plan. • Plan communicated to and understood by all staff.
FINANCIAL PERFORMANCE AND MANAGEMENT	• Indemnity commission/initial income dominates. • Capital constraint to growth. • Poor management information. • Recurring revenues less than 10% of turnover. • Falling profit. • No formal budgeting process.	• Running costs covered by recurring income. • Capital 'readily' available for development. • Management information reviewed at least monthly. • Regular achievement of profit and turnover targets. • Clear and consistently applied financial management disciplines.
MARKETING	• No clear target market. • Client demands drive activity. • Ill-defined image – inconsistent tone, style and design. • No structured marketing plan. • Campaigns are ad hoc and ill defined. • Low rate of new client acquisition. • No website.	• Clarity of target clients. • Strong profile and image. • Clear proposition. • Straightforward, well managed marketing plan. • Marketing activity is accountable. • Productive sources of new clients.
CLIENT SERVICE AND RELATIONSHIPS	• No differentiation between clients. • No service proposition. • All clients treated the same. • Long tail of unproductive dormant clients. • Advisers decide on service – not the business.	• Proactive concentration on profitable clients. • Clearly defined and priced service. • Absolute transparency for clients of what they receive and how much it costs. • Many profitable long standing clients.
DATA MANAGEMENT	• Reliance on paper files. • No client categorisation. • Basic accounting and record keeping only. • Data keyed several times. • Inaccurate and incomplete data. • No data disciplines.	• Clear data management policies applied by everyone. • All data clean and on the system. • Clients categorised. • Software to support all main business and advice processes. • Data keyed once.
PEOPLE PROCESSES	• No job descriptions. • No appraisal system. • No training plans. • Gaps in knowledge across the business. • High staff and adviser turnover. • Support staff work in isolation – no teamworking. • Poor recruitment record	• Job descriptions in place and correctly used. • Appraisal system in place and used effectively. • All staff have development plan. • Clear disciplinary and dismissal procedures. • Staff are well trained. • Low turnover of staff and advisers. • Lots of teamwork. • Excellent recruitment record.
BUSINESS PROCESSES AND IT	• Several ways of doing the same thing. • Processes in place but ignored. • New joiners rapidly become confused. • Back office software not used to full effect. • Hardware insufficient to support the business. • No standard processes.	• Well defined processes which everyone follows. • Clear induction programme. • All relevant back office software functionality used effectively (e.g. valuations and management). • Extensive use of appropriate software and external provider and specialist internet services. • Clients can be segmented and profiled in many different ways.

CASE STUDY

Strengths and weaknesses: sorting out the priorities

Blue and White Financial Services are at the Goldstone Hotel and have started the first part of their planning workshop: strengths and weaknesses. In setting up the meeting, Brian had circulated a short questionnaire using **Template 1.4** which helped to home in on the more important areas.

As Siobhan Martin, who was facilitating, built up the flip chart, an overview of strengths and weaknesses emerged: summarised in Table 1.3.

Siobhan said, "We need to sort out those which are a real problem and those we can live with; which are the most important on this list?"

There was quite a debate, and the strengths/ weaknesses assessment model (opposite) was used to provide structure. Brian said, "If we can sort these out now, it should make identifying the key issues a lot easier."

Lucy said, "That's not a bad summary of the major strengths and weaknesses and shows us where we need to concentrate. If you think of Palace Pensions Services, who we know well, they sorted out their back office a couple of years ago and it has made a real difference. That's our biggest problem, and this really brings it out."

Siobhan decided that the picture was good enough. It had reinforced what they all knew, but at this stage everyone shared exactly the same view — a good point to break for coffee.

At the end of the session, the matrix created looked like Figure 1.6.

Table 1.3

	STRENGTHS	WEAKNESSES
TREATING CUSTOMERS FAIRLY	Plan in place, most issues dealt with.	Service changes behind schedule, management information needs extending.
STRATEGIC PLANNING	Planning meeting is first step.	No plans and no agreed direction at present.
FINANCIAL PERFORMANCE AND MANAGEMENT	Almost 50% of turnover recurring, profitable.	Capital can constrain development (e.g. recruitment).
MARKETING	Good local image, longevity, retirement market expertise.	Poor professional connections, no structured marketing plan, reception needs decorating.
CLIENT SERVICE AND RELATIONSHIPS	New clients by 'word of mouth', around 1,000 loyal and active clients.	Irregular client servicing (e.g. the middle 'B' group).
DATA MANAGEMENT	Data clean-up almost complete.	Disciplines not adhered to by everyone (mainly advisers).
PEOPLE PROCESSES	Loyal and hard working staff, well qualified (but short of RDR needs for some).	Job descriptions out of date, some advisers (two) low productivity.
BUSINESS PROCESSES AND IT MARKETING	None at present.	Current software inadequate. (change is being progressed), hence muddled back office processes, duplication of effort, too much paper!

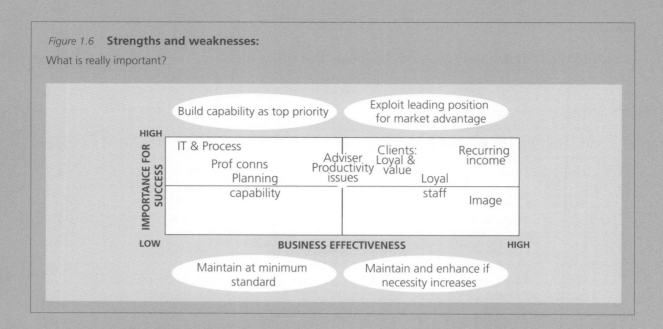

Figure 1.6 **Strengths and weaknesses:**
What is really important?

CASE STUDY KEY POINT

Sometimes the major strengths and weaknesses are obvious and the assessment is not needed. However, if it is not so clear, working through what is important for success and where the business stands is a good way to summarise competitive position. Also, thinking of what competitors do much better or worse is always a useful benchmark. Copies of the strengths and weaknesses **Templates 1.4 and 1.5** are included in the Strategic Planning section of the website.

Figure 1.7 **Opportunities and threats:**
Main influences in the advice market

THESE ARE INCREASING THE DEMAND FOR ADVICE

Treating customers fairly

Awareness of need to plan

More people aged 45+

People are time pressured

Government trying to expand the market

Inheritance monies

Retail Distribution Review

Recession

Pensions proposals

Negative image of financial services

Consumer confidence

THESE ARE REDUCING DEMAND OR CREATING UNCERTAINTY

3 Take account of the market place

This section will help you to identify the external events that are expected to have an effect on your business. You are likely to produce an extensive list, and some of the events may have unpredictable consequences. There is no doubt that you will be dealing with complexity in this section.

3.1 Where does change come from?

In broad terms, you need to concentrate on the following categories of change:

- Political.
- Economic.
- Social.
- Technological.
- Legal and regulatory.
- Environmental.

Relating these to the advice market throws up a number of issues illustrated in Figure 1.7. As this shows, there are many long term factors, such as demographics, that are increasing the demand for advice. At the same time, there are changes and events, such as trading conditions and confidence, that are holding it back. In addition, the key initiatives, Retail Distribution Review (RDR) and Treating Customers Fairly (TCF) have a mixed effect.

In the long term, they will favour advice businesses through the operation of good practice and clarity of who is qualified to give advice. However, in the short term, they have diverted energy and resources toward preparation and implementation.

The pension changes scheduled post 2012 (the National Employment Savings Trust or NEST) are slightly different from RDR and TCF as, on balance, they will have a negative effect, because the total number of people who are likely to be members of company-sponsored schemes will fall. However, this is offset by the opportunity to give advice in the period up to implementation and the demand for higher quality schemes by wealthier clients after implementation.

3.2 The impact of external change on your business

You should use the framework outlined in Table 1.4, which should make the analysis directly relevant to your business. It will identify the issues that are really important, and those that can either be ignored or considered secondary in their effect.

A blank copy of this Table can be found as **Template 1.6** on the website. The description column is relatively generic, but the implications, importance and time frame will all vary by business. This example, which relates to our case study, Blue and White Financial Services, demonstrates how this framework could be applied to an individual business. It is not a set of market predictions.

To help you work through this, the following questions should be addressed:

- What are the big changes in the external environment for the next three to five years?
- How will they affect your business?
- Which ones worry you most and which are secondary?
- How certain are you that these changes will happen?
- Are there any show-stoppers that could prevent you from trading?
- Which parts of government policy will influence what you do or what you give advice on?
- Where are the greatest opportunities?
- How well placed are you to respond to these changes?
- Are there any actions you need to take now or within six months?
- If the picture is unclear, what is your working assumption?

Use **Template 1.7** from the website to circulate these as a formal questionnaire.

Table 1.4 **Impact of external factors**

SOURCE	DESCRIPTION	IMPLICATION	TIME FRAME	IMPORTANCE
POLITICAL	• General election in 2015. • No change in political landscape in medium term. • •	• Steady fall in government spending and deficit. • Maintenance of high personal tax rates.. • RDR will go ahead as planned. • No change in pensions (NEST) proposals.	• Election 2015. • No real recovery until 2012 earliest. • RDR deadline end 2012 earliest. • NEST phased implementation 2012 onwards.	• Tax planning = HIGH. RDR = HIGH. • Pensions = MEDIUM.
ECONOMIC	• Slow recovery. • Low interest rates 2011. • Eurozone sovereign debt problems — not resolved until medium term. • Poor stock markets to mid-2009.	• Rising unemployment to medium term. • Unpredictable stock markets. • Fragile consumer confidence. • Brand new clients reluctant to invest. • Strong demand for income from traditional savings account savers.	• Unemployment rising to 2012. • Inflation rise in 2011 and then fall back. • Interest rate increases — more likely 2012 onward. • Income requirement short and medium term.	• Economic cycle = MEDIUM. • Stock market changes = HIGH. • Redundancy advice = HIGH. • Demand for income = HIGH
SOCIAL	• Negative image of entire FS industry. • Rising retirement ages. • Lower pace of movement between jobs. • Falling real incomes.	• People postpone retirement. • Consumer concern about what to do — increased demand for advice, but reluctance to take action. • Less disposable income to invest.	• Rate of retirement slows — permanent change. • Consumer concern — short and medium term. • Lower real income — long term (at least 5 years).	• Image = LOW. • Retirement = MEDIUM. • Lower disposable income = HIGH.
TECHNOLOGICAL	• Increased development of all e-based services.	• Continue to review current software set-up. • Increased use of on-line services RDR increases take up of wrap.	• Ongoing.	• Wrap = HIGH. • On-line developments = LOW (to medium term).
LEGAL/ REGULATORY	• RDR implemented from 2012. • Simplified products (no cap) initiative — similar timescale. • Capital adequacy requirement increased. • Introduction of 'Adviser Charging'.	• QCA4 required for all advisers. • Service design essential to support adviser charging. • Change in processes and way some advisers operate. • Up to 15% of advisers leave at RDR deadline. • Consolidation of advice businesses. • Rise in business values post RDR.	• Qualifications 2012/3. • Adviser charging from RDR • Disposals — short term linked to falling business value. • Values rise — medium and long term.	• Qualifications = HIGH. • AC and service = HIGH. • Consolidation = MEDIUM.
ENVIRONMENTAL	• Demand for green investments falls. • 'Green' agenda continues to roll forward.	• No change in overall approach to investment policy. • Undertake sensible green policies — introduce scanning.	• Up to end of recession 2011.	• Demand for green product = LOW.

3.3 Assessing the impact of external changes

As with strengths and weaknesses, there is often disagreement about the relative importance and impact of particular external events. The model in Figure 1.8 helps facilitate this discussion and looks at two dimensions: the scale of the change and the expected impact on the business. It also summarises the generic action that you should take.

We return to Blue and White Financial Services to show how this model can be applied and how it brings out the more important areas. Complete **Template 1.8 from the Strategic Planning section** of the website for your business.

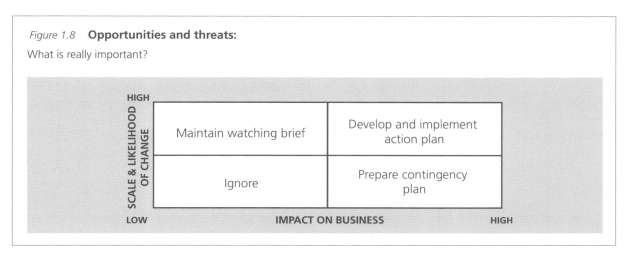

Figure 1.8 **Opportunities and threats:**

What is really important?

	IMPACT ON BUSINESS	
	LOW	HIGH
HIGH	Maintain watching brief	Develop and implement action plan
	Ignore	Prepare contingency plan

SCALE & LIKELIHOOD OF CHANGE

As with strengths and weaknesses, there is often disagreement about the relative importance and impact of particular external events

CASE STUDY

Sorting out the external environment

Back at the Goldstone Hotel, Siobhan had moved the team on to think about the external environment. Compared to strengths and weaknesses, there were fewer issues raised, but they were confident they had not missed anything from their collective understanding of the market. They also decided that getting higher levels of qualification was particularly important.

Siobhan built up the chart (see section 3.2) and summarised a lot of views and opinions. She decided that they needed to draw this to a close and that plotting these on the assessment matrix would be useful to home in on the bigger issues. The chart is illustrated in Figure 1.9.

Lucy commented that some of the changes were hard to predict, but that they had to make their best judgement. "We need to keep an eye on some of this, especially the capital adequacy issues and the way in which the RDR implementation actually unfolds," she said. They agreed there were no 'show-stoppers' and that they were fortunate that they did not operate in the corporate pensions market, which for them removed a particular threat.

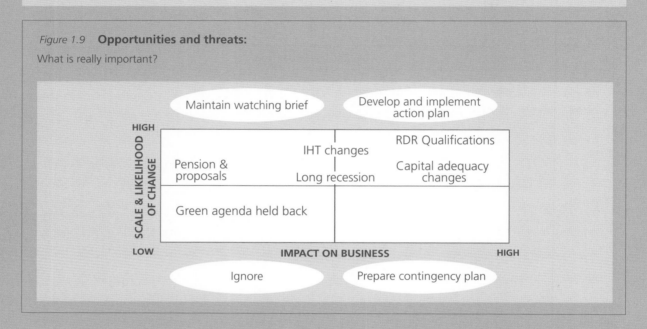

Figure 1.9 **Opportunities and threats:**
What is really important?

CASE STUDY KEY POINT

It is difficult to be precise with many of the external changes, because their timing and impact is often unknown. The best approach is to ask, "What is our best working assumption?" and move on, especially if the impact on the business is relatively low. In the end, you need to be sure that there is nothing going on in the market that could really help or hinder you that may have been missed. A blank copy of the matrix is in Part 1 — Strategic Planning on the website as **Template 1.8**.

4 Opportunity analysis: getting more detailed

The more rigorous your analysis of your competitiveness and the external environment, the more robust will be your plan. This section contains two additional models that you will find useful: one deals with the client base, while the second links your view of the main markets with business capability.

4.1 How loyal are your clients?

You can analyse this by using the loyalty ladder shown in Figure 1.10. It works particularly well if you have profiled your clients, but is still useful if you have to make estimates.

You can ask the following questions to get the best out of this model:

- How many clients are in each group?
- Do all the advisers categorise their clients in the same way?
- What is the split by adviser?
- Do you currently offer different levels of service and contact between these groups?
- What is your policy on newsletters, investment commentaries and mailshots between these groups?
- Should you proactively approach the customer and client groups, or leave them as dormant?
- How much recurring income arises from each of these groups?
- If you have group scheme members, where would you categorise them?

A version of the loyalty ladder is included in the Strategic Planning Part of the website as **Template 3.1**.

You may not have profiled your clients using the exact categories, but if you can estimate how many will be in the loyal, vulnerable and lost groups, it will provide you with a broad overview. Typically, no more than 20% of clients will

be 'loyal' and these are likely to provide 80% of your profit. If you are operating a three tier service model, all of your top (gold) clients and all or most of your middle (silver) clients will be in this group.

However, those in the 'vulnerable' group will be of value, particularly if they are expected to become wealthier as time passes. Indeed, if those who have made two transactions have made them in the past two or three years, they are highly likely to be in the middle (silver) group and you will want to retain them.

At an overview, this model helps identify:

- How many clients should receive a high level of service and a structured retention programme.
- How many additional clients are of value to the business and require a level of service and retention activity that will prevent them from going elsewhere.
- The number of transactional customers where you need to decide if they are to be left as dormant or if you will approach them through structured marketing campaigns.
- The number of new clients for the top group that need to be found or 'promoted' to help achieve your future business targets.

4.2 What is the potential of specific markets?

This model draws together your view of the market potential for the main products and services that you offer, and how you rate your business capability to deal with and deliver them. This model helps you:

- Identify market opportunities that are not fully exploited.
- Confirm where you should concentrate training, development and investment.
- Identify products or services that are important to you,

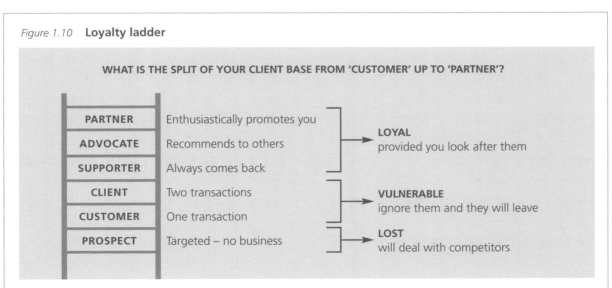

Figure 1.10 **Loyalty ladder**

WHAT IS THE SPLIT OF YOUR CLIENT BASE FROM 'CUSTOMER' UP TO 'PARTNER'?

PARTNER	Enthusiastically promotes you	**LOYAL** provided you look after them
ADVOCATE	Recommends to others	
SUPPORTER	Always comes back	
CLIENT	Two transactions	**VULNERABLE** ignore them and they will leave
CUSTOMER	One transaction	
PROSPECT	Targeted – no business	**LOST** will deal with competitors

but which may be declining in market importance.

The model is shown in Figure 1.11, and includes the generic policies for each segment.

To implement this model, you should list all the products and services that are important, either as current lines of business or highly likely for the future (say, within 12 months). You then need to take each one and plot it on the chart by asking the following questions:

● Is this a good market to be in over the next two to three years? Combine your view of size, profitability, growth, competitiveness, cyclicality and opportunity to differentiate.
● How good are you in this market right now? Consider your knowledge and depth of understanding of the market, and your technical and administrative skills.

When you have covered every product and service, check their relative position to make sure you have really differentiated between them. **Template 3.2 in the Strategic Planning section** of the website provides a blank matrix for you to use.

An example of a completed matrix is shown in Figure 1.12 for Blue and White Financial Services, which majors in retirement planning and investments as opposed to corporate and personal pensions. Product markets are shown in light blue, and specific services offered by the firm are in bold.

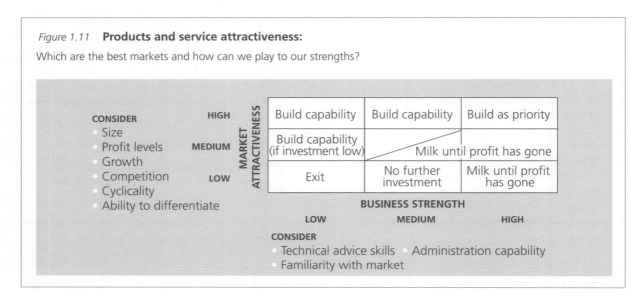

Figure 1.11 **Products and service attractiveness:**
Which are the best markets and how can we play to our strengths?

THE PRODUCT AND SERVICE MATRIX is designed to facilitate a discussion about the main product and service offerings. The discussion is more important than their precise position on the chart.

FOCUS POINT

Where does Blue and White play best?

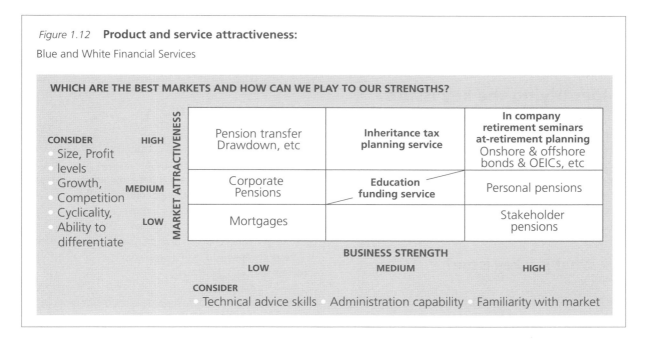

Figure 1.12 **Product and service attractiveness:**

Blue and White Financial Services

WHICH ARE THE BEST MARKETS AND HOW CAN WE PLAY TO OUR STRENGTHS?

		BUSINESS STRENGTH	
	LOW	MEDIUM	HIGH
HIGH	Pension transfer Drawdown, etc	**Inheritance tax planning service**	**In company retirement seminars at-retirement planning** Onshore & offshore bonds & OEICs, etc
MEDIUM	Corporate Pensions	**Education funding service**	Personal pensions
LOW	Mortgages		Stakeholder pensions

MARKET ATTRACTIVENESS

CONSIDER
- Size, Profit levels
- Growth, Competition
- Cyclicality, Ability to differentiate

CONSIDER
- Technical advice skills
- Administration capability
- Familiarity with market

As the chart shows, for Blue and White, there is a strong demand for its retirement seminars and tailored planning services along with associated products. The firm is clearly proficient in the investment markets, but has an equally clear view of the relative attractiveness of the other product markets.

While understanding that the market for pension transfers and drawdown is strong, Blue and White recognises that it lacks capability in these markets. The education funding service is a less positive market, and the business needs to improve its proposition, while the mortgage market is seen as poor along with business capability.

The generic responses would indicate:

- Continue to sustain the retirement and lump sum investments work in the top right hand box.
- Enhance capability for IHT planning and transfer and drawdown products — move them to the right.
- Place no additional resources or training into the other pensions products.
- Maintain the education funding service as the market improves, but devote few resources at present.
- Outsource mortgage business to a trusted partner.

It is important to note that all advice businesses will have different views on the individual service and product markets and, inevitably, will have different degrees of capability depending on specialisation. There are no right or wrong answers for this analysis; the most important issue is to ensure a full and detailed debate and think about how the business should react.

- Further development of management infrastructure.
- Considering/reviewing acquisition policy.

The relative importance of these will vary, but generally across the market the priorities are close to those above.

Complete **Template 1.9 in Part 1 – Strategic Planning** from the website to identify the key issues for your business.

5 Identifying the key issues

You need to identify key issues, because they are essential for prioritisation; the final list should be agreed by the key decision takers. In practice, you will find that this always happens, but it depends on the rigour of the internal and external analyses. If you have been very thorough up to this point, there is usually little debate and much agreement about the key issues list.

5.1 What is a key issue?

The identification of key issues is designed to make sure your plan deals with the right things and that scarce resources are not wasted. Key issues are:

- Really important.
- Under the control of the business.
- Essential for the completeness of the plan.

You should aim for no more than five key issues to make certain that you are prioritising correctly. The range of key issues that arise in advice businesses includes the following:

- Ensuring financial strength/increase recurring income.
- Defining pricing strategy and associated service levels.
- Identifying/shifting to profitable markets.
- Sourcing and retention of the right clients.
- Increasing client and adviser productivity.
- Exploiting electronic commerce and technology.
- Developing and enhancing database.
- People – recruitment, retention and training.

6 Chapter summary

This chapter has dealt with the constituents of the business that drive profit and success, and the analysis stage of the business planning process. It has provided you with a benchmark for businesses that operate either the employed or self-employed model up to a turnover of £5m.

The use of the benchmarks and analysis tools in this chapter will have provided you with a detailed picture of where your business stands in the market.

The management skills you have developed as a result of this chapter mean that you can:

- Objectively compare your business to other similar operations.
- Apply specific techniques to identify and evaluate the competitive position of your business.
- Analyse the external operating environment and evaluate the impact of change on your business.
- Identify the most important issues that you must include in your plan.
- Recognise the difference between issues that are strategically significant and those of lesser importance.

KEY ISSUES are the best way of agreeing what is really important and what must be dealt with in the plan.

CASE STUDY

Key issues and priorities

It is almost lunch time at the Goldstone Hotel, and Blue and White Financial Services have moved on to key issues. Siobhan, who is facilitating the workshop, asks the question, "What do you see as the five key issues that we must make sure the plan deals with? Please write them down independently and then we can collate them on a flip chart."

Brian asked, "Do we include major changes that might affect us, but over which we have no control?" Siobhan decided that, as key issues were issues that the plan had to deal with, they should note the external factors that might be significant, but concentrate on those which they could do something about.

Silence descended as the group made their lists. Lucy broke the silence and said, "This is a bit like a party game, but at least we all get an equal say and it is a quick way of gathering the information." They made sure that everyone had time to think about and complete their list before Siobhan asked them

to call out their responses. She grouped them under the business functions to try to achieve a co-ordinated list. As she expected, there was a wide measure of agreement and the final list, after she had tidied it up over lunch, looked like this table.

The right hand column was included to double check why an issue was so important. Most were obvious, but they agreed that the rationales would also help them think about the implementation plan.

Siobhan decided to stop for lunch and give people a break before checking that this was exactly the right list.

After lunch, the first comment was, "We all know the business inside out — let's just check that this is the right list. Is this what our implementation plan should be based on?" It was agreed that these were the right key issues, and the workshop moved on to talk about vision and what the business could realistically look like in three years time.

Table 1.5

KEY ISSUES	RATIONALE
INFRASTRUCTURE: • Complete the software change and implement as quickly as possible. • Deal with process changes and job content that will be linked to this. • Specific training on the new software.	• To enhance client service. • To increase efficiency. • To reduce costs.
SERVICE: • Complete the pilot for the three tier service. • Implement across all advisers.	• To complete major TCF project. • To enhance service. • To increase revenues.
MARKETING: • Develop additional professional introducers. • Increase client numbers in the A and B groups, and also increase client value.	• To reach higher value clients. • To increase client value. • To concentrate on the more profitable clients.
TRAINING: • Develop technical knowledge of transfer and drawdown product markets. • Set plan to ensure advisers gain the required professional qualifications.	• To improve our offering. • To retain ability to deliver advice at whole of market status.
EXTERNAL ISSUES: • Keep a watching brief over RDR implementation.	• To make changes to plans if necessary.

CASE STUDY KEY POINT

The key issues distil all the previous analyses and start to concentrate on what is really important. There is usually a high degree of overlap between each person's list and, for this part of the process, the need for people to make their own lists is very important. All perspectives have to be covered to make sure that nothing important is missed. A blank key issues **Template 1.9** is included on the website.

Chapter 2
Setting direction

By the end of this chapter, your business will benefit from:

✔ Clarity of vision and long term direction.
✔ Confirmation of planning objectives and strategies.
✔ Control of destiny and reduction of risk.

This chapter will help you to define and agree a clear direction for the business and set out the main strategies under each of the business functions. This is the point at which you move from analysis to action.

1 Vision: where are you heading?

In practice, articulating a vision often reconfirms the current operating style and market position of the firm, but with a different scale and scope. However, it is an opportunity for you to consider a change in direction or emphasis, and, for the key decision takers, a part of the plan that needs their full agreement. You should normally take a three year perspective, because anything less is too short and falls into the day to day operation of the business. Also, it is difficult to read the market if we extend past three years.

The benefits of setting a clear vision are:

- Everyone understands where the business is going.
- There is a context for the implementation part of the plan.
- It identifies the difference between the current and desired positions.
- It can be shared with staff and potential employees to demonstrate how the business will develop.

1.1 The issues to cover when developing the vision

The range of questions to be asked, and the best order for thinking about them, is summarised in Figure 2.1.

As you can see from these questions, articulating the vision can take some time, and we will cover how to manage this in Chapter 3 on the implementation of this process in your business.

To develop the vision, you need to take the following headings in the order shown, use the questions above and describe what the business will look like in three years.

Purpose:

- What the business does and who it does it for.

Scale:

- Key financials: turnover and profitability.
- Clients: numbers and types.
- Advisers: numbers, types and productivity.

Resources:

- Administration and other staff: skills, job types, numbers.
- Organisation structure: reporting lines.

Marketing:

- Service and charges: bespoke or tiered.
- Sources of business: diversified if possible.
- Business mix: by product or area of financial planning.

Back office:

- Processes: the degree of streamlining and consistency.
- Technology: the contribution from IT.

Figure 2.1 **What will the business look like in three years time?**

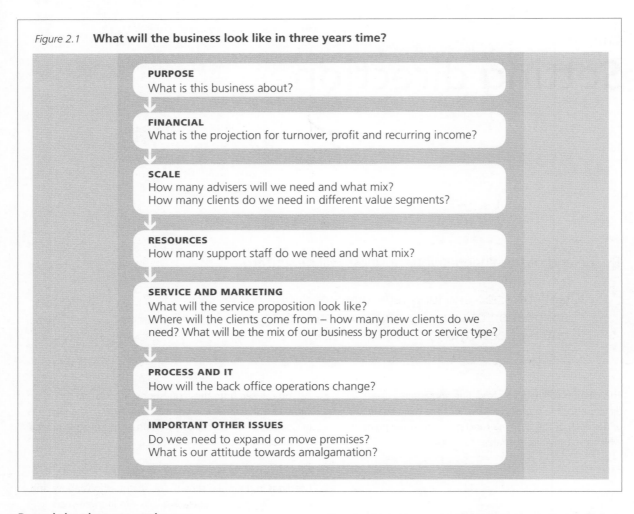

PURPOSE
What is this business about?

FINANCIAL
What is the projection for turnover, profit and recurring income?

SCALE
How many advisers will we need and what mix?
How many clients do we need in different value segments?

RESOURCES
How many support staff do we need and what mix?

SERVICE AND MARKETING
What will the service proposition look like?
Where will the clients come from – how many new clients do we
need? What will be the mix of our business by product or service type?

PROCESS AND IT
How will the back office operations change?

IMPORTANT OTHER ISSUES
Do wee need to expand or move premises?
What is our attitude towards amalgamation?

Remaining important issues:

- Premises: staying or moving.
- Acquisition policy: to acquire or be acquired.

1.2 Example vision statement

Table 2.1 demonstrates what a typical vision statement will look like. We will use Blue and White Financial Services as our example.

As you can see from the example, quite a detailed picture can be developed.

At the very top of the statement is a summary of what the business is about. This will provide you with a point of focus for the detail that follows. You can use the market positioning statement that will be developed in Chapter 5 on service in this section.

You should make sure you verify the turnover targets by:

- Referring to past performance.
- Linking to typical client values and realistic numbers of clients (ideally categorised by annual value to the business).
- Considering expected adviser numbers and production (either using realistic averages or projections for individuals if possible).

Of course, there is no certainty that the vision will turn out exactly as expected, but the value of developing it is that you can compare what actually happens to your desired vision. That enables you to adjust the vision if necessary or change the implementation to get back on track. We will deal with how we track this through performance measures further on. **Template 2.1 in Part 1 – Strategic Planning** on the website provides a blank vision template for you to use.

Table 2.1 **Blue and White vision towards December 2015**

PURPOSE	Blue and White Financial Services will be recognised as a specialist financial adviser for personal clients, making key decisions when they retire and in retirement.
FINANCIAL	Profit target = 15% of turnover rising to 20% + toward 2015. Turnover rising as follows: **ACTUAL** • 2010: £1.2m, including £580,000 recurring: 8 advisers with new business avenues = £78,000. • 2011: £1.3m, including £600,000 recurring – 8 advisers @ £88,000. **FORECAST** • 2012: £1.2m, including £650,000 recurring – 7 advisers @ £79,000. **VISION** • 2013: £1.3m, including £650,000 recurring – 7 advisers @ £93,000. • 2014: £1.5m, including £750,000 recurring – 8 advisers @ £94,000. • 2015: £1.8m, including £800,000 recurring – 9 advisers @ £111,000. **ASSUMPTIONS** • Economy will grow slowly toward to 2012. • Revenue dips in 2012 when we move to adviser charging. • Recurring revenues are fund-based but remain stable as we continue to cover service cost with recurring revenue. • Economies of scale increase rate of profit. **COSTS** • Staff costs will increase directly in line with recruitment. • We assume inflation salary increases (note: profit bonus included in labour cost budget). • No additional infrastructure costs are anticipated above software change detailed below and already budgeted.
CLIENTS	Client numbers and annual value to the business to rise as follows: **2012:** A: 300 @ £1,750 pa = £525,000. B: 600 @ £800 pa = £480,000. C: 1,000 total = £295,000. **2015:** A: 400 @ £2,000 pa = £800,000. B: 750 @ £1,000 pa = £750,000. C: 1,000 total = £250,000.
RESOURCES	**ADVISER NET INCREASE:** From seven to nine (2012–2015): note total recruitment will be four to cover two retirees. **SUPPORT NET INCREASE:** One additional para-planner (2014) to give: 1 × senior admin, 3 × admin, 2 × para-planner, 1 × compliance manager, 1 × office manager (IT, projects, etc). Note: finance, IT support and additional compliance outsourced.
MARKETING	**SERVICE:** Full introduction of three tier service model currently in pilot with four advisers. Upsell of B clients into A, and proactive marketing to C group to increase numbers in B. **MARKETING:** In-company retirement seminars (currently four contracts to provide this service) plus potential for redundancy counselling and advice. Further development of professional connections and enhanced website. **BUSINESS MIX:** likely to be 80% investment-orientated with increasing pension transfer and drawdown work.
PROCESSES	Completion of process and back office software review. The latter replaced and implemented over 2012–2013 alongside final phase of data clean-up for A and B clients. All processes streamlined in line with roll out of back office software.
PREMISES	No change.
ACQUISITIONS	No desire to be acquired at this stage, and not favourably disposed to acquiring until back office changes complete.

1.3 Strategies to achieve the vision

When you are satisfied that the vision is a realistic description of where you want to get to, you have set out how you will get there. The question is:

- What do we need to do under each of the business functions to achieve the turnover and profit targets?

You should always take the three year financial targets as the objective, because they are specific, measurable and time-scaled.

Table 2.2, based on Blue and White Financial Services, uses the business function headings to detail what will be done to achieve the business objective. Incidentally, we do not want to get side tracked into theoretical planning issues, but one useful point is that the objective always starts with 'to. . .', while the means of achievement, the strategies, start with 'by . . .'

Note that the words in *italics* that follow each strategy are the justification for it. They answer the question, "Why are you doing this?"

Table 2.2 **Blue and White financial services business strategy**

	The **business objective** is to achieve a turnover of £1.8m and profit of £400,000 (15% rising to 22%) by December 2015. This will be achieved by . . .
FINANCE	• Recruiting additional RIs — *to provide additional revenue.* • Continuing to build the proportion of income which is recurring — *to build value into the business and further enhance liquidity.* • Maintaining all costs at current levels (apart from staff costs as in the vision) — *to achieve profit targets.* • Maintaining the monthly financial review and forecasting process — *to manage costs effectively.* • Reviewing costs — *to secure profitability.*
CLIENTS AND MARKETING	• Increasing client numbers in each of the categories as in the vision — *to achieve the financial targets.* • Increasing the value of clients in the A and B categories — *to achieve the financial targets.* • Providing retirement seminars for in-company delivery — *to ensure a steady flow of new leads.* • Sustaining relationships with the current four corporate connections — *to maintain access to retiring clients.* • Identifying three additional productive professional introducers — *to reach higher value clients.* • Acquiring additional clients through professional introducers — *to diversify business sources.* • Upgrading the website — *to promote the image of the business more effectively.*
RESOURCES: PEOPLE	• Recruiting additional RIs — *to replace retiring members of staff and to enhance production.* • Recruiting additional para-planner — *to provide additional capacity, specialist capability and support RI production.* • Maintaining the current organisation structure — *to ensure effective staff management and direction.* • Undertaking appropriate training and professional development — *to support delivery of specialist advice and meet RDR requirements.* • Increasing productivity of RIs — *to take advantage of infrastructure.*
RESOURCES: TECHNOLOGY	• Replacing existing back office software — *to reduce unit costs, enhance processes, increase productivity and retain and service clients.* • Reviewing back office processes in line with software implementation — *to maximise efficiency.* • Reviewing the opportunity for scanning (post software implementation) — *to enhance service and efficiency.* • Maintaining an effective hardware configuration — *to ensure robust IT services.*
PROCESSES	• Reviewing processes as above — *to increase efficiency.* • Reviewing resource support required to deliver compliance process — *to increase productivity and reduce costs.* • Refining service delivery in line with pilot — *to enhance service and retain clients.*
PREMISES	• Renewing lease at 2013 break point — *to avoid moving.* • Upgrading reception area — *to project a better image to clients.*
ACQUISITIONS	• Maintaining a 'no sale' position — *to provide time to build further value into the business.* • Maintaining our 'no buy' position — *to enable full implementation of IT changes.*

This Table includes at headline level all the things you and your colleagues will do to achieve the turnover and profit objectives. You are likely to already be doing a large proportion of these, but it brings together all the main activities in one place. Any new projects will be included above but detailed in the implementation section that follows. **Template 2.2 in the Strategic Planning section** of the website sets out a blank business strategy template for you to use.

2 Vision and strategies: one additional model

It is possible that your debate on vision will involve discussion on finding new clients or selling new services or products to existing clients. The following model will provide a structure for this debate.

2.1 New opportunities: client/ service matrix

Figure 2.2 shows how this works, as well as the generic actions at each stage.

The degree of complexity and risk tends to increase as you move from box 1 to box 4, although this depends on what is planned. The actions can be summarised as follows:

Box 1: Current clients and current services/products

- Sell more to the existing clients and find more in the same target market — that is market penetration.

Box 2: Existing clients being sold new services/products

- It is always easier to sell something new to an existing client than to find a new client.

Box 3: New clients for existing services

- Find new target client groups for services that you are good at selling.

Box 4: Brand new target clients and brand new products/services

- This is the most difficult, risky and (probably) costly route to pursue.

An example for Blue and White Financial Services, Figure 2.3, follows. **Template 3.3 in Part 1 — Strategic Planning** on the website provides a blank matrix for you to use.

To make sure this model works, you have to use the headings (either client groups or products/services) as they are shown. That way you will be able to develop the boxes as summarised above.

Figure 2.2 **Client/Service matrix**

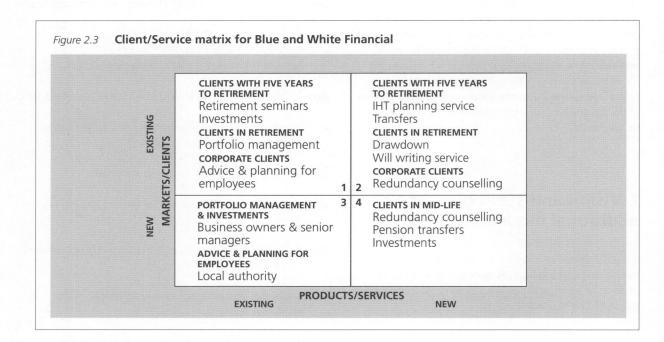

Figure 2.3   **Client/Service matrix for Blue and White Financial**

3 Chapter summary

The management skills you have developed as a result of this chapter mean that you can:

- Develop a clear vision for your business.
- Make sure that your vision is realistic and achievable.
- Work out what needs to be done to achieve the vision.
- Take the initial strategic steps to guide your business in a direction that you have decided (as opposed to the market).

As you will have seen, this is quite a difficult part of the planning process. You have moved from analysing the past and dealing with many known factors to predicting what your business will look like. However, you have past performance as a guide, as well as your experience and intuition of what works and what can be achieved. In addition, you have your colleagues and fellow principals to support the development of the vision, which is why, when this process is applied in practice, it has an uncanny tendency to come true. Take your time and test your assumptions, and your vision will be a far more practical guide than you might initially expect.

Chapter 3

Implementing the plan

By the end of this chapter, your business will benefit from:

✔ Prioritisation of projects to fully implement the plan.
✔ Specification of individual projects.
✔ Identification of risks to the plan and how they can be reduced or removed.
✔ Effective monitoring of the progress of the plan.
✔ Identification of key measures to test the robustness of the plan and help track progress.
✔ Development of a process to implement the planning framework and techniques.

Many would argue that this is the most important part of the plan, because it deals with the actions that will help you to move the business from where it stands today to where you want to get to, as described in the vision. This is partly true, but you can only be confident that the implementation plan covers the right issues with the right priorities if the previous analysis is thorough.

1 Identifying the projects to go into the implementation plan

To make sure that the implementation plan includes the right projects, you need to check back to section 5 in Chapter 1 on key issues, and section 1.3 in Chapter 2 on strategies to achieve the vision.

The key issues list always provides the starting point for the implementation plan. Quite simply, if you have listed something as a key issue, it is highly likely that you need to take action on it. However, you also need to check the list of strategies to pick up any that are not already being dealt with or not included in somebody's job as 'business as usual'. There are three reasons for doing this:

- To make sure the implementation plan only picks up new projects that are not already being dealt with.
- To make sure you only deal with priority issues.

- To keep the list manageable — ideally, as short as possible.

This does not mean that you should ignore certain problems or issues, but you have to be realistic.

There is only so much time and resources available for projects, which is work that is effectively in addition to 'business as usual'. It is far better to work on a small number of top priority projects and complete them successfully than try to do too much and achieve nothing.

1.1 Constructing the implementation plan

To construct the implementation plan, you should use the techniques covered in Chapter 19 on how to design and manage projects. **Template 2.4 from the Strategic Planning section** of the website can be completed for the main projects in your business.

CASE STUDY

Too much to do, and too little time to do it!

The team from Blue and White had been working hard, and energy levels were falling. Vision had taken well over an hour, and at 4pm they turned their attention to implementation.

Siobhan suggested that at this stage all they needed to do was list the implementation projects and agree the main actions that would be needed to get the issue sorted. "There is a lot of detail here which is best worked up after this session; we will make sure we check it all through at our second half-day meeting to review and verify the plan after I have drafted it," she said.

The key issues were split into two groups: issues that were being dealt with, and those which were not and for which a plan was needed.

The 'business as usual' list included:

- The software change and associated process changes (Patrick Fuller and Siobhan had this under control already).

The project list included:

- Full launch of the new service proposition, following the pilot.
- Developing four new professional connections.
- Securing additional clients in the A and B groups.
- Professional training for advisers.
- Training on the new software and processes.

For each of the projects, they listed around five bullet points to summarise the main actions, and they also thought about who could take responsibility for each and over what timescale. Brian said, "We need to make sure we have got this right, so let's do exactly what Siobhan suggested and check this carefully in our next meeting; we don't want to take on too much and fail, particularly as we have a plan that looks as if it is taking good shape."

There was full agreement, and the workshop moved to the final short section on risk and monitoring.

CASE STUDY KEY POINT

In practice, planning sessions take a lot of energy, and the implementation plan is quite challenging because of the detail. The main aim should be to draft the main parts of this section, so that everyone has a clear idea of what actions will follow when the overall plan has been approved. The facilitator can take this away, and tidy up the implementation plan and make sure nothing major is missed. The 'cold light of day test' in the second meeting is a very effective way of checking that the implementation section is in good shape.

2 How to manage risk and monitor progress

The final part of the plan is to identify and manage risk and monitor progress.

2.1 Identify and neutralise the risks

To deal with risk, you need to identify any risks that could prevent the achievement of your plan. These can be internal or external. You also need to rate the risks in terms of their potential to occur and their impact on the business. The typical risks for advice businesses are:

Internal

- Loss of key people.
- Failure to monitor and manage the plan.
- Poor implementation of project management.
- Major compliance failure.

External

- Major stock market or economic disruption.
- Unforeseen distraction from regulator.
- Unexpected distraction from possible amalgamation.

If you think about these risks and their impact assessment, there are actions you can take to avoid or reduce them as outlined in Table 3.1.

The risk section of Blue and White Financial Service's plan would look like this. **Template 2.5** on the website provides a blank version of this Table for you to use.

2.2 Keep track of progress

You should undertake monitoring at two levels:

- Individual projects within the implementation plan.
- The key business performance indicators (KPIs) related to the overall financial objective and key supporting strategies.

The first of these is covered in Chapter 19 on project management; the second is dealt with here.

2.3 Monitoring key business performance indicators

These are based on the key numbers that are contained in the vision. You should be particularly interested in:

- Turnover.
- Recurring income.
- Costs.
- Profit.
- Client numbers.
- Productivity per adviser.
- Productivity per head of staff.

Table 3.1

RISK	LIKELIHOOD OF OCCURRENCE High, Medium or Low	IMPACT ON BUSINESS High, Medium or Low	RISK REDUCTION
Loss of key people	Low	Medium	Key-man cover and diversification of management and client responsibilities.
Failure to monitor and manage the plan	Medium	High	Robust monitoring and reporting processes.
Poor implementation project management	High	High	Robust project management processes.
Major compliance failure	Low	High	Full attention to good compliance practice and procedures.
Major stock market or economic disruption	Medium	Medium	Well trained clients who understand the risks — and plenty of communication if circumstances become difficult.
Unforeseen distraction from regulator	Medium	Medium	Keep up to date with industry issues — this makes unforeseen events become visible.
Unexpected distraction from possible amalgamation	Low	Medium	This is manageable if you instigate the discussions; if not there is little you can do in advance.

Table 3.2

RISK TO BLUE AND WHITE	LIKELIHOOD OF OCCURRENCE High, Medium or Low	IMPACT ON BUSINESS High, Medium or Low	RISK REDUCTION
Loss of key people	Low	High	Continue to develop other advisers to reduce dependence upon Brian and Lucy. Continue to delegate to Mary and Chris. Maintain key-man cover.
Failure to monitor and manage the plan	Low	Medium	Give Mary accountability to prepare review reports and place on agenda of appropriate monthly and quarterly meetings.
Poor implementation project management	Low	High	As above.
Major compliance failure	Low	Medium	Continue our high % file checking policy and ensure we review relevant MI at management meetings.
Major stock market or economic disruption	Medium	Medium	Make sure client details are maintained and up to date so we can make timely contact if this issue arises.
Unforeseen distraction from regulator	Low	Low	Ask Brian to make formal report on industry developments at quarterly Board meetings.
Unexpected distraction from possible amalgamation	Low	High	Cross this bridge if we come to it.

Table 3.3 **Business performance indicators**

BLUE AND WHITE FINANCIAL SERVICES	2010	2011	2012	2013	2014	2015
TURNOVER (£m)	1.2	1.3	1.2	1.3	1.5	1.8
RECURRING INCOME (£k)	580	600	650	650	750	800
RECURRING INCOME % OF TURNOVER	48	46	54	50	50	44
COSTS (£m)	1.02	1.105	1.02	1.105	1.225	1.4
PROFIT (£k/%)	180 (15)	195 (15)	180 (15)	195 (15)	275 (18)	400 (22)
CLIENTS	A: 275 B: 520 C: 1,200	A: 300 B: 600 C: 1,000	A: 325 B: 630 C: 1,000	A: 350 B: 670 C: 1,000	A: 375 B: 710 C: 1,000	A: 400 B: 750 C: 1,000
ADVISER PRODUCTIVITY (INCLUDING RECURRING) (£k)	150	163	170	186	188	200
ADVISER PRODUCTIVITY (EXCLUDING RECURRING) (£k)	78	88	79	93	94	111
PRODUCTIVITY PER MEMBER OF STAFF (£k)	80 (15)	87 (15)	86 (14)	93 (14)	94 (16)	106 (17)

This example, using the vision outlined for Blue and White Financial Services from section 1.2, should make this clear.

There are several points to note:

- The turnover, recurring income and profit targets are taken directly from the vision in Table 2.1.
- Costs increase in 2014 and 2015 to reflect recruitment.
- The rate of profit increases toward the end of the period to reflect economies of scale.
- Adviser productivity is ahead of industry averages (circa £100,000) for total income.
- Productivity per member of staff is just ahead of the typical range of £60,000–£90,000.

We will return to productivity in the next section.

The benefits of constructing a key business performance indicators matrix are as follows:

- It summarises the aims of your business on one side of paper.
- It provides a benchmark for you to measure progress and an opportunity to respond if actual performance differs from the plan.
- Inclusion of client numbers is important, because if the business acquires the numbers at the average values set out in the vision, it will achieve the headline turnover target.

Template 2.3 in Part 1 – Strategic Planning on the website provides a KPI Table for you to complete.

You can break down the data by month or half-year if required, and progress should be monitored on a monthly basis. In addition, you should prepare budgets and forecasts to make sure that the plan is fully costed and financially viable.

2.4 Productivity data

The productivity data in the preceding Table requires additional explanation. High levels of recurring income can inflate the average productivity of the advisers. It is important to note that the existence of recurring income implies that advisers will be servicing the clients as well as producing 'brand new' business (some of it from existing clients). Therefore, high levels of servicing would normally be associated with lower levels of brand new business, as is the case above.

The productivity of the total staff (advisers plus support) is influenced by:

- The mix of business (e.g. high levels of group pensions business tends to require more back office support).
- The efficiency and deployment of back office software.
- The ratio of support staff (that is, everyone excluding advisers) to advisers.

The starting point for the ratio between advisers and support staff is 1:1. This would apply in the following situation:

- Employed advisers (as in the first section in section 1).
- Mainly personal clients.
- High level of service.
- Para-planning to enhance adviser productivity.

The ratio will be higher if more than 40% of the business is group pensions (although this has become far less labour intensive with the introduction of e-services by the main providers), and if the advisers are producing in excess of £500,000 each and spending over 80% of their time with clients.

The ratio falls with the level of adviser support, and will often be much lower in the self-employed model, as shown in section 1.1. This is because self-employed advisers have to be more self-sufficient or hire their own support staff, who are separate from their host company. However, this is usually associated with lower levels of adviser productivity, while the hiring of support staff external to the company makes the productivity appear better than is actually the case.

3 Implementing the planning process in your business

This section will help you to put this chapter into practice in your business. Essentially, you need to follow the chapter section by section, using the tools and techniques that you find useful. However, to get the very best from this, you need to set up the planning process in a particular way.

MONITORING CHANGES IN CLIENT NUMBERS AND VALUE is a key part of measuring performance; if this stays on track, then the turnover targets will be achieved. Don't forget to combine this with monitoring costs and productivity to ensure the right profit outcome.

3.1 Select a good facilitator

As you will have seen, a lot of work is required to make sure you develop a robust plan as time-efficiently as possible. Clearly, you need to be heavily involved throughout the process, and this is best achieved if somebody else is responsible for running the process and the meetings. That gives you time to concentrate on the content and final outcome.

The facilitator must be able to:

- Turn work around quickly.
- Sort out main trends and direction from a wealth of detail.
- Write quickly and clearly on a flip chart.
- Use the templates in this document.
- Keep a meeting on track, in terms of both topic and time.

You would be wise to use a very capable and respected senior member of your team to do this; don't give it to the graduate trainee. If you do not have the right person, it is recommended that you use an external specialist who has a track record in facilitating this type of activity. It is more difficult than it may appear.

3.2 Before you start the process and run the first meeting

You need to consider the following:

- Whom to invite.
- What information to give in advance.
- What work (if any) you would like people to do before the first meeting.
- What you will do with the outcome.

It is recommended that you invite people who are:

- Key decision takers.
- Able to make a good contribution to the process.
- Vital to help deliver the plan and from whom you need acceptance from the outset.

The information is best set out in a clear document (an example follows). This tells people about the process, what they will cover and what you are trying to achieve. This is important, because the term 'business planning' can mean very different things, so setting expectations from the start is highly desirable.

In some cases, you can ask people to complete a template on strengths and weaknesses or issue the questionnaire you've created from **Template 1.4** before the first meeting. The facilitator should collate the results before the meeting for use in the strengths and weaknesses section.

FACILITATION is key to the success of business planning workshops. The quality of the outcomes varies directly with the effectiveness of the facilitator.

FOCUS POINT

Agenda for planning meetings, to be issued before the first meeting

BLUE AND WHITE FINANCIAL SERVICES LIMITED: STRATEGIC BUSINESS PLANNING

INTRODUCTION

The business is at a point in its development where it needs a clear three year strategic plan. The strategic planning exercise has the aim of producing:

- A three year strategic plan for the business.
- The initial one year implementation plan to support delivery.

PROCESS AND OUTPUTS

The process is split into three parts:

- Initial meeting: a full day workshop.
- Second meeting: a half-day workshop approximately two weeks after the main workshop to confirm the strategy and finalise implementation — this will be based on the written plan prepared after the first workshop.
- Review meetings: quarterly to track progress, and annually to review the entire plan and roll it forwards a further three years.

This is summarised in Figure 3.1.

WORKSHOP FORMAT

The workshop format will follow a straightforward business planning route map which is designed to take a wide range of information and analysis and distil it to key issues from which the plan can be derived.

The process was summarised earlier in Figure 1.4.

The approximate timings are as follows:

- Strengths and weaknesses: 2 hours.
- Opportunities and threats: 1 hour.
- Key issues: 30 minutes.
- Vision: 1 hour.
- Headline implementation: 1 hour.
- Risk and monitoring: 30 minutes.

The workshop will be facilitated by Siobhan Martin, and the aim is to be both creative and realistic and to provide a 'working' plan that will guide the business over the next three years.

BENEFITS

The benefits of this will be:

- Development of a clear direction for the business.
- Opportunity to express and debate our views on development of the business.
- Opportunity to prioritise and test ideas.
- Time for strategic thinking in contrast to the day to day operation of the business.
- Teambuilding within an agreed direction and plan.

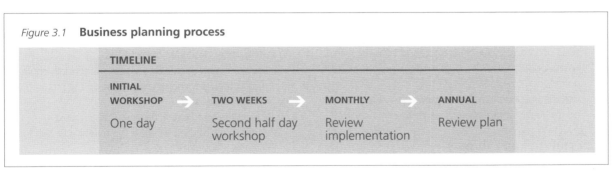

Figure 3.1 **Business planning process**

TIMELINE			
INITIAL WORKSHOP →	TWO WEEKS →	MONTHLY →	ANNUAL
One day	Second half day workshop	Review implementation	Review plan

3.3 The first meeting

The aim of this meeting is to work through the process as set out in this part of the book. The recommended running order is:

- Strengths and weaknesses: 2 hours.
- Opportunities and threats: 1 hour.
- Key issues: 30 minutes.
- Vision: 1 hour.
- Headline implementation: 1 hour.
- Risk and monitoring: 30 minutes.

You should set aside a full day and, if possible, run the meeting offsite to reduce distractions. You don't do this exercise very often, so creating the right conditions to achieve the best outcome is important.

In practice, the timings shown above vary a lot. This depends on the number of people involved, the experience of the facilitator, whether or not work has been done in advance and the scale of the issues to be discussed.

You should not worry about getting every last detail sorted out in this meeting, as long as there is enough clarity and agreement for the facilitator to prepare a first draft of the plan.

3.4 Tips for facilitating the first meeting

This is the meeting where all the hard work is done and there is a lot to cover. It is important that everyone makes a good contribution as well as keeping to time. To achieve this, the following activities work well.

Strengths and weaknesses:

- Ask people to write down as many strengths and weaknesses they can think of on post-it notes. Cluster these on two flip charts, and you will quickly get a detailed and collective view of what people think.
- Use Table 1.2 in Chapter 1, section 2, and ask "On a scale of 1 to 10 (where 1 is poor, and 10 is excellent), where do we stand?" This gets to the main areas quite quickly.
- Use the questionnaire from **Template 1.4** and home in on the really strong or negative areas.

Opportunities and threats:

- Run the same post-it exercise as under strengths and weaknesses.
- Take Figure 1.7 in Chapter 1, section 3, and ask if all of the generic issues are relevant and how they will affect the firm.
- Use the Table in the same section, split people into three or four groups (these can be groups of one) and give them different sections to complete; ask them to present back and give others an opportunity to comment.

Key issues:

- Ask people independently to write down their five key issues; give plenty of time for this, and suggest they review the flip charts on strengths, weaknesses, opportunities and threats. Record the responses on a flip chart under the business function headings, and you will find there will be a strong measure of agreement.

Vision:

The way you approach this is very much an individual choice and what you think will work best. This is also the point where you may want to take the lead, as principal. There are two approaches, and both work:

- Ask everyone to write down independently their key desires under each of the headings: record these on flip charts and debate the differences.
- Take the lead and give your view: it provides the others with a good starting point to respond to and build on.

To build up the vision:

- Take the financials first, outline the desired turnover figures and then think about the number of advisers and what contribution they would need to make.
- Using the same turnover numbers, try to factor in the contribution from client segments. This, along with the adviser contribution, is a good test of the feasibility of the plan. Always ask the question, "What are the trends from the past two or three years?" If your projections are way ahead of the trends, you have to ask the question, "What is it about this plan that gives us confidence that we can achieve these higher numbers?"
- When you are happy with the financials, move to resources and ask the question, "Can we operate on the same level of support or do we need more, less or different?" Drawing the organisation chart often helps this debate, but always base the chart on jobs, not people. You should deal with any people issues in the manner described in Part 6.
- The remaining parts of the vision are normally more straightforward, and you can build up the picture from the collective view.
- You will need to check the financial and cost implications of the plan after the meeting to test for viability.

Strategies:

These should be drafted by the facilitator after the initial meeting. There will be enough in the vision to work these out. Just ask the question, "What do we need to do (or continue doing) under each of the functional headings to achieve these turnover and profit targets?"

Implementation:

The important point is to concentrate on setting up the project, not solving the problem. That is what the project is designed to do. Work through the process covered in Chapter 19 on project management.

Key business performance indicators:

These should be drafted by the facilitator after the meeting based on the numbers in the vision.

Risk:

The final part of the initial planning meeting should identify risks to the success of the plan. List them on a flip chart and ask how they can be reduced. It is likely that most actions are already being taken; if not, draft them into the implementation plan.

Monitoring:

You should agree how frequently you will check on progress. The following is recommended:

- Projects contained in the implementation plan: weekly.
- Key business performance indicators: monthly.
- Overall plan: quarterly.
- Review and update of the plan to roll it forwards a further year: annually.

3.5 After the first meeting

The facilitator should draft the plan based on documents created using the templates listed in section 4 of the templates document for the Part 1 —Strategic Planning on the website. They should highlight any gaps or inconsistencies, and circulate it to all those who attended in advance of the second meeting. You need to be satisfied that the draft is as accurate as it can be and that you will be happy to present it to the team at the second meeting.

In the brief for the second meeting, you should remind participants of the desired outcome (a robust three year business plan) and that the aim of the second meeting is to review the outputs from the initial meeting and complete any outstanding work.

3.6 The second meeting

The aim of this meeting is to review the draft plan, fill in any gaps, and in particular make sure the implementation plan is clear and achievable.

The recommended running order is:

- Review of draft plan, section by section: 1 hour.
- Overview discussion to check the plan is realistic and achievable: 30 minutes.
- Detailed review of the implementation section to make sure that each project is clearly specified and that those responsible will be able to complete the work in the time: up to 1 hour.
- Communications plan to inform rest of staff: 30 minutes.

3.7 After the second meeting

The facilitator should finalise the plan and circulate it one final time for any remaining amendments.

You should secure formal endorsement of the plan at the next senior management meeting and agree arrangements for the staff presentation. Some firms present the entire plan, while others take out sensitive material (which is perfectly reasonable) and cut the presentation to the key slides. Your formal presentation to staff should be no more than 30 minutes and, as suggested in Chapter 24, this often works well if it is operated as a special event which may be combined with annual awards (if you have such a scheme) or refreshments. It is good to go offsite, but you have to judge the benefits against the cost.

3.8 Drafting the plan

The plan should have the following contents, which follow the process we have described in this chapter:

- Context: short profile of the business.
- Executive summary: headlines from each main section.
- Business capability: internal audit (strengths and weaknesses).
- Market analysis: implications for the business (opportunities and threats).
- Key issues.
- Vision: three to five years (variable).
- Business objective and strategies.
- Implementation.
- Key business performance indicators.
- Risks.
- Monitoring.

4 Chapter summary

This chapter has provided you with an overview to construct the implementation plan and identify and manage risks. In addition it has detailed a process to use the tools and techniques from the previous chapters to prepare a robust three year business plan. As you will have seen, you need your top team to devote almost two days to this, and the person who facilitates the process will be required for much longer. However, this is a small investment of time to prepare a plan designed to take the business through the next three years. At the very least, you have a favoured direction and vision to work with, and against which you can evaluate any changes in the market or opportunities that are outside your initial plans.

There are no particularly good or bad times to undertake planning, although avoiding business peaks is sensible. In effect, there is never a perfect time, because as much as it would be nice to stop the clock or start with a blank sheet of paper, that luxury rarely happens.

There are very few instances where not having a strategic planning is a good thing. It does not guarantee success, but it increases the chances of moving in the direction that you desire, as opposed to being forced to respond to the whims of the market and regulator.

The management skills you have developed as a result of this chapter mean that you can:

- Confirm where development resources should be used.
- Work out what you need to do to implement the plan.
- Use key business performance indicators to test the plan and manage its outcome.
- Identify and manage planning risks.
- Organise your team to develop a plan for your business which everyone supports.

Part 2: How to develop an effective service proposition

What are you offering, who is it for and how will you deliver it?

"Being on par in terms of price and quality only gets you into the game. Service wins the game."

Tony Alessandra

"Although your customers won't love you if you give bad service, your competitors will."

Kate Zabriskie

Introduction: Design service to sustain your business

When you have completed this Part, you will be able to:

✔ Define and describe your target market.
✔ Evaluate the potential of target markets.
✔ Design and implement a comprehensive service proposition.
✔ Design and implement a transparent pricing policy.
✔ Ensure your service and pricing policy supports TCF.
✔ Clearly explain your service offering to clients.

Over the past few years, the term 'service proposition' has become common. This is because many advice businesses have decided to define their services formally, particularly as part of the Treating Customers Fairly (TCF) initiative and in response to the development of adviser charging.

We are defining a service proposition as 'a coherent set of services that are designed for a specific group of clients'. It is perfectly reasonable for you to have two or three propositions aimed at different client groups, but you must ensure a clear distinction between them. For example, many advisers offer a different service to business owners from that offered to pension scheme members.

Service propositions have important benefits

You can easily think of businesses that have 'joined up' service. John Lewis Partnership is a widely used example, where the service standards and style of delivery are consistent between departments and stores. There are also plenty of examples where this is not the case and you know that, despite the fact you are a customer, doing business will be difficult and frustrating.

The main benefit of a clear service proposition lies in the word 'consistency'. Clients will know what they are going to receive, and you and the others in the business will know what has to be done. That means that you can be confident in selling your services to clients and setting a price that is

profitable, in the certainty that you and your support team will provide the service to the right standards at the right time.

Firms that can achieve this have a competitive advantage. All advisers have the same generic proposition, which is 'advice services', but it is the style and consistency of delivery that sets businesses apart. This is particularly the case in the service sector, where products are intangible, so it makes processes and behaviours – what you do and how you do it – even more important.

Service proposition: where do you stand?

The Table that follows asks Ten Killer Questions about service. They summarise what is 'good' in service design and delivery. Whatever your score, this book is designed to help raise it, possibly by a substantial amount.

For each question, give your business an objective score (1 is poor, and 10 is excellent) and ask others what they think. **Template 1.1 in Part 2 – Developing a Service Proposition** on the website lays this out as a questionnaire for you to circulate.

If you have scored around 50%, you will be close to the majority of advice businesses. A score of less than 30% means that there is a lot of work to be done. If you have over 70%, you will be in the top 10% of firms who are already securing a competitive advantage through service delivery.

These questions imply tough standards, and most advice businesses will have low scores for numbers 1, 2, 5, 6, 9 and 10. This is because the majority of firms do a good job for their clients and have a good service ethic in the back office. However, they are less thorough when it comes to stating formally what clients will receive and following up service in a timely manner. This is one of the reasons for the rising trend in client complaints about service, ie where client expectations have not been established at the outset and communication has broken down.

The practicalities of developing an effective service proposition

The rest of this Part will take you through the steps required to define your proposition, and the final chapter includes a specific process that you can use in your business.

We will cover:

- Targeting clients — who they are and why they will come to you.
- Designing service — the detail of what you will offer.
- Pricing policy — what you will charge.
- Practical processes to support implementation in your business.

SERVICE: Ten killer questions

Score: 1 = poor, and 10 = excellent

To what extent:

1. Do you have a well defined service and pricing policy?

2. Do you have a clear description of your main target clients?

3. Do you sell advice, not products?

4. Do your clients know what service they will receive and how they will be charged?

5. Is your service delivered consistently, by all your advisers?

6. Do you always deliver ongoing service on time?

7. Have you achieved your turnover and profit targets in at least seven of the last ten years?

8. Are roles designed to enable excellent service delivery?

9. Does service provide the basis for client segmentation?

10. Are advisers spending 80% of their client time with those who are most profitable?

Chapter 4
Be clear about your target market

By the end of this chapter, your business will benefit from:

✔ A clear description of target market.
✔ A detailed understanding of target market.
✔ A segmented client base.
✔ A clear link between client segments and services.
✔ A shared knowledge of which clients are the most valuable.

This chapter is about concentrating on a part of the market where your expertise and service will excel, to the benefit of your target clients and the profitability of your business.

If you ask advisers to describe their target market, they will often say, "Anyone with money", "High net worth", "People over 40 years old" and "Everyone who is upmarket". While these descriptions give some direction, they are too broad and open to different interpretations. The more specific you can be, the more effectively you can tailor your service proposition. This will provide clarity and consistency both within the business and when you promote your services through marketing or networking.

It is good practice to have a core target market that is expected to sustain profitability into the longer term. In reality, a number of clients (typically up to 20%) may be outside the target market, but that is no great problem — if they like your service and are prepared to pay for it, why should you turn them away? However, you should always concentrate on your main target market and avoid dilution of your client base.

Many advisers have used the exercise of targeting to introduce a discipline in the business that clearly states who will be taken on as a client and who will not. In some cases, clients will 'self-select', particularly when service is well defined and prices are transparent. There is no doubt that this really concentrates the business on what it does and who it does it for, but you must be certain that the selected target market is viable and receptive to the service proposition.

TARGET CLIENTS are a group of people with similar characteristics who have predictable behaviours in a particular marketplace.

1 You can benefit from a clear target market

If a specific group of people regards your business as being specialist and understanding them, then you will have achieved a point of distinction that cannot be easily copied. No other adviser can come straight into your market and compete head-on. The advice market is not an easy place to build sustainable points of distinction, so concentrating on a particular segment of the market and delivering highly tailored advice and service is an effective way for you to achieve this.

To review where your business stands, ask your advisers to answer the following questions:

- Can all of the people in the business describe our main target markets?
- To what extent do we, the advisers, target the same groups of clients?
- Do we lose out collectively because we do not share the same target clients, or are we genuinely so different that we have to accept this?
- When was the last time we reviewed exactly what our target clients want from us?
- How close is our desired target market to our existing client profile?
- How good is our understanding of our existing client base?
- Is our target market viable and expanding?
- Will our target market be the same in five years' time?

Use **Template 1.2 in Part 2 – Developing a Service Proposition** on the website to circulate the questionnaire.

If you and the advisers have answered "No" to any of these questions, this chapter will help to improve your business and enable you to benefit from the detail on service design that follows.

Clear targeting increases profitability because:

- You can tailor your service and expertise to fit closely with what your clients need. This will give the perception of specialisation.
- You can streamline your processes and minimise variations. This will cut your costs and make your business efficient.
- Your marketing (networking, developing introducers, advertising, etc) can be specific in content and direction to maximise returns and minimise wastage.
- You gain a positive reputation in a particular part of the market, and enjoy the benefits of client recommendation and referrals.

CASE STUDY

Define the target and reap the long term rewards

Red Retirement Financial Planning (RRFP) is a very focused business. It was set up ten years ago to provide retirement planning services to the employees of companies exceeding 100 people. The research it conducted showed that people wanted a comprehensive picture of retirement to provide a context for the financial issues that were likely to arise. Health and time use were just as important as income and 'how long the money would last'.

The business put together two main propositions: the first was for in-house programmes for large firms, and the second was for open programmes to which smaller businesses could send their employees. The programmes were seminar-based, ran over three months, and included a full range of retirement issues as well as those referred to above. Specialists such as doctors and lawyers were used in conjunction with the financial advisers from RRFP.

RRFP used business directories to identify and target firms in a 50-mile radius, concentrating upon those with higher value employees and a positive attitude toward employee benefits, of which this service was one. With an aging population, the demand for this service and the financial planning that inevitably flows from it has increased steadily, particularly as RRFP has gained a reputation as a specialist in its field.

When asked why the firm adopted this approach, the managing director refers to other businesses that had successfully concentrated on particular parts of the market, such as will writing and trust planning, nursing home fees and education funding. She says, "We wanted to concentrate our efforts and expertise in one part of the market to really stand out – this market (financial planning) is so crowded that we thought a point of distinction would be really important. Our business figures suggest we made the right choice."

Claret and Blue Financial Services (CBFS) is owned by Euan Macdonald and Amanda Holland. Their current location is just off the high street in a town in the Midlands that is thriving less now than when they set up 25 years ago. CBFS has a shop front and, as the lease is running out, debate is raging about the importance of 'walk-in' business.

Euan makes the point that, "Anyone can walk in, they know where we are and if they have just won the lottery we are well placed to sort them out". He recalls the £500,000 case from ten years ago that "paid the rent for a year" from a client who had recently inherited two properties and needed advice.

Amanda is not convinced. She asks, "How many times have we spent an hour or more with people who are very genuine, but should really be in the Citizens Advice Bureau rather than in our office?" To make the point more firmly, she recalls the number of times they had discussed concentrating on "higher value clients" to make better use of their time and increase their profits. "Our problem is that we have a very laudable service ethic, which is to deal with whoever walks through the door, so look at our client bank built up over 25 years – over 15,000 names on a list, in files stacked from floor to ceiling, and only a few hundred really longlasting clients of good value, who we have never got time to deal with properly – not much to show for 25 years of hard graft!"

CASE STUDY KEY POINT
The benefits of concentrating on one part of the market can be significant in terms of streamlining, building up expertise and gaining a reputation that others find difficult to copy. This can be based around a specific need, such as the retirement planning example, or particular types of people in certain circumstances.

Where does your business stand between these two extremes? If it is close to Claret and Blue then, shop front or otherwise, it is never too late to change. However, the longer you leave it, the greater the problem will become and potentially the lower the value of your business.

2 Identifying and changing target markets

There are some important practical issues that will influence your approach to this. The majority of advice businesses have been around for at least five years, and many for much longer. That means that they have an existing client bank which will often be quite diverse, particularly if there have been acquisitions or high adviser turnover. As a result, there could be a difference between the selected target market for the business and the existing client base.

If this is the case for your business, it should not stop you identifying your core target market for the future. There are often circumstances where advisers and advice businesses will want to change direction and redefine who they really want as clients. It may take five years to change the profile of the client base, but if that enables you to shift to a more profitable client group then it is clearly worthwhile.

2.1 Evaluate your target market

In terms of identifying target markets, there are no right answers. So much depends upon the location and history of your business, as well as the capabilities and experience of your advisers. But there are ways of evaluating whether or not your target market is worthwhile. You will need to answer the following questions — use **Template 1.3 in Part 2 — Developing a Service Proposition** on the website:

- Can your target be clearly defined — particularly in terms of what it requires from you?
- Is your target viable in terms of numbers of potential clients and buying power?
- What is the range of products and services they are likely to buy from you, how often should you see them, and how much will they invest?
- Can you reach the target, either directly or through introducers? Will they be receptive to referring you to similar prospective clients?
- Will it be easy to communicate with them, and what methods should you use?
- Can you obtain lists of names and addresses, can you use their professional or business community, and do they respond to e-mail or prefer formal letters?
- Do you have the knowledge and capability to successfully attract and service this target market? If not, how long will it take to build up?

If you are seriously considering devoting time and money to developing a new target market, you should share these questions with as many colleagues as possible. By their nature, some of the answers are difficult to quantify, which means that well considered commercial judgement is necessary. An hour spent debating these questions and testing the depth of the answers will always be time well spent.

2.2 Examples of successful target markets

It is always good practice to be clear about your target market, and to make sure everyone in the business knows what type of person (or business) you are targeting. You will then secure the benefits of good targeting listed above.

However, the vigour with which you advertise, network and promote to a target market will vary, depending upon the life stage of the business.

For example, it may be that you have a mature and profitable client base, and have developed your firm so that 60% of new business comes from existing clients and the rest from recommendation and a small amount of marketing. If that is the case, you have achieved an ideal benchmark. Your client base is self-sustaining and profitable, and there is little pressure or need to identify and pursue new target clients.

However, if the business is at the start-up stage, you will need to identify the target market and work very hard in securing a share of it. In the early days, financial pressure often means businesses will accept a wide range of clients. You should avoid this, because it will save the time and complexity of reviewing and refining the client base at a later date.

Here are some examples of client groups that advisers have successfully targeted:

- **Specific professions:** doctors, dentists, lawyers, bankers, city traders, computer specialists, footballers and rugby players.
- **Business sectors:** information technology, sport, marketing and advertising, print and publishing, media and service industries.
- **Businesses:** often defined by sector as above, but also

TARGET MARKETS must be reachable, viable, sustainable and profitable.

by size, number of employees, turnover and profit, recruitment policy (attitude toward employee benefits) and acquisition activity.

- **Life stages and life events:** pre- and post-retirement, mid-life (often linked with redundancy services), retired and older age, divorced, family providers, personal injury litigants, will writers and tax planners.
- **Very specific groups requiring a specific service:** pension scheme wind-ups, trustee investors, people with over £1m to invest, pension transfers and nursing home fees.

2.3 Look for complementary target markets

Many advice businesses have more than one target market, although there are often links between them. Business owners and their employees are a common combination, comprising up to four sets of client needs, as demonstrated in the following Figure. As Figure 4.1 shows, there are four different sets of needs, with the business owner having both a corporate and personal perspective. These can be summarised as follows:

- **Business owners:** corporate decision taker for pension schemes, additional employee benefits, group risk and key person cover.
- **Business owners:** private individuals for their own financial planning.
- **Senior employees:** financial planning.
- **Other employees:** scheme membership, straightforward advice and transactional services.

To satisfy these needs, you could easily develop three clear propositions: one which is corporate, another for 'wealth management' and a third for straightforward planning and transactions. These would all wrap together as a very cohesive set of services to discuss with the business owners or key decision takers.

2.4 Describe the target market as clearly as you can

This is about writing down the description of the identified target market. At first glance, you may think this is not necessary – and if you have been advising for more than ten years, you may well feel that you know clients and their needs in great detail. However, you will achieve real benefits from a clear and detailed description, particularly when it is shared with others in the business.

Benefits from target market description:

- Shared understanding across the business of who the main target clients are.
- Concentration of service and attention on the target group.
- Rapid build-up of expertise and understanding across the business.
- Acts as a key benchmark to test that the business is on track to achieve its strategic objectives.

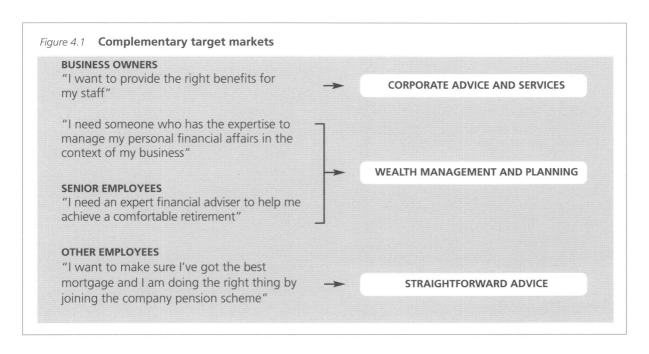

Figure 4.1 **Complementary target markets**

BUSINESS OWNERS
"I want to provide the right benefits for my staff" → **CORPORATE ADVICE AND SERVICES**

"I need someone who has the expertise to manage my personal financial affairs in the context of my business"

SENIOR EMPLOYEES
"I need an expert financial adviser to help me achieve a comfortable retirement" → **WEALTH MANAGEMENT AND PLANNING**

OTHER EMPLOYEES
"I want to make sure I've got the best mortgage and I am doing the right thing by joining the company pension scheme" → **STRAIGHTFORWARD ADVICE**

FOCUS POINT

Target descriptions

'WEALTH BUILDERS'

Wealth builders are aged between 35 and 50 (when they tend to become pre-retirement planners) and are employed in senior management or professional positions. Their partners are likely to be working, often in similar level jobs, and their teenage children will be independently educated.

The total household income will be between £100,000 and £150,000, and there will be additional annual lump sum bonuses for one of the partners. This group will have a desire to retire early and the motivation to plan for it.

They will make large regular pension contributions, as well as lump sum investments; their aim is to build a sizeable retirement fund to sustain their standard of living.

This group will tend to be very busy, and will favour online communications (where relevant) and a businesslike approach to financial planning. They will want to keep on top of their investments, and will rely upon their adviser to make them aware of any tax or legislative changes that need to be taken into account.

They will expect to meet at least once a year and to be able to access the value of their investments online. From time to time, they will call or e-mail and will expect a prompt response, but they are unlikely to waste your time with trivial issues.

'PRODUCT BUYERS'

Product buyers will have straightforward financial affairs and will be valuable clients over their lifetimes, but there may be long gaps between direct contact and product purchase.

Their needs are driven much more by life stage and triggered by events than a long term financial plan. They will span the age ranges, and are likely to become clients for mortgages and protection before moving on to pensions and other one-off savings, such as ISAs. They want a reliable and local adviser who keeps in touch (often by bi-annual newsletter) and who will be around when they need him. They will tend to grow more anxious about their financial affairs as they pass 50, and pre- and at retirement advice will be extremely important to them. At this stage, they may have up to £100,000 to be dealt with and are likely to want 'peace of mind' for retirement with products and investments that are low maintenance.

Product buyers are not very demanding, and financial planning is a low priority for them, except when events demand greater involvement. They will not expect to see their adviser very often, and then only when there is a particular issue or product purchase to be dealt with.

3 Profile your existing client base

As you have seen, target marketing is about splitting **prospective** clients into well defined categories. The same principle applies to an **existing** client base.

If your client data are up to date, comprehensive and held on a modern back office system, you can obtain a detailed picture of your client base. All the back office systems enable you to profile by age, product holdings, investment values and other variables, provided you have collected the data. In practice, the data are not always sufficient, so you will require a shortcut approach.

There are two ways to achieve workable results:

- Profiling by client value.
- Profiling by adviser perception.

3.1 Profile by client value

This is a very effective way of profiling your client base, because it concentrates on the value of your clients to the business. Most businesses have a record of the annual recurring income for each client (renewal commission, fund-based commission, fees, etc), and will typically split their client base into three parts. The following segments are often used:

- Over £1,000 pa.
- Between £500 pa and £1,000 pa.
- Less than £500 pa.

This will give you an overview of how many clients fit into each band. You may need to run the exercise more than once to achieve a typical profile, which has 20% of the client base in the first group, 50% in the second group, and the rest in the third group.

There is a degree of trial and error required here. It is best to stick to three bands for simplicity, but you may need to alter the ranges. Using the previous examples, the 'wealth builders' will be in the first group and the 'product buyers' in the second.

Clients in the first group will receive a proactive service with a lot of contact, whereas those in the third are likely to be handled on a transactional basis. This approach will enable you to tailor your service to the value of the clients, and will be covered in detail further on.

It is inevitable that profiling in this manner will place some clients at the margin of the bands in the 'wrong' group. There are many reasons for moving clients up and down (their contacts with other potential clients, they are less than two years from retirement, they are far too demanding in relation to their value, etc), but you must maintain a consistent approach across all your advisers. So, changes like this should be done with all advisers present, and should never involve more than 10% of the active client bank (the

first two groups). If it exceeds 10%, the bands are probably incorrect and you will need to revise them.

3.2 Profile by adviser perception

Profiling by adviser perception is very rough and ready, and you should only use it as a last resort, although it has the benefit of simplicity. The challenge is to get all your advisers to agree on the criteria for each segment. Inevitably, mature advisers are likely to have higher value clients than junior advisers, and so will place their clients in the first group, whereas the junior advisers will have most clients in the third or second group.

If your business has a policy of dealing with clients by category, then it has to recognise that the 'top clients' of a junior adviser are important to that adviser and must pitch the level of service and contact accordingly. We will deal with this in the next chapter on service design; it will always be a matter of judgement as to what level and quantity of service you provide to the different groups.

In the absence of useful data, there is a framework which you can use to help this process, but it is only as good as the knowledge of the client bank held by the advisers. Typically, knowledge is good for top clients, patchy for secondary clients, and non-existent for the third group.

The framework that follows is based on client loyalty, determined by the number of transactions.

If advisers can be provided with a list of clients, they can normally identify all their advocates and supporters, and many of the dormant customer group. By elimination, this leaves the client group in the middle.

With this model, the differences between the client groups of individual advisers have to be accepted, but at least it enables categorisation to take place with a common approach across the adviser team.

The real value of this model is its practicality, because there are clear implications for how each group should be dealt with. You can vary the level and types of contact between the groups, as well as the range of service.

CASE STUDY

Simple models can crack difficult questions

Sarah Davies runs a successful advice business in the south-west. She has eight employed IFAs working for her, and has a clear view about corporate standards and the importance of sticking to them. This is particularly the case with service and client management, and she has welcomed the TCF and RDR because these initiatives have helped her sustain this approach.

In spite of this, she has struggled with one of the most difficult issues, involving standards. "We all categorise our clients, mainly by value, and deal with them in different ways that reflect this. However, we all do this slightly differently; I have been in the business for several years, so my client bank and method of working differs from Alan Smith, who is a junior adviser with a very different group of clients. We just can't seem to crack this one."

Sarah shared this view with a business client, who mentioned how he had used the 'loyalty ladder' as a way of pulling this together. He was in the wholesale market for building products, and had a wide range of clients served by a small team of account managers. He faced exactly the same problem.

At the next 'adviser away-day', Sarah decided to raise this issue. Before the event, she asked Jackie, her senior administrator, to categorise all of the clients by value. This was a very revealing exercise, partly because there were some gaps in the data that Sarah was not aware of, and also because the value of several clients was different from her perception. Jackie used quite a bit of trial and error to come up with categories that seemed to work, and eventually she and Sarah decided on over £1,500 pa for 'supporters and advocates',

£750–£1,500 pa for 'clients', and less than £750 pa for 'customers'. They then allocated all these clients to their advisers, so they could see the pattern from the perspective of the client loyalty ladder and the adviser client lists.

At the away-day, most of the advisers shared the same degree of surprise as Sarah. The actual lists looked different from what they had thought. Sarah observed, "We are all busy, and it is easy to forget, and get clients muddled – especially in the middle range, where we have over 2,500 people listed."

Laura Austin, who had been advising for over ten years, suggested that the firm look at the possibility of tailoring its service to reflect the value of the different groups. "What about some minimum service standards for each group, such as how often we should see them, whether or not they get newsletters and investment commentaries? If you put together what we all do as individual advisers, it looks a bit of a muddle, even though we do look after our clients."

Laura continued: "I bet this happens in many advice businesses, when time pressure means that, in the absence of clear guidelines, advisers work out their own service standards."

It took some time to finally sort the clients into the three groups, but once that was done Sarah was able to set up minimum service standards and communications to run across the entire client base. The advisers were happy with the clarity that this brought, and Jackie was able to streamline a lot of the administration processes linked directly to service delivery.

CASE STUDY KEY POINT

Straightforward models can often be the most useful. They are easy for people to understand and apply. They provide a 'common language' and a framework around which service and communications can be standardised.

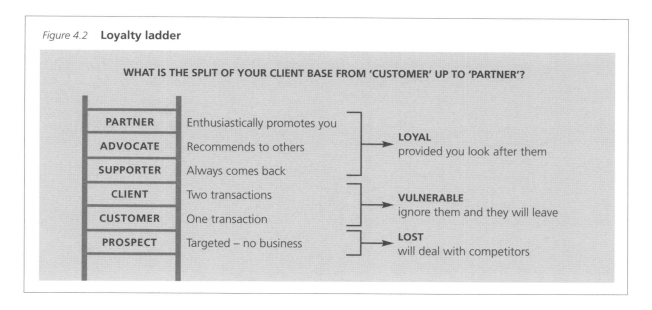

Figure 4.2   **Loyalty ladder**

4 Chapter summary

The management skills you have developed as a result of this chapter mean that you can:

- Describe your target market.
- Communicate it to others in the business.
- Segment your clients by value.
- Direct your efforts to the right clients.
- Use your client profile to support service design.

This chapter has dealt with the fundamentals of service design. You cannot do this properly if you do not have clear picture of your existing client base and your desired target market. It is highly likely that these will overlap, but, if they don't, then understanding the differences is important. In addition, if all the people in the business have a shared understanding of the target market and the key clients, you will deliver more effective service. It will help with the consistency of service delivery and make sure that back office processes line up with client needs.

Chapter 5

Why service design is fundamental to your business

By the end of this chapter, your business will benefit from:

✔ A clear definition of service and price.
✔ More profitable clients.
✔ Fewer loss-making clients.
✔ A consistent approach to communicating service to clients.
✔ Consistent service delivery.
✔ The achievement of a major part of Treating Customers Fairly.

While service design is one of the most important activities that you need to get right, it is also one of the most time consuming. As a result, we will present a practical approach to designing service in Chapter 7. In practice, it often takes businesses at least a year from the initial meeting on service through to the first stages of implementation with new clients.

This is for three main reasons that are best recognised at outset:

- The process involves a lot of detail which is very important and must be right.
- Implementation often requires advisers to change the way they do things, and we are all creatures of habit. We individually work out an approach that suits us best, so change − even if we know it is right − will take some time and space.
- The back office processes and jobs often need to be revised, which always takes time, particularly as the current business must be dealt with. In practice, you cannot close your business for six months while you make this change.

1 Design service to integrate business

In the introduction to this part, we used the phrase 'joined up' to describe good service delivery. There is a framework that many successful advisers have used that shows how service design influences all other parts of the business. Everything that is summarised on Figure 5.1 will be covered in detail later in the book; at this stage, you should only be concerned with how the different parts link together to emphasise the benefits of well defined service.

SERVICE DESIGN is about detail, taking time to get it right, and making sure everyone is involved.

As you will see, the Figure summarises a clear sequence of events that begins and ends with people. Clients are at the beginning, and the people in the business are at the end.

Figure 5.1 **Six steps to service design**

1. IDENTIFY CLIENT NEEDS
Why will they come to us?

2. SUMMARISE SERVICE PROPOSITION
What will you do and how will you do it?

3. DEFINE SERVICE CONTENT
What actions will you take and when will you take them?

4. DEFINE COMMUNICATIONS
What information and documents will you provide and when will you do it?

5. DETERMINE PROCESSES AND ORGANISATION
How will your business processes and IT (what you and your back office do) ensure you deliver this service consistently?

6. CONFIRM WHAT PEOPLE WILL DO
Have you got the right people in the right jobs doing the right things?

These six steps to service design provide you with a clear process to work through and a set of questions to answer. As indicated above, all of these will be covered in this chapter or other parts of the book.

You should begin with **client needs**, and a clear description of what your clients will require and what benefits you will bring to them. We will cover this in detail in the next section when we deal with target markets.

You can then summarise your **proposition** to use with clients to demonstrate the worth and value of what you do and how you do it. This is something many advisers do towards the end of their first meeting with a client: "So, in summary, we will undertake a detailed review of your affairs, analyse where you stand now against where you want to be, and then work out a plan with clear steps and reviews along the way." This is just one example, and we will look at some alternatives further on in this chapter.

Service content means the specific activities you will undertake for your clients, and **communications** include everything that you will send them, regardless of format. This ranges from newsletters and reports through to hard copy and web-based materials.

Finally, you need to make sure that your back office processes and software are set up and **organised** in a way that ensures you can deliver the service your clients require. This goes hand in hand with the jobs **people** do and how well trained and organised they are to do them. It includes everyone in the business: advisers, technical support and administrators.

This is a lot to ask, but if you can link these parts together you will achieve the benefits of consistently delivered service.

CONSISTENCY is key to providing a joined up service proposition that will give you a real competitive advantage.

CASE STUDY

Investigate the symptoms to diagnose the problem

Bill Batham had built up his advice business over 15 years and had successfully steered it through many market changes and economic cycles. He worked hard and admitted that his was a classic case of "working in the business as opposed to working on the business".

So, one particularly bright morning in early summer, he decided to take a step back and try to look at his firm through the eyes of his clients. He did not have much time, so he was drawn to the more visible aspects of the business, especially his brochures, letterheads, business cards, website and logo. There was no doubt that they looked 'tired and dated' and this underlined the fact that he had been trying to get round to sorting them out.

His first client appointment was with a local businessman, Adrian Evans, who he knew well and with whom he enjoyed a good open relationship. In Bill's view, this client ran a 'very tidy business', and he asked him what he thought of the materials he had assembled.

Adrian was a straight talker and told Bill all of the material needed to be "freshened up", but — and this was the key point — if the image was tired and muddled, it was likely that other parts of the business suffered the same problem.

Adrian said to Bill, "From a client perspective, I come to you because I trust you and you know your stuff — so I put up with having to remind you that it is time for the annual valuation or that you need to send me certain documents at the end of the tax year."

Adrian paused and then said, "I can never really pin down what service I should expect and, if I am honest, exactly what it costs me." Adrian's final comment really hit home: "This is why I never feel comfortable recommending you to my friends and family."

Later in the day, Bill reflected on this conversation and realised he had experienced one of those 'moments of truth' that arise from time to time. The logo and marketing materials were just a symptom of an underlying problem. The entire business needed to be 'freshened up' and reviewed in the cold light of day.

Adrian was right: the service and pricing were not well defined, the back office processes were not geared around client service and there was nothing clear in Bill's mind (let alone in tangible form) about where the business really stood in the market and what the service proposition was.

CASE STUDY KEY POINT

Businesses that have their service really well defined and deliver it consistently normally have everything else in good shape. This is because much of what advice businesses do flows from service, and if it is well organised, everything else becomes easier to organise. It also means that they can make the most of their expertise and capabilities by concentrating on what is important for their clients and, importantly, what they can charge for.

Where does your business stand? Look at the symptoms on the surface and then dig deeper; ask your colleagues and a few trusted clients. You will quickly be able to gauge the current position.

2 The practicalities of design and implementation

In practice, advisers tend to be good at designing service, while their senior administrators are good at developing the supporting processes. This is because much of this process requires the formalisation and tidying up of something you have been doing for many years. Provided you recognise that it will take time, because you have to take all your people with you, you can complete this task.

There is often a lot of pressure associated with 'day one', when you launch your new service propositions. Despite all your best judgements, you cannot be certain how clients will react when you discuss your new advice services and pricing policy for the first time. However, you can reduce the risks that are often perceived around this by working through the job in a structured manner, giving sufficient time for each part. This is summarised in Figure 5.2.

Figure 5.2 **Service design and implementation – Timeline**

2 MONTHS
Initial service design

1 MONTH
Research with sample of existing clients

3 MONTHS
Pilot: brand new clients and sample of advisers

1 MONTH
Review pilot and make changes

1 MONTH
Train and role play other advisers

12-24 MONTHS
Roll out to existing clients over 12-24 months

To be certain that your service proposition and content are robust and work well with new and existing clients, you need to:

- Test your proposals well in advance with respected clients whom you know will give you a genuine opinion.
- Implement the new propositions with brand new clients first for a pilot period of three months, possibly starting with one or two advisers as opposed to the entire group.

- Share the experience of the pilot with all the advisers and make changes if required.
- Train all advisers, and role play the new conversations and predicted objection handling that may emerge.
- Introduce the new propositions with existing clients only after the pilot and decide whom you need to see and who can be contacted remotely. A sample marketing plan to help organise this exercise is in Chapter 12, section 2.1.
- Roll out the new service to existing clients over a period of 12–24 months.
- Be prepared to make adjustments if necessary.

This checklist is contained in **Template 3.1 in Part 2 – Developing a Service Proposition** on the website.

This project is one of the most complex that you will undertake, because it affects everyone in the business and many of the clients. Indeed, it is the heart of the business, because it is what everyone works on to deliver effectively, and it is what the clients receive as the tangible output of all your efforts and hard work.

2.1 Use Treating Customers Fairly (TCF) to support service design

Well designed service, clearly communicated to clients and consistently delivered, lies at the heart of TCF. It also lies at the heart of good business practice. There is a clear link between the aims of the TCF and Retail Distribution Review (RDR) initiatives. Firms which have developed and applied an effective TCF plan will be well placed to enhance their service further.

Specifically, from a TCF perspective, this approach to service design will make sure you give your clients what you have promised and what they are paying for. That is one of the reasons you should take time to get it right and be prepared to make changes if experience guides you to do so. Setting clear service expectations with clients at the outset also gives you a commercial benefit, because it means everything you do is paid for.

Figure 5.3 shows you the link between TCF and service design; the two go hand in hand.

A majority of clients will be taken through a logical sequence of activities, or 'customer journey'. TCF concentrates on all the parts of this journey and how they are delivered. That is why much of the management information relating to TCF, covered in Chapter 16, measures the performance of the business and its people through this journey. Regardless of your service proposition, it is essential that consistency is maintained in how advisers operate as well as in the service that is provided.

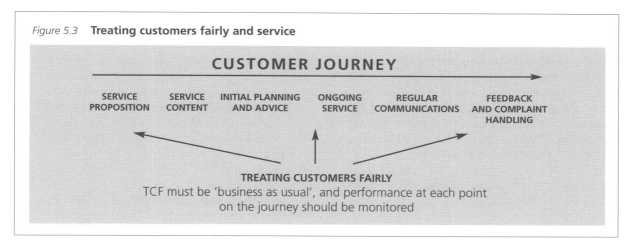

Figure 5.3   **Treating customers fairly and service**

Service frameworks and processes

It is not unusual for advisers in the same business to deal very differently with similar types of client. It is accepted that the detail of advice, implementation and ongoing service may vary, but it is very hard to defend why in one case the client is charged full initial commission, and in another a lower initial plus ongoing renewal. There is no doubt that this makes a business vulnerable to TCF investigation and will create a problem if the two clients should meet and discuss their differing experiences.

Principals of businesses where this occurs must ask themselves the question: "Can I defend this variation in practice to regulators, clients or myself?" There are often reasons why this happens, which are more related to how advisers wish to derive their income, as opposed to what may be right for the client.

This is not about criticising advisers who concentrate on initial commissions, because in many cases this is often used as the 'down payment' for service that is delivered in the following years. The issue is that the market is moving away from commission which will be banned (apart from protection products) when the RDR is implemented. Furthermore the regulator does not favour them, and there is a clear requirement to link ongoing service more closely with ongoing payments. So if this is the reality for your business, you will need to achieve a degree of conformity.

TREATING CUSTOMERS FAIRLY is mainly about good business practice, and well defined service lies at the heart of getting this right.

CASE STUDY

TCF shines a light

The principals of Green and Red Independent Advice Services Limited (GRIAS) were sceptical when they heard about the Treating Customers Fairly (TCF) initiative back in 2005. The main shareholder, Gareth Bond, said, "We have always treated our clients properly — if we didn't, they would not come back to us. I am not certain this initiative applies to us, and I cannot see any benefit to the business that will come out of it."

His partners agreed and thought it was likely that TCF would be consigned to the long list of failed initiatives that never get completed.

Two weeks later, the principals attended a business briefing held by one of their main providers, at which TCF was the main topic. Although the briefing concentrated upon compliance and meeting the FSA deadlines, the more positive aspects of the initiative were discussed. Gareth prided himself on seeing the opportunities in any problem or challenge and, after the briefing, decided to "turn TCF on its head".

He called a meeting of the other principals and senior people in the business, and suggested that "we ignore, for the moment, the compliance aspects of TCF and think about the opportunities. This project is all about how we treat our clients; maybe we could learn something from it, and perhaps we can look at the business from a slightly different perspective."

They decided to take the first part of TCF seriously, and initiated the gap analysis by issuing a survey to their staff and a similar one to clients. The clients seemed pretty happy with the service and advice, but the staff survey revealed a slightly different picture.

Later, Gareth found that the reactions of his staff were very similar to other firms. They did not think that the firm had a good clear service proposition, or that the way they priced their services was clear to clients or consistently applied by the advisers.

Of even greater concern was a view that the back office systems and processes were "set up solely for the convenience of the business, as opposed to serving the clients", as one staff member stated.

As a result of this, GRIAS decided to review and overhaul their service proposition 'from top to bottom'. They realised that TCF was as much about good business practice as compliance, and that they could use the initiative to build a head of steam around the service project.

It took them almost two years to complete the new service proposition and make all the changes in processes and procedures. However, this placed them in a strong position as they moved toward adviser charging and the Retail Review deadline.

CASE STUDY KEY POINT

TCF processes provide a very good framework for dealing with service design. The gap analysis is a good starting point and, in over 80% of cases, advice businesses conclude that they need to review and often amend or formalise their service proposition. The process of formally defining service is central to TCF and adviser charging and will bring clear benefits to the firm and its advisers.

2.2 Link service, costs, revenues and profit

In the context of the financial implications of launching a new service proposition, you will have two genuine and fundamental questions:

- How will changing how I charge for my services influence my **revenues** in terms of the total and the mix between initial and recurring income?
- How can I be sure that I will make a **profit** when I launch a range of new services, when all the components have a **cost** attached to them?

Chapter 6, on pricing, will deal in detail with the different approaches that you can adopt when service is formally designed, particularly recognising the end of the trend away from the traditional commission-based model. Chapter 13 will cover budgets and costs.

At this stage, you should concentrate on service design and use your experience to make initial judgements around costs and profit. However, that cannot replace the more rigorous approach referred to above. The overriding principle is to make sure that you design service so that the cost of delivery reflects the value of the client.

In most service businesses, the level and amount of service will vary by client value. Figure 5.4 shows the relationship between the cost of service and complexity and value of the client.

The vertical axis shows rising client value and complexity of need as found in many adviser client bases. The horizontal axis shows the associated levels of service based on the typical three-tier service structure, which will be detailed later in this chapter. It is clear that the cost of service delivery rises with client complexity, along with changes in the nature of the client relationship.

If you grade your clients in three tiers ('A' being high value, 'B' middle value and 'C' lower value), then you can think about different levels of service for each, determined in part by their value. With 'C' clients, many advisers adopt a reactive stance, as they are generally dealing with them on a transactional basis. At the other extreme, they will be far more proactive with 'A' clients, where ongoing relationships are important. 'B' clients present a challenge, because there is a need to balance the frequency of face to face contact and provision of other services with client value.

For many advisers, this is obvious and reflects how they have worked for many years. However, there are others who will give all clients the same level of service, regardless of value. In other words, they will make a loss on some clients because the cost of service delivery exceeds client value. It is hard to criticise such a strong service ethic, but advisers need to find a way to be true to their values and make a profit. We will deal with that issue later.

It is important to keep this framework close by as you get into the detail of service design, because it will help maintain the balance between cost of service delivery, expected revenues, service levels and content.

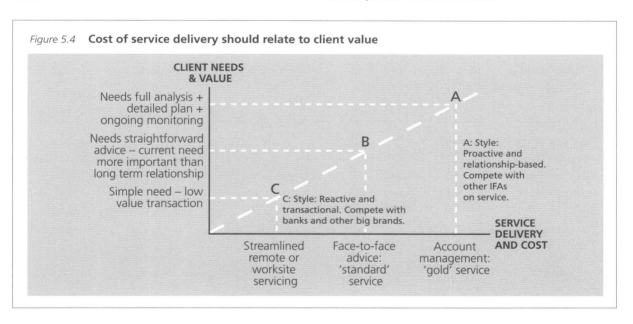

Figure 5.4 **Cost of service delivery should relate to client value**

CASE STUDY

Tailor service and prices to client value

Magenta Investment Services were deep into discussion on service design and how much to charge. The five advisers (including the business owners), para-planner and senior administrator had a good feel for what they would charge if they went to hourly rates, and had a good measure of agreement on how they would structure fees based on percentages of funds invested, if they chose that route.

The sticking point was costs and profit. As Simon, the senior administrator, observed, "We know our overall costs and how they break down, and we have a clear objective for incomes and profit margin – but we don't have any detail below that in terms of the cost of undertaking individual tasks". Huw, the business owner, was worried that they would set prices at a level that would not yield a profit, or worse still fail to cover costs.

He suggested that a "root and branch review and analysis of all our costs will be needed before we can set prices", but, as Simon stated, "that will take months and hold us up – we really want to get this issue sorted out".

After more deliberation, they decided that, in the short term, they should work out the cost of providing the main services they were offering to clients. As Meena, the para-planner, said, "We know it takes 30 minutes to undertake an electronic valuation, tidy it up and quickly common sense test it, so if you charge me at £50 an hour, that is £25,

plus a share of the web services that send us the data and the software that pulls it together. That gives a cost of provision in the range of £30–£40, so if you add on something for profit, you could charge £50 for each one."

Huw recalled the exercise that had been done to work out what the advisers would need to charge as an hourly rate to achieve the same revenue as currently earned through commission.

Given that the total was sufficient to cover costs and make a profit, he suggested that up to £200 per hour for senior advisers and £125–£150 per hour for junior advisers would be about right. "That would mean that one three-hour meeting (including preparation and travelling) and valuation a year for a standard client should produce at least £650 if it were my client, and £500 if it were one of the junior advisers. On that basis, our middle 'B' group clients must produce at least £500 for us to provide the annual review service".

They recognised that this was an approximation, and decided to take a more detailed look at their costs. However, Huw decided that if they were reasonably confident in the cost of undertaking the main tasks that came up frequently, then that would be sufficient to set prices, which could be reviewed when the more rigorous work was complete. As Meena said, "I doubt we will ever go to hourly rates, but they are an incredibly useful starting point when working out what to charge."

CASE STUDY KEY POINT

It is good practice to know what it costs to provide the main services. This means that you can take a view as to how much clients should be worth on an annual basis, either through recurring income or standing order, to receive a particular level of service. If you do not have the data, your experience should allow you to estimate the main costs, so you can complete your service proposition, which can always be amended when more accurate data is produced.

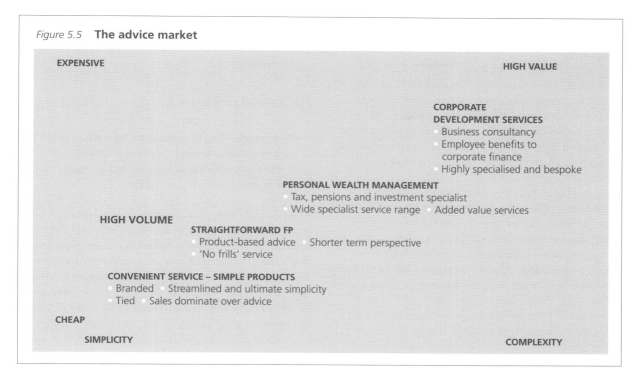

Figure 5.5 **The advice market**

2.3 Where do you stand in the market?

We have made the point that a clear service proposition that is well targeted provides the basis for sustainable competitive advantage. You can strengthen this by deciding which part of the advice market you want to operate within. This is where you feel most comfortable, and where you can play to your strengths.

You will know that all firms are different and that there is a wide spectrum across which advice businesses operate and compete.

Figure 5.5 summarises the main parts of the advice market, and is designed to help you think about where you stand now and if that is where you want to be in the future.

The vertical axis runs from 'cheap' to 'expensive', and the horizontal from 'simple straightforward' advice to 'complex'. As with the previous chart, the price of advice is linked to its complexity and, by inference, the value of the client.

From a client perspective, this picture of the market has been stable for many years and is unlikely to change. However, the relative attractiveness of different client segments to the various players in the market is influenced by the RDR. The high volume/low value segment in the bottom left of Figure 5.5 has traditionally been served by high street banking brands with a streamlined offer which has typically been multi or single tied. As time passes, it is expected that non-financial services brands will enter the market and an increasing proportion of business will be transacted remotely with a combination of telephone and on-line service.

This is because the cost of providing advice to this part of the market requires extensive use of technology to minimise the use of relatively expensive people. In these circumstances, some of the high street players may radically

alter their bancassurance, offering or moving towards the more profitable parts of the market. In terms of RDR business status, it is expected that most firms operating in the high volume markets will be 'restricted', i.e. offering a limited range of products and funds, and will retain a tied model.

All other positions in the market are expected to be dominated by advice businesses with IFAs being the major players up to the point of RDR implementation. After this date, all distributors must decide on 'whole of market' independent status, restricted status or a combination of both. The important issues for IFA businesses as they consider this include:

- The structure of the client bank and whether or not access to every product, fund and tax solution in the market is necessary to meet their requirements.
- The changed and more onerous requirements for IFA businesses after the deadline, particularly related to the cost of researching the entire market and staying up to date, increased compliance requirements and the possibility of higher professional indemnity costs.
- The importance of professional introducers (who will only refer clients to the independent category).

Following the RDR deadline, the advice market will develop into a mix of 'restricted' and 'IFA' businesses with firms coming to different conclusions depending upon their response to the issues listed above. Many pre-deadline IFA firms operate a restricted model under the new definitions which works very well for their clients, principals and advisers. As a result, many are expected to continue successfully with this model unless they depend heavily on professional introductions. It is important to note that there should be no difference in the quality of advice between restricted and IFA firms (all advisers at QCA level 4), but that some firms will have access to a wider range of solutions than others. Restricted firms can be tied or simply decide that certain product or fund types are not appropriate for their clients.

After the RDR deadline, whole of market IFA firms will be able to operate panels with the obligation to select 'off panel' if necessary. Panels must be regularly and comprehensively reviewed to retain whole of market status and the firm must keep up to date with the widest range of products, funds and other solutions that are available.

You should note that no single position on Figure 5.5, or in the market generally, is any better than the others. The 'right' answer is the one that fits with the needs of your client base and the capabilities of your business. Of course, some firms, when reviewing the broad structure of the market and the range of opportunities, will decide to change position, which should be part of the broader strategic plan.

The nature of competition changes with different market positions, and you should recognise that banks operate in the 'straightforward' advice market alongside advice businesses. If you operate here, you must be aware of the strength of the banks and the need to work hard at client retention to maintain your competitive position. This will be covered in Part 3 on marketing.

When you have confirmed where you are concentrating, and the needs of your clients (covered in Chapter 4), you can move to the detail of proposition and service design.

3 Summarise your service proposition

The term 'service proposition' has many definitions and can be the source of much confusion. For the proposition to be useful it should cover what you do and how you do it. You will know when you have got it right because you should be able to use it with clients to demonstrate your value and justify the price of your advice.

The proposition is made up of three parts:

- A client provision statement — a concise summary of what is on offer.
- A description of what you do for clients from initial work through to ongoing service — to show there is more to your work than many clients realise.
- A summary of how you do it — to show the skills and expertise required to do the job properly.

3.1 Client provision statement

You should start with a short client provision statement which describes what you do as concisely as possible, ideally in less than 20 seconds. This provides the basis for the more detailed 'what and how' which follows. Here are

three examples that many advisers use or adapt to suit their business.

Private and corporate financial planning

'We provide financial consultancy for business and private clients with complex affairs — we work with other professionals to create and manage a comprehensive and evolving plan.'

As you would expect, the words are carefully chosen to create an image of the service. This is very important because the aim is to attract certain clients and avoid others. This is clearly for clients who need ongoing management of their financial affairs and whom you might expect to see at least twice a year. Also, use of the words 'consultancy' and 'professional' implies fee based work which may well be a feature of the pricing policy for this type of proposition.

Straightforward advice

'We provide straightforward financial advice to make sure you have the right products for your future needs.'

This presents a very different image to financial planning and is much more product based and generally less strategic in delivery. As we saw in Chapter 4, up to 50% of the client base of a typical advice business will comprise clients who need this service. For many clients this is attractive because it implies that financial issues can be dealt with in a straightforward manner and almost forgotten until the next life stage or event prompts a need for review or change. In addition, many clients do not enjoy dealing with financial issues, so if your service looks accessible and easy, with no frills or catches, is very attractive.

Corporate advice

'We will provide, manage and communicate employee benefit packages and services to the directors and employees of the business. This will bring additional expertise and capacity to the human resources and finance functions and allow them to concentrate upon their core specialist activities'.

This is an example of the provision of employee benefit services. In this part of the market the tone and style must be 'business-like and professional' and the business benefits to the employer should be explicit. It is very clear about where the added value comes from and, by implication, why it is worth the fee.

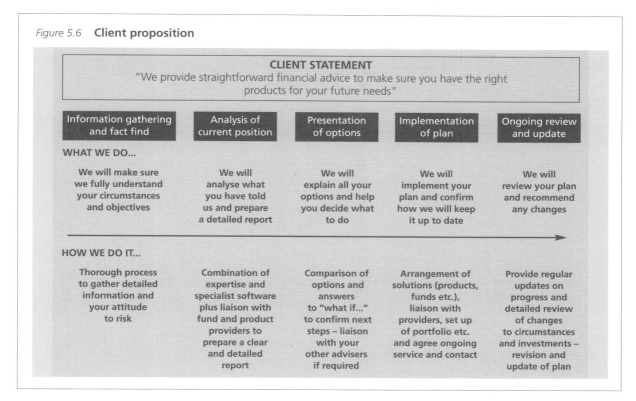

Figure 5.6 **Client proposition**

3.2 What you do and how you do it

Use the generic 'customer journey' to structure this — it can be applied to a transactional (single transaction) offering through to full financial planning. As advisers will know, the main sections are:

- Information gathering and fact find.
- Analysis of current position.
- Presentation of options.
- Implementation of plan.
- Ongoing review and update.

For each section, summarise what you will be doing for the client and how you go about the work. Use a conversational style avoiding all jargon. Many advisers are very good at translating complex issues into layman's terms and this is an opportunity to use those skills.

Figure 5.6 provides an example of a client proposition with the client provision statement, followed by what we do and how we do it.

You need to remember that the aim of this exercise is to show clients why you are worth the price of your advice and that what may appear straightforward to them is usually more complex and time consuming. There is nothing in proposition statements that you will not be familiar with, but with the transparency of adviser charging it is important that clients see the benefit in the services you offer. Communicating this at the early stage of a client relationship, and repeating it at the appropriate points, is vital until adviser charging is understood and accepted.

An increasing number of advisers use this type of proposition summary directly with clients to talk through and demonstrate

what is involved in advice, planning and transacting products and funds.

So with your target market made clear, its needs understood and the service proposition, you can move on to the content of the service you will be offering.

4 Work out the detailed service design

In the context of TCF and the introduction of adviser charging, it is essential that service is designed with great care. Clearly your service needs to be competitive and attractive to clients, as well as straightforward and economical for your business to deliver. 'Less is more' has direct relevance here because it is tempting to offer extensive service to medium and high value clients on the assumption that you may lose them if you don't. The problem is that this can raise the cost of service delivery and increase its complexity.

- The capability of the firm and the adviser to prepare an initial plan.
- The effectiveness with which funds are invested.
- The frequency and type of adviser contact (e.g. face to face, telephone, internet or letter).
- The frequency of updates and reviews.

This is not to suggest that other elements of service are unimportant because they often provide the 'added value' that clients really appreciate. But it is essential to deal with the basic components of service and get their delivery right in terms of what the client needs, how much they are prepared to pay and the cost of delivering the service.

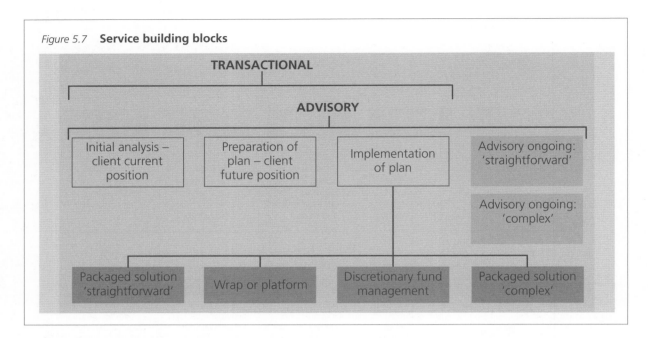

Figure 5.7 **Service building blocks**

You also need to work out your approach and processes toward investment and build this into your service design. While you need the freedom to select the right investment solution for any type of client, many advisers tend to use different solutions for different ranges of funds. For example, up to £50k may be multi-manager, £50k – £400k may be wrap and in excess of £400k may be discretionary fund management.

The service building blocks that cover the important client issues listed above are summarised in Figure 5.7. As the figure shows, service is split into three main parts:

- Initial work and implementation of the plan – often the same for transactional and advisory clients.
- Ongoing service for advisory clients – often split into two but can be bespoke.
- The product and fund solutions.

As a minimum you need to be clear about what you will offer at each stage of the process and, for monies to be invested, what products and services you will use. Straightforward packaged solutions could include pensions and bonds from product providers as well as multi-manager funds; complex solutions could include venture capital trusts, film partnerships, commodity based investments and so on.

An example of how this might work for a firm that is mainly involved in investments is summarised in Table 5.1.

A framework such as this should be applicable to a majority of clients. There will always be some clients who do not fit, but the building blocks can be assembled differently in those cases. If your service is well structured, it is easier to manage any variations, because they will still be within the overall framework.

The benefits of structuring your service at high level are:

- Clients can see what is available and work with their

Table 5.1

SERVICE BUILDING BLOCK	CLIENT SERVICE
Initial analysis	Same for all transactional and advisory clients
Preparation of plan	Same for all transactional and advisory clients
Implementation of plan	Same for all transactional and advisory clients
Ongoing service – straightforward	Advisory clients with up to £400k under advice
Ongoing service – complex	Advisory clients with more than £400k under advice
Packaged solution – straightforward	Transactional clients and up to £50k
Wrap or platform	Advisory clients with between £50k - £400k
Discretionary fund management	Advisory clients with more than £400k
Packaged solution complex	Advisory – higher value clients

adviser to select what is right for them.
- Everybody in the business knows what is and is not available for clients.
- There is a clear basis for charging clients.
- Processes can be set up to support building blocks with opportunities for streamlining and cost reduction.

Transactional service is not the main activity of a majority of advice businesses. However, there are instances when this could be offered:

- Pension scheme members for whom a financial advice service is also being provided.
- Clients who do not require (and typically cannot afford) ongoing service, but have potential to come

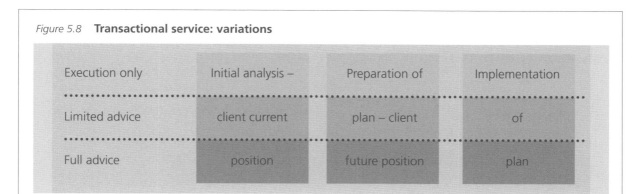

Figure 5.8   **Transactional service: variations**

Execution only	Initial analysis –	Preparation of	Implementation
Limited advice	client current	plan – client	of
Full advice	position	future position	plan

back from time to time, particularly if you maintain marketing contact. This is often referred to as 'repeat transactional' and may become important if the banks step back from financial advice through their branches.

As indicated above, many firms will apply the same approach for both advisory and transactional clients. However, there are alternative routes which should be considered, particularly as this group is likely to be less profitable than the others. Figure 5.8 shows the variations that could be used. There are three routes:

- Execution only – where the client effectively places an order, often in response to direct marketing.
- Limited advice – where the client makes it very clear exactly what they want (e.g. £30 a month invested in a personal pension).
- Full advice – the same process as applied to advisory clients.

You need to decide which of these approaches you will adopt depending upon the volume and type of transactional business you expect to undertake. In a majority of cases, firms will continue to use the second two options, but on-line services are expected to grow and, with the development of corporate wraps, opportunities may emerge that are relatively straightforward to implement.

5 Bespoke or packaged service

Both the TCF and RDR initiatives push the market towards streamlining and uniform processes so you need to decide, for ongoing service, if you will provide bespoke service, service packages or a combination of both. Clearly there are cost, complexity and process considerations, but the greatest issue is consistency of treatment across the client bank. A packaged service overcomes these issues, particularly if you have a large number of clients and advisers. But there are circumstances where bespoke service is the right approach.

5.1 Bespoke ongoing service

This approach is appropriate in the following circumstances:

- The client bank is dominated by a small number of high value clients with different and complex circumstances — typically personal clients, but could be corporate.
- Advisers have lengthy experience and are well qualified, so have the ability to judge the make-up of ongoing service for individual clients.
- Your operating model is self-employed with a wide range of advisers with different types of client bank.

To ensure this works in an effective and compliant manner you need:

- Back office processes that can accommodate variations in ongoing service at client level.
- Rigorous controls to demonstrate an overall consistency in approach and to show that clients are clear about the service they will receive and how much it will cost.
- A consistency framework strictly applied as covered in section 2.1.

In effect you have to set the framework and standards within which advisers can recommend ongoing service. You must avoid a completely laissez-faire approach because it will result in inconsistencies and TCF-related issues around differential treatment of clients in similar circumstances. This is relatively straightforward to apply with the small, high value client bank, but much more difficult with a number of self-employed advisers. These businesses tend to be fragmented and harder to control, so you have to use careful judgement when setting standards and the consistency framework. Ideally you should work with the advisers to establish the framework and standards in the context of increasing scrutiny from the regulator at adviser level and particularly around adviser charging.

For all advisers, it is essential that they recognise that autonomy implies responsibility and that they must adhere to the standards and guidelines. A less prescriptive and bespoke approach is often favoured in self-employed firms and it is absolutely right for principals to expect that it is implemented responsibly and consistently.

CASE STUDY

Laissez-faire or prescription – a key decision

Orange Pensions Services has over 50 advisers and operates throughout the UK. The business runs the employed model, but has a philosophy of encouraging advisers to 'build a business within the business'. This has proved very successful, because each adviser and branch is effectively a profit centre which provides a transparent and effective means of monitoring and managing performance.

When the business started to think about the service implications of TCF and defining a clear proposition, it faced a dilemma. As Graeme, the managing director, stated, "Our 50 advisers all operate slightly differently with their own clients; they are successful and we know from our T & C processes that there are no issues with standards or compliance. If we put a service straitjacket on them, we will lose the flair and individuality that makes us and them very successful."

The business debated this issue for some time, and set up a small working party of advisers to take soundings from the rest and come up with recommendations. The working party presented its findings to the board, and, as Janine, its spokeswoman, suggested, "We need to set some standards, but also give flexibility to allow individual advisers to deal with clients in their own way."

The result was the establishment of clear frameworks and processes with minimum standards for service and documentation. The board were challenged on this approach by their external consultants, who asked how they could be sure that this would achieve the consistency that was needed.

Alexandra, the chairwoman, said, "Most of our advisers have been in the business for at least ten years and, importantly, have stable and mature relationships with their clients. They will understand that if we give them some freedom they will act responsibly, plus we will monitor closely how effectively the guidelines are working." As Graeme said, "If this does not work, we can always tighten up, but if we go in too prescriptive then it is very difficult to pull back and maintain an effective policy."

CASE STUDY KEY POINT

The extent to which the business should dictate how advisers operate is a key issue and will differ for all advice businesses. Only the principal can make the judgement, but it is extremely important to consider how advisers will operate if they are given frameworks as opposed to more precise rules. Different principals and advisers will warm to different approaches. When you have made this judgement, you can decide how detailed you wish to be in designing service and rolling it out across all the advisers and their clients.

5.2 Consistency frameworks

Your aim here should be to ensure that all your advisers operate according to the same standards and that they have a relatively uniform approach to dealing with clients. You can achieve this by using the following to achieve consistency:

- Standard fact finding and risk analysis forms to ensure that everyone collects the full range of data that is required to manage the client relationship and make sure that the business provides comprehensive and compliant advice.
- Clear processes and disciplines in the back office to ensure that all the relevant data are keyed into the back office software.
- A standard letter or 'service agreement' that explains what service the client will receive and how they will be charged. Clients should sign this to show that they understand it and that they agree to the service and pricing they have been offered.
- Guidelines on charging. Under the commission model, this would be ranges of commission, or it might be a clear statement of maximum levels or mixes between initial and recurring. With adviser charging it will be a 'price list' used by all advisers with all their clients.
- Minimum service standards such that all active clients are reviewed at least annually, with the type of contact at the adviser's discretion, as described later in the section on the 'financial advice' service.
- A process for producing review lists on a regular (monthly) basis, and a system for monitoring the action taken by the advisers.

Template 3.2 in Part 2 – Developing a Service Proposition on the website sets these out as a checklist that you may find useful to work through.

Finally, you will require a formal sign-off process for any circumstances that fall outside the frameworks. As always, these would be exceptions, and should never exceed 5%–10% of cases.

As an overview, the key parts of the process are summarised in Figure 5.9.

The two key sets of guidelines feed into the service agreement. In practice, you may want to combine this with the client agreement, or convert the latter. The important point is to make sure there is clarity about what you will give the clients and how much they will pay for it.

5.3 Service content

By its nature service content is about detail and, to avoid complexity, you should use the building block approach with each level of service adding to the previous. The reasons for this are:

- As many processes and tasks as possible should be repeatable to increase efficiency.
- Advisers need a framework which is straightforward so that they can easily explain to clients why they have recommended a particular level of service.
- Clients need to be clear about service choices.
- You can easily show the differences between service levels to justify the differences in price.

Service content is based upon the three main building blocks for service structure. These are:

- Analysis and planning.
- Implementation.
- Ongoing service.

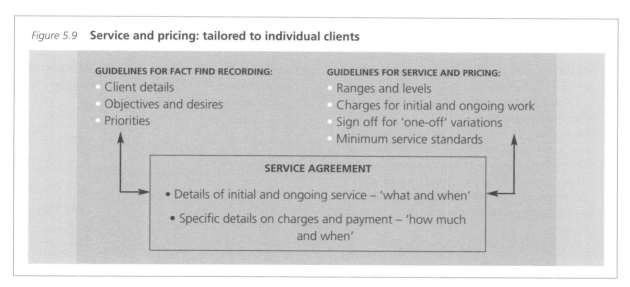

Figure 5.9 **Service and pricing: tailored to individual clients**

GUIDELINES FOR FACT FIND RECORDING:
- Client details
- Objectives and desires
- Priorities

GUIDELINES FOR SERVICE AND PRICING:
- Ranges and levels
- Charges for initial and ongoing work
- Sign off for 'one-off' variations
- Minimum service standards

SERVICE AGREEMENT

- Details of initial and ongoing service – 'what and when'
- Specific details on charges and payment – 'how much and when'

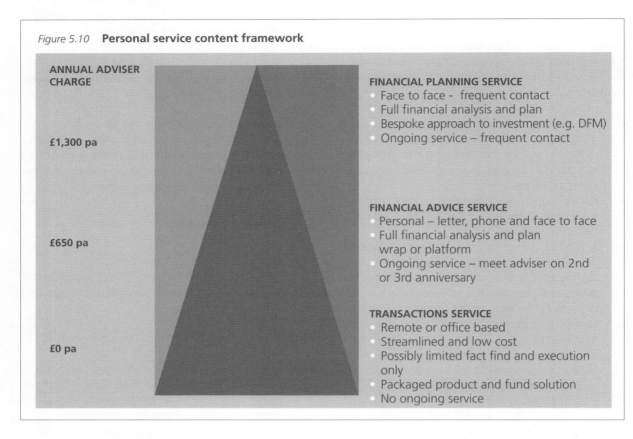

Figure 5.10 **Personal service content framework**

ANNUAL ADVISER CHARGE

£1,300 pa

£650 pa

£0 pa

FINANCIAL PLANNING SERVICE
- Face to face - frequent contact
- Full financial analysis and plan
- Bespoke approach to investment (e.g. DFM)
- Ongoing service – frequent contact

FINANCIAL ADVICE SERVICE
- Personal – letter, phone and face to face
- Full financial analysis and plan wrap or platform
- Ongoing service – meet adviser on 2nd or 3rd anniversary

TRANSACTIONS SERVICE
- Remote or office based
- Streamlined and low cost
- Possibly limited fact find and execution only
- Packaged product and fund solution
- No ongoing service

The combination of these changes with client needs and ability to pay for advice is summarised in Figure 5.10.

- The transactions service has no ongoing service or annual charge. It is low cost and streamlined and any investments will be placed in products and funds that self-manage.
- The financial advice service has a full financial fact find and, because a majority of clients tend to be in this group, a wrap or platform is used for investments. This supports the annual review, but it should be noted that this does not involve a face to face meeting with the adviser every year. The annual charge of £650 is based upon an average investment of £130k at 0.5% or £100k at 0.65% or a monthly retainer of approximately £55.
- The financial planning service builds upon the advice service, but has greater frequency of valuation and adviser contact plus the option for discretionary fund management. The charge is based upon an average investment of £230k with the same percentage charges or a monthly retainer of £110.

We will deal with pricing in Chapter 6 but, to give an indication of how much needs to be earned from the large proportion of personal clients, the percentage rates and client values are relatively typical across the market. Indeed, analyses of hourly charge out rates indicate that £650 pa for a middle range client and £1,300 pa at the higher end are necessary to cover costs and make a profit.

We are now at a stage where we can review each service level in detail. Table 5.2 summarises the service.

We will start with the transactional service (client group 'C' in Figure 5.10), because this is straightforward and will enable you to become familiar with the template that you can use to describe your service offering.

Table 5.2 **Personal service summary**

TRANSACTIONAL SERVICE	FINANCIAL ADVICE	FINANCIAL PLANNING
A straightforward transactional service instigated by client request or direct marketing activity. Also appropriate if initial analysis indicates that a single transaction with no requirement for ongoing service is right for the client.	A straightforward advice service typically centred around immediate client issues that are expected to require review and re-planning in the future.	A comprehensive specialist service that typically encompasses investment and pension planning, financial, estate and tax planning often delivered in partnership with other advisers.
INITIAL SERVICE	INITIAL SERVICE AS TRANSACTIONS SERVICE PLUS	INITIAL SERVICE AS ADVICE SERVICE PLUS
Fact find and risk analysis. Analysis, report and recommendations. Implementation of recommendations. Self-maintaining investment solution.	Funds managed by wrap or platform	Full review of tax position and capital and income needs. Funds managed through wrap or platform based and/or DFM investment solutions.
ONGOING SERVICE	ONGOING SERVICE	ONGOING SERVICE AS ADVICE SERVICE PLUS
None	Annual valuation. Face to face meetings typically every 2–3 years. Letter and/or telephone conversation linked to valuation annually. All records maintained and updated. Access to named adviser.	Bi-annual valuations. Face to face meetings typically twice per year. Access at any time to named adviser and support staff. Annual review to update all elements of initial plan. Pro-active contact linked to tax and legal changes.

Transactional service

Many IFAs do not proactively offer transactional service, but it is inevitable that from time to time some clients will require this approach with no ongoing servicing, unless they choose to come back (repeat transactional).

Table 5.3 below summarises the contents of a typical transactional service, where, as you will see, there is no recurring income.

The template is designed to contain all aspects of the service and to make it clear to advisers, administrators and clients what is and is not included. This is the minimum level of service that will be provided, and can be used to show clients how much additional value they will receive as they move to higher levels of service.

Financial advice

We now move to the middle level of service. There is an important aim here, which is to ensure that it is sufficiently different from the transactional service and gives you room to offer more services to the very top clients.

Using the same template, you will immediately see in Table 5.4 the differences in service content.

This is very close to what many advisers offer the majority

of their clients. As you know, there is no need for all clients to be seen every year, and a frequency of once every two or three years for a face to face meeting may well be enough, for both adviser and client.

Unfortunately, in practice, it is often this group of clients that gets neglected. This is because it is typically large in number and, if the back office is not able to provide service reminders, the years will pass by and some of these clients will defect to other advisers or become dormant. This is why the client receives an annual valuation and letter or telephone call, plus a newsletter, to make sure that contact is retained and that the client is confident that their affairs are being monitored. However, as face to face contact is infrequent, the time pressure in looking after this group becomes manageable and the cost of service delivery is matched to client value.

The key to maintaining and retaining this group of clients is to ensure the back office provides monthly lists of who is due for review, and that advisers proactively decide what they will do: arrange a visit, send a letter, or send a letter with telephone follow-up. One of the most important parts of management information for TCF is the effectiveness with which the advisers carry out this activity.

We now move to the top level of service. Again, you have to make sure that there is enough difference compared to the middle level to show top clients that they are receiving the additional value of more time and expertise.

Table 5.3 **Transactional service**

OVERVIEW	A reactive service instigated by client request or direct marketing activity.
PROPOSITION	A simple service for 'one-off' transactions. 'Pay as you go'.
CLIENT BENEFITS	In summary: • Time saving. • 'One-off' access to advice. • Minimal paperwork and hassle. • Can come back again, or shop around.
METHODOLOGY	Remote (where possible) or at adviser office.
CORE SERVICES	Fact find and risk analysis. Analysis, report and recommendations. Implementation Self-maintaining investment solution.
CLIENT CONTACT	Remote, at adviser office or at workplace.
PRICE	Initial adviser charge. No recurring charge.
MARKETING COMMUNICATIONS	Aim to retain and move up to next level. Likely to include ad hoc product/fund based communications (e.g. product maturity review, newsletter etc.)

Table 5.4 **Financial advice service**

OVERVIEW	A straightforward advice service typically centred around immediate client issues that will require review and re-planning in the future.
PROPOSITION	An uncomplicated service for clients who recognise the need for expert advice and who are expected to have increasingly complex financial affairs as time passes.
CLIENT BENEFITS	In summary: • Peace of mind. • Access to expertise. • Minimal paperwork and hassle. • Satisfaction that affairs are being properly looked after.
METHODOLOGY	Mix of face to face and remote contact with named adviser and back office team. Meetings held at IFA office.
CORE SERVICES	Fact find and risk analysis. Analysis, report and recommendations. Implementation Funds managed via wrap or platform. Annual valuation. Face to face meetings typically every 2–3 years, but once pa for certain clients. Letter and telephone conversation linked to valuation, every year. All records maintained and updated. Named adviser.
CLIENT CONTACT	Typically even split between face to face and remote – frequency agreed with client and based on corporate standards.
PRICE	Initial and ongoing adviser charge.
MARKETING COMMUNICATIONS	Annual review pack: 1 x valuation 1 x investment commentary 1 x personalised letter. Aim to retain and move up to next level. Likely to include newsletter plus ad hoc marketing and service communications.

Table 5.5 **Financial planning service**

OVERVIEW	A comprehensive specialist service that typically encompasses investment and pension planning, financial, estate and tax planning, typically delivered in partnership with other advisers.
PROPOSITION	A bespoke financial planning service for private clients with complex affairs that require continuous management, often in consultation with other specialist advisers.
CLIENT BENEFITS	In summary: • Peace of mind. • Delegation to experts. • Access to expertise and information. • Clarity out of complexity.
METHODOLOGY	Predominantly face to face meetings with adviser at convenient location for clients and other advisers. Additional contact with support team.
CORE SERVICES	Fact find and risk analysis. Analysis, report and recommendations. Full review of the position and long-term capital and income needs. Funds managed through DFM or wrap/platform. Face to face meetings typically twice pa or additionally as required. Access at any time to named adviser and technical support. Annual review to update all elements of initial analysis and plan and recommendations for re-balancing portfolio. Proactive contact linked to relevant tax and/or legislative changes. Liaison with other professional and specialist advisers. All records maintained and updated.
CLIENT CONTACT	Typically face to face meetings with frequency, as above, at location convenient to client and other advisers.
PRICE	Initial and ongoing adviser charge.
MARKETING COMMUNICATIONS	Annual review pack: 1 x valuation 1 x investment commentary 1 x personalised letter. Aim to retain and move up to next level. Likely to include newsletter plus ad hoc marketing and service communications.

Financial planning

As you will see in Table 5.5, the range of service provided is far more extensive. It uses the same template, which enables comparisons between the different service levels, and shows in bold everything that is additional to the middle level of service.

As you might expect, the level of expertise that you bring to these clients is much greater, as reflected in how you look after their investments, the depth of planning, the depth of reviews and the need to work with and often co-ordinate other professionals. It is also here that some advisers operate discretionary fund management, which makes a real difference between this service level and the others.

There is little doubt that this service is right for higher value clients, and there are some very clear differences compared to the middle level of service.

Service for corporate clients tends not to lend itself to structuring in the same way as for personal services. All of the principles and templates that have been used for personal clients apply here and Table 5.6 provides an example of a corporate service.

5.4 Service content – an overview

This completes the structured service model, which an increasing number of advisers are formally adopting. They are publishing their service levels in hard copy and on websites, and have made the move from selling products and funds to selling service. This is a significant and important step, because service is what clients value and appreciate, far more than the act of arranging a product or investment fund.

To decide whether or not you should adopt this approach, ask yourself the following questions:

Table 5.6 **Corporate services**

OVERVIEW	A tailored service for corporate clients concentrating on risk management, pensions and a wide range of employee benefits.
PROPOSITION	An efficient and high value service designed to manage the cost and distraction related to the provision of employee benefits and protection of the business.
CLIENT BENEFITS	In summary: • More time to work on your business. • Reduced business risk and increased staff retention. • Less distraction and hassle for your HR team/person. • Tailored advice specific to the needs of your business and its employees. • Employee welfare enhanced (provision of pension, communications and personal FP where appropriate). • Development of best solutions in a complex and ever-changing market.
METHODOLOGY	Predominantly face-to-face meetings with advisers and, where necessary, external experts and specialists. Face to face meetings with employees.
CORE SERVICES	• Fact find and risk analysis. • Analysis, report and recommendations. • Implementation of recommendations. • Liaison with other specialists as required. • Annual review of plan and product solutions.
CLIENT CONTACT	Face to face — always at client premises.
PRICE	Bespoke and based around a tariff of charges.
MARKETING COMMUNICATIONS	Service-specific communications only. Selected hospitality for higher value clients.

- Is your business undertaking a lot of unpaid work for clients?
- Do you have some advisers who are already running this type of model very effectively?
- Could this approach be a catalyst to streamlining your processes and back office?
- Can you find enough clients to sell the top level of service to?
- Are you vulnerable because all your advisers operate very differently?

Template 1.4 in Part 2 – Developing a Service Proposition on the website sets these questions out in a questionnaire. If you have answered "Yes" to at least three of these questions, then you have a strong case for introducing a more formal service structure. More importantly, your business will benefit through lower risk and increased profit. Use **Template 2.1** to help you design the service content for your business.

6 Chapter summary

The management skills you have developed as a result of this chapter mean that you can:

- Define your overall service proposition.
- Describe the proposition clearly for clients and others in the business.
- Define the specific services you will offer.
- Make sure that TCF principles are interwoven into your service proposition.
- Implement a pre-defined service across your business.

You have dealt with one of the most complex issues facing advice businesses. As you have seen, defining, developing and changing service has implications for how the business operates and how people work. It affects the back office and the approach to customer service just as much as it leads to changes in how advisers operate. You can make sure you implement this effectively by using the process in Chapter 7.

Chapter 6

How to work out the price of your service

By the end of this chapter, your business will benefit from:

✔ Clarity of pricing for advice and transactional services.
✔ Consistently applied pricing policy.
✔ Concentration upon pricing for value and profit.
✔ Greater profit and far less cross-subsidisation between clients.

How clients are charged for services has been debated for many years, with as many answers as there are advisers. It is not the purpose of this chapter to rehearse the fees versus commission debate with which we are all familiar, but to set out the various approaches that could be used. The Retail Distribution Review (RDR) sees adviser charging replacing commission which moves the issues of pricing advice services to a new level.

The days of cross-subsidisation between clients have long gone and clear service and pricing definition takes the market further in the right direction. That does not mean that you should never discount in particular circumstances but, if you have structured your pricing correctly, that should be a rare event. The aim is to be as consistent with pricing policy as you will be with a structured service proposition.

Supporting materials

Given the complexity of pricing we have included two **spreadsheets** to help you undertake the analysis. These are in Part 2 – Developing a Service Proposition on the website.

The first spreadsheet, 'The cost of providing advice', covers the cost of delivering initial and ongoing service. It encompasses the main tasks, who will undertake them, how long each takes and how much you should charge your client if you were working on an hourly charge out basis.

The second spreadsheet, 'Hourly charge out rates, target revenues and productivity', helps calculate hourly charge out rates for individual job roles in the context of your overall

revenue target. Working out the hourly charge out rates has two advantages:

*   They provide the basis for calculating project fees, minimum charges and 'rates for the job'. Even if you use a different pricing policy for most of your work you will need these in certain cases.
*   They give you a benchmark for comparing the outcome of any other pricing policy that you are considering.

1 Pricing is complex

This is often the most contentious area within a service design project. It has a direct effect upon the level and pattern of revenue of your business and the level and mix of income for your advisers. This means that any changes made at the firm level directly affect the advisers, and often in different ways.

We will deal with the wider issues of transforming the revenue pattern of the business (the move from indemnity commission to initial plus recurring income) Part 3. However, it is worth emphasising that it typically takes an advice business up to five years to make such a change. This is why changes to pricing policy can be difficult to implement and why the issue is often not dealt with effectively.

However, this can no longer be the case because of the market trend toward servicing and the application of adviser charging, a fee based policy, after the RDR deadline. If it is proving difficult to deal with this issue because of resistance, inertia or complexity, ask the advisers these questions the next time you meet with them:

- Do we operate a completely consistent pricing policy across all advisers and clients?
- Can we successfully argue the case for any variations that may occur?
- Do our clients understand exactly what they are paying for our services?
- Is there a sound case for us, as a group of advisers, to adopt the same pricing policy?
- How often do we operate outside any existing pricing guidelines that we may have?
- Have we got a clear fee structure for the situations when we need to use it?
- Do we talk about 'taking commission' as opposed to 'charging clients'?

These questions are set out in **Template 1.5 in the Part 2** section of the website.

The aim of this is not to identify dissent or bad practice (because your T & C processes should do that), but to initiate a genuine discussion on an issue that has to be dealt with as part of service design. Even more importantly, resolving any issues around pricing will bring benefits in terms of client understanding and confidence, which is always a long-term benefit to your business.

This chapter will take you through the process to enable you to determine your pricing policy. You need to:

- Understand the market and regulatory context — this includes the client perspective, the rules on adviser charging and the application of value added tax.
- Take account of the cost of service delivery.
- Use your service structure to underpin your pricing structure.
- Combine all of the above to work out exactly what you will charge.

and transactions or as an 'offset' for the payment of fees. From the RDR deadline, this is replaced with adviser charging which has instigated important changes and developments, including the widespread formalisation of service design. Hence, the RDR deadline represents a watershed in terms of regulation and the way in which the market operates. However, this section will begin with the client perspective, much of which is not changing, but which will be influenced by the way firms deal with and inform clients of the pricing and service changes.

2.1 Consider the client perspective

It is very important that all firms, in all markets, think about pricing from the client perspective. What is going on in the client's mind may differ from yours, but it gives you some essential clues in how to set prices for post RDR circumstances.

In essence you need the combination of your service and pricing policy to answer all these questions. When discussing the price of your services with a client you need to:

- Use your service proposition and credentials to demonstrate value and worth.
- Use the detailed service content to justify your prices.
- Present your prices in a way the clients understands — whether or not you use the word 'fee' should be immaterial, it is up to you.
- Remove any doubts or confusion in the client's mind about how they pay you and what alternatives they have.
- Base your prices upon the cost of service delivery and your profit target to make sure you are properly remunerated.

If you can achieve the above, you can confidently present your service and prices in a way that minimises the risk that a client will claim you are too expensive. You will have the rigour of analysis and substantiation to support your position in the same way as professional advisers in other markets.

2 Market and regulatory context

Over the past 20 years the market has been accustomed to the commission system of remuneration. It has been applied in many ways, either as a direct payment for advice

Table 6.1 **Advisers and clients have different perspectives about price**

ADVISER	CLIENT
"Am I going to be too cheap or expensive?"	"How do I know that this is good value?"
"Could I justify my charges if pressed?"	"Does the advice cost come out of my pocket or product?"
"Will my clients pay fees?"	"Is this adviser really an expert?"
"Will I make any money out of this client?"	"Should I postpone this and spend it on a holiday?"

CASE STUDY

Value must dominate over price

The directors and advisers of Silver Financial Advice had finally decided how they were going to charge clients. They had been right through the debate, looked at costs and were confident their prices were fair and that they would make a profit.

As Danielle, the managing director said, "I am 100% happy that I can justify these charges to clients – I think we are good value for money, not the cheapest, but I know we will do a good job". Everyone knew there was a 'but' coming. "But", she said," I am still worried that we will struggle to convince clients, even though we are confident in the service and ourselves".

Michael, who had responsibility for marketing, had been thinking for some time about what support material he could provide to help get over this problem at least until the advisers were happy they could handle the situation. "What about a one-pager that summarises everything we do. I recall a company that makes up-market jeans which has listed on its packaging all the processes and activities it goes through to show how much care is taken and all the work that goes into their quality product. Why don't we do the same thing?"

Michael drafted the leaflet (which was also a page for the website) and headed it up, 'These are all the things you need to do to be your own expert financial planner'. It was a long and impressive list including getting qualified, acquiring special software and skilled support staff and keeping up to date on a huge range of issues. Danielle was so impressed she sent it to all new clients in the first letter confirming their appointment and it provided a really good talking point in the first meeting to discuss everything that would be done to make sure the client's affairs were properly managed.

CASE STUDY KEY POINT

The best way to be confident about prices is to make sure they are based on good analysis. However, clients cannot be expected to know all the things that have to be done to deal with their finances. There are different ways of communicating this, but this type of leaflet makes the point very effectively. Another approach is to use your service proposition ('what we do and how we do it') with clients to demonstrate your value and the benefits they receive.

2.2 Adviser charging

After the RDR deadline all firms providing financial advice, whether they are whole of market independent or restricted, will use adviser charging with their clients. This switches distributor remuneration from provider led to client led, with advice businesses agreeing prices with clients as opposed to commission with providers. Providers are not allowed to offer commission or factoring to support indemnified arrangements. The only exception to this is protection products.

In summary adviser charging means:

- You set your own prices using hourly rates, fixed fees, minimum charges, percentage of monies invested or a combination. It will be same for all advice businesses, from banks to one-person IFAs: the tariff of charges must be formal and available to all clients.
- You must present the tariff of charges at the first meeting and as soon as practical the actual cash sum to be paid must be disclosed – charges can be renegotiated in the future if appropriate.
- You can only levy ongoing charges if an ongoing service is agreed and delivered.
- You cannot recommend any retail investment product which pays commission.

This means that:

- All products will be available at 'factory gate' prices so that clients can see the manufacturer and distributor charges separately – enhanced allocations and similar 'special offers' will not be allowed and any benefit of this type has to be passed in full to the client.
- You need to consider the implications of advice charges within the advice that is being given, particularly with regard to tax outcomes (e.g. VAT and capital gains and differential tax treatment between product types).
- You do not need to rejustify legacy trail commissions (arranged before the RDR deadline) but you must take them into consideration when the client receives service under your new pricing arrangements after the deadline.
- You can expect most providers and fund houses to facilitate adviser charging, although it is not compulsory for them to do so.
- An increasing number of clients will use the cash facility in wraps and platforms to enable payment of advice charges.
- You need to ensure you have processes for issuing fee notices, tracking revenues (either from clients or via third parties) and chasing bad debts.

Payment for advice can be made in a way that clients find most convenient and you can offer a choice from:

- Facilitation via products with the charge being agreed between you and the client and then paid from the investment on a 'pound for pound' basis – importantly not mixed in with any product charges.
- Withdrawal with the client's agreement from the cash fund in a wrap or platform.
- Direct payment via cheque and direct debit.

You should approach this in two stages:

- Present the price of the advice service to the client and secure agreement.
- Provide the client with any payment alternatives that you decide to offer making plain any differences between them, particularly in relation to tax.

The outcome we are seeking is for clients to be presented with a clear and transparent set of adviser charges to enable them to decide if what is offered to them represents good value for money. While this is not expected to encourage any more shopping around than the defunct menu of charges, it is likely to increase competition because advice charges will be explicit. It will be the same as any market where the client can see what is on offer, how much it costs and if the brand and the service meet their requirements. The better you can present this, the more business you will win.

2.3 Value added tax

The rules on VAT have been clear for some time, but the custom and practice of their implementation has been confusing. For clarity the defining principles for charging VAT are:

- If the activity is advice only (e.g. full financial health check and plan) then VAT is payable.
- If product arrangement (intermediary services) is the dominant activity then VAT is not payable.

These principles apply regardless of how the activity is paid for (e.g. fees, commission before the RDR deadline or adviser charging paid directly or facilitated through a product, platform or fund after the deadline).

You are responsible for determining the predominant activity and applying the rules accordingly. The guidelines make it clear that this must be based on what is actually provided and not the achievement of a desired outcome that, by implication, avoids VAT. Do not forget that many corporate clients will be able reclaim VAT, which means your approach to pricing may be slightly different compared to your personal clients.

FOCUS POINT

Adviser charging: initial service VAT rules

HM Revenue & Customs (HMRC) and the Association of British Insurers (ABI) guidance is:

- Financial advice only – VAT applies.
- Product arrangement only – VAT exempt.
- If the service proposition has separate charges for advice and product arrangement then VAT is applied to the advice element only.
- If the proposition combines the charges and advice is the dominant activity, VAT will be applied to the entire service (advice and arrangement). If product arrangement dominates, the entire service is VAT exempt.

Adviser charging: ongoing service

The application of VAT for ongoing service is determined by whether or not the agreement to provide such services was made as part of the initial work and whether or not this was subject to VAT.

The guidance is:

- If the predominant activity under the initial agreement was product or investment arrangement **and** the agreement also provided for ongoing review then the

entire arrangement (initial and ongoing work) would be VAT exempt. In addition, if the services (i.e. exactly what services the customer will be provided with and over how many years) are **agreed** at outset the client can pay for ongoing service when it is delivered.

- If the ongoing service proposition has separate charges for advice and product arrangement then VAT is applied to the advice element only.
- If the ongoing service proposition combines the charges and advice is the dominant activity, VAT will be applied to the entire service (advice and arrangement). If product arrangement dominates, the entire service is VAT exempt.
- **Example 1**: Single 'bundled' charge for all initial work (planning and transactions) and same for ongoing service (e.g. 2% of value of investments for initial work and transactions and 0.75% for ongoing work) – **VAT is payable on all the activities.**
- **Example 2**: Separate 'unbundled' charges for initial work (charge for the advice and charge for arranging funds and products) and same for ongoing service (e.g. £1,500 for initial plan and 1% of value of investments for arranging transactions and £1000 pa for ongoing service and 1% of value of subsequent transactions) – **VAT is payable only on the service element of the activities.**

What this means in practice

Adviser charging is based upon the service that you provide. So a well-structured and presented service proposition can be used to justify the charges for initial and ongoing services. It is also the case that clients value the provision of analysis and advice and delivery of service far more than product and fund arrangements which they perceive as a routine and lower value activity.

Higher value clients will generally buy more service (greater frequency and depth of review and contact) while medium value clients may require less (e.g. biannual and straightforward reviews and less adviser time). In both cases service clearly dominates but the application of VAT will depend upon the way in which you structure your charges as shown in the Focus Point.

To decide on the approach you should:

- Structure a service proposition which you are confident clients will favour and that the firm and its advisers can deliver profitably.
- Determine a pricing policy that is straightforward, transparent and can be clearly communicated to clients and managed within the business (e.g. invoicing and VAT processes etc.).
- Review the implications of the VAT guidelines for the chosen policy and only reconsider if the application of VAT renders the policy uncompetitive or too complicated to explain, understand and (very importantly) to administer.

In brief, avoid the issue of VAT dominating your pricing policy. Clearly it is important, but design your price against market, client and cost circumstances before you consider the VAT position.

To work out the hourly charge out rates you need to list all the processes that have to be undertaken for initial work with a new client and also for ongoing service. Then attach a job role with its hourly charge out rate to each of these. A straightforward spread sheet will provide you with the numbers. You will find one, '**Cost of providing advice**', already set up to be applied to your business in **Part 2** on the website. This contains full guidance on how to use the spreadsheet and make changes that tailor it to your specific processes and job types.

The spreadsheet calculates the hourly charge out rate for delivering service so when setting the individual hourly rates for advisers and support staff you should account for **all** your overheads and profit margin. The process for working out individual charge out rates for advisers and other is covered further on.

When charging on an hourly basis, the cost to the client of bringing them into the business is at least £1,000 for typical advice practices. The client cost of providing ongoing service for middle range clients (annual valuation with face to face adviser meeting biannually) is close to £600 per year and top range clients (two valuations and face to face meeting annually) £900 per year.

An example of how the spreadsheet works is in Figure 6.2 and you can see the list of processes, job types and hourly rates that make up the final total. The example is based on hourly charge out rates as follows:

- Adviser: £150.
- Para planner: £60.
- Support: £30.

3 The cost of service delivery

When you have understood the market trends and regulatory issues, you need to think about the cost of delivering the service you have designed. The best way to consider this is to use hourly charge out rates as a benchmark. This is not to suggest that all firms should operate on hourly rates but that this data provides you with a benchmark for any other pricing policies you intend to use.

Table 6.2 **Hourly charge spreadsheet**

TASK	RESPONSIBILITY	TIME TAKEN	CHARGE OUT RATE	COST	RUNNING TOTAL
Gather data, set up file, confirm meeting, adviser pack	Sales support	1.50	30	45.00	45.00
Initial client meeting	Adviser	2.00	150	300.00	345.00
Finalise meeting notes - check fact find and risk profiler	Adviser	0.50	150	75.00	420.00
Brief para planner/technical	Adviser	0.50	150	75.00	495.00
Research and analysis	Para planner	4.00	60	240.00	735.00
Obtain illustration/ applications/ fund info.	Sales support	0.75	30	22.50	757.50
Prepare draft client report	Para planner	1.00	60	60.00	817.50
Check and revise client report	Adviser	0.50	150	75.00	892.50
Prepare covering letter	Adviser	0.25	150	37.50	930.00
Confirm 2nd meeting	Sales support	0.25	30	7.50	937.50
2nd client meeting	Adviser	2.00	150	300.00	1,237.50
Brief para planner and admin	Adviser	0.50	150	75.00	1,312.50
New business submission	Sales support	1.00	30	30.00	1,342.50
New business chase up	Sales support	1.00	30	30.00	1,372.50
Receipt and check	Sales support	0.50	30	15.00	1,387.50
Prepare suitability report	Para planner	1.00	60	60.00	1,447.50
Check and sign suitability report	Adviser	0.25	150	37.50	1,485.00
Set up service and prepare invoice and payment method	Sales support	0.50	30	15.00	1,500.00
Covering letter with documents, suitability report and invoice	Sales support	0.50	30	15.00	1,515.00
Ongoing file preparation (incl. set up on platform/wrap etc.)	Sales support	0.50	30	15.00	1,530.00
File check and review plus compliance check	Para planner	1.00	60	60.00	1,590.00
TOTAL (Engagement to implementation)					**1,590.00**

4 Pricing structure

It is at this stage that your service structure becomes particularly important. If you have a clear picture of this and have used the building blocks of service design, you can easily structure your pricing. As you will see, each main service block is a pricing point and you can price separately or bundle using hourly rates, percentage of monies invested or a combination.

The structure which you adopt depends upon how you decide to present the service proposition and the type of clients that you deal with. You need to be aware of the application of VAT as summarised in section 2.3 and recognise that unbundled services and pricing allows you to apply VAT only to the advice parts of the structure.

The benefits of structuring price around the main service blocks are:

- You can show very clearly what the client receives for what they are paying – the client benefits at each stage can clearly demonstrate this.
- You can charge at each stage so if the client decides to stop, or only needs the initial parts of the service, you get paid for the work you have done.
- Client understanding and confidence is increased because this is a very transparent model.
- You should be able to work out VAT liability more clearly.

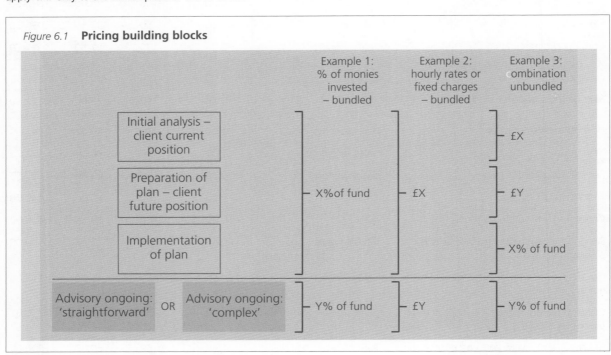

Figure 6.1 **Pricing building blocks**

CASE STUDY

Minimum charges

The team at Silver Financial Advice were struggling over whether or not to introduce minimum charges. They had decided their overall pricing policy which was based on percentage of monies invested but they wanted to avoid the position of undertaking work and not being paid for it.

Danielle, the managing director, said "For our clients, we have chosen the right approach — which is to bundle our charges for initial work — and then charge separately for ongoing service, again in a bundle. X% plus Y% is nice and straightforward". Laura, who was an experienced adviser, supported this but recalled, "We've had a few cases in the past where clients have not gone ahead with our recommendations and we have done all the work up to that point for nothing — because we received no commission and had no minimum charge. I know it doesn't happen very often but I think we need to bring it in".

"Surely there is a danger of putting people off", stated Tom, a new adviser to the business. "Where I worked before we had a minimum charge of £500 for the initial plan and if this wasn't put to the clients in the right way some would walk at that point — again, not many, but we did lose a few".

Laura added, "There is also the case where you have a client with a small sum to invest when our percentage rates don't cover our costs — the ISA has always been an example of this. This is not our main market, but it does happen and we always lose money!"

Danielle said, "Let's see if we can sort this out — we have two scenarios, the first is where we don't get to our charging point, after implementation, and the second is where the percentage rates don't cover our costs for low value investments. A minimum charge would deal with both of these and we need to be very careful where we set it, because, as we have said, there are not many instances of this, whichever scenario you look at".

Tom suggested setting the charge at the point where costs are covered, which Silver had estimated was £500 in many cases. "This may put off some lower value clients but, unfortunately, if they cannot afford our service we cannot give it away. We will need to explain this clearly, but we know virtually all clients who come to us need the full process and a solution to their issues."

"Let's test this for six months and see how it works", suggested Laura, "we need a short training or role play session on how we put this to clients".

Danielle observed that this issue would be less likely to arise if their charges were unbundled and they charged at every stage of the process. "With unbundled charges it is clear to clients from the very start what they pay for, but if we prefer the simplicity of our bundled approach then we must run with minimum charges which, in practice, will only affect a small number of clients."

CASE STUDY KEY POINT

The use of minimum charges depends upon the pricing structure that you adopt and your experience of the number of low value loss making clients or those who might be lost if you introduced a minimum charge. If this is not an issue for the business, or you are unbundling your charges, then you can make a quick decision and avoid an additional element of your charging structure. If this is not the case introduce a minimum charge at a relatively low level and see what happens. After six months you can make a judgement about whether to raise it so you at least cover costs, or remove it because you are losing valuable clients.

5 Pricing policy: the specifics

We should remind ourselves of the different approaches that can be used independently or in combination. These include:

- Hourly rates.
- Percentages of monies invested.
- Rate for specific jobs.
- Project fees, made up of individually costed activities.
- Percentages of tax saved.

In considering which to adopt you should account for the following:

- Your client bank — the range, income, wealth and buying power of your typical clients and how you expect them to react to a different approach to charging.
- The main types of business that you are involved with because the approach could differ between a practice that is heavily involved in personal investments and another which concentrates upon the corporate market.
- Your current method of remuneration and the ease with which you can move to a different approach from the perspective of adviser training and back office processes.
- The expected impact on your total revenue and its mix and if that requires 'funding' in the short term.

Ideally you should adopt a pricing policy that will be used in over 90% of cases. This means you will achieve consistency across the business and be able to monitor how the policy is working. That does not mean that if you have distinct client categories you have to treat them the same. For example, you may use percentage of monies invested for personal clients but project fees and hourly rates for corporates. As stated above, it is consistency of approach across all the advisers which is essential.

There are two basic approaches that most businesses will use:

- Hourly charge out rates which can be used to support the calculation of project fees, minimum charges and rates for the job — more prevalent in the corporate market but will work equally as well for personal clients.
- Percentages of monies invested — typically for personal clients.

5.1 Hourly charge out rates

A good starting point is the calculation of hourly charge out rates in the context of targeted levels of revenue. Even if you do not intend to use hourly rates this is an extremely useful benchmark, and a sound basis for working out project fees or to compare with your forecast outcome from using an alternative approach.

In any event you should be clear about hourly rates for all the main tasks because there are bound to be pieces of work or projects which fall outside your normal charges for initial work or ongoing service. Ideally you should be able to provide clients with typical charges for certain projects, or extra service which is additional to their service agreement. This could include tax analysis arising from a change in circumstances, complex pensions analysis, dealing with an inheritance or simply providing additional valuations. It is one of the benefits of a formal service agreement that clients can see exactly what they should receive for ongoing service which means that, quite rightly, you can charge for additional work which is outside this.

There is an '**Hourly charge out rate**' spreadsheet in the Developing a Service Proposition section of the website for you to use with your business. The process for working out your hourly charge out rates is relatively straightforward but you have to make some careful judgements about the availability of people across the year.

You need to work through the following process (all of which is repeated on the spreadsheet):

- Estimate the number of working weeks available by excluding holidays, training, internal meetings etc. — you can normally estimate how many days a week would typically be spent on these activities.
- Confirm the total hours available in a typical working day — ideally this should be no longer than eight hours because study time, additional reading, external evening events should be accounted for in the working weeks available analysis.
- Confirm what percentage of a typical day could be charged to a client — you can discount general administration, travel time, background research not specific to a client etc.

At this stage you will have the number of hours for which you can charge out. The final step is to divide these into the target revenue for the various job roles.

Your initial analysis gives you the opportunity to check the entire picture for sense and, if necessary, make changes which are as realistic as you can achieve. This is not a perfect science, but it is a framework that enables you to think about all the essential issues and to develop a starting point as opposed to using an informed guess. In any event you must have a basis for the pieces of work and projects for which hourly charge out rates are either used or form the basis of your project fee.

The preceding process is included in the spreadsheet so you only have to key in the assumptions and revenue targets.

Table 6.3 shows how this works.

In this example, the hourly rates in practice could be set at £250 for the senior adviser, £140 for the junior, £60 for the para planner and £50 for the administrator. The working weeks available and charge out time have been assessed as follows:

Table 6.3 **Hourly rate calculator**

HOURLY CHARGE OUT RATES, TARGET REVENUES AND PRODUCTIVITY

1. Complete **availability** calculator
2. Complete **hourly charge out rate** calculator

Availability calculator

1. Estimate number of weeks available for work (e.g. account for holidays, training, internal meetings and sickness)
2. Confirm typical total number of hours worked per day
3. Estimate % of **daily** time available to be charged to clients (e.g. take out general admin., travel time, ad hoc non chargeable issues etc.)

Job role	Working weeks available	Daily hours available	% of daily time available to charge out	Chargeable hours
Senior adviser	35	8	55	770
Junior adviser	30	8	60	720
Para planner	40	7	70	980
Administrator	43	7	50	753

Hourly charge out rate calculator

1. Check chargeable hours from **availability calculator**
2. Confirm revenue target in £k

Job Role	Charge out hours available	Revenue Target £k	Hourly Rate
Senior adviser	770	200	260
Junior adviser	720	100	139
Para planner	980	60	61
Administrator	753	35	47
Total revenue		395	

- The senior adviser (who we assume is also the principal) has to devote time to running the business and this, plus an estimate of training time, reduces the working weeks which are available. However, there is benefit in terms of daily charge out time from the presence of a para planner and junior adviser
- The junior adviser has to undertake much training and supervision which reduces the working weeks but the charge out time benefits from client work supporting the senior adviser plus some para-planner support
- The para-planner has no management tasks but will need training and, like the others, attend internal meetings. However the weeks available and charge out time are quite high. After all, para planning time should be dominated by client work, particularly if they are client facing and act as a point of contact for straightforward pieces of work and servicing
- The administrator only has the internal meetings to reduce the weeks available but a wide range of general administrative tasks which are not client specific which means the percentage of charge out time is lower than the others.

You should make your own estimates using the process and example above. The spreadsheet will save you a lot of time and you can analyse as many 'what-ifs' as you wish.

As indicated above not all practices will wish to use hourly rates, but they must be fully debated before you make your final decision on pricing. The arguments in favour of hourly rates are:

- Clarity and transparency for clients.
- Direct fit with other professional practices.
- A method of charging understood by professional introducers.
- All good back office software has time charging functionality.
- All work is paid for and very little will be given away.

The arguments against are:

- In some cases valuable expertise may be provided at a relatively cheap rate; this is where minimum charges or fixed rates for the job or project become important.
- Many clients have a perception that advice services are free and the suggestion of charging by hourly rates, even if facilitated through the product, may be a barrier.

5.2 Percentage of monies invested

It is expected that many advice businesses will adopt this approach as the implementation of the RDR progresses. It is a smaller step than moving to hourly rates and is intuitively easier to handle because we have previously worked in percentages.

There are two approaches as suggested by the 'pricing building blocks'. The first uses only percentages; the second combines them with fixed charges. Figure 6.2 is a typical example of how this works.

Example 1 is the typical tiered structure with a minimum charge at the lower end, to avoid losing money on investments below £20k, and bespoke pricing at the top where the nature of the work and the risks involved with larger sums warrant a tailored approach.

The bands are deliberately close to avoid the inevitable range of overlap at the cut-off points. There is overlap between £50k and £60k and £200k and £225k and you have to judge what to charge depending upon the amount of work and the complexity of the client's circumstances.

The cut-off points will differ across the market and you should choose those which make sense in the context of your clients. You should not have more than three main bands to avoid complexity and stick to a single rate for ongoing service. The latter will mean that clients in higher ongoing service categories will pay more to reflect the fact they receive more, as indicated in our ongoing service examples in Chapter 5. In addition there is a risk premium to be attached to greater levels of investment and complexity so your tiering should reflect this along with fair treatment in terms of 'reasonable' prices.

Example 2 combines fixed charges and percentages and you will see that, compared to example 1, lower value clients pay more and higher value clients pay less. At £100k invested the total cost to the client in example 1 is £2,000 while in example 2 it is £2,500. However, at £300k invested the example 1 client charge is £5,250 as opposed to £4,500. Of course, this can be altered by varying any of the charges in either example but the unbundled combination structure normally reduces client charges and revenue at the higher investment levels.

Before the RDR deadline you should test your planned prices against current revenue patterns to analyse the effect of moving from a commission basis to this tiered structure. This can be done by analysing your business activity over a three-to-six month period, then reworking the revenues on the proposed model and comparing against their earnings under the commission model. Again, this is an approximate approach but provides an initial indication as to whether or not the proposed rates are in the right area.

The advantages of the percentage of fund approach are:

- Clarity and transparency.
- Simplicity for clients and advisers.
- Inherent 'fairness' through the tiered structure.
- Ease of facilitating payment through products, funds, wraps and platforms.

We will deal with costing and the setting of profit and turnover targets in Chapter 12. All of these have an obvious bearing upon the level at which you finally set your prices.

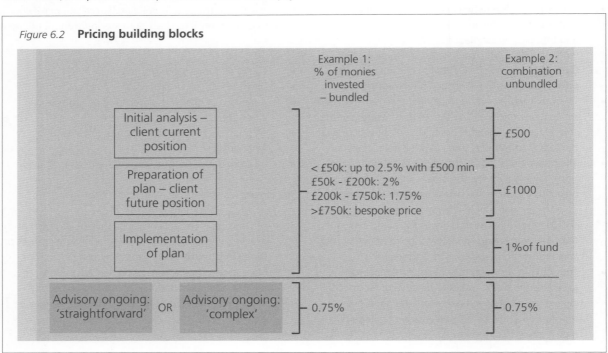

Figure 6.2 **Pricing building blocks**

Example 1:
% of monies invested – bundled

Example 2:
combination unbundled

Initial analysis – client current position

Preparation of plan – client future position

Implementation of plan

< £50k: up to 2.5% with £500 min
£50k - £200k: 2%
£200k - £750k: 1.75%
>£750k: bespoke price

£500

£1000

1% of fund

Advisory ongoing: 'straightforward'   OR   Advisory ongoing: 'complex'

0.75%

0.75%

6 Chapter summary

The management skills you have developed as a result of this chapter are the ability to:

- Define a clear pricing policy.
- Apply the policy to your service offering.
- Use pricing to increase concentration on client value.
- Implement an essential part of the TCF and RDR initiatives.

Setting prices is as challenging as designing service. A modern pricing structure requires many advisers to work in new ways and experience a different pattern of remuneration. This is one of the critical changes that you have to test and be prepared to adjust. |However, if you adopt a methodical approach initially you will reduce the risks associated with changing your pricing model, moving to a clear set of advice charges linked directly to a predefined set of services.

Chapter 7

A practical approach to designing service

By the end of this chapter, your business will benefit from:

✔   Full development of the service proposition.
✔   Acceptance and support from everyone in the business.
✔   Service and pricing design dealt with efficiently.

The aim of this chapter is straightforward: to provide you with a process to implement everything we have already discussed on designing and delivering excellent service.

This is supplemented by a **Powerpoint Roadmap in Part 2 – Developing a Service Proposition** on the website.

1 Use a structured framework to design service

Earlier in this part, we recognised that reviewing and re-designing the service proposition is one of the most difficult and important pieces of work that you have to deal with.

The entire process from initial design meetings through to full implementation can take at least a year, and it may often take an additional two years before all existing clients have been contacted and transferred to the new regime. However, this is certainly one of the projects where it is right to implement changes over a reasonable time period, and you should not try to complete the work in three months and expect a good outcome. There will be a need to continuously review progress and make adjustments, as well as ensure acceptance right across the business.

This chapter will deal with the initial stages of service design and, through two workshops, shows how to make best use of the time and experience of those involved.

2 Workshop One

This workshop is where all the hard work and co-operation is required. There is quite a lot to do before the workshop to make sure that the groundwork is done and you can get into the detail quickly.

2.1 Prior to Workshop One

- Gather all the existing service templates and agreements from across the business and review them for examples of good practice.
- Issue a brief for all those taking part in the process with some background on why the initiative is necessary and what benefits it will bring advisers and the business.
- In the brief, make it clear that this is a joint effort involving all parts of the business, and that participation and agreement is key to success.
- Invite everyone if the business is no more than six people; if it exceeds that, invite a sample that represents all parts — administration, para-planning and advisers.
- Identify a 'facilitator' for the workshop, who can keep an eye on time, capture the key points on a flip chart, and ideally write up the first draft using the templates in this chapter.
- Decide (with other principals, if appropriate) how prescriptive you wish to be. It is reasonable for the principal to have an initial view regarding how far you wish to go in prescribing service levels and activity.

2.2 Workshop One: running the day

- Allocate a full day, recognising that less time may be needed but making sure that the exercise is not time-pressured.
- Open the session by repeating the importance of the exercise and the need to gain full involvement and eventual agreement and acceptance. Also, ask people to set aside existing clients and to consider this as if it were a brand new business; this is because there will always be examples of existing clients who do not fit what is being suggested, which takes the focus away from what you are trying to achieve for the future.
- Introduce the overall approach from good practice frameworks and processes through to the detailed three-tier structure.

It is your decision as to whether or not you simply rehearse the arguments about the degree of prescription and explain your decision, or allow the group to decide. There is a danger here that stopping short of the structured approach seems easier and less of a change. That is not necessarily the case, and is the reason why you will need to take the lead on this.

- Use the diagrams and charts in this book to discuss market position, headline proposition and, if appropriate, detailed service content.
- Introduce the examples at an appropriate point, but after some debate, because there will always be fresh ideas to consider.
- The three-tier service examples usually work very well, and many advisers take them as a good starting point and then amend them accordingly to suit their business and target clients.
- The same approach can be used with the examples from Chapter 6 on pricing.
- You may find that pricing is difficult to tie down in the workshop, and that the best outcome is to solicit views and, if possible, decide on overall policy. It will take time to arrive at the precise numbers, and these should be worked through in detail and then discussed at a subsequent meeting.
- Identify any changes to process, back office software or jobs and responsibilities that will be needed to deliver the service proposition. If these are extensive, they will need to be part of the overall implementation plan (note: we will deal with processes, IT and jobs in Part 5 and Part 6).
- When you have completed the first drafts on a flip chart, ask participants to apply the 'common sense' test. Would the advisers be happy to work with this and recommend it to clients, and are the para-planners and administrators happy that the back office can support delivery of the service?

2.3 After Workshop One

- Circulate the outputs; brief the facilitator that this should be presented as the first draft of a service plan using the templates. Do not simply write up the flip charts.
- Check with fellow principals if the outputs are in line with what you would expect, if they support your overall strategy and direction, and decide on pricing policy – include this in the draft to be circulated.

3 Workshop Two

Run Workshop Two to work through the draft and refine, revise and discuss how you think pricing will work. If you have agreement at the end of this second workshop, you will be in a position to work towards implementation through the project planning processes, which are covered in Chapter 19.

SERVICE DESIGN can take at least a year, and it may often take an additional two years before all existing clients have been contacted and transferred to the new regime.

4 Chapter summary

The management skills you have developed as a result of this chapter mean that you can:

- Design and run (or preferably delegate) a service design process.
- Secure the agreement of colleagues on a major business change.

Remember you can use the **Roadmap on Service Design** from the website.

Over the past five years, one of the most frequent action points to arise from business planning exercises involving advice businesses is service design and development. There are many reasons for this, including:

- A desire to provide consistent service for clients, regardless of the adviser that they deal with.
- A need to increase efficiency through streamlined processes and back office activity.
- A concern that inconsistencies are contributing to business risk and that advisers are promising service that cannot be delivered.
- A wider objective of 'joining up' all parts of the business to maximise expertise and capability and stand out from the rest of the market.

As you will have seen, your service proposition links with all other aspects of the business, and many would argue that if you have a well defined service proposition you will have an efficient and low risk business. It is also the case that service design involves far more than satisfying the needs of the TCF and RDR initiatives, although this has proved to be a very good spin-off and catalyst for change.

Part 3: Marketing your business

How do you promote your business to acquire and retain your target clients?

"In the factory, we make cosmetics. In the drugstore, we sell hope."

Charles Revson

Introduction: Get the best outcome from your marketing effort

When you have completed this Part, you will be able to:

✔ Develop a marketing communications plan.
✔ Construct a cost efficient marketing budget.
✔ Split the plan and budget between profile, client acquisition and retention.
✔ Develop effective marketing campaigns.
✔ Select the right marketing techniques for the right tasks.
✔ Make sure you project your brand effectively.
✔ Acquire more target clients.
✔ Retain the clients you wish to keep.
✔ Evaluate the effectiveness of your marketing.

The best marketing activity is low in cost and high in productivity. You do not need 'marketing flair' to achieve this; well tested ideas, clear objectives and organisation are the basic ingredients for success.

This Part will cover the three main marketing tasks that advice businesses need to undertake:

● Raising profile and promoting image.
● Acquiring new clients.
● Retaining existing clients.

We will also look at the main techniques for each of the tasks, and use a practical approach to planning and budgeting to make sure you build a manageable and cost effective marketing plan.

The term 'marketing' is widely used and has a variety of meanings and applications. The theoretical definition is 'the process by which goods and services are designed,

MARKETING for advice firms is about acquiring and retaining enough of the right type of clients to achieve the long term expansion, profit and value targets of the business.

produced, promoted, distributed and sold to their target market to provide a profit to the producer and satisfy the needs and expectations of the consumer.' There are some who confine marketing to advertising and promotions, and others who interchange the word with 'sales'.

We will consider the parts of marketing that concentrate on communicating to our target market. You can take heart that much of the material in the chapter on service design provided a firm foundation for this. The sections on target markets, client needs, clear propositions and consistency of approach are as important for effective communications as they are for effective service delivery.

How effective is your marketing?

The table that follows asks Ten Killer Questions about marketing and summarises what is 'good' for cost effective marketing in advice businesses.

For each question, give your business an objective score (1 is poor, and 10 is excellent) and ask others what they think. Use **Template 1.1 from Part 3 – Marketing Your Business** on the website.

If you have scored around 30%, you are close to the market average. A good score would be around 70%.

This shows that a majority of advice businesses have an incredible opportunity for improvement and could gain competitive advantage from effective marketing. For many businesses, the big constraints of lack of time and budget mean that the job is not done as well as it could be. Some of the 'good practice' that is listed above simply does not happen, because it gets squeezed out in the daily pressures. If you look at the list again, you will see that most of it is common sense and, if you had time, you would probably recognise it all and put it into practice.

However, we are dealing with reality, which means that this chapter will give you the most effective approach to marketing, which maximises outcomes and minimises resource and time.

To do this, we will concentrate on:

- Using a checklist for testing all marketing ideas and activities.
- Using the right techniques for tasks related to profile, acquisition and retention.
- Effective marketing planning, from logistics to budgeting.

MARKETING: Ten killer questions

Score: 1 = poor, and 10 = excellent

To what extent:

1. Does one person have responsibility for making sure your marketing plan works?

2. Is your marketing person trained, and do they have time to do the job?

3. Do you have a marketing plan that runs at least six months ahead?

4. Do you measure the result of the majority of your marketing activity?

5. Is the marketing budget sufficient for the task and well defined?

6. Is your marketing budget carefully split between profile, acquisition and retention?

7. Do you all share responsibility for making marketing campaigns happen?

8. Is your approach to marketing well organised?

9. Do your clients compliment you on your marketing?

10. Do your marketing materials (brochures, website, business cards, etc) have the same design, style and colours? Do they look 'joined up'?

Chapter 8

Marketing communications

By the end of this chapter, your business will benefit from:

✔ Marketing plans that use the right techniques for the required tasks.
✔ Well tested campaigns and materials.
✔ Productive marketing campaigns which are well designed.

You should concentrate on the communications part of marketing more than anything else, because advice businesses are directly involved with clients and the selling of products and funds as well as advice services. You are less likely to make extensive use of marketing planning and research, or get into the detail of complex product development processes. We will refer to these where appropriate, but you have to make sure that your marketing communications are well designed and conducted.

1 Marketing communication comes in many forms

The previous (Figure 8.1) shows which marketing techniques are best suited for the three tasks of raising profile, acquiring clients and retaining them.

Figure 8.1 **Marketing techniques**

THREE MAIN TASKS	THE BEST TECHNIQUES
PROFILE **RAISING THE PROFILE OF YOUR BUSINESS** – reminding people of your presence, creating the right impression	Website/Social media Premises Public relations Sponsorship Corporate brochure
ACQUISITION **ACQUIRING NEW CLIENTS** – specifically targeting a segment of the market	Professional introducers Networking/Social media Client seminars Direct marketing Advertising
RETENTION **RETAINING EXISTING CLIENTS** – making sure you keep clients who will sustain your growth	Newsletters Targeted e-mails Website client area/Social media Service calls Hospitality

Figure 8.2 **Marketing family tree**

As Figure 8.2 shows, the wide range of techniques that you have at your disposal can be more effective for some tasks than others. The lists above are not mutually exclusive, because marketing is about being as precise as possible, recognising that it is difficult to be 100% accurate. For example, a series of well placed press articles will always raise profile but, at the same time, generate a few enquiries.

However, a well targeted mailshot should generate a lot of enquiries, but may have less affect upon the overall awareness and profile of the business. The mailshot may go to a few hundred people, but several thousand may see and read the article.

We will look at the relative merits of each technique later in this chapter. At this point, you simply need to be aware that the use of the right technique for the task in hand is a major way of increasing the productivity of your marketing.

Finally, you need to make an important distinction between marketing materials and marketing activities. **Materials** cover all printed and electronic items that are used to support marketing **activities**. The range is vast and will typically include brochures, newsletters, service leaflets and investment commentaries, as well as the website and promotional e-mails.

2 How does this fit together?

We have now introduced all the different terms that we need to use. The jargon has been minimised to aid explanation and to give you a 'common' language to use in the business. Figure 8.2, 'marketing family tree' reminds us how this all links together.

The marketing plan is split into the three types of task: **profile**, **acquisition** and **retention**. As we saw earlier, there is a range of techniques that you can use to carry out these tasks. Most of the techniques are **activities** that you carry out, but they will be supported by **materials**, either hard copy or electronic.

We will deal with developing the marketing plan in Chapter 12. At this stage, it is worth noting that many advice businesses have conducted their marketing by using the family tree structure to good effect, because it is very organised and highly practical.

3 Getting the best out of your marketing

Because time and resources are limited, there are several things you can do to maximise your chances of success.

To maximise marketing effectiveness, you should:

- Give the job of 'marketing' to someone who has time to do it.
- Take time to plan ahead.
- Work through the detail of individual marketing activities, particularly how and when prospective clients will be followed up.
- Use the right marketing techniques for the job.
- Measure the outcome of all marketing exercises and use this to improve future campaigns.
- Test all marketing ideas (from brochures through to mailshots) with a checklist to be covered later.

This chapter will cover all of these issues to make sure your marketing is as productive as possible, and that you can achieve excellent results with the most efficient use of your time.

4 Use the checklist for testing marketing activities

In the introduction, we saw three main reasons for undertaking marketing (to build profile, acquire clients and retain clients) and many different ways of achieving this. There is a straightforward way of testing these approaches, which has the following benefits:

- You can filter out very poor activities or initial ideas before time and money are devoted to them.
- You can prioritise different activities, because the process should reveal their relative strength and viability.
- The criteria will become standard practice, and you will begin to apply them to all marketing activities.
- You can continuously refine and improve your marketing activities by using this approach.

4.1 The checklist

To test and improve all marketing ideas and techniques, you should ask the following questions:

- What are we trying to achieve?
- What is the activity about?
- Who are we trying to influence?
- What do we want them to know?
- How will we communicate?
- When will this happen?
- Who will do the work and what will it cost?
- How will we know if it has worked?

The best way to see how this applies to your business is to take your most recent marketing activity and put it to the test using **Templates 2.1 and** 2.2 in the Marketing Your Business section of the website.

The example in Figure 8.3 shows how this works. You will see that we have taken a straightforward case of issuing a seminar invitation, and have added in the marketing shorthand for each of the questions. Note that we cover the questions on 'how and when' in one column.

The figure shows how you can apply the questions, and at first sight it may look simplistic. However, most advisers can recall apparently simple marketing exercises that have failed due to lack of organisation or attention to detail. These questions may take you a few minutes to answer, but they can save a lot of time, money and effort when they are correctly used.

An additional benefit of this approach is related to internal communication. This chart makes sure that everyone knows what is going on and who is involved, as well as providing a basis for checking progress. Getting out a few letters may seem simple, but the column on method and timing shows that there is more to it. Many of us have been involved with communications to several hundred clients, and setting up lists and making this happen can be a logistical challenge.

Figure 8.3 **Marketing seminar invitation**

ACTIVITY	Seminar invitation: 'Pensions in divorce'
OBJECTIVE What are we trying to achieve?	To achieve 15 attendees directly in our professional introducer target market
PROPOSITION What is the activity about?	Seminar to professional introducers on pensions in divorce – to encourage them to refer appropriate clients to us
TARGET Who are we trying to influence?	15 key contacts in ten accountants and solicitors
KEY MESSAGES What do we want them to know?	"We are experts in pensions planning" "This is complex – you must be aware of it" "This is relevant to some of your clients" "We provide specialist, impartial advice"
METHOD & TIMING How will we communicate? When will this happen?	Set up list 15/1 Draft letter and invite 15/1 Mail out letter and invite 22/1 Follow up phone call – 29/1 Letter reconfirming all details – one day after positive response Reminder phone call one day before event Event 22/2
RESOURCES & BUDGET Who will do the work and what will it cost?	Andrew and Joanne Letters and invitation – £50
MEASURE OF SUCCESS How will we know if it has worked?	15 attendees in target group

CASE STUDY

Filtering out a bad idea!

Reena Frank knows that the most difficult part of her planning sessions is 'idea generation'. Sometimes it is the challenge of getting the ideas flowing, and it is always about filtering out ideas that sound great but have no substance. She is also conscious that she needs to be objective when it comes to filtering, particularly if the idea originated from one of her more enthusiastic people.

As happened in most years, Alan Smith, one of her more flamboyant and successful advisers, came up with the idea of large posters advertising the business on the four main roads into town. "This will give us great name awareness — no one will miss these, and our competitors will wonder what's hit them!" His enthusiasm was boundless, and he went into some detail about the pictures and messages that would be included.

Reena was rigorous about applying objective criteria to all the ideas, no matter how enthusiastically they were proposed. Her list included costs, target audience, key messages, timings, logistic of implementing and finally measuring success.

The poster idea failed on several of these counts. It was too expensive; over 50% of the firm's clients and prospects lived outside the town, and did not come into it; and the posters would be seen by all passing motorists, most of them outside the firm's target market. As Reena said, "We will be wasting quite a lot of money, and could attract people that we will have to turn away politely — also, we know that just advertising that we exist won't make the phone ring; you have to focus on something that people are interested in, like retirement or education funding. We can't cover all of these on one poster."

Alan was slightly crestfallen — nobody likes to have their ideas rejected — but he accepted that, on careful testing, this was not the best way to spend a limited marketing budget.

CASE STUDY KEY POINT

The checklist really does sort out what is worth pursuing and what should be rejected, and takes some of the subjectivity out of the final decisions. It is human nature to have an instant reaction to an idea, but this has to be tempered with a logical review to make sure that the judgement is right.

Also, we need the 'Alans' of this world to generate lots of ideas, so you need to treat them appropriately when their suggestions are rejected.

4.2 Apply the checklist to marketing materials

In section 1, we made a small distinction between marketing activities and marketing materials. Activities are marketing campaigns that we carry out (e.g. seminars, mailshots, advertising, sponsorship), and materials are documents and brochures (hard copy or electronic) that we use as part of those exercises. Examples of materials include:

- Corporate brochures.
- Service leaflets.
- Information packs.
- Seminar invitations.
- Newsletters.
- Investment commentaries.
- Websites and social media.

All of the above can be hard copy or electronic, which is why the website is included in this list.

You should apply the same discipline of the key questions to materials as you would to the wider range of marketing activities. We have varied some of the questions slightly to make them completely relevant, and you will find that they work for all materials, including reports and recommendations, especially if you decide to standardise these.

The checklist for testing marketing materials is as follows:

- What is the purpose of the document?
- When will it be used?
- Who are we trying to influence?
- What do we want them to know?
- What do we want them to do?
- How do we want it to look and sound?
- Who will do the work and what will it cost?
- How will we know if it has worked?

As with activities, use **Templates 2.3 and 2.4 from Part 3 — Marketing Your Business** on the website, take a recent example for your business and apply these questions.

Figure 8.4 shows how these questions can be applied to a corporate brochure. This is often hotly debated, and many advice businesses decide that they do not need this type of document, as they 'sit on the shelves and gather dust'. For those who do use them they tend to have a specific purpose, as the case study will show. For simplicity, we have combined two questions on what we want the target market to know and to do. As with activities, we have added in the marketing shorthand.

As the figure shows, the questions allow all of the contentious issues around corporate brochures to be debated. The final set of answers may appear straightforward, but many businesses will take at least an hour and often longer to arrive at their conclusions. This is time well spent, because these documents take time and money, and must be evaluated in that context.

You will see that we have referred to digital print. This will be covered further on, but in this example it is important, because it can help you to avoid the cost of traditional lengthy print runs and potential wastage if your brochure goes out of date. Modern techniques mean that you can update and make changes at very low cost and drastically reduce your print charges. This can give you both a cost and an environmental advantage.

Figure 8.4 **Material development: corporate brochure**

DOCUMENT	Corporate brochure

OBJECTIVE
What is the purpose of this document?

To set client expectations prior to first meeting; to demonstrate credibility and expertise to substantiate our charges; to re-enforce image with introducers

APPLICATION
When will it be used?

Mail to new clients prior to first meeting
Leave with introducers to give to clients they refer to us

TARGET
Who are we trying to influence?

New client
Introducers

KEY MESSAGES & CALL TO ACTION
What do we want them to know and to do?

KEY MESSAGES:
"We are expert", "We are long established", "We have no ties with insurance and investment companies",
"We listen and plan before we act"
CALL TO ACTION:
"We want to work with you"

TONE & STYLE
How do we want it to look and sound?

Business-like and professional
Two colours – designs as opposed to photographs
Mandatory statements to be included
Timeless

RESOURCES & BUDGET
Who will do the work and what will it cost?

Who: Marilyn and external agency
Design cost: £1,000
Digital print cost: £3 per unit (min 100 units)
Deadlines: Design: 15/8.
Initial print: 30/9

MEASURE OF SUCCESS
How will we know if it has worked?

Client and introducer observations
Adviser use (eg in client meetings)
Introducer use (prior to their client meeting us)

CASE STUDY

Talking fees – the case for a corporate brochure

Black and Gold Financial Planning Consultancy Limited had decided to move to a 'fee-based' proposition.

Sheila Martin, one of the most experienced advisers, rehearsed the well known arguments concerning talking about fees with clients. She said, "The problem is in our heads; we have a mental block about this and it is ridiculous!"

Black and Gold had decided that if they went 'fee-based' they needed to be clear about their proposition, which would give them justification and confidence when discussing fees. They had done this, but something seemed to be lacking. "The problem is that we often leave that first meeting having talked fees, and I am worried that this is what remains uppermost in the client's mind," reflected Sheila.

Sanjay Singh suggested that this might be time for a corporate brochure. He reminded the others that the written detail on service came later in the process, and that leaving clients with the brochure would be a tangible 'summary' of the firm and would provide a more balanced impression.

The argument was accepted and, for the first time in its history, Black and Gold had a corporate brochure and specifically used it at the end of the first serious meeting. The aim was to demonstrate the quality of the business and breadth of expertise to justify a fair charge for the advice services.

They decide to review their policy after one year, and agreed it had worked. As Sheila said, "It was an incredibly good way to justify the price of advice – without using many words, the brochure does the job."

CASE STUDY KEY POINT

All materials need to be justified, and confirming in which particular circumstances they will be used is a good way to do this. It is worth remembering that an idea that was rejected or did not work in the past should always be re-considered. Times and regulations change, which means that you should always explore the widest range of solutions to each marketing problem.

5 Chapter summary

The management skills you have developed as a result of this chapter mean that you can:

- Use the best communication techniques for the job.
- Apply a rigorous approach to designing campaigns and marketing materials.
- Distinguish between activities that raise profile, and acquire and retain clients.

This chapter has provided you with the fundamentals of effective and organised marketing planning. You will have the opportunity to apply these techniques throughout the rest of this part to make sure that your marketing is successful and accountable.

Chapter 9
Profile and image

By the end of this chapter, your business will benefit from:

✔ A clear brand image.
✔ Co-ordination of all the parts of the brand.
✔ A well defined market position.
✔ A website strategy that supports the business objectives.
✔ Targeted public relations.
✔ Well chosen sponsorship.
✔ Effective selection of the profile-raising techniques that are right for the business and manageable for the principals.

Profile and image are about the overall impression you create and how many people you create it with. More specifically, it is about empathy and awareness between the business and its clients. All businesses will have an image, regardless of whether or not they promote it — and it may be different from what they expect.

1 People and tangible items are major parts of the brand

This is particularly important in markets where the role of the person (in this case, you, your fellow advisers and your support staff) is a central part in the delivery of the service and in the eyes of the client. Your main 'product' is based in the intangibles of advice and future expectations. For much of the time, you work with words, concepts and ideas in the context of your clients' hazy expectations of the future. This is very different from tangibles such as cars, shoes, beer and clothes.

This means that you have to work hard at promoting your image and take full advantage of anything tangible that you produce or use, including yourself, to create the right impression. Above all, it is essential that everything that contributes to your image is consistent.

FOCUS POINT

Self-awareness

Many of us have been on 'self awareness' courses. Most are designed to help us think about the image we project to other people. There are many parallels to be drawn with the image that firms project. Figure 9.1 below, sums up some common differences between how advisers see themselves and what clients see.

It is quite common for people who deal with technical issues to come across as remote, because the subject matter can place a barrier between them and their clients. Advisers often see themselves as 'financial guides', but complexity, regulatory constraints and the need to ask a lot of difficult and challenging questions can often project a very different image.

This is exactly what comes out of self awareness courses. What makes this more complicated is that different people see things in different ways, and want different things from us.

Let's take the first part: the difference between our perception of ourselves and what others see. The surprise usually comes when the gap between the two is greater than we expect. There will always be some observations that we will recognise and others that we had not thought of. This makes us start to think about the second part: what would others like to see more of, and less of? We cannot second guess this; we have to ask.

There can be some uncomfortable moments on these courses – and when thinking about it all on the way home after the event. It is one thing to find out that people see us very differently from what we thought, but we then have to work out what to do about it.

All firms and organisations have exactly the same problem – and many use market research and image consultants to develop the answers. Whatever you think about this, you cannot ignore it. If you put your business through a self awareness course, it would probably have the same uncomfortable experience. This is because, to an extent, advice businesses are made up of combinations of the people (and their images) that work in them.

Key point: Much of what your advice business does relates to facts and numbers. Image and brand (either personal or business) are very different, because they are imprecise and there is often more than one 'right answer'. This means you need to take a structured approach to this issue, because it is just as important to small firms as their larger counterparts. Indeed, because so much of what you deal with is intangible, anything that influences your image will be heightened in importance. From experience, you will know that clients see you and your business in many different ways – you need to be sure that you direct this in a way that suits your business and continues to keep and attract the right type of client.

Figure 9.1 **Sarah: Two perspectives**

SARAH: AS SHE SEES HERSELF

As an adviser, I see myself as:
- A guide
- Someone who shows the way
- Essential to my clients
- Good at sorting out clients' 'financial journey'

SARAH: AS HER CLIENTS SEE HER

As my adviser, I see Sarah as:
- Asking lots of questions
- A bit difficult to understand
- Technical
- Somewhat distant

2 Recognise that brand is everywhere

Your brand is far more than logos and brochures, because it encompasses everything that the client sees and hears. In marketing terms, brand is every part of the business that touches the customer. This creates your image, and you need to make sure that this is consistent and has sufficient profile with prospective and existing clients and introducers. Figure 9.2 emphasises the point.

Everything creates an impression, which is one of the reasons why effective service design has to be supported by consistent delivery. It makes it much easier to join everything else up if you are clear about what you are doing and who it is for.

To check the extent to which your brand is consistent, answer the following questions:

- Are the colours and logo on your website the same as on your printed materials?
- If you placed all your marketing materials side by side, would they look as if they came from the same firm?
- Do you have corporate standards for all personalised communications (e.g. letters, reports, valuations, etc) that everybody sticks to?
- Is the décor in your offices colour co-ordinated with your logo and other marketing materials?
- Do all of your staff answer the telephone with the same welcome?
- Are you convinced that your advisers and other staff represent your brand in the way you want them to — and is it consistent?

The questions are set out in **Template 1.2 in the Part 3 — Marketing Your Business** on the website.

Many small businesses think that 'brand' is for large organisations, and that it simply does not apply to them. This is certainly not the case: smaller firms can be more practical about their brand, but they certainly cannot ignore it. Think about other advice businesses or your own corporate clients. You should immediately be able to distinguish between those who have given some thought to their overall image and those that have not.

A really practical exercise is to ask one of your trusted clients to describe all that they see and experience when they visit your offices. The following case study is based upon an actual report that a client produced for his adviser when asked to do this.

This emphasises that you must be certain that you have the right image before you promote it, or go about client acquisition and retention.

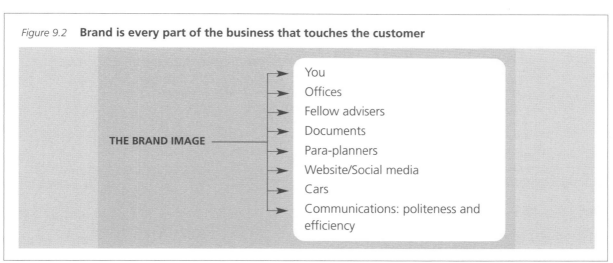

Figure 9.2 **Brand is every part of the business that touches the customer**

THE BRAND IMAGE

- You
- Offices
- Fellow advisers
- Documents
- Para-planners
- Website/Social media
- Cars
- Communications: politeness and efficiency

CASE STUDY

The dead flowers

Report: The experience of Peter James when visiting the offices of Red and Amber Financial Services.

I had trouble parking, which is not unusual, although the telling-off from one of the other firms on the trading estate got me off to a bad start.

The intercom at the main doors is difficult to hear because of the traffic noise, but the challenge is to get past all the boxes in the shared hallway. I know this is communal space, but it is pretty shabby and always untidy — a bit like the smokers clustered around the front doors.

Your receptionist is always friendly and offers me a coffee. She must find the dead flowers in the corner a bit depressing, and, if she is not around, I am never sure who to approach to tell them I am here.

I know you are busy, and you do a really good job for me. But if I was meeting you for the first time, I would think you were under constant pressure and that I was a bit of an interruption to your day. These meetings are 100% to me, even if they are a much smaller percentage to you. I realise that, but like most clients I like to feel important.

I am pleased that we no longer meet in the open office and that you have separate consulting rooms. Next time you walk into the one we used, look at the carpet, the window blinds and all the debris from staff training programmes in the corner. Incidentally, I know that all businesses have sales targets, but the flip chart that lists them should be out of public view!

The content of our meeting was excellent; it is a shame that your assistant had not checked the valuation and that the printer smudged the replacement, but at least the value is holding up!

Incidentally, my car was blocked in, so if you can organise a visitor space next time, I would really appreciate it.

CASE STUDY KEY POINT

Your firm needs to look in the mirror every day, the way that you do. The office and the experience of visiting it are very important to clients, especially new ones. The types of detail referred to above provide context for the service you provide and how you deliver it. The quality of your advice is what people pay you for, but they need to be reassured that the business has substance and is as good as you tell them. A vase of dead flowers can ruin the whole effect.

2.1 How you can establish the right brand image

This is important, because if you are clear about your brand image you can make much better and more consistent decisions about logos, brochures, office design, cars and even people. Everything needs to fit in with and support the brand image. As with service design, this provides another source of clarity and helps your business stand out from the rest.

As we all know, some businesses spend a lot of money on branding; smaller businesses need to be more practical and cost-conscious. To help, we can use some marketing theory here: market positioning. Your position in the market can be established by answering these five questions:

- What do you do?
- Who do you do it for?
- How do you do it?
- Where do you do it?
- Do you do it consistently?

You don't have to produce a finely crafted market positioning statement, but you do need precise answers to these questions. Use **Template 1.3** on the website to circulate this questionnaire. You will see that this links closely with the work you undertook on service design, and it should give you a good summary of what your business is about.

Here are two examples of market positioning to show how this works.

These two market position statements give very different impressions. Without any more information, you can visualise the offices, décor, brochures, website and people in these businesses. More importantly, if you were running one of these businesses you would be in a good position to talk to office designers, decorators and marketing agencies (e.g. brochure designers, website builders) about the image that you want to convey.

The market positioning exercise does a similar job to the service proposition summary that we covered in Part 2. This is because both summarise what the business is about, and you have to make sure that they are individually and jointly consistent.

The headline service proposition for Gold could be:

> "We provide financial consultancy for business and private clients with complex affairs — we work with other professionals to create and manage a comprehensive and evolving plan."

Whereas Bronze would have:

> "We provide straightforward financial advice to make sure you have the right products for your future needs."

This shows the direct link between the market positioning statement and the service proposition. It will move you even closer to achieving excellent consistency throughout your business.

Figure 9.3 **Market position**

GOLD FINANCIAL CONSULTANTS

WHAT DO WE DO?
Expert financial and tax planning to enable the long term management of investments through a detailed plan that is regularly reviewed

WHO DO WE DO IT FOR?
Private clients with over £500,000

HOW DO WE DO IT?
Working with other professional advisers from a consultancy perspective to use our in-house technical skills and expert software to proactively manage clients' affairs

WHERE DO WE DO IT?
In traditional style offices in the 'professional quarter'

BRONZE INSURANCE ADVISERS

WHAT DO WE DO?
Streamlined advice in one meeting to make sure that people have the right policies for their needs

WHO DO WE DO IT FOR?
Families and working people between the ages of 30 and 50

HOW DO WE DO IT?
Straightforward fact find and product/fund selection software – automated reports and other documents

WHERE DO WE DO IT?
In our high street 'shop-front' office or in people's homes

2.2 How to promote your business and brand

As we summarised earlier, this is about promoting the image that you have created. In many ways, this type of marketing activity provides a backdrop for the more direct and specific work related to client acquisition and retention.

There are particular circumstances when promoting the brand is recommended:

- At start-up, when you need to make your presence known with potential clients and introducers.
- When you are breaking into a new target market, and particularly if you need to reach it through a new route.
- If you have acquired another business and want to announce your presence in the new locality and, very importantly, create the right first impression.
- If you have acquired a business and have decided to replace the name of the acquired business with your own.
- When you are expanding into a new geographic area and need to support your advisers.
- When a new competitor comes into your area, particularly if they are heavily promoting their presence.

As suggested above, there are few circumstances when there is no case for promoting your brand. The judgement will always be based on the presence of the issues listed above, and the extent to which your business is attempting to acquire new clients. Profile raising tends to be more important in support of this task than client retention, provided that the latter is well organised and executed.

The effect of promotional activity tends to be more difficult to measure than acquisition and retention. Sponsoring the local rugby side is bound to raise your profile, but you cannot specifically identify how many additional people know about you or how much extra business it will generate. However, what we do know is that these types of activity – if you stick with them consistently – will have an effect over a period of time. Realistically, if it puts you 'on the radar' of potential clients and introducers, it gives you a head start over competitors who have no profile at all.

As we saw in Chapter 8, typical methods of raising profile and reinforcing image include:

- Website and social media.
- Premises.
- Public relations.
- Sponsorship.
- Corporate brochure.

Each of these works slightly differently to the others, but they all place your business name in the public eye and certainly create an image.

BRAND PROMOTION puts your busine on the radar of potential clients and introducers, and gives you a head start over competitors with no profile.

CASE STUDY

Gold and Bronze compared

3/21

We know that Gold and Bronze are very different businesses, which means that they will use profile raising techniques in different ways. The following table summarises how this could work, and you will see that both businesses take account of their very different target markets. This gives us some clear differences in how the firms portray themselves and how they 'speak' to their clients. You will also see how the different techniques fit together for consistency.

CASE STUDY KEY POINT

The approach to profile raising is very different for different types of business. That is why you should think about market position, because it makes it relatively easy to work out what to include and what to avoid. You do not have to use all the techniques referred to above; the mix will depend on the scale of the task and budget.

Techniques	Gold	Bronze
CORPORATE BROCHURE	**DESIGN:** • Full colour. • High quality photos. • Traditional colours (blue, gold, racing green, etc). • Low on text, high on 'white space'. • High quality paper. • More 'book' than 'leaflet'. **TONE AND STYLE:** • Professional and businesslike. • Concepts & ideas: 'this is how we like to work'. • Third person.	**DESIGN:** • Bright colours. • Designs and charts. • Less space and more text. • Lower paper quality for longer print runs. • More 'leaflet' than 'book'. **TONE AND STYLE:** • Chatty. • Personal — 'you' and 'we'. • Action-orientated — 'this is what you do next'.
WEBSITE	**DESIGN, TONE AND STYLE: AS ABOVE.** **CONTENT:** • High on consultancy approach. • High on 'solutions' to complex issues. • Case studies of wealthy clients. • Accent on added value and depth of planning. • CV majoring on qualifications and expertise. • No technical material or generic descriptions of funds and products.	**DESIGN, TONE AND STYLE: AS ABOVE.** **CONTENT:** • Easy and simple explanations of products. • High on ease of doing business — 'click here or phone this number'. • Online trading. • Links to popular sites. • Latest offers heavily promoted.
PUBLIC RELATIONS	**MEDIA:** • Glossy 'free' magazines circulated in wealthier locations. • Business pages of regional press. **CONTENT:** • Corporate financial planning (with personal angles). • Tax issues for higher rate taxpayers. • Inheritance planning. • Macro-economic change, implications for clients.	**MEDIA:** • Local free sheets. • Local evening papers — personal finance pages. • Radio — popular financial questions and answers. **CONTENT:** • Latest rates — mortgages, savings, etc. • How to save money on insurance. • ISAs and tax planning. • Good practice financial housekeeping.
SPONSORSHIP	Theatre, golf, rugby, less mainstream charities.	High street flowers and Christmas lights, popular charities (national or local), annual pantomime, local football.
PREMISES	Office in 'professional' area, Georgian house, wood panelling, quality wallpaper, solid wooden desks & chairs, paintings, thick pile carpet.	High street shop front, bright lights, modern furniture, play area for children, open plan, posters with product offers

3 You need a website strategy

Your website is a unique marketing technique, because it can be used for all three marketing tasks: profile, acquisition and retention. The balance between these depends on your overall business and marketing objectives, and you should subject your website to the same checklist tests that you would for brochures and specific campaigns. The comparison between Gold and Bronze shows how the approach can differ, depending on the target audience, market position and tone and style of communication.

Over 90% of advice businesses use their website as a corporate brochure to promote their image and as a means of client retention. It is now common practice for potential clients to look at websites as part of their initial search, even if they have been recommended by an existing client or professional introducer. As we saw with the focus point on self awareness, first impressions count, and your website is the shop window. You need to think about what people see on the shelves and behind the counter, as well as how far you want them to come into the shop.

The latter is important, as it will influence the contribution of the website to client retention. Many sites are relatively passive and simply carry newsletters and investment bulletins along with broader corporate information. However, many advisers have password-protected areas that are exclusive for clients and provide access to fund values and enable communication of changes to personal information and addresses.

For businesses that decide to trade online and acquire clients (even if they are transactional), the website is performing a very different function. All the factors that relate to brochure type sites still apply, but you need to add the rigour of the checklists that apply to client acquisition and campaign planning. These are covered in detail in Chapter 10 (client acquisition) and Chapter 12 (campaign planning).

3.1 Set a clear website strategy

This section is about making sure that you construct a website that supports your overall business objectives. You need to consider the following questions:

- Is my proposition based on face to face advice?
- Am I offering a bespoke service to all or some of my clients?
- Does over 70% of my business come from existing clients?
- Do the majority of my new clients come from referrals?
- Is my expertise in the more complex parts of the market?

You can work through these using **Template 3.1 in the Marketing Your Business section** of the website.

If you have answered "Yes" to at least three of these questions, then your site should concentrate on supporting your **profile** and client **retention**. You can still use the site to make clients aware of specific opportunities, but not to sell products or funds direct. To do so clashes with your proposition and your image as a specialist adviser who deals with clients on a personal level. It may be tempting to try to become an internet millionaire, but the development and operation of such a site requires a very specific set of skills that are unlikely to reside in purely advice-based businesses.

Of course, if you answered "No" to at least three of the questions, you may well be in the minority of advisers for whom online trading is appropriate for client **acquisition**. However, without wishing to remove enterprise and dynamism, you will need the capital and specialist skills to set up a site that can compete with the large and well established online businesses. Take a look at these sites, and ask yourself if what you have in mind could truly compete, and if you have the time and money to set up the site, promote it and proactively manage it day in, day out.

YOUR WEBSITE is your shop window. You need to think about what people see on the shelves and behind the counter, as well as how far you want them to come into the shop.

3.2 Websites are good for raising profile

Your overall approach to this should be similar to a corporate brochure. Indeed, many businesses do not have the latter and always point prospective clients to their website.

Taking the shop window analogy a little further provides some guidelines for developing a website that effectively raises profile. These are:

- Make sure the design, tone and style fit with your other marketing materials.
- Use photographs to break up the text and contribute to tone and style.
- Keep each section relatively short and free of technical jargon.
- Include your service and pricing proposition, or a summary of it.
- Exclude lots of detail about products and complicated financial planning issues.
- Use case studies to demonstrate your services and the types of client you like to work with.
- Include personal details and photographs of all your key people, because the familiar term 'this is a people business' applies, and you need to put a human face to your business.
- Make sure contact details and location maps are clear and up to date.

If you look at your competitors' sites, much of the content is similar. This is not surprising, as you are offering the same generic service, so there is a limit to how much your site can stand out. Keeping the site completely up to date and sticking to the guidelines listed above will help, because so many sites break these simple rules.

3.3 Use your website for client retention

Websites designed for retention must encourage frequent client visits, and the extent to which they achieve this depends in part on the service proposition. For example, if you offer access to online valuations, the frequency of visits will be greater than if you simply post your newsletter or investment commentary on the site.

The best way to support retention by raising the frequency of visits to the site is to:

- Include all forms and documents for people to download when needed.
- Post newsletters, investment commentaries and other regular communications on the site, even if you also send some of these by hard copy.
- E-mail clients when you add something new to the site, with the link embedded in the e-mail.
- Include news about the business and the people in it, particularly any charitable work and donations.

- Provide links to other relevant sites (e.g. business partners, charities, new services, etc), including your business Facebook pages or Twitter account (if you have them).
- Remove everything that is out of date and any news that is more than two months old.

Finally, if you offer online valuations, you will have more clients looking at the site. This provides you with an excellent opportunity to strengthen client relationships when fund values are falling, particularly if there is uncertainty of direction. Under these circumstances, most clients will be confused, and if you proactively e-mail them and post your views on the website, it will remind them that part of your role is to guide and advise them in difficult times as well in more favourable conditions. There is nothing worse than the accusation "I only hear from you when times are good and you want to sell me something."

3.4 Should you use your website for client acquisition?

This requires you to adopt a highly proactive approach and, if your business is entirely web-based, a permanent team to manage the site. If you are thinking of acquiring a large number of new clients on the internet, you will need to develop a promotional campaign to raise awareness of the site. This is likely to include a combination of advertising (online as well traditional) and public relations. The market is competitive, and this is very expensive. A quarter-page advertisement running permanently in one national newspaper on Wednesdays and weekends in the business pages will cost several thousand pounds. For most advice businesses, this is prohibitive and, with the current online players well established, a route that is not recommended.

However, there are plenty of circumstances where the web-based acquisition of business from existing clients is a sound strategy. Answer these questions to see if this could work for you:

- Do we have a large number of dormant or transactional (single sale) clients?
- Do we have their e-mail addresses?
- If not, do we have their postal addresses so we can contact them to tell them about the site?
- Are we happy to offer products that are transactional and might cut across face to face advice?
- Will clients be receptive to being offered insurance, such as protection, travel, household and motor?
- Can we gain access to these products at terms that are genuinely competitive so that clients will see that we are trying to help them as well as gain sales?
- Are we sure that if we offer these products they will not clash with our image as a 'bespoke financial adviser'?
- Do we have the skills and resources in the business to set up the agreements and links with providers, and manage them on an ongoing basis?
- Can we trust these providers to treat our clients

properly and fairly?

- Do we have the resources to manage, maintain and monitor our site and the returns from these arrangements?

Circulate these questions among your team using **Template 3.2 from the Marketing Your Business section** of the website.

If you have answered "Yes" to the first question and at least five others, then you should consider this approach. As with any marketing idea, you should subject it to the checklists and make sure you prioritise it along with all the other potential marketing initiatives and business projects. This is an area of development that often looks attractive, but anecdotal evidence suggests that it often fails to live up to expectations.

3.5 Take care when setting up the website

This section deals with the practicalities of setting up the site, which depends on the skills and resources that you have in the business. There are two basic approaches: a templated service or bespoke development.

The first is supplied by a number of companies, and typically includes:

- A range of designs and colours to choose from.
- Specialist content that is generic across the market (overviews of taxation, product types, etc).
- Your logo and specific content about your business.
- Live feeds from relevant sites (e.g. stock exchanges, BBC business news, etc).
- An updating service for all the generic content.

This is the most cost effective way for advice businesses to establish their first site, and many will use it as a permanent way of maintaining their presence on the internet. The benefits are:

- Simple, straightforward and very time efficient.
- Highly flexible to enable your brand to stand out.
- No major updating apart from content specific to your business.

- Low cost.
- Very little pressure on internal resources.

Bespoke sites have the obvious benefit of being tailored exclusively to your business, which means that you do not have to compromise on any style or content issues. Bespoke websites are very similar to bespoke advice services, as they cost more to set up and require time and specialist resources for ongoing maintenance. It is a commercial and cost decision as to which route you follow, and consideration must be given to the relative importance of the site in the context of all other marketing activity. Chapter 18 on out-sourcing will deal with the issues which you need to consider.

3.6 Spring clean your website

If you have a website, you need to run the 'dead flowers' exercise (discussed earlier in section 2) on it at least four times a year. Have a look at your site and answer the following questions:

- Have any of the listed advisers left the business?
- Have you included all new joiners (key staff and advisers)?
- Is there any news on the site that is over two months old?
- Is there any generic information that is clearly out of date (e.g. announcement of pensions A-Day, or budget changes that have been overtaken by events)?
- Are the contact and location details completely accurate and up to date?
- Are the photographs out of date?
- Do all the internal links work?
- Do you have links to external sites that no longer exist?
- Are there 'urgent' news items that are no longer urgent (e.g. the failure of Northern Rock or the Budget before the last one)?
- Are the client testimonials the same as the ones you started with?

These questions are listed as **Template 3.3 in Part 3 – Marketing Your Business** on the website.

Finally, ask someone who does not normally use the site to look at it. A fresh pair of eyes will often spot something that you have missed.

FOR AN EXISTING WEBSITE, you need to run the 'dead flowers' exercise at least four times a year.

4 Social media

Social media encompasses an increasingly wide range of on-line services that support networking. These can be accessed through PCs and mobile devices which means that communication is very fast and can be shared between high numbers of users. A majority of these services have a strong social bias, but there are many business applications that are rapidly gaining use.

The best known example is Facebook which has in excess of 500 million users across the world and, for professionals, LinkedIn which has over 70 million members worldwide, including four million in the UK. Many large organisations have Facebook pages and LinkedIn profiles, with the latter listing all the employees that are also listed as subscribing individuals. Twitter facilitates communication of short messages between subscribers and followers and can be used for social as well as business purposes.

There is no doubt that these are powerful forms of communication that can play a part in developing profile and acquiring and retaining clients, and it is clear that many businesses do this very well. However, as we know from the example of television advertising, it does not follow that, just because a communications technique is very effective in many markets, it works in the financial advice market. You should apply the normal marketing criteria and checklist (see Chapter 8 section 4.1) for social media as you would all other marketing activities. An example of this will follow.

Many of the issues and practices that relate to websites also apply to social media. In particular, you need to be clear about what you want to achieve and you must have sufficient time to manage and respond to content and contact. If you cannot do this, avoid these techniques because out-of-date Facebook or LinkedIn pages are just as damaging to your brand as a website that is not maintained.

You should also set some very clear rules about the distinction between social and business use. In a majority of cases these should be separated. Most of your friends will not be interested in changes in business taxation any more than your client community will be interested in what you are doing at the weekend. Of course there can be some crossover, but keeping the messages relevant is as important with social media as any other form of communication.

If you decide to use social media for business purposes then Facebook and LinkedIn are the services that you should use. There is a wealth of information on the internet about using these for business development as well as the specialist guidance on the sites themselves. There are some basic rules to follow which should help achieve a positive outcome.

Present the right image by:

- Making your personal profile as complete as possible and remember that clients will be viewing this as well as or instead of private friends — for example, you probably don't want to share photographs on Facebook with business contacts.
- Understanding the codes of practice for business use of Facebook and LinkedIn.
- Carefully controlling your privacy — on Facebook you can manage this by segmenting 'friends and followers' into separate lists.

Build and manage your network by:

- Adding your Facebook, LinkedIn and Twitter links to your email signature and any other marketing materials.
- Frequently adding 'business updates' — it is essential to keep content and communication as up to date and lively as possible.
- Posting (or linking to) useful articles, information and links to presentations that are relevant to your clients — charity activity and personal successes are highly appropriate for Facebook, articles and industry related topics work well for LinkedIn.
- Using the search facilities to identify potential contacts in the corporate markets as well as background before meeting a new client —a shared interest or acquaintance will make your initial contact much easier.
- Marketing your service on Facebook.
- Encourage people to follow you on Facebook by clicking the 'like' button.
- Promoting future events where you will be present.
- Join industry groups on LinkedIn to increase your presence as well as to keep up with current debates.

For business use, Twitter can be very useful for communicating short and time-bound messages. Critical deadlines (e.g. end of year or close of special offer etc.) work well, or very short snippets of news (with links) that your clients will find relevant. This is very good for client retention, but it is always possible that your message will be forwarded to others which could result in a new client.

When using any social media, you do need to remember that there may be compliance issues around how you discuss both your business and any products or providers. You should take particular care with this and warn any other staff who may be involved in keeping your website, Facebook page or Tweets up to date that they need to think carefully about every post. This is a growing area of concern for the Financial Services Authority, but following agreed sensible rules should avoid potential embarrassment or, at worst, disciplinary problems.

Finally, there is no better way to consider how social media could support your business by going online to see what others have done. In addition to the many sources of information and ideas to be found, you can form an initial view of whether or not to consider these services for your business and apply the checklist referred to above.

5 Don't forget your premises

Premises and offices are not always considered as part of marketing. This section will show you how important they are, particularly in a sector where there are no tangible products. As the 'dead flowers' case study showed, your premises really do count. They sit alongside websites, corporate brochures and initial meetings with clients, as they contribute to the first impression.

In essence, your offices need to fit with your brand and project the image you desire. In practice, you cannot always achieve this as effectively as with more traditional marketing materials, such as brochures and websites. It is clear that many businesses do not occupy premises in keeping with their brand because of financial circumstances, life stage (especially if they are at start-up) or tenancy constraints. What were perfect offices on day one may be out of line by the fifth year, particularly if the business has grown and achieved many of its early ambitions.

On the few occasions when the business moves, you have the opportunity to acquire the premises that fit with the image. You can also decorate and fit out the offices to your brand guidelines and set new rules for housekeeping. Policies related to smoking outside, eating in the office, clear desks, etc, are much easier to change when relocating than in existing premises where day to day practices have grown up over many years.

Because the clean sheet of a business move is rare, here are some suggestions to present the best impression you can using your existing premises. Incidentally, these may seem obvious, but they are very frequently missed — and they do stand out.

- Thoroughly clean and decorate throughout, particularly the public areas.
- Decorate in colours sympathetic to your corporate colours.
- Have a concentrated campaign on tidiness: remove all rubbish, old computing equipment, used flip charts, broken furniture, etc.
- Review and reset the rules for dress code, smoking, eating and clear desks.
- Remind the cleaners of all the tasks they should be undertaking.

- Tidy all external areas, including car parks, gardens, shrubs, etc.
- Replace all broken or outdated signage, and clearly mark visitors' car parking.
- Ensure reception is manned with people with the appropriate personal skills.
- Organise reception so that it is a pleasant place to wait (plasma television, magazines, drinks, comfortable seats, etc).
- Finally, if they are still around, remove the dead flowers!

6 Will public relations work for you?

The area of public relations that is most useful and practical for advice businesses is the press. This includes trade press, such as *Money Marketing* and *Financial Adviser*, and consumer press, such as local papers, free sheets and the nationals. That is not to rule out radio and television, but for the majority of advisers the press provides the most cost effective opportunities to gain publicity. As with all other marketing activity, the role of the press should be determined by the business and marketing objectives. The checklist for marketing activities in Chapter 8 will work here, and will ensure that any time you spend developing press relations will be well spent.

There is a misconception that the press will print any news release that you send them, and that 'all news is good news'. The latter is patently nonsense, as the coverage of the banking crisis clearly demonstrated.

In addition to applying the checklist, there are some additional questions you need to answer to decide if the press is right for you and your business — use **Template 3.4 in the Marketing Your Business section** of the website if you want to circulate these.

- Do you have time to develop and sustain relationships with journalists?
- Are you prepared to spend as long cultivating a relationship with a journalist as you would a professional introducer?

THE TRADE PRESS is good if you want to raise profile to recruit or be involved in acquisitions.

- Are you flexible enough to adopt a 'ten minute' rule for getting back to journalists if they call you?
- Are you prepared to take the chance that you will be misquoted?
- Have you got time to write a series of articles to a deadline on a monthly basis?
- Do the people you are trying to influence read the publications that you are likely to appear in?

Despite the attraction of publicity at no cost, there can be a substantial time commitment. Local public relations agencies can help you make contact with journalists and place stories, but you still have to prepare articles and news releases and speak with journalists — and that is where the time goes. If you cannot commit to this, then do not use public relations as a marketing technique, because it will fail.

Advisers often talk about appearing in the trade press to 'raise their profile'. However, if there is no clear reason for doing this, then there is little point in pursuing it. Coverage in the trade press is useful as a support to:

- Recruitment.
- Acquisitions.
- Promoting a service you are offering to other advice businesses.
- Promoting a charitable cause.

If none of the above apply to your business, you are likely to gain greater benefit from local press. This is particularly useful if you wish to:

- Raise local profile.
- Demonstrate financial planning knowledge and expertise.
- Promote a particular service (or range of services) that you offer.
- Target a particular group of prospects.
- Support a charity.

To an extent, the success of this will depend upon the range of publications that are available to you. These include the free sheets and local newspapers referred to above, and the glossier paid-for or free magazines, which tend to be aimed at higher income groups. All publications can provide details of the readership size and profile, so you can judge the extent to which you will reach your target audience.

CASE STUDY

Local press: friend or foe?

Joanne Brown is taking over the running of Brown Financial Planning from her father Edwin and wants to make changes. She has decided that the business needs "dragging into the 21st century" and that it needs to make more of its local strengths and heritage.

Her father has prided himself on building the business over a long time period, and rather favours the low profile approach which he says "makes us seem more exclusive." He has never courted the local newspaper, despite the fact that the readership fits quite well with the target market and the paper has a business and personal finance section.

Joanne decided to show her father that this could work. She invited Brian Major, the business editor, for lunch and, in getting to know him, talked about a wide range of issues from the strengths of the business through to the ongoing liquidity crisis. Joanne thought the lunch was a great success, and anticipated that Brian would call her from time to time for her views on personal finance and what readers should do.

Three days later, her father stormed into the office, waving the local paper above his head. "I told you not to bother with the local press — look at this headline on the business pages!" he shouted. Joanne read: 'Adviser predicts meltdown, keep your money under the bed.' The article concentrated on the few words over lunch about the economy, and a passing comment that Joanne had made, taken out of context. "We want people to have confidence in us and ask for advice —this headline will have the opposite effect," remonstrated Edwin.

It dawned on Joanne that she had gone into her lunch meeting badly prepared. She had not given enough thought to the real purpose of the meeting, what she would and would not talk about, and whether the journalist recognised that this was an initial social meeting as opposed to a discussion that he could write about. Joanne wanted to pursue her PR plans, but needed to make amends with her father and achieve far better results.

She spent an hour thinking about why she wanted to be in the press, who she wanted to influence and what should be the main key messages of any article or interview. The key messages were easy:

- We understand personal financial planning.
- We have been in this town for 25 years.
- We are experts.
- We are a family business, so we understand the financial issues that face most of the readers.

She thought this would develop empathy with the readers and that she should aim for the personal finance pages, not the main paper — that should cover the more likely prospects. Joanne then wrote a short proposal for Brian Major, suggesting six articles on practical financial planning to run every other month.

Two weeks passed, and Joanne heard nothing. She was beginning to think that her father was right when Sandy, her PA, called through to say Brian was on the phone and wanted to ask her about the latest figures on property prices. Joanne had heard of the 'ten minute rule' and said that she would call him back in a few minutes. She had a quick look on the internet to get the facts, quickly reminded herself of her key messages and then called back.

Joanne's disciplined approach paid off, and her advice to readers to take a long term view and seek professional advice on all financial planning issues was accurately quoted.

Brian did not take up the offer of the six articles, but he did ask for one-off pieces and often called her for comment on market and legislative changes. It took several months for this to develop, and the level of coverage gradually increased. Joanne knew her strategy had worked when her father told her that one of his clients had seen her quoted in the press and commented, "That gives you real credibility, and reminds us that you are just a phone call away."

CASE STUDY KEY POINT

The press should be treated as one of your best clients. Always prepare for meetings, think about what you are going to talk about, and be prepared to be challenged. If you do not know the answer, be honest, but get back to them quickly. Finally, treat them with respect and you will invariably get the same treatment back.

7 How to make sponsorship work

For most advice businesses, sponsorship falls into two parts:

- Charities.
- Local organisations encompassing sport, education, theatre and the arts.

You should approach this from a business perspective and recognise that it is one of the few areas of marketing activity where personal interests and preferences play a part; the other is hospitality, and the two are often linked. Any sponsorship will work better if you are interested or involved, but you have to take the initial decision in exactly the same way as any other marketing opportunity. Hence, make sure you use the checklist for marketing activities to bring an objective perspective to your decision.

The need for a sponsorship budget is vital, not just for efficient financial management but to help deal with the large number of requests that you will receive. To enable you to manage this, you need to undertake the following:

- Decide if sponsorship is to be a part of your marketing activity.
- Set a budget exactly as you would for the rest of the marketing plan.
- Decide what you will sponsor and allocate budget accordingly (use the checklist to help make this decision).
- Set a small contingency (no more than 10% of your sponsorship budget) for small opportunities that may arise.

If new opportunities arise, you can consider them for the following year, provided they fit with your criteria.

7.1 How to develop charitable sponsorship

Charitable sponsorship can be based on individual opportunities or a long term commitment. The major difference between this and all other sponsorship is that you should not do it for the primary purpose of achieving publicity. It is a good spin-off, but you should support charitable causes for the right ethical reasons. This may sound purist, but any individual or firm that uses charity work as an obvious means of publicity will suffer a negative response.

Advice businesses take a wide range of approaches to charity involvement, including:

- Charitable foundations into which a percentage of profit is paid, supporting several charities.
- Charities which are adopted for a specific time period.
- Charities that are chosen by staff and have events and opportunities for their involvement.

There are some specific questions you need to ask before you support a charity:

- Am I happy for the business to be associated with this charity?
- Does the charity have a sound image with the public?
- Are there opportunities for the staff to take part in events, if they wish to?
- Is there anything about this charity that could offend a particular group of clients?

You should also apply these questions to any political organisations that may approach you. They can be turned into a formal questionnaire for use in meetings using **Template 3.5 in Part 3 – Marketing Your Business** on the website. These are likely to fail the test, which shows us that overt political support should be avoided. The rule of thumb is that politics is personal and not for business involvement.

7.2 There is a wide range of sponsorship opportunities

Sponsorship of local organisations is a very good way of raising profile and getting to your target market. It is relatively cheap, can secure good publicity and may provide hospitality opportunities, thereby supporting client acquisition and retention. Opportunities include:

- Schools and universities – e.g. prizes for the best business student.
- Theatres and arts groups, usually one-off productions.
- Sports clubs, ranging from school competitions through to local football, cricket and rugby teams.
- Areas of historical or natural interest, such as nature reserves, Roman remains and museums.
- Seats, floral displays and monuments in public places.

There are many more examples, and you should approach them with an open mind and always use the checklist to make sure they fit with all your other marketing activity.

CASE STUDY

Bowled over!

Gordon Godfrey is one of the principals of Purple Independent Advisers Limited and is an avid bowls player. He was approached by the club president to sponsor the annual dinner at a cost of £500 and automatically agreed.

When he told his fellow directors, they were far less enthusiastic. Ghurinder Patel thought the money could be better spent on upgrading some outdated IT equipment, while Alison Crosby suggested that the local hospice would be a better recipient. Quite clearly, Gordon had started a debate that he had not expected, and he was faced with going back to the bowls club and withdrawing his offer.

Purple were due to hold a senior management meeting two days later, and Gordon decided he needed to work out how to respond to the objections. He decided to go back to the club president and suggest that, in return for the sponsorship, he be given the opportunity to write to all the members about Purple's services and to run six hospitality days for key clients at a discounted rate. It was fortunate that Gordon knew the president well, and there were no objections; Gordon realised that sponsors will often give something in return, particularly if it does not cost them anything.

The senior team accepted the new proposal, which prompted a wider discussion about sponsorship and charities. They recognised that this issue had often come up in the past, that there was no consistency to their decisions and that sometimes disagreements arose. As a result, they decided to set an annual budget for this type of activity and agree a set of criteria for deciding what they would support. Each opportunity had to:

- Provide potential for hospitality (for key clients and prospects).
- Be popular in the locality.
- Be of interest to some of their target market.
- Provide opportunity for press coverage.
- Stimulate their own personal interest.

They allocated £2,000 to the budget, and before the start of the next year arranged the following:

- Bowls club for second year (£500), including member contact and reduced rate hospitality.
- Schools rugby sevens competition prizes (£250) with free advertisement in the schools magazines and Purple posters at the competition.
- Costumes for a local drama group (£1,000), including 30 tickets to use at the local theatre for hospitality and programme advertising.
- Contingency fund of £250.

After the meeting, Gordon felt that, despite the initial friction, his initial decision to support the bowls club was right. He had secured a good return for the money and, more importantly, provoked a discussion that lead to a clear policy and a manageable and diverse range of sponsorship activity. The three principals split the responsibility for making the three sponsorships work and, in the following meeting, adopted a similar approach to charitable donations.

CASE STUDY KEY POINT

You should apply the same disciplines to sponsorship as any other marketing activity. Setting a budget is vital, along with making sure you can commit the time that may be required to make the sponsorship really work. The more you can secure associated hospitality and press coverage opportunities, the better.

8 Are corporate brochures worthwhile

These are documents that aim to promote the business and its services. They are normally used at the beginning of a relationship with a client or professional introducer, and have the core purpose of strengthening the relationship in its early stages. For example, some advisers will use a corporate brochure when discussing adviser charges and a fee-based proposition. Clearly, the aim is to convey that price is only one aspect of the client's decision and that expertise and service are also extremely important.

The best practical test of whether or not you need a corporate brochure is to think about occasions when you would use it. If you find there are circumstances when you would want to leave it with a client, then you know that it will be used. If this never happens, then do without it, but make sure the corporate information on your website is up to date and presents the same information and impression that a brochure would have achieved. Whichever medium you use, you do need to present the corporate style of the business either through a traditional brochure or on the website, or both.

Corporate brochures work best in the following circumstances:

- If a majority of your target market is high value and likely to seek a long term relationship.
- When you are competing with well known brands and need to demonstrate the depth of your business.
- If your target market includes businesses where you are dealing with professional finance or human resource managers or other senior people.
- When you are proactively developing new professional connections.

You should write the brochure in a style that does not go out of date, so avoid naming people or referring to specific pieces of legislation. You also need to check that other advisers in the business will use the brochure, otherwise the money will be wasted.

Finally, remember that the brochure is designed to convey an impression of your business. This means technical product and financial planning information should be avoided; you can include this in other leaflets, newsletters or on the website. Remember that corporate brochures are about impression and image, and that photographs and designs can play an equal role to the words on the page.

9 The relative merits of the profile raising techniques

9.1 Website

What we are talking about?

A website specific to your business — either individually designed or based on one of the generic frameworks that is available.

What is the best use?

Most advice businesses use the site as a 'corporate brochure' and direct new clients to it. Far fewer businesses use it to sell direct — this leads to a very different type of site.

Think about this...

Do:

- Be clear about the main purpose of the site before developing it.
- Look at competitor sites: you soon see what works and what doesn't.
- Make certain that the style (design, colours, etc) is the same as other materials.
- Include details of the key people in the business and professionally taken photographs.
- Look at the generic frameworks before spending a larger sum on a bespoke design.
- Provide your web designer with a clear brief.

CORPORATE BROCHURES are about the way you do business _ it is more about HOW you do you do it than WHAT you do.

Don't:

- Directly lift your hard copy materials onto your man web pages — the media are different, so some changes will be needed.
- Design the site yourself — this applies to the 'look and feel', as well as the technical operation of the site.
- Ignore the site and fail to update it after it has been launched — you need to appoint a 'webmaster'.
- Include content that requires frequent updating — keep it manageable.

9.2 Social media

What are we talking about?

Communications with clients and prospects through interactive media such as Facebook and LinkedIn.

What is the best use?

To promote the business through the development of an online network which enables frequent contact. For Facebook, you can bias content to more social issues such as charity events, staff successes and local involvement.

Think about this . . .

Do:

- Follow the same rules as for websites.
- Make sure you have time to keep the sites up to date.
- Pay particular attention to your profile.
- Add or change content at least once a day.
- Be certain that you will maintain this for at least two years to give you worthwhile experience.

Don't:

- Neglect the sites.
- Lift copy directly from your website.
- Forget to provide links from all your other hard and soft copy material and sites.
- Overtly sell your services.
- Post potentially uncompliant comments that could reflect badly on your business.

9.3 Premises

What we are talking about?

This is clearly different from other marketing techniques but has an immediate impact on image.

What is the best use?

Your offices say as much about your business as you do. This covers the location, design, décor, greeting, reception area, furniture and so on.

Think about this...

Do:

- Ask some trusted clients to do the 'dead flowers' test.
- Change whatever you can if problems are identified.
- Take full advantage of your next office move to get everything right.
- Recognise that attention to detail is key.
- Pay particular attention to the treatment of people when they arrive — first impressions are critical in this market.
- Make sure colours, décor and design fit with your brand image.

Don't:

- Ignore this issue — you can find something today to improve.
- Forget that this includes disciplines such as where people can smoke, eating at the desk, tidy desk policy, etc.
- Underestimate what clients will spot — everyone has a different perspective.
- Forget that clients will favour your business if visiting your offices is a positive experience.

9.4 Public relations

What we are talking about?

This is about using the press and/or radio to gain publicity — if it works well, it is extremely good value compared to paid-for advertising.

What is the best use?

There are three parts:

- Articles or speech slots — you control the content and will be regarded as 'expert'.
- Press releases — you control the content, but your release must be of interest to the audience.
- Availability for interview — acknowledged as expert, but you must be confident with the topic and comfortable with the interview situation.

Think about this...

Do:

- Think very carefully about whether or not you have time to do this.
- Recognise that it takes time (months and years) to gain the confidence and recognition of journalists (who also have a habit of moving on).
- Consider how comfortable you will feel being interviewed — the interviewer is in control, not you.
- Undertake 'media training' if you are serious about doing this.
- Realise that you have to adopt the 'ten minute rule' if

you are going to be available to the press — if they call, they need the answer quickly, so call back within ten minutes.

- Issue releases about business success and recruitment — local press like these.

Don't:

- Miss deadlines or ignore the brief for an article (e.g. topic and word count).
- Lie — if you do not know the answer, be honest and say so.
- Offer to deal with topics where you are not expert.
- Arrive late for an interview — you will be in the wrong mindset.
- Forget to use words, tone and style that fit with the image of your business and that people will understand.
- Worry if, on radio, you slip over a few words — no one will notice, unless you continue to do it.

9.5 Sponsorship

What we are talking about?

This is where your business gives money to a cause it wants to support and be identified with.

What is the best use?

There are two parts:

- Charities
- Local projects such as theatre and the arts, sport, education etc.

There can be a PR spin-off, and you must decide if this is one of the reasons for sponsoring an activity. As a rule of thumb, it is perfectly acceptable to gain publicity as part of sponsoring local projects, but far less so for charity support.

Think about this...

Do:

- Make sure you sponsor activities that involve your target clients as participants (e.g. sports clubs) or as audience (e.g. theatre, school sports).
- Sponsor activities that fit with your brand (e.g. Gold would sponsor theatre and rugby, while Bronze would support football and flower displays in the high street).
- Take part in the activity where appropriate (charity activities are a good example, and firms often adopt a charity for the year and support several events and conduct fundraising).
- Take full advantage of the PR opportunity — apart from the charity events (except where you have raised money).
- Set a budget for these activities.

Don't:

- Expect results unless you sponsor for at least three years.
- Expect one single event to produce instant results.
- Be afraid to turn down charity and sponsorship offers — make sure they fit with your brand and target audience.
- Allow anyone but yourself or your marketing person to decide on sponsorship.
- Ignore the legitimate spin-offs (e.g. sponsor the local golf club, but in exchange for an opportunity to write to the members).
- Let emotion rule your decision — we are all human, but we must treat this as a business decision first and a personal commitment (where appropriate) second.
- Force your staff to take part in sponsorship or charity events.

9.6 Corporate brochure

What we are talking about?

A document that describes the scope and style of the business.

This is about the way you do business — it is more about HOW you do it than WHAT you do.

What is the best use?

Brand new prospects and clients and introducers.

New businesses working hard to create a positive initial impression.

Think about this...

Do:

- Use the right colours and layout to support your brand.
- Use the right 'tone and style' for the words.
- Use digital print to economise on print costs.
- Use fewer words wherever possible.

Don't:

- Include time-specific statements and lists of people.
- Have long print runs.
- Use a lot of text with little 'white space' — the document needs to look inviting or 'accessible'.
- Include any technical detail.

10 Chapter summary

The management skills you have developed as a result of this chapter mean that you can:

- Co-ordinate all the factors that influence brand image.
- Recognise when brand promotion is necessary.
- Decide which promotional techniques to use.
- Develop a website strategy.
- Work with the relevant social media outlets.
- Evaluate the worth of public relations and sponsorship.
- Deal with the press.
- Secure awareness and enhanced image from sponsorship.

Answer the following questions to decide the extent to which brand promotion is a priority for your business:

- Does over 60% of your new business come from existing clients?
- Is the greatest source of new clients from existing client and introducer referrals?
- Are the competitive pressures from other advice businesses or local branches of banks low or non-existent?
- Is there low turnover in your adviser team?
- Have you been in your present location for more than ten years?

You will find these questions in **Template 3.6 in the Marketing Your Business section** of the website.

If you have answered "Yes" to at least three of the above, including the first one, then you should not need to spend very much on profile raising. Your brand and image are just as important, but your marketing budget should have a bias toward client retention and acquisition which are dealt with Chapters 10 and 11.

Chapter 10
Client acquisition

By the end of this chapter, your business will benefit from:

✔ Clear objectives for acquiring clients.
✔ Recognition of the full range of client acquisition techniques.
✔ Selection of the best techniques to acquire target clients.
✔ Management of the detail of client acquisition campaigns.

This chapter will cover the main methods of acquiring new clients, which are through:

- Professional introducers.
- Networking.
- Client seminars.
- Direct marketing.
- Advertising.

This is not to rule out enquiries that may arise from a press article or sponsorship of a local school sports competition, but you can target the techniques above more accurately, as they are specifically designed to generate enquiries or, in some cases, product sales. Even more significantly, you can measure the effect of direct marketing campaigns or the number of client referrals from an accountant, whereas measurement of the effect of a website is less precise.

You will know from experience that advice businesses differ in their use of acquisition techniques, and what works for one can be a failure for another. While you may have preferences, your starting point should always be to identify what is the best technique for the job.

Over the past few years, many advice businesses have shifted their targeting to higher value clients, using professional introducers as one of the key routes. For every business that makes this route work, there at least three others who cannot, and that is usually based on the experience of a previous attempt that failed.

While learning from past experience is important, you should always keep an open mind to the various approaches that are available. There are only a certain number of routes to market, and you should only discount them if you are certain that they will not work.

CLIENT ACQUISITION techniques are accountable: you know exactly what returns you get for the time and money invested.

1 Set clear client acquisition objectives

Many advice businesses proactively target new clients as part of their growth plans. If you have a clear revenue target, you should work out how many clients will be needed to contribute to this. The focus point opposite shows how this can be done and how useful it is to know how many clients you need, over what time period and to what value. This will give you a clear acquisition objective, and you will be able to measure progress and make adjustments to the plan if required.

When you complete this, you will immediately recognise that much of the content is based on estimates. The typical costs are covered in Chapter 12. Despite the need to estimate costs and outcomes, the benefit of adopting this approach to acquisition planning is summarised below. It:

- Makes you think about the detail of the overall task in terms of what has to be achieved.
- Provides a test of reality in terms of your ability to achieve the number of clients at a particular value.
- Enables you to tailor your marketing budget to the task and techniques.
- Allows you to compare different approaches.
- Provides an initial benchmark against which to measure success and make adjustments in the light of actual results.

Client acquisition is the most difficult of the three marketing tasks. Finding the right route to market, developing activities and running them at the right time and intensity are hard to get right. You have to plan as much as you can, because that reduces the risk of failure, but be prepared to pilot and make changes at every stage.

If you adopt this approach, then over time you will identify what works well for your business and target markets, and will be in a position to refine your activities and predict the outcomes more accurately.

THE NUMBER OF CLIENTS TO ACQUIRE must have an objective related to an income target and expected average client value. This allows progress to be measured and adjustments to be made.

FOCUS POINT

Objectives, targets and measures

This is a process for testing if you can actually acquire as many clients as you need and where they are likely to come from. This makes your marketing accountable, so you know exactly what returns you get for each campaign.

Table 10.1

QUESTION	ANSWER
How much revenue must brand new clients contribute over the next three years?	YEAR 1: very little due to time lag. YEAR 2: £90,000. YEAR 3: £165,000. YEAR 4: £220,000.
What is the main target market?	People within one year (possibly two years) of retirement.
How will you reach them?	In company and open seminars.
How many clients do you need to achieve the revenue target?	YEAR 1: run seminars, build prospects and commence communication. YEAR 2: assume 30 new clients with £100,000 to invest on a fee of 3% for initial work and 0.5% for ongoing service, and reviews in following years = £90,000. YEAR 3: 50 new clients on same assumptions = £150,000 plus service charge for initial 30 clients @ £500 each = £15,000. Delivers total of £165,000. YEAR 4: 60 new clients on same assumptions = £180,000 plus service charge for initial 30 = £15,000 plus second 50 = £25,000 delivers £40,000 recurring income. Delivers total of £220,000.
What is the cost of the marketing?	Includes: time to develop the corporate and other networking connections to offer the service; invitations and seminar operations based on total of 750 invites and 250 attendees = £20,000.
What is the potential contribution?	£475,000 revenue less £20,000 direct costs = £455,000.

Key point: It is quite possible that more than one approach will be needed, but this level of detail is important. Even if the outcome is different, this initial analysis will provide you with a benchmark for measurement. This gives you the chance to change your plans much earlier than if you had no measures or expectations. Use **Template 4.1 in Part 3 – Marketing your Business** on the website to create your own evaluation.

2 Think about developing professional introducers

This is an increasingly important route to market for many advice businesses, as it supports development of high value personal and corporate clients. The term 'professional introducer' normally relates to accountants and solicitors, but also includes general insurers, estate agents, housebuilders and bankers involved with mergers and acquisitions. This range of introducers can provide the full spectrum of business and financial planning from simple protection through to complex pension scheme work.

The extent to which professional introducers will be an important source of new clients for your business depends on your target market and the amount of time you are prepared to devote to developing these connections. Many advisers have spent a lot of time in initial meetings, but failed to follow up. The typical result is little or no business, because the relationship has not been cemented. All advisers who are successful with introducers recognise that trust lies at the heart of the relationship, and this takes time to develop.

Before approaching potential introducers, it is important to answer the following questions:

- How much time are you prepared to devote to developing the connections?
- What are your measures of success in terms of business value and client numbers?
- How do you want to work with them — order taker or business partner?
- What do you need them to commit to in order to make the relationship work?
- What will your service agreement contain?
- Will you make payments for the introductions or work on a reciprocal basis?
- How much reciprocal business can you offer?

Formalise your answers using **Template 3.7 in the Marketing Your Business section** of the website.

This covers your proposition, and if you are clear about these items, you will stand out from the majority of advisers who do not think this through before the initial meeting. If you consider the perspective of the introducer, you will know that they have been courted many times before, and have often been let down in practice.

The range of potential benefits that you can offer an introducer includes:

- **Service:** provision of complete service for their clients.
- **Compliance:** no risks or worries, because you carry the responsibility.
- **Simplicity:** you deal with all administration and communicate back to the introducer.
- **Client retention:** enables the introducer to compete with others who have advice businesses in-house.
- **Client confidence:** the introducer and his clients will be up to date with changes and developments in financial markets.
- **Remuneration:** subject to professional body guidelines.

You should develop the initial campaign to attract introducers in the same way as any other marketing campaign using the planning guide in Chapter 12. This ensures that your approach is thorough and that initial contacts, be they letters or seminars, are followed up by the right person in a timely manner.

2.1 Sustaining the relationship

The majority of introducer relationships fail because the adviser has no plan to sustain the relationship. One of the parties has to be the driving force and, if you think about it, financial advice will not be at the forefront of the introducer's mind. Table 10.2 shows how you can develop and sustain the relationship.

This takes considerable time and is a test of whether or not you have found a source of clients that you can successfully pursue. In addition, the early conversations with introducers should cover this way of working to test their commitment to the overall process and the time they will need to devote to it.

2.2 Consider joint venture companies

Some advisers have set up joint venture companies with introducers to provide a real focus for activity and to secure commitment of all parties. The advice business provides services to the joint venture, thereby securing payments for the service as well as a profit share. The revenue stream for the venture comes from the charges for advice and transactions that are undertaken with introduced clients. The benefits of these arrangements are:

- Costs and revenues are transparent to both parties.
- The level of commitment is likely to be much greater.
- The introducer secures remuneration through profit share and does not have to discuss fees or commission with the client.
- The advice business has a source of revenue for providing adviser and back office services as well as profit share.

In practice, the majority of arrangements with introducers are less formal, and advisers who actively use this approach typically have five 'live' introducers who may provide up to ten opportunities over a year. There will be wide variations to this, but it provides a benchmark if you are considering developing this source of business. Many of the issues to consider are dealt with in Chapter 18 on outsourcing.

Table 10.2 **Professional connections: maintenance and growth**

The following is a range of activities that can be used with introducers to develop the relationship.

TRAINING/BUSINESS DEVELOPMENT —
lunchtime seminars at their offices
(you supply the lunch)

OBJECTIVES:
- To develop the range of business areas acquired from the connection and the number of partners placing business.
- To demonstrate expertise and personality.
- To link the topic with an area of obvious and (ideally) immediate interest to the partners.

KEY MESSAGES:
- We have depth of expertise.
- We have many ideas from which your clients will benefit.
- We work across the full spectrum of tax and financial planning.
- We are committed to you (and will take time to work with you).

BUSINESS DEVELOPMENT

OBJECTIVE:
- To ensure business flows at a steady pace.

PROCESS:
- Regular meetings with individual introducers.
- Link to ongoing client work.
- Identify clients who fall into particular categories.
- Potentially offer seminars for specific client groups — with shared presentation.
- Alternatively, invite the introducer to write to clients, introducing and endorsing your services.

ADDITIONAL SUPPORT

OBJECTIVES:
- To maintain contact.
- To build a personal relationship.

PROCESS:
- Specific password-protected area of website (technical information, log of work, calculators, etc).
- Professional connection newsletter.
- Specific e-mail contact — on particular issues.
- Entertainment.

3 Does networking work?

Networking is about directly meeting a specific group of people with the aim of developing the business. The major attraction is that this tends to be relatively cheap, although it can be demanding on time. There are several target groups for whom networking is an effective means of contact:

- Potential clients.
- Introducers.
- Potential employees, including advisers.
- Principals of firms who might be looking for an acquirer or opportunities to acquire.

You need to find out where these different groups are likely to meet, and make a clear distinction between professional meetings and more social events. At the former, it is perfectly legitimate to talk about business and explore opportunities. Organisations such as rotary clubs play an important role in business development in addition to the charitable work they carry out.

By contrast, your approach at golf and sports clubs should be very different. You should adopt an extremely relaxed

approach to business and judge carefully if it is appropriate to make someone aware of your services. Despite the fact that such venues will have many potential clients, you should join as much for the sport and exercise as the business opportunity. This is likely to develop, but you must take a three-year view and be prepared to join in and give time to the club and its operation, as well as meeting people.

Because networking involves a lot of personal time, you should answer the following questions to consider if it is a route you wish to follow.

- Are you prepared to spend at least one evening a month attending professional business meetings?
- Can you keep this up for at least two or three years, and often longer?
- Do you enjoy meeting new people?
- Do you have the patience to let relationships develop over a long time period?
- Are there networks open to you where a good number of potential clients exist?
- Are there networks or activities that you enjoy that will also provide contact with the target audience?
- How much are you prepared to contribute to the operation of the network?

- Are you completely clear about the business objectives of developing network relationships?

Keep a record of your answers using **Template 3.8 in Part 3 – Marketing Your Business** on the website.

Many advisers will claim that networking is highly rewarding in terms of new clients and potential advisers. There is no doubt that advisers who are well known in their region stand a much greater chance of being approached by potential new joiners or clients than those who are anonymous.

4 Client seminars are very direct

This can be a very effective way of acquiring new clients, because it is direct and you have the opportunity to demonstrate expertise and make people aware of particular financial issues that they should deal with.

Invitations to seminars can be made in a variety of ways:

- In conjunction with a professional introducer, inviting some of his clients as well as yours.
- Inviting clients and suggesting that they also invite a friend or relative.
- Buying lists and writing to people in a particular area or post code.
- Promoting the seminar on your website.

The optimum number of attendees is usually no more than 20, which means you have time to welcome and meet them all before the formal session begins. You have to decide which approach is likely to attract the best response. If your business is based on a relatively small number of clients, you can offer 'exclusive' seminars to those with greater value and ask them to bring another person. It is important to choose a topic that will be of interest to them and those they invite, and that you have speakers and content that live up to the exclusivity of the event.

4.1 Using external speakers

This provides breadth and added interest to the seminar. Speakers do not have to be well known, but they should represent organisations that invitees will recognise. Fund managers, business gurus and writers are good examples.

It is essential that you give them a very clear brief, including:

- When to arrive and location details.
- How long to speak for.
- Exactly what you want them to talk about.
- The profile of the audience.
- Who else will be speaking and where they appear in the running order.
- How much you will pay and if you are including accommodation.

If they are using slides, it is best to obtain them in advance, so you can check the content and load them onto one laptop. As always, the professionalism with which you run the event will be instantly recognised by the attendees.

4.2 Think carefully about venues and organisation

Venues need to reflect your brand image and be cost effective. You should consider the following when making arrangements:

- Access and parking for venue.
- Comfort, décor and general ambience of the venue.
- Size of presentation room.
- Potential for noise from other activities.
- Access time to the room to enable you to set up equipment before the seminar.

When organising the seminar, don't forget the following:

- The level of catering: do not under-cater, as it creates a very bad impression.
- Timing of catering: before or after, depending on how you wish to meet the attendees.
- The time that is likely to be most convenient for attendees.
- The total running time of the formal part: no more than 45 minutes is typical.
- The number of speakers: having at least two is advisable.
- Presentation materials with pictures, simple diagrams and few words.
- Content that is clear and easy to understand, with the minimum of technical jargon.
- The process of following up the attendees, particularly those who expressed an interest in more details or a further meeting.

After the seminar, you need people to think the following:

- "The content was relevant to me."
- "That guy knows his stuff and can explain it in simple language."
- "The slides were easy to read and understand."
- "I need to do something about this; he seems the right person to deal with it."
- "I trust him to do a good job."
- "The surroundings were comfortable and conducive to talking to the speaker (and his colleagues)."

Importantly, they do not need to leave with a full technical understanding of the issue or to be so worried that they end up doing nothing. They simply need to believe they have an issue to be dealt with and that you can help. This places you in the strongest position when you make the follow-up call to arrange an appointment.

5 Does direct marketing work?

This is about communicating directly with a potential client by post, e-mail or telephone. Response rates depend on many factors, but will tend to be around 1%, so this can be quite wasteful if it is a postal exercise.

You can maximise response rates by:

- Making the offer specific: a particular product or service, as opposed to generic financial planning.
- Setting a clear deadline: this always concentrates people's minds.
- Emphasising any opportunity to save money: often tax savings.
- Making the offer simple to understand.
- Running the campaign in tranches, depending on timing and numbers involved.

In planning campaigns, you need to use the checklist in Chapter 8, and also think carefully about the following direct marketing guidelines:

- The covering letter: this should never exceed one side of A4.
- Additional contents: minimise these to save postage or download time, and to avoid confusion and information overload.
- Timing: for initial contact and when you may follow up.
- The 'call to action': response needs to be as easy and low cost as possible.
- The quality of your data: either from your own prospect file or purchased lists.

Because direct marketing tends to involve large volumes of contacts (at least 200), there is a generic process that should be followed. This is summarised in Figure 10.1.

As the chart shows, there is a specific route to follow, which you can easily adapt if you use e-mail communications instead of traditional methods. This process is just as important as the offer and the contents of the pack, because if the data is poor or the time lags are too great between each stage, responses will drop.

For many advice businesses, there is no requirement to generate enquiries in large volumes, which means this complex and potentially wasteful approach can be avoided. However, there are times when a large number of existing clients should be contacted using these methods. These are:

- Regulatory reviews.
- Change of ownership or adviser.
- Product reviews, when many clients need to make changes.
- Fund reviews, for the same reasons.
- Issue of client surveys: often linked to service quality.
- Despatch of regular communications, such as newsletters.

In these cases, the generic process above can avoid wastage and large numbers of returns, and keeps the exercise as manageable as possible. The larger the exercise, the more important it is to despatch material in tranches, partly to spread cost, but also to ease the workload of the administration team.

6 Does advertising pay?

This is paid-for space in a wide range of media, including newspapers, magazines, radio, television, posters, the internet and many more. For a majority of advice businesses, this is not recommended, for the following reasons:

- It is relatively expensive compared to other more direct and precise targeting methods.
- The expense relates to the number of times your advertisement is seen; it has to be high frequency to register with consumers.
- Most advice businesses do not need to be high profile: they just need to be good at keeping their best clients and acquiring some more.
- Advertising is wasteful, because even with good targeting there will be many people who see your advertisement who are not in your target market.
- The cost of producing effective advertisements is relatively high, which clearly adds to the cost.

There are certain instances where advertising can be justified:

- Magazines linked to organisations which you are sponsoring: this includes theatre programmes, school magazines, sports club yearbooks, etc.
- Highly targeted local magazines in which you can write articles that are distributed to the wealthier areas.

For these opportunities, you need to have a good generic advertisement that is professionally produced and which can be used many times. This makes the production cost effective and means that you only have to go through the preparation and production process once.

There is one type of publication (hard copy or electronic) that does not quite fit with those referred to above: directories, including examples such as Yellow Pages or www.unbiased.co.uk. The decision about using these depends on your target market and what you intend to offer them. In broad terms, directories are useful in the following situations:

- If you operate across all main areas of personal financial planning.
- If the product range you work with is broad and runs from mortgages to pensions and ISAs to unit trusts.
- When you are seeking to attract a middle income client group and offering 'straightforward' advice, as opposed to more strategic financial planning.

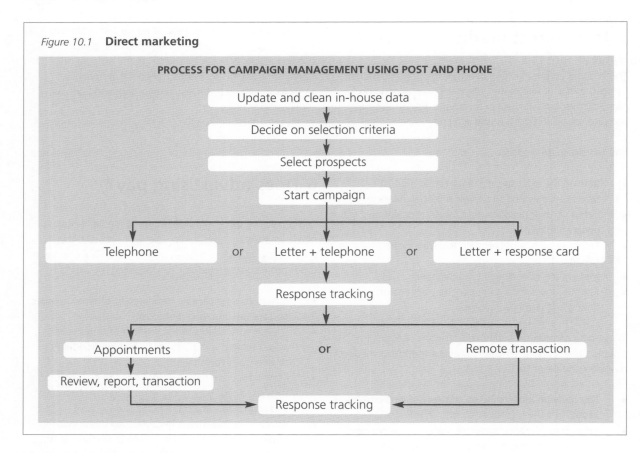

Figure 10.1 **Direct marketing**

In these cases, the volume of enquiries is important, and many people turn to directories or search engines to find advisers in their locality. However, if this does not apply to your business, then directories will most likely lead to wasteful enquiries that do not fit with your main target market.

7 The relative merits of the client acquisition techniques

7.1 Professional introducers

What we are talking about?

This is the introduction of clients from accountants and solicitors.

It can be extended to estate agents, general insurance brokers, housebuilders, bankers involved with acquisitions, etc.

What is the best use?

To acquire higher value clients from the personal and corporate markets.

To enable you to major in a particular area of expertise (e.g. IHT, pensions in divorce, investing trust monies, pension scheme wind up, etc).

Think about this...

Do:

- Work out how you want to work with introducers (e.g. order taker or equal in the relationship) — your proposition to introducers is as important as your service proposition.
- Set out in writing what you will do and what you expect the introducer to do, to make the relationship work for both parties.
- Consider if you have the time to develop and nurture these relationships.
- Consider if you are prepared to pay for the introduction in money or reciprocation.
- Work out how you will develop and sustain the relationship.
- Work with introducers to identify the types of client or circumstances where financial advice is important.

Don't:

- Forget that these relationships are based on trust — an introducer has to be confident that you will treat their clients properly and professionally.
- Forget to track the business flow and value from each introducer.
- Fail to communicate with the introducer on the overall progress of each client's case.
- Miss any opportunity to update introducers on issues that are important to their clients but that only you can deal with.

7.2 Networking

What we are talking about?

This includes attendance and membership at sports and business clubs and associations, with the objective of raising the profile of your business and acquiring new clients.

What is the best use?

To target specific types of client who are very difficult to communicate with using other methods. This is useful when relationship-building and development of trust is going to be particularly important.

Think about this...

Do:

- Confirm your target market before selecting networking opportunities.
- Choose organisations and events with care — you need to be interested and have empathy (e.g. play the sport, follow the club, support the charities, etc).
- Be prepared, at some point, to take a proactive role in supporting the network (e.g. committee roles, etc).
- Recognise that this takes time — for each event and through regular attendance.
- Accept that it takes time for business to flow from networking.
- Consider networking to identify potential recruits or other principals interested in acquisition.

Don't:

- Overtly press for business.
- Over-commit — develop one or two networking areas properly.
- Expect everyone in the business to take part — people have different preferences and ranges of social skills.

Simply follow a personal interest — always test for business benefit first; if they both combine, that is a bonus.

7.3 Client seminars

What we are talking about?

These are seminars on specific topics for a carefully targeted audience. Depending on the topic, these can be viable with 15 or 50 people — it is the quality of the attendees that is most important.

What is the best use?

To target a very specific group of people, often in conjunction with professional introducers and their client base.

The aim is to create such a positive impression that those attending develop a strong desire to do business with you.

Think about this...

Do:

- Be as precise as possible when targeting potential attendees.
- Avoid clashing with key national events and sports occasions.
- Write to those accepting to reconfirm the details, and phone one day before.
- Make sure that you concentrate on the targets' specific area of interest.
- Consider splitting the content with others (e.g. retirement planning often includes doctors and solicitors as well as financial advisers).
- Use examples and case studies.
- Use your best presenters and think about using external presenters.
- Practice thoroughly before the event.
- Think hard about which venue to select (practical issues such as car-parking and access, and wider issues which fit with your brand).
- Ensure that follow-up with attendees is well organised and co-ordinated to make sure all potential new business possibilities are pursued.

Don't:

- Use out of date material.
- Use jargon and technical language.
- Cut corners on hospitality.
- Speak for more than 20 minutes before switching topics or to another person.
- Use a lot of Powerpoint charts with lots of text — pictures and diagrams work much better.
- Forget to get your follow-up process worked out in advance.
- Be late or forget that first impressions count.

7.4 Direct marketing

What we are talking about?

This is communication by post, telephone or e-mail with the aim of generating an enquiry or, in some cases, selling a product under execution only.

What is the best use?

The aim is to generate a high volume of leads from a well defined target market and bring new clients to the business.

Think about this...

Do:

- Define your target market as precisely as possible.
- Make your message as relevant as possible.
- Check the age and frequency of use of any lists that you purchase.
- Clean your data before the exercise.

- Communicate in tranches so you can manage the leads that are generated and make any changes to the campaign.
- Consider communication by e-mail or post, followed up by telephone call.
- Make the 'call to action' crystal clear.
- Make sure you follow up leads or enquiries within five working days.

Don't:

- Include any technical detail in the main communication.
- Have more than three key messages.
- Contact people who have asked you not to.
- Forget to measure initial responses as well as business generated.
- Forget to review the experience when the campaign has finished.
- Fail to communicate the benefits of what you are proposing to the client.

7.5 Advertising

What we are talking about?

This is paid-for space in a wide range of media, including newspapers, radio, posters, websites, magazines, etc.

What is the best use?

This is often used to raise profile as well as generate enquiries. However, it is NOT recommended for profile raising for advice businesses, because it is relatively expensive and there is high wastage — many other people will see it besides your target market.

Think about this...

Do:

- Take great care to check that your target market uses the media you are considering and that use by non-target clients is low.
- Minimise key messages — no more than three, and ideally less.
- Concentrate on client benefits.
- Test different sizes/lengths and positions/times for advertising.
- Make sure the tone and style fits with your brand.
- Make the 'call to action' crystal clear.
- Make the 'call to action' crystal clear.
- Ensure you can fulfil enquiries (manning phones or responding to a deluge of coupons).

Don't:

- Appear in your own advertisements.
- Design your own advertisements.
- Use media that are not compatible with your brand.
- Commit to advertising before you test it or it is proven to work for you.

- Forget to filter the enquiries, and work out how you will handle those which are not viable.

8 Chapter summary

The management skills you have developed as a result of this chapter mean that you can:

- Set clear objectives for acquisition campaigns.
- Decide which acquisition techniques will work best.
- Develop campaigns to acquire clients.
- Develop business from professional introducers.
- Organise seminars.
- Decide if networking is likely to be productive.
- Run direct marketing campaigns.
- Decide if advertising is likely to be productive.

As we have seen, there are at least five different ways of acquiring new clients, and how you use them will depend on the numbers that you wish to acquire and the target market.

As the focus point in section 1 showed, you need to estimate the scale of the job and take a high level view to think about how many new clients you need, how you will find them and, importantly, how much this will contribute to your growth targets.

Chapter 11
Client retention

By the end of this chapter, your business will benefit from:

✔   Retention of key clients.
✔   Retention of all clients who are valuable to the business.
✔   An organised and targeted retention plan.
✔   Deployment of a variety of retention methods.

This chapter will cover the main methods of retaining clients, which are:

- Newsletters.
- Targeted e-mails.
- Website client area.
- Service calls.
- Hospitality.

Of course, the most effective method of client retention is to provide them with ongoing service to the standards and timescales that you have agreed. These may be set as minimum levels or may vary if you operate a tiered service model. The service example in Chapter 5 showed how the frequency of contact (face to face as well as other communications) varied by client value. If you apply your service standards consistently, then you will have very little extra to do by way of client retention. Servicing will do the job for you.

However, the five techniques listed above can play a very useful role in supporting retention, and there are particular client groups with which they work best.

1 Is client retention important for your business?

To decide the extent to which you need to undertake retention activity, answer the following questions.

- Do you have a lot of clients (say, over 40% of your client base) who are of value to you, but whom you do not see or contact regularly?
- Do you find that clients you see less frequently have made their own financial decisions, or seen another adviser or the bank since you last saw them?

CLIENT RETENTION works best when the ongoing service is delivered to the standards and timescales agreed with the client.

- Are you concerned that you have not informed clients about important tax and legal changes?
- Do you find that clients do not recognise the full breadth of your expertise and services?
- Do you tend never to use hospitality as a means of sustaining relationships with the really top clients?

Distribute these questions among your advisers using **Template 3.9 from Part 3 – Marketing Your Business** on the website.

If you have answered "Yes" to at least three of the above, you should seriously consider running a formal retention programme using the techniques which follow.

2 The usefulness of newsletters

These have been widely used by advice businesses for many years, come in many different formats and perform different functions. The range can be summarised as follows:

- Provision of information through to updates about the business and its people.
- Generic coverage of financial issues through to content related to specific topics, such as investments or pensions.
- Product offers or generic information.
- Up to six times a year or just once.
- Produced in-house or purchased.
- High production quality or black and white.
- Mailed hard copy or e-mailed (or a combination).
- Sent to all clients or selected group.

The approach that individual businesses should adopt will vary depending on the importance of client retention, the number of clients, costs and the frequency of client contact through service delivery.

NEWSLETTERS are an effective method of keeping in touch with clients who you want to retain but only see every two or three years.

CASE STUDY

Newsletter survey

Caroline Chan is in charge of marketing at Grey Financial Advisers, and has been challenged by the managing director of the firm to prove that the bi-annual newsletter is worthwhile. "I am not convinced that this is money well spent; we never seem to get any business when we send it out, and the number of returns and gone-aways grows each time," he complained.

Caroline held the same reservations, but had an instinct that the newsletter was worthwhile from the occasional comments that clients and other advisers had made. The newsletter had been running for five years, and they had included a short questionnaire at the start of the third year to find out what clients thought. The response rate was not very good, but those who did mail back generally liked what they received. However, at the time, the MD asked, "If the response is so low, should we conclude that people just throw it in the bin?"

Caroline decided that another survey was required, but that this could be used to proactively support the newsletter. She designed a short questionnaire that would be used by the administrators in a telephone-based survey. The questions were:

- Do you remember receiving the newsletter?
- Did you read most of it?
- What did you like about it?
- What did you not like?
- Do you find it interesting?
- Was the length too short, about right or too long?
- Would you like to receive these more or less often?

She mapped out a response sheet that the administrators could use to gather the answers, and randomly selected 100 names from the mailing that was about to go out.

The survey ran two weeks after the mailing (including those who were e-mailed) to allow time for the post to deliver. Caroline added a further question which was:

- Would you like us to give you further personal advice on the issues covered in the articles on inheritance tax or pensions contributions?

Caroline was pleased with the results, as it appeared that 90% remembered receiving the newsletter and 50% had read it. Those who read it liked the content, and 10% asked for personal advice. The latter were followed up by the advisers, and the result was two pieces of business that covered the cost of the newsletter for a further year.

The MD thought this was a good outcome, and they decided to plan the follow-up service calls for the next edition well in advance and call at least 250 recipients, excluding those who had been seen by an adviser in the previous six months. The MD said, "This is a really good way of getting extra business in a difficult market, and it more than justifies sending the newsletter — I wish I had thought of the follow-up phone calls before!"

CASE STUDY KEY POINT

There are three good practice points here:

- Always survey the readership at regular intervals to make sure the newsletter is worth sending: do this at least every three years.
- Make sure the survey is short and well structured, and that it is easy for the administrators to capture the answers.
- If you are going to follow up with the offer of advice, do so within two weeks.

Many practices only send newsletters to the top client group, whereas others send them to everyone on the database. In some cases, they ask the individual advisers to make up the list. The best approach is to use the checklist for marketing activity as a starting point, and then think about how many clients you have who are of value to you, but who you rarely see. If you have over 500 of these, and they really are valuable, then newsletters can be a very good way of reminding them of your existence.

Typically, advice businesses will produce or buy in two or three editions a year and that, with a covering letter, should make a good contribution to client retention. It follows that if you are sending to the 500 middle value clients, you should also include the high value clients.

You need to make a careful judgement about what to do about low value or dormant clients. If these are simply names on the list with no contact for over ten years, then it is not worth sending to them. However, if you contact them from time to time or use them to provide leads for new advisers, then you should include them.

Finally, you need a consistent approach across the business, so it is not advisable to let individual advisers decide on the list. If you have segmented your client base by value and service delivery, then that should be the basis for your circulation list.

3 Using electronic communication

This is a very cost effective and immediate communication process, and you should make full use of it, provided you have the e-mail addresses of a sufficient number of clients.

3.1 Targeted e-mails are very cost effective

You should use targeted e-mails or Twitter in the following circumstances:

- If the content is specific to the recipient.
- If recipients need to take some action (even if it is to do nothing).
- When you need to communicate quickly and with urgency.
- At times of uncertainty, when you want to manage expectations and pre-empt enquiries and questions.
- When there is confusion about a change in economic or taxation policy that needs to be clarified.

If you use targeted e-mails or Twitter in this way, your clients will perceive you as proactive, up to date, keen to look after them and helpful. That is a good outcome, which means you only need to use them in the circumstances referred to above. This means clients will always open e-mails from you, because they know they are important and will not waste their time.

3.2 Website client area

This has been covered in the main section on websites in Chapter 9.

4 Make genuine service calls

The purpose of service calls is to retain contact with clients and not to directly offer products, funds or additional service. Calls that do this are part of acquisition and should be treated like any other marketing campaign.

It is highly likely that your ongoing service delivery will include calls, particularly for clients you will not see face to face every year. These calls are often about the annual valuation or the products that the client holds with you.

The types of service call referred to in this section are often centred on keeping client records up to date. Inevitably, they will have the spin-off of reminding the client that you exist and sometimes prompting enquiries.

Service calls can cover the following:

- Data clean-up: checking addresses, post codes, e-mail addresses.
- Genuine surveys on service (often a month or so after a client has transacted business with you).
- Surveys on a recently sent newsletter or similar communication.

You need to log on your client database who has been called, for what purpose and when. You should use administrators who have a good telephone manner, and train them to listen for business opportunities and how to handle technical issues (which will typically require a call back from an adviser).

Finally, it is best to undertake this exercise in tranches so that any issues or advice enquiries that arise can be responded to in a timely manner. You can always suspend this exercise at busy times, but always remember to pick it up when it becomes quieter. It will help to keep clients, and business enquiries will always arise.

5 When to offer hospitality

Advisers' views on this vary from enthusiastic to the opposite. For some, it is an essential part of retaining clients and meeting new ones; for others, it is time and money wasted.

This is one of the few marketing techniques that you have to enjoy to make it worthwhile. You should apply the questions in the checklist and, if it makes sense to spend part of your budget on hospitality, you should think carefully about what you and your clients will enjoy. The reason for considering your personal view is because your feelings will come across to your guests. If you take them to a good restaurant with a sense of duty, they will be able to tell. They will definitely detect your feelings if you take them to a sporting event that is of no interest to you.

There is quite a lot of judgement involved in hospitality. In general, clients like it if it is a genuine 'thank you' for being a long-standing and valuable client. For the most part, hospitality of this nature should stay firmly in this category and not be used to sell new products or services. For certain events, it is perfectly reasonable to give clients the opportunity to bring another guest, but you should use the event purely to make their acquaintance.

5.1 Take care with budgets and organisation

You need to think carefully about how much you are going to spend. You should be generous with entertainment but not lavish. A decent wine with a meal is correct, but never-ending supplies of champagne create the wrong impression. You do not need the best seats in the theatre or the top corporate package at Twickenham, but you should not buy the cheapest. Think about what clients might expect or buy for themselves: that is always a good guide.

Generally, you should invite small numbers (no more than 20), because you need to speak to them all and give yourself an opportunity to be a good host to everybody. This means choosing events where there is opportunity for conversation, which places golf at the top of the list and theatre at the bottom. However, drinks or a meal before theatre can remedy this.

You do not need an extensive hospitality programme for retention. This is because it will always be your top clients for whom hospitality is appropriate, and they probably see you quite frequently as part of service delivery. One event a year may be enough, but make sure you vary it so that the majority of interests are catered for. If you can include partners, it really enhances the power of the 'thank you', particularly because partners often miss out on such events.

For an event to be successful, you need to:

- Invite no more than 20 people.
- Invite them personally and well in advance.
- Check dietary requirements before the event.
- Ask your secretary to call invitees two days before to make sure they have the time and location (clearly this acts as a reminder).
- Carefully check the venue and arrangements beforehand.
- If appropriate, arrange seating plans with care.

- Make sure you speak with everyone, and don't just stick to your favourites.
- Keep a very close watch to ensure that people are enjoying themselves — do something about it if they are not.
- Brief your fellow advisers on the guests and their backgrounds.
- Thank guests for coming to the event.
- Ensure that there is a systematic process for follow-up if new business opportunities are identified.

6 The relative merits of the main retention techniques

6.1 Newsletters

What we are talking about?

These are regularly produced communications, typically sent (by e-mail or post) to a large number of clients (and sometimes prospects). They usually cover a range of topics — and sometimes include a product offer.

What is the best use?

If the aim is to keep in touch with clients, then the best use is with the middle (C or silver) group of clients who are not seen every year.

For clients seen once every two or three years, a bi-annual newsletter is an excellent way to remind them of your presence. This would not preclude your sending newsletters to the top (A or gold) clients as an additional means of sustaining the relationship.

To keep clients informed of important tax or legal changes, and to give them an opportunity to contact you.

Think about this...

Do:

- Segment your client bank to make sure you do not waste this exercise on completely dormant clients.
- Check the contact list each time you undertake the exercise.
- Decide on frequency and stick with it for at least three years.
- Carefully consider whether to produce in-house or buy in one of the externally produced newsletters.
- Recognise that in-house production requires time and deadline commitments, plus positive support from others in the business.
- Use the opportunity to promote your brand as well as your expertise.
- Use this as an opportunity to tell clients about important changes that might affect their position,

and invite them to contact you if they think they are affected or concerned – this is very useful from a TCF perspective.

Don't:

- Make the content too technical – talk about concepts and issues to generate interest.
- Forget to include a covering letter to draw attention to particular issues – this is very useful if you buy in generic content.
- Buy in newsletters unless they can carry your brand.
- Forget to ask clients if they prefer hard copy or e-mail.
- Stick to a small number of topics – you need a good range to have broad appeal across the client base.
- Run this exercise for more than three years without including a short survey to find out if people are reading it and what they do and don't like.

6.2 Targeted e-mails and Twitter

What we are talking about?

These messages should be specific to clients (or groups of clients), the products or funds they hold, and the service they expect from you.

For retention, you should only use them when you have something important to communicate.

What is the best use?

- To inform clients of changes directly relevant to them (if individual or group use e-mail; messages on Twitter will be received by all your followers).
- To cover product- or fund-specific issues.
- To manage expectations at times of financial crisis.

Think about this...

Do:

- Keep these short and to the point.
- Make it plain what action clients need to take – even if it is do nothing.
- Personalise where appropriate.
- Provide links to any sites the client needs to look at. Make sure the links are live and the content you are linking to do not contain anything that could be detrimental to your firm or your clients. This is particularly true when using Twitter, which can encourage quick reactions.
- Read through carefully before sending – especially if you have written the content under pressure.
- Make sure e-mail addresses are up to date and that advisers collect them.

Don't:

- Over-use this method, or some clients will delete or ignore.
- Send large attachments by email– use links (including back to your website) where possible.

6.3 Website client area

What we are talking about?

These are often password-protected areas that are exclusive to clients. They often provide access to fund values, and may allow communication to you about limited data changes, such as new address.

What is the best use?

- To offer to higher value clients as part of their higher level of service.
- To present the impression of exclusivity – 'member of the club'.
- To avoid phone calls from clients on routine issues that are best dealt with by internet.

Think about this...

Do:

- Ensure that links to valuation software are robust and accurate.
- Ensure that the site has sufficient capacity to manage high levels of demand.
- Be prepared for high levels of contact when markets are fluctuating.
- Post market comment at times of uncertainty.
- Make sure other people in the business look at this part of the site.
- Proactively manage this part of the site – place newsletters here five days before anyone else sees them.

Don't:

- Allow any content to become dated.
- Make the password access over-complicated.
- Allow clients to make any direct changes to data on your back office software.

6.4 Service calls

What we are talking about?

These should fit in with the other servicing activities, and are best used with clients who are not seen every year.

These are calls (phone is best, but e-mail also works) which are designed to remind clients of your presence but have a genuine purpose that is not to sell directly.

However, enquiries often arise as a result of this contact.

What is the best use?

- To monitor service delivery.
- To identify if client circumstances have changed.
- To make clients aware of an important change in the business.
- To offer clients a review if an important tax or legal change affects their holdings.

Think about this...

Do:

- Run this as a regular exercise, undertaking a certain number of calls each week.
- Use people in the business with the best telephone manner, and/or the client's regular adviser.
- Keep a record on the central database of who has been called, when and about what.
- Make sure that your main reason for contact is genuinely service-based.
- Practise how you intend to open the call and introduce yourself.
- Monitor the outcome of the calls (e.g. comments, answers to short client survey, enquiries).

Don't:

- Call at obviously inconvenient times (this is your judgement).
- Persist with a call if it is clear that the timing is wrong or the individual does not appear interested.
- Use word-for-word scripts — prompts are much better and more natural.
- Try to deal with any difficult issues that come up unless the answer is straightforward — always get the facts and call back.
- Ever forget a call back.

6.5 Hospitality

What we are talking about?

This is genuine 'entertainment', which is to thank people for their business and potentially gain additional business, particularly if you involve friends and relatives of your main guests.

What is the best use?

- To sustain and deepen important and valuable relationships.
- To provide a genuine 'thank you'.
- To gain an introduction to potential new clients (if appropriate).

Think about this...

Do:

- Consider the full range of client interests (e.g. meals, sport, arts, active events, participation or spectator).
- Rotate events over time (e.g. sport, wine tasting, time of year, etc).
- Consider inviting partners (they often miss out, so this is usually seen positively).
- Keep the numbers manageable so that you can talk to everyone.
- Invite people well in advance.
- Limit this to a small number of clients.
- Reconfirm acceptances by letter and then phone the day before.
- Ensure that there is a systematic approach to following up any new business opportunities that are identified.

Don't:

- Make events so regular that people expect to be invited each time.
- Clash dates with major national events.
- Run more than one per year (typically, two is maximum) — that way they become special and exclusive.
- Choose an event that you personally will not enjoy.

7 Chapter summary

The management skills you have developed as a result of this chapter mean that you can:

- Set clear objectives for retention campaigns.
- Decide which retention techniques will work best.
- Develop campaigns to retain clients.
- Use hard copy and electronic retention techniques.
- Manage corporate hospitality.
- Set up service calls.
- Link retention activity to ongoing service content.
- Identify and efficiently follow up new business opportunities.

This chapter should be relevant to all advice businesses, and particularly to mature ones. It costs much more to acquire a brand new client than it does to sell additional service or products to an existing client. Retention of the middle band of clients is often poorly organised, as most of the effort is spent on the top group. That is not surprising, but a small amount of well organised retention activity for the middle band should reduce the rate of client attrition.

Chapter 12

Effective marketing planning

By the end of this chapter, your business will benefit from:

- ✔ Well specified marketing plans.
- ✔ Realistic plans that can be achieved.
- ✔ Concentration on the marketing activities that support the business objectives.
- ✔ An effectively deployed marketing budget.
- ✔ Accountable marketing activity.

This chapter draws together the tasks and techniques that we have covered so far. For the most part, marketing in advice businesses is relatively tactical, and is managed through clear objectives related to acquiring and keeping clients. Despite this, it is important to take a strategic perspective to make sure that all you do supports your business objectives and that you make your marketing as effective and accountable as possible.

1 Guide to budgeting

The split between profile, acquisition and retention will allow you to organise your marketing activity and prioritise where you want to use the majority of your marketing budget and resource (typically time). Mature advice businesses will tend to spend up to 60% of the budget on client retention, 30% on new client acquisition and the rest on profile. This is because keeping the existing clients, built up over many years, is a priority. Provided that they continue to be viable and refer you to similar clients, they are an asset that you would wish to keep. There will be less pressure to acquire large numbers of brand new clients and further raise the profile of the business in these circumstances.

Alternatively, a brand new business may well have to spend 30% of its budget on profile, 60% on acquisition and just 10% on retention. Clearly, the priorities are very different, as reflected in the budget split.

2 Develop a structured marketing plan

We reviewed the structure of business plans in Chapter 1, and at this point we need to look at the link between the top level business objective and the marketing objective. This is to make sure that all your marketing, individual campaigns and the overall plan help to move the business toward its long term objectives.

The link is very straightforward, and the following example, using the firms Gold and Bronze, helps explain. Gold is very focused on its high value clients, whereas Bronze operates with lower value clients and high volumes.

Table 12.1 **Structured marketing plans for Gold and Bronze**

	GOLD	BRONZE
WHAT WE DO	Expert financial and tax planning to enable the long term management of investments through a detailed plan that is regularly reviewed.	Streamlined advice in one meeting to make sure people have the right policies for their needs.
WHO WE DO IT FOR	Private clients with over £500,000.	Families and working people between the ages of 30 and 50.
BUSINESS OBJECTIVE	To increase turnover from £2m to £2.5m, and raise the proportion of income that is recurring from 45% to 60% over the next two years.	To increase turnover from £1m to £2m by taking full advantage of high street position over the next two years.
MARKETING OBJECTIVE	To acquire an additional 25 high value clients, and continue to sell our premier service to existing clients.	To sell products to an additional 2,000 people (at £500 initial charge).
TASK BIAS	Majority of activity biased to retention.	Majority of activity biased to acquisition supported by profile.
TECHNIQUE BIAS	<ul><li>Sponsorship of local theatre and rugby club.</li><li>Network with professional introducers through Rotary Club.</li><li>Continue to proactively sustain professional introducers.</li><li>Bi-annual newsletter and investment commentaries. Selected hospitality.</li></ul>	<ul><li>Sponsorship of local football team, plus flowers and Christmas lights in the high street.</li><li>Direct marketing via leaflets on a regular basis.</li><li>One-off/tactical local press advertising for very competitive deals.</li><li>Regularly changed promotions in the shop window.</li><li>Local store vouchers to reward referrals.</li></ul>

As you can see, the split between profile, acquisition and retention is very different. This reflects the need for Gold to keep existing clients and sell them more service, and for Bronze to find 20 new paying clients a week (recognising that up to 10% of these will be previous clients).

The marketing plan is made up of all the individual campaigns that are planned for the year ahead. In practice, you should design a 12 month rolling plan that is reviewed and updated every quarter. The immediate three months should be confirmed, the next three should be in preparation and the remaining six are provisional. This is to allow you to make short term changes to exploit market opportunities or to extend an existing campaign that is working particularly well. As you can see, the aim is to be well organised but retain as much flexibility as possible. That means you only commit time and money when you are confident that individual campaigns should go ahead. **Template 4.2 in Part 3 – Marketing Your Business** on the website sets out a blank grid for you to use.

This plan is designed to be as manageable as possible, by:

- Sharing the work.
- Spacing campaigns throughout the year, but reflecting when the opportunities are likely to be greater.
- Spreading the spend throughout the year, as much as the plan will permit.
- Repeating types of activity to enable learning and also gain some economies of scale.

The benefits of having a plan like this are:

- Everyone can see what is happening and when.
- The overall plan made up of the individual campaigns can be reviewed against workloads.
- The plan provides for a strategic and longer term approach, and prevents the waste of a series of unrelated one-off tactical campaigns.
- Future campaigns can be started in good time, as soon as they have been confirmed.
- The overall structure of the plan and budget can be 'common sense' tested to make sure it really does support the overall business objectives.

2.1 How to construct individual campaigns

We have already seen what the plans for these look like in Chapter 8, when we applied the checklist to seminar invitations. All campaigns must be subject to the rigour of these questions to give you the best chance of success. You need to avoid campaigns which are badly thought out and concentrate on maximising the benefits of those which are confirmed to run.

The checklist for testing marketing activities is:

- What are you trying to achieve?
- What is the activity about?
- Who are you trying to influence?
- What do you want them to know?
- How will you communicate?
- When will this happen?
- Who will do the work and what will it cost?
- How will you know if it has worked?

Table 12.2 **Proposed marketing plan for Bronze**

	Q1	Q2	Q3	Q4
Profile Total cost for profile: £5,000 (= 33% of total budget)	**WHAT:** sponsor local football team **WHEN:** all year **COST:** £1,500 **WHO:** Adrian	**WHAT:** sponsor flowers **WHEN:** 30/5–15/9 **COST:** £2,000 **WHO:** Sally		**WHAT:** sponsor Christmas lights **WHEN:** 30/11–10/1 **COST:** £1,500 **WHO:** Sally
Acquisition Total cost for acquisition: £6,500 (= 43% of total budget)	**WHAT:** direct marketing ISAs **WHEN:** 15/1–15/2 **COST:** £1,500 **WHO:** Adrian	**WHAT:** direct marketing mortgages **WHEN:** 15/3–15/4 **COST:** £1,500 **WHO:** Adrian		**WHAT:** direct marketing to be decided **WHEN:** 15/10–15/11 **COST:** £1,500 **WHO:** Adrian
	WHAT: tactical press advertising, four ads **WHEN:** February **COST:** £1,000 **WHO:** Sarah		**WHAT:** tactical press advertising, four ads **WHEN:** September **COST:** £1,000 **WHO:** Sarah	
Retention Total cost for retention: £3,500 (= 23% of total budget)	**WHAT:** referral rewards **WHEN:** all year **COST:** £1,000 **WHO:** Sally			
	WHAT: newsletter **WHEN:** January **COST:** £1,250 **WHO:** Sally		**WHAT:** newsletter **WHEN:** September **COST:** £1,250 **WHO:** Sally	
Budget Total = £15,000	**TOTAL Q1:** £6,250	**TOTAL Q2:** £3,500	**TOTAL Q3:** £2,250	**TOTAL Q4:** £3,000

We will apply these questions to the implementation of a new service proposition and a product review, which are more complex than our previous example of the seminar invitation.

As you can see, these are relatively complex exercises which can be broken down into their constituent parts and tested for viability for the investment bond review. The estimates of client numbers and investment values will be influenced by the quality of the firm's data, as well as the ability to generate client lists and record progress at each stage of the campaign.

While it takes time to prepare marketing campaigns for the first time, the job becomes far more manageable as you become familiar with the process.

There is a list of good practice suggestions that many advisers who use this process adhere to. Table 12.3 brings this together, and you will see that it contains a number of points that have been covered in this chapter.

This practical guide provides a checklist to run against the detail of any campaign as you develop it. You will see that the investment bond and earlier examples reflect this.

Table 12.3 **Campaign plan: practical guide**

OBJECTIVE	Specific, measureable and achievable
PROPOSITION	Exactly what the activity is
TARGET	Be as precise as possible
KEY MESSAGES	Maximum of three
MEDIA	Relevant and used by the target
TIMING	Avoid obvious fixed calendar dates
RESOURCES	Share the load and plan in advance
MEASUREMENT	Easy to forget, but essential to do

3 Implementing marketing planning in your business

This section will provide you with a practical approach to using this chapter's tools and techniques to best effect. As you know, the scale and importance of the marketing task varies between businesses, but in all cases the disciplines and processes that we have covered should be applied.

All businesses will differ in terms of their marketing expertise and experience. In the majority of advice businesses, the role of a full time marketer cannot be justified. There will not be enough work, and much of what is required will be relatively straightforward, although it can often be time consuming. The best way to decide how much time is needed is to develop your plan and, as carefully as you can, work out

Table 12.4 **New service launch**

ACTIVITY	Launch of new service and pricing proposition with existing clients.
OBJECTIVE What are we trying to achieve?	To move over 90% of existing clients to the new proposition within 2 years.
PROPOSITION What is the activity about?	Communication to clients by letter, phone and face to face (determined by client segments) to explain new service and prices and to secure their agreement to move to the new proposition.
TARGET Who are we trying to influence?	All existing clients split as follows: • 2,000 'transactional' clients (currently infrequent and low level of contact — low value to the business). • 1,200 'advisory' clients (usually come back to us, irregular contact — collectively of important value to the business). • 400 'planning' clients (frequent contact and important).
KEY MESSAGES What do we want them to know?	**Transactional** (communicated by letter) • We have reviewed and enhanced our service. • If you would like to receive our 'advisory' or 'planning' service please call us. • If we do not hear from you we will assume you no longer wish us to act for you.
	Advisory (communicated by letter) • We have reviewed and enhanced our service. • We will contact you in (name quarter of year) to ensure your financial affairs are up to date. • If you have more immediate requirements please call us.
	MONTH 0 — MONTH 12 **Planning (face to face when client is next seen):** • Confirm what advisers will cover in next meeting with this group of clients (e.g. role play positioning of new service and pricing proposition, client benefits, reasons for change, what it specifically means for the client). • Work out any service or price changes before the next scheduled meeting and if any discounts to be offered to enable transition to increased charges in such cases. • Record outcome of meeting.
METHOD AND TIMING How will we communicate? When will this happen?	**MONTH 3 — MONTH 9** **Advisory (letter to face to face if client to be seen in first month):** • Draft letter 1 (initial contact) and letter 2 (follow up if no response) and confirm list. • Letter 1 mailed in tranches over 6 months. • Letter 2 (no response follow up) mailed *if required* 4 weeks after letter 1. • Responses (including nil returns after letter 2) recorded. • Adviser to call any client who requests more immediate contact to confirm and make appointment if required.
	MONTH 12 — MONTH 24 **Transactional (letter):** • Draft letter 1 (initial contact) and letter 2 (follow up if no response) and confirm list. • Letter 1 mailed in tranches over 10 months. • Letter 2 (no response follow up) mailed *if required* 4 weeks after Letter 1. • Responses (including nil returns after letter 2) recorded. • Adviser to call any client who requests advisory or planning service to confirm and make appointment if required.
RESOURCES AND BUDGET Who will do the work and what will it cost?	**Timing:** • To note this is phased over 24 months to prioritise contact and to make the task manageable.
	Materials: • 2 x letters for transactional clients. • 2 x letters for advisory clients. • 1 x service brochure. • Additions to website covering new service and prices.
	People: • Senior administrator to oversee process. • Administrators to run process (mail out in tranches, record responses and mail out follow ups). • Advisers to call clients as indicated and to discuss changes with planning clients at their next scheduled meeting).
MEASURE OF SUCCESS How will we know if it has worked?	**Budget:** • Increased revenue (depending upon service levels and prices). • Retention of all 'Planning' and 'Advisory' clients — immediate. • Loss making clients moved to profit (could be over 1 — 2 years depending on specific circumstances) — no more than 2 years. • New service process with its streamlined approach replaces current ad hoc approach — within 12 months. • Large number of transactional clients decide to use alternative adviser (free up our time to concentrate on higher value clients) — within 24 months.

Table 12.5 **Investment bond review**

ACTIVITY	Review of investment bonds to identify if clients should move to cheaper and more flexible alternatives
OBJECTIVE What are we trying to achieve?	To be certain that clients have the right product and fund solutions to meet their objectives; to produce £170,000 initial fees at 3% and recurring fees for ongoing service of £25,000 at 0.5% Assumption that 75 clients make the change with an average of £75,000
PROPOSITION What is the activity about?	Bespoke letter to clients referring to their specific current holdings and suggesting that this could be improved
TARGET Who are we trying to influence?	All holders of A, B and C investment bonds where we have identified potential to improve their position — 500 clients
KEY MESSAGES What do we want them to know?	The market has changed since you acquired this product", "We can get you a better deal", "We provide specialist, impartial advice" Call to action "Call us to arrange an appointment"
METHOD AND TIMING How will we communicate? When will this happen?	Identify providers, product and funds, and identify clients Set up list 15/1, draft letter 15/1, mail out letter 22/1, follow up phone call — 29/1, second letter if no reply — 15/2 Arrange appointments through normal process Record outcomes
RESOURCES AND BUDGET Who will do the work and what will it cost?	Andrew and Joanne Letters and postage, etc — £200
MEASURE OF SUCCESS How will we know if it has worked?	Achievement of objective: Client offered opportunity to change to better product £150,000 initial fee and £25,000 recurring

how long each campaign will take to implement and the extent to which you can confidently share the work across the business. This is difficult, and you need to be as realistic as possible; some apparently simple tasks can take hours, particularly those related to data and preparing lists of target clients. This really is a case of the 'devil in the detail'.

You can also draw on experience. Ask yourself: how well have you coped in the past with marketing? You will probably need to dedicate some resources (for example, 30%–50% of somebody's time) if the following is the case:

- Have some really good ideas not been taken to fruition?
- Have good campaigns not been followed through and a lot of leads wasted?
- Do you have poor data on the productivity of previous marketing activity?

- Have you missed clear market opportunities?
- Does the preparation of brochures, etc, greatly overrun, in terms of time and cost?
- Are some of your competitors obviously doing a better job than you?
- Have the majority or all of the prospects you come across ever heard of your business (or hadn't prior to a recommendation)?
- Do your marketing planning sessions ever lead to a clear, written plan?
- Is marketing rarely reported on at the senior management meetings?

This can be used as a formal questionnaire with **Template 3.10 in the Marketing Your Business section** of the website..

FOCUS POINT

How much does it cost?

Table 12.6 summarises the typical costs of a range of marketing activities. These will vary across the country and by the scale of the task, but they give an overview of sums involved.

Table 12.6

ACTIVITY		COST
WEBSITE	Set up of site using a template service. Annual charge from template and content provider. Bespoke set up. Hosting costs.	£300–£750 £600–£1,200pa £2k–£3k £100–£300pa
ADVERTISING – press, posters, radio	One quarter page advertisement for four weeks in the local newspaper. One full page advertisement in the glossy free magazine.	Production: £500 Media: £3k–£4k £500
	Series of radio commercials – 30 seconds at morning and evening peak (Mon–Fri) for five weeks. Sponsoring the weather forecast on local radio. Large '48 sheet' poster at four sites for two weeks.	Production: £500 Media: £3k–£5k
	Facebook	Starts at £25/day
PUBLIC RELATIONS – press articles and interviews	Series of articles – six per year.	Free
	Interview on local radio.	Free
	Advertorial – half page.	£500
	Support of local PR agency to gain media coverage.	£250–£500pm
NETWORKING – introducers, business clubs, sports clubs	Membership of rotary club.	£75–£125pa
	Golf club membership.	£500–£1,500pa
	Sponsorship of three business meetings per year.	£300
MAILSHOTS – door-to-door or via purchased mailing lists	1,000 one-sided leaflets delivered by postman. As above, delivered by local distribution company.	£500–£750
	Pack cost for typical ISA campaign (letter, application form, key features, product brochure).	£1 per pack
	Mailshot enclosing letter of invitation to seminar and pre-paid response card to 1,000 people.	£1k
FACE TO FACE – seminars, presentations, exhibition stands	Seminar in 4-star hotel with 30 guests and light refreshments.	£750–£1,000
	Stand at exhibition for two days.	£2k–£3k

Key point: It is often possible to secure discounts if you intend to place a lot of work with one supplier or commit to campaigns that run over a long time period. Always negotiate to secure better value, and always obtain more than one quote where possible.

If you have answered "Yes" to most of the questions, you are in line with the majority of advice businesses. The common denominator is time pressure, but it is unfortunate when some really creative approaches are wasted, particularly if they could take the business forward.

As suggested above, you will need to dedicate up to half of someone's time to marketing or, if this is not possible, assign 20% of their time to act as co-ordinator and share the work across the business. In the end, you have to make a judgement about what will work best and always be prepared to trial your approach for 6–12 months, making changes if necessary.

The other important action you can take is to develop a rigorous plan and then monitor and update it on a three monthly basis as described in section 2.

3.1 Running a marketing planning workshop

This section is supplemented by a **Powerpoint Roadmap on Marketing Planning in the Resources section** of the website.

If you have no plans, there is a point where you have to take the time to develop them. This is the only way to break the cycle of incomplete campaigns and lost opportunities.

Fortunately, this does not have to be at the beginning of the year, because once the main task is complete the activity is more manageable and is based on quarters. A full day is suggested, because there is a lot of detail that has to be as accurate as possible, and if you are looking for others to be involved, they need to play a full part in the development of the plan.

Before the workshop:

- Select all the people that can make a positive contribution and who you will need to help implement the plan – make sure this includes those with ideas as well those who will have to deal with data, lists, invitation processes, etc, because there is a need to test the practicality of ideas and campaigns.
- Issue the agenda in the context of the need to

undertake marketing to help achieve the turnover and profit targets – state what these are, as this will provide a good point of concentration.
- Issue the checklist (section 2.1) with the agenda and explain its purpose.
- Arrange for someone who is good and quick at using the flip chart to run the meeting and, if they have the experience, draft the first plan to be circulated after the meeting – brief them well and make sure they understand how the templates in this chapter work.

The agenda for the workshop is as follows.

Marketing planning day: agenda

- Purpose of day: to develop a manageable rolling marketing plan that helps the business achieve its objectives.
- Confirmation of objectives: typically turnover for current and next one to two years.
- Debate on balance between profile, acquisition and retention.
- Idea generation and filtering: using eight key questions.
- Confirmation of best campaigns.
- Detail each campaign using the checklists and the templates – be rigorous and detailed (if you have sufficient people, split into groups to do this).
- Map the proposed campaigns on a quarterly timeline and apply reality test (see below).
- Confirm the campaigns to run in Q1 and to be prepared for Q2.

You will need to allocate times to each section. The first three points should not exceed 45 minutes, so you can allocate at least an hour to idea generation and filtering. If this is going really well, let it run on, but cut it short if ideas are flagging.

You need to be quite tough in selecting campaigns. This is the point where you are starting to commit time and money, so pet ideas that have no hope of working have to be filtered out. Importantly, the checklist gives objective criteria which will make the decisions less subjective.

Allow up to two hours to detail the campaigns, depending on how many there are and how many people can share the task. If you split into groups (which can be individuals if

THE SUCCESS OF THE PLAN depends on shared and joint responsibility and frequent ongoing monitoring.

necessary), make sure each campaign is presented to the rest of the group to allow others to add ideas and ask questions to get the very best outcome.

Mapping onto the timeline takes ten minutes, but allow 20 minutes to apply the reality test (see below).

After the workshop, make sure you work with your facilitator to tidy up the outputs of the workshop and prepare the first draft. Circulate it so that participants can pick up any errors or make improvements.

When you are happy with the plan, initiate the work on the first campaigns in the first quarter, and circulate the final plan to everyone so they know exactly what is happening when and who is doing what.

You should monitor progress against the plan in the subsequent management and team meetings. This gives the opportunity to provide support if plans run off track or adjustments are needed. The closer you operate as a team and the more everybody takes joint responsibility, the greater the chance of success.

3.2 Test the reality of the plan

The phrase 'less is more' applies to marketing in advice businesses. Time will always be at a premium, so you should undertake a relatively small number of campaigns, but run them very well. Taking on too much is bound to fail, and this thought should be paramount when undertaking the reality test.

- Is the activity spread as well as possible throughout the year?
- Are there any unrealistic demands on specific individuals, taking into account their other work?
- Have you made absolutely certain that you can run these campaigns (e.g. availability of data, lists, logistics of implementation, etc)?
- Do all of these campaigns contribute to your growth targets?
- Is the balance between profile, acquisition and retention right?
- Does the total budget and budget split look reasonable?
- Have you been specific on start and finish dates?
- Have you missed any critical dates that clash with national events?

Template 4.3 in the Marketing Your Business section of the website sets this out as a checklist. There are no guarantees, but this final test of the overall plan means that you have been as rigorous as possible — at the campaign level, as well as at the overall strategic level.

CASE STUDY

Fail to plan and you plan to fail

Reena Frank has a business philosophy that she drums into all her staff: "Fail to plan and you plan to fail."

The repetition of this often annoys her team, but they know she is right. So when it is time for Reena's business to undertake the annual marketing workshop, they know it will be a day of detail, but that it will save time and money over the coming months.

Reena's approach is relatively straightforward, because she knows exactly what she wants to achieve: a clear one year marketing plan. She gathers her advisers and key support staff together, because she wants to make sure that the responsibility for marketing is shared across the business. She knows that if one person has to do the job, they will fail; lack of time will always beat them.

Reena splits her planning day into four parts:

- Review of last year.
- Idea generation and filtering.
- Planning the individual marketing exercises.
- Finalising the overall plan and 'common sense' testing it.

Review of last year

The first hour is spent reviewing all the marketing activity from the previous year. The typical questions are: "What went well?", "What went badly?" and "What are our learning points to factor into this year's plan?"

Idea generation and filtering

This fills the second hour and, to make it fun, Reena awards prizes for the best and worst ideas. She makes sure everyone is involved, and uses different brainstorming techniques to help with this. The first part of this section is about generating as many ideas as possible; the second part evaluates the ideas, using the checklist for testing marketing activities.

Planning the individual marketing exercises

For the individual exercises (or campaigns), Reena splits the team into groups of one or two to work these up. She uses a simple template to make sure all angles are covered and to help everyone else understand what the campaign is about. She insists on clear objectives to make sure she can measure the outcome.

Finalising the overall plan

Finally, the team take all the individual campaigns and log them onto the 12 month calendar. They work on the basis that the first quarter is confirmed, the second is in initial implementation and the final half of the year is provisional. At each quarterly review, they roll the plan forward, so the provisional quarters gradually move forward and are confirmed.

The 'common sense test' allows them to sort out any bunching of activities and workloads, and to make sure the whole plan is manageable and viable. Reena calls this the 'common sense test'; her question is, "Does this stack up, does it look sensible, can we do it?"

There is some reworking after the session to tidy up the plan, but they then press on with the first quarter.

Reena admits that there are many other things she and her team could do with the day, but reckons it is time well spent to have her marketing organised a year in advance.

CASE STUDY KEY POINT

Reena's approach is good practice, because she gets her marketing organised well in advance. The benefit of spending a day on this is that she gets the key people involved, and each marketing exercise runs smoothly, because everyone knows in advance what is going to happen and what they have to do. Success in marketing comes as much from good organisation as it does from good ideas. The 'fail to plan and plan to fail' mantra is well known, but it really does apply in this case.

4 Chapter summary

The management skills you have developed as a result of this chapter mean that you can:

- Design achievable marketing plans.
- Link the business and marketing objectives.
- Prepare a well balanced marketing budget.
- Measure all marketing activity.
- Ensure that marketing is delivering good value for money.
- Run a successful marketing planning workshop.

It is often observed that much of what is needed for good marketing is obvious. To an extent, this is true, and it is very likely that you will have previously come across many of the ideas and approaches contained in this part. The greatest challenge is time, and the greatest enemies of robust and successful marketing campaigns are lack of planning and attention to detail.

It is not possible to create additional hours in the day, but you can use your time more effectively. This is where the rigour of the processes and templates will pay dividends, plus the good practice of sharing the work and ensuring that everyone plays a part in marketing the business. As principal, you cannot develop and execute the plan yourself, so the support of others is critical.

To encourage the support of others, you can pose the following questions:

- Do we want the business to grow in the medium and long term?
- Do you want to earn more?
- Do you want to raise the value of the client bank?
- Would you like to work for a business that prospects have heard of?
- Are there activities (e.g. sport, charities, seminars, talking to the press, etc) that you would like to take part in?
- Do you want the chance for your marketing ideas to be properly considered and potentially developed as campaigns?

This normally raises interest and elicits positive responses, which will give you a good platform to develop your marketing and involve many of the others in the business.

MARKETING PLANS work best when they comprise a small number of well defined and executed campaigns

Part 4: Finance, growth, acquisitions and sales

Making sure you control, grow and maximise the value of your business

"Price is what you pay. Value is what you get."

Warren Buffett

Introduction: Control and manage your business for growth and sale

When you have completed this Part, you will be able to:

- ✔ Monitor and manage the performance of your business.
- ✔ Set financial targets for your business.
- ✔ Design and manage budgets and cash flow forecasts.
- ✔ Identify financial risk, strengths and weaknesses.
- ✔ Prepare your business for sale.
- ✔ Manage the value of your business and assess the value of others.
- ✔ Evaluate potential acquisitions.
- ✔ Secure and manage funding.
- ✔ Select the right legal structure.

This Part will help you manage and develop your business by using good legal and financial practice, and being rigorous if you are involved in buying and selling. The way in which you structure your business has a direct bearing on raising finance, personal liability and longer term growth. If you are starting a business, you need to take particular care with these issues; if you are running an existing operation, it is always useful to review the structure to make sure it is still right for the current size and scale. This relates as much to risk management, tax planning and succession management as it does to funding growth and day to day operations.

It is a regulatory requirement that you adopt effective financial management processes and take any action required to maintain financial strength and control. You must avoid taking short cuts to sensible budgeting and

CONTROL AND GROW YOUR BUSINESS by regularly getting into the detail of the financial and management information. Doing this in the short term will help you maximise value in the long term.

meticulous cash flow management; this section will provide you with frameworks to make this straightforward and effective.

We will cover:

- Why budgeting is good for you.
- Using financial data to manage your business.
- Using management information.
- Growing, buying and selling.
- Selecting the right business structure.

How effective are your control processes?

The Table that follows asks Ten Killer Questions about control processes. These questions also summarise what is 'good' for controlling, structuring and growing your business.

For each question, give your business an objective score (1 is poor, and 10 is excellent) and ask others what they think. Use **Template 1.1 from Part 4** on the website to share with others in the business.

There is no doubt that advice businesses have improved their processes around all these issues in the last five years, and if you have scored over 70% you will be in line with market. The three areas that advice businesses cover less well are:

- **Management information:** this is the information that is wider than that produced by financial data, which provides a broader perspective on business operations and efficiency.
- **Succession planning:** plans tend to be vague, which means actions are often taken late, thereby impairing the value of the business and constraining the potential for internal purchase.
- **Legal structure:** there are still many businesses operating without limited liability, which, given the market we operate in, is not recommended.

CONTROL AND GROWTH: Ten killer questions

Score: 1 = poor, and 10 = excellent

To what extent:

1. Do you have preset budgets that are monitored on a regular basis?

2. Are you happy with the legal structure of your business?

3. Do you use structured management information to monitor and manage progress?

4. Do you maintain accurate and up to date cash flow forecasts?

5. Have you developed and agreed a succession plan with your colleagues?

6. Have you developed clear criteria for reviewing a potential acquisition?

7. Do you know which parts of your cost structure influence operating profit?

8. Do you set and agree revenue and cost targets with others in the business?

9. Do you have access to finance to grow the business in the way you want to?

10. Do you have management information that enables effective TCF monitoring?

Chapter 13

Using financial data to manage your business

By the end of this chapter, your business will benefit from:

✔ Recognition of financial risk.
✔ Effective and realistic budgeting.
✔ Better management through understanding of financial accounts.
✔ Robust cash flow management.
✔ Regularly using key data to manage the business.

You need to use as much financial management information as possible to control your business on a day to day basis and develop it in the longer term. Many advisers concentrate on turnover, assets under management, and adviser and client numbers, and fail to take full advantage of what their financial data could tell them.

1 Recognise your financial risks

The regulator requires all advice businesses to develop and maintain a risk management plan, and one of the most important parts relates to finance. To consider your level of financial risk, answer the following questions:

- Is the business exposed to commission clawback and non-payment of fees?
- Is the business often close to running out of cash?
- Is there over-reliance on high producing advisers?
- Is there over-dependence on a small number of key revenue-producing clients?
- Is your awareness of financial issues impaired through inaccurate or unavailable financial data?
- Is your recurring income influenced by stock market movements?

Work through these questions using **Template 1.2, Part 4 —Finance, Growth, Acquisition and Sales** on the website.

If you have answered "Yes" to the majority of these questions, you need to take steps to reduce the level of risk.

In practice, most of these risks can be reduced over time, which means you have to pay close attention to them in the shorter term.

A low financial risk business will have the following characteristics:

- A policy of low initial and high recurring incomes.
- A mix of recurring income between client direct debits, traditional renewal commission, fund-based commissions and ongoing fees. The latter will reduce as a proportion after the RDR deadline.
- An effective invoicing and debt management system.
- Diversified sources of business and a steady flow of new clients.
- Up to date and accurate financial data that is regularly reviewed.

The most difficult risk to reduce is over-dependence on high revenue-producing advisers. Clearly, you cannot hire additional advisers simply to mitigate this risk, and in practice smaller businesses have to live with heavy reliance on key people. It is a consideration when you think about expansion, but should never be the principal reason.

2 Benefit from a wealth of data

To make sure you get the most from your financial data, you need to:

- Use dedicated financial management software: to minimise the number crunching and maximise the analysis.
- Construct financial statements: balance sheet, profit and loss account and cash flow statement.
- Prepare them accurately and regularly: at least once a month.
- Review them for detail and the longer term trends: you need to look at the wood as well as the trees.
- Continuously compare current financial performance with external benchmarks or previous experience: to identify any problems at an early stage.

This will provide you with the basis of a good financial management process, from which other benefits will flow. These include:

- Clarity of your current and projected cash position.
- Better longer term forecasting.
- More effective debt management and invoice payment control.
- Analysis of profit and where it comes from.
- Ability to provide a well presented and rigorous case for potential investors, acquirers and banks.
- More efficient completion of Retail Mediation Activities Returns (RMARs).
- Starting point for valuation of your business.
- Easier calculation of your tax bill.

You may well decide that your time could be better spent with clients. This means outsourcing or employing a specialist to make sure the numbers are entered correctly and to add real value by undertaking the regular analyses that are required.

3 Why budgeting is good for you

You can use budgets as part of the process for running your business, because as it becomes more complex as it grows, the development and monitoring of budgets is essential.

The purpose of the budget is:

- To set cost and revenue targets for the coming year.
- To make sure plans fit with the overall strategy and objectives of the business.
- To enable effective financial planning, particularly financing for additional equipment or people.

The benefits are:

- Progress can be monitored.
- Remedial action can be taken early if problems arise.
- Financial management is disciplined.
- Adherence to the overall strategy is supported.

You should prepare cost and revenue budgets, and use them to monitor performance on a monthly and year to date basis. As well as reviewing actual performance against budget, you should make forecasts of expected outcomes for a full year ahead.

For effective financial control, you should prepare three versions of the budget:

- **Realistic scenario:** what you expect to happen.
- **Aspirational scenario:** based on the revenue targets agreed with the advisers.
- **Worst case scenario:** based on revenue performance below target.

The reason for this is the need for you to make a careful judgement about the actual level of revenue that you expect, which might differ from what has been agreed with advisers. For example, from experience, you may know that one group of advisers always underperforms and another group typically overperforms. If this is the case, it is entirely sensible to factor this into your financial planning.

The worst case scenario may be less important when the market is buoyant, but vital in the opposite circumstances. At the beginning of 2009, many advisers adopted this practice to help their contingency planning if the market continued to decline. This means that, as the year unfolds, you can take a more informed judgement on what actions might be needed if you have already thought about them in advance.

3.1 The challenge of the revenue budget

You need to prepare this as thoroughly and realistically as possible. Clearly, it will be based on:

- Expected recurring income arising from existing clients.
- Fees for work that is already contracted.
- Projection of new business: both initial and recurring revenues.
- Adjustment for anticipated loss of clients.

It is very easy to be over-optimistic, and it is very important to talk in detail with advisers about what they expect to achieve and the goal you will agree with them. Many advice businesses do not use **targets** or even seek projections from advisers about the likely levels of business. You must avoid this, because you cannot possibly manage your business if you have not taken a serious approach to budgeting the revenues.

The culture of your business will determine how you use the process of targeting and the terms you use to describe it. However, you have to get to a point where you have a realistic revenue plan that can be monitored alongside the cost plan.

3.2 How to develop the cost budget

Within an advice business, there are two ways that you can approach this. The first is baseline budgeting, the second is zero-based budgeting.

The majority of advice businesses use **baseline budgeting**, which takes the previous year's budget as a starting point. If the business is relatively stable and has a straightforward financial model, this is a good way to start. It is relatively time-efficient, and the existence of previous budgets and outcomes means the common sense test can be applied easily. It is important to question every line, because there will be circumstances when it is wrong to simply roll the budget forward with a few percent added for inflation. This applies particularly to the larger entries, including:

- Staffing.
- Information technology.
- Marketing, travel and entertaining.
- Rent and office costs.

Zero-based budgeting requires each part of the budget to be built from scratch and each item of expenditure to be justified on its merits. The advantages are:

- Every item of expenditure has to be considered for the value it brings to the business.
- It helps you to think about the most effective way of doing things.
- It should remove waste and lead to a better use of the firm's resources.

This is not recommended if your business is in a stable position and you are satisfied that costs are realistic and under control. It can be very time consuming and, for smaller businesses, is over-complicated. However, if you are setting the budget for a newly merged business, the range of issues that you will be dealing with will probably call for zero-based budgeting. You would not automatically assume that you need all the resources of the combined businesses, or that the current ways of doing things are right for the new company.

When constructing a cost budget, you should ask the following questions:

- What am I going to get for this item of expenditure?
- What will we actually do with this part of the budget?
- Have we factored in inflation?
- How will this extra expenditure affect clients?
- What percentage of the budget did this account for three years ago?
- Did we spend the total budget for this item last year?
- Why did this part of the budget overrun last year?
- Does this extra expenditure give us a clear increase in productivity?
- Is this line an 'investment' or a 'cost'?
- If we had to lose 10% of the total, where would it come from?

These are all ways to test the thinking behind the budget, even if you have a one person business. It pays to be inquisitive, and always consider how you would justify a line in the budget being the same as the previous year plus inflation. The questions are set out in a formal questionnaire in **Template 2.1 in Part 4** of the website.

3.3 Monitoring costs and revenues

You should monitor costs and revenues on a monthly and year to date basis. This will allow you to review the progress of the business and make any necessary changes in a timely manner.

The structure of the template for monitoring costs and revenues is shown in Table 13.1 and in **Template 2.2 in Part 4** of the website.

As the Table shows, the main lines of expenditure are included, with rolling totals for year to date as well as individual months. Many businesses split the revenue Section by advisers so they can track exactly how the individual sources of income are performing.

Table 13.1 **Costs and revenues**

	JAN (ACTUAL	JAN (BUDGET)	YTD (ACTUAL)	YTD (BUDGET)
RECEIPTS				
Initial revenue				
Recurring revenue				
Fees				
Others				
TOTAL				
PAYMENTS				
Employment-related				
Property-related				
Travel and accommodation				
Marketing-related				
Postage, etc				
Telephone				
Others				
TOTAL				
EXCESS OF RECEIPTS OVER PAYMENTS				

CASE STUDY

Looking the wrong way

Mohand and Roshan Khan are father and son, and jointly run Vermillion Financial Planning Limited. Stephen Norman retired five years ago, which provided the opportunity for Roshan to play a greater role in the business.

There are six advisers, including Mohand and Roshan, and the final payments to purchase Stephen's share of the business were made 12 months ago. Mohand and Roshan both agreed that this was the point at which to expand and to use the 'money we have freed up' to recruit advisers and support staff.

The business was making around 10% operating profit and, as Mohand said, "There is no reason why we shouldn't put more business through the back office and lift the profit to at least 15%."

As luck would have it, two advisers approached Mohand as they completed Stephen's buy-out payments, expressing a desire to join the business. "This sounds like great luck and perfect timing; we know Alison and Parvez very well and they should fit in perfectly. We had better recruit another administrator to take up the workload," said Mohand.

Roshan agreed in principle, but half jokingly warned his father that "this will add a lot to our costs, and it will take them a while to produce revenue for us. Should we take them on as self-employed and reduce our risk?" Mohand had never liked the self-employed model, and dismissed the idea. "We have always had a healthy balance sheet, so I am sure we can cope with this; they are both good advisers."

Six months after Alison and Parvez had arrived, Roshan was feeling increasingly uneasy. It had taken longer than expected to transfer their FSA registration and their previous company had been rigorous in making it plain that, if the embargo on client contact was broken, they would seek redress. Roshan had an uncomfortable feeling that the finances were out of balance, and lots of talk about 'large clients coming across' was no more than talk. Nothing had actually happened.

Mohand was enjoying a quiet Sunday evening, contemplating how his own retirement might look. The phone rang, and it was Roshan. "Dad, we have a real problem. I need to see you tonight, and if we don't act quickly we'll be out of business!"

Roshan, who generally left the finances to his father, had been through the data on money in and money out, where they stood now and how the situation would look at the end of the year. Some of the information was not readily accessible, because the book keeper they employed part time was not fully up to date. "We are literally running out of money," he told his father. "We may have millions under management and a profitable set up, but right now the cash is going to run out. Just compare the next three months' bills that we know we have to pay and actual revenue."

Roshan's analysis was slightly pessimistic, but they both realised that they had not planned the financing of two new advisers and had not built in any contingency for the slower than expected flow of income.

They worked out a plan which involved increasing their overdraft and the possibility of Mohand putting an additional £50,000 into the business for at least six months. In addition, they planned how they would approach Alison and Parvez, as they needed to raise their production as quickly as possible.

The outcome was that Parvez left the business and Alison embarked on a detailed review of all Mohand's 'silver' clients, who were of medium value and had not been contacted for some time.

As a result, the business pulled through, with Parvez being seen in hindsight as an expensive mistake. The book keeper was replaced by external accountants to provide proper financial control. From that day on, the business prepared detailed cash flow statements and monthly management accounts to keep a close track on things. It was a discipline they did not give up as the position improved. As Mohand said, "It had been too easy to just let everything wash through the finances, but it seemed to work — we must never allow that to happen again; we may not be so fortunate next time."

CASE STUDY KEY POINT

This happens many times with advice businesses. They run their finances on perception as opposed to fact, and if they make a recruitment mistake often end up with a loss. The profit and loss account and balance sheet have an important role to play, but they tend to look back, whereas the management of the business needs to look forward and be supported with clear and accurate information.

3.4 Budget best practice

In many cases, firms assemble this information into a profit and loss budget to help chart and monitor their way through the year. In addition, you should construct the cash budget, which is very similar to the cash flow (see section 6 in this chapter), and, if required, a capital budget to ensure that major expenditure is appropriately timed and funded.

If you wish to be really thorough, you can bring all of this together in a budgeted balance sheet, set out on a monthly basis. You will certainly require this if you are going to approach external sources or the bank for additional finance.

4 Prepare the financial statements and decide what you want to know

The financial statements perform two important functions:

- They enable you to manage your business effectively.
- They provide essential information in the buying and selling process.

The full financial statements or 'accounts' comprise:

- Profit and loss account.
- Cash flow statement.
- Balance sheet.

At this point, we will introduce the statements; their full application will be covered in Chapter 14. Each has a specific function and will provide a different perspective on the financial health and performance of the business.

When analysing the accounts, you should be clear about what you want to know and recognise that this applies to reviewing your own business performance as much as analysing the potential of a possible acquisition.

The important issues will include:

- Rate of growth of turnover and profitability.
- Mix of turnover.
- Level of profitability.
- Financial strength.
- Mix and value of assets.
- Financial structure and the mix and level of borrowings.
- Efficiency of operation.

If you are planning to sell your business, you need to concentrate on maximising performance on these financial KPIs over a period of time. This is also the benchmark you should set when reviewing other businesses for acquisition.

There are some good practice approaches to analysing accounts, which include the following. You should:

- Use ratios and percentages to 'common size' data over time to enable more effective identification of trends.
- Be sceptical and always look for verification of headline numbers; don't take them at face value.
- Take account of seasonality and changes in adviser numbers between accounting periods.
- Review reasons for changes in adviser numbers.
- Look at the notes to the accounts; once again, the devil is in the detail.

5 Explore the profit and loss account

The profit and loss account shows you how much revenue has come into your business, what costs have been incurred and thus what profit or loss you have made over a given time period. Notes to the accounts will show any transfer to or from the company reserves and any dividends proposed or paid.

The profit and loss account is normally prepared annually, but you should produce it monthly or quarterly as management accounts to compare actual performance against budget, as covered in section 3 of this chapter.

When you review the profit and loss account, you should remember the following:

- Sales are not the same as cash receipts: sales will include services that have been paid for and also those where payment is still outstanding.
- Purchases are not the same as cash paid out: this will include purchases that have been paid for as well those where the payment is still outstanding.
- Profit is not the same as cash flow: businesses can have a healthy profit but suffer from severe cash flow pressures.

5.1 What does a profit and loss account look like?

The structure for the profit and loss account is summarised opposite, and is based on Scarlet Independent Financial Advisers Limited, whom we will use throughout this chapter. The first part of the case study deals with the structure of the account; we will look at the detail in Chapter 14.

CASE STUDY

Scarlet Independent Financial Advisers Limited: profit and loss account

Scarlet is based in Leicester and has been operating for a number of years. In the past three years, turnover has increased from £940,000 to almost £1.4m, and recurring income accounts for around 30% of the turnover.

The personnel structure is:

- Three directors, who also give advice.
- Four advisers (one recruited toward the end of 2011).
- Two para-planners.
- Five administrators.

The profit and loss account is structured as shown in Figure 13.1.

The **income** is split into direct expenses and gross profit.

Direct expenses are the reward for the professional staff, who, in an advice business, are the directors (in their work role, as opposed to their ownership role) and other revenue earners.

Gross profit is what is left to pay the overheads and produce an operating profit. This demonstrates clearly how a lack of control of overhead expenses can rapidly eat into operating profit.

Overheads are all the main running costs of the business, including support staff, IT, buildings, management, depreciation, marketing and so on.

Operating profit, as indicated above, is what is left and is the reward to the owner for all the risks and challenges of setting up and running the business. There are two additional lines that should be included here to arrive at **profit for the year:** adjustments for payment, and receipt of any interest and tax.

Figure 13.1 **Profit and loss account**

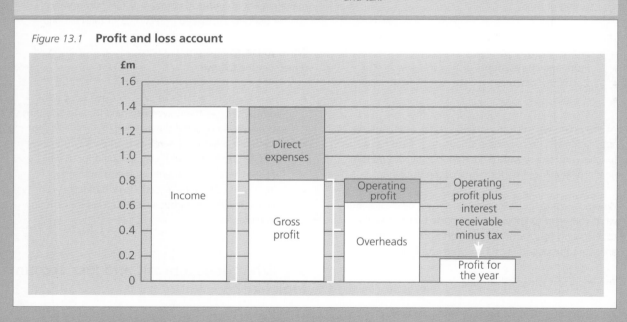

6 Why cash flow is so important

Many advice businesses will know why cash flow is important, particularly those who rely on initial commissions and revenues. For the majority of advice businesses, the percentage of annual operating costs that is covered by recurring income is less than 25%. Indeed, if the figure for your business exceeds 50%, you are in the top 20% of all advice businesses.

You need to be clear that cash flow is different from profit, because:

- Sales are credited to the profit and loss account when the work takes place and often before payment is received.
- Purchases are debited to the account as they are made, with payments often being made later.
- Fixed asset purchase immediately affects the cash position, but has little short term bearing on profit.
- Creation of a bad debt reserve in the profit and loss account will reduce profit but have no effect on cash.

In effect, the financial statements produced at the end of the trading period look back, whereas you have to look forward to manage cash flow. This is achieved with a cash flow forecast that predicts when payments will be received and bills have to be paid.

There have been many instances when growing and profitable businesses have failed because they have not managed their cash flow. Indeed, principals of advice businesses will often cite lack of funding, partly linked to cash flow, as a reason for being unable to recruit additional advisers.

You need to make sure that you can fund expansion, and that the excitement of growing the business does not take your concentration away from the need to manage cash flow and working capital.

6.1 How to prepare a cash flow forecast

The concept is straightforward. As summarised above, you need to forecast as accurately as possible when monies will be paid to you and when bills have to be met.

For the majority of advice businesses before the RDR deadline, the largest source of income is commission from product providers and fund managers. After the deadline, the principal source of income will be payment of invoices by clients. Many will use products, funds, wraps or platforms to facilitate this, but a slowly rising proportion will pay directly. You need to maintain accurate records in the 'new business book' to track income and manage the inevitable pipeline. This is particularly important if the type of business and client means you receive small numbers of large sums, which are likely to be irregular, whereas many of your costs will have to be made with predictable frequency.

The cash flow forecast provides a clear picture of what is expected to happen, against which outcomes can be evaluated. For example, if trading conditions deteriorated rapidly, as they did in 2008, then the initial income line will need to be reforecast and the effect of a lower stock market on fund-based recurring income will require a similar adjustment.

Many advice businesses manage cash flow by regularly reviewing their bank statements. While this is not a bad thing, it is a snapshot that is too short term. You need to prepare the cash flow statement as accurately as you can, and update and review it on a monthly basis.

CASE STUDY

Scarlet Independent Financial Advisers: cash flow statement

Table 13.2 **Cash flow statement**

	2013	2012	2011
Net cash flow from operating activities	220,250	211,850	225,700
Returns on investment and servicing finance	–	–	–
Net cash inflow on investment and servicing	–	–	–
Taxation	(38,850)	(37,730)	(36,690)
Net cash outflow for capital expenditure	(35,000)	(30,000)	(25,000)
Increase/decrease cash in the year	146,400	144,120	164,010

As the Table shows, Scarlet has a relatively healthy cash flow position, although the deteriorating trends from 2011 to 2013 should be noted and will be returned to.

If we express cash as a percentage of turnover (see Table 14.3 in Chapter 14 for turnover data), the figures are:

- 17% (2011).
- 13% (2012).
- 11% (2013).

It would be expected that this ratio would be fairly constant over time, which suggests insufficient attention has been paid to financial management, with too much concentration on the top line income.

CASE STUDY

Scarlet Independent Financial Advisers: cash flow forecast

Scarlet reflects the typical cycles of revenue around the start of the year and the end of the tax year. As would be expected, there is less fluctuation of recurring income. The main cost variations relate to the timing of rent payments and marketing activity. Clearly, a dip in revenue or uncontrolled cost in January, March and June could result in an unfavourable and possibly unpredicted cash flow position.

Table 13.3 **Cash flow forecast (2013)**

RECEIPTS	JAN	FEB	MAR	APRIL	MAY	JUNE
Initial revenue	40,000	70,000	80,000	75,000	75,000	80,000
Recurring revenue	33,000	33,000	34,000	34,000	35,000	35,000
Fees	6,000	6,500	8,000	6,500	6,500	6,500
Others	1,500	2,000	1,500	1,500	1,500	1,500
TOTAL	80,500	111,500	123,500	117,000	118,000	123,000
PAYMENTS						
Employment-related	68,000	68,000	68,000	68,000	68,000	68,000
Property-related	3,000	3,000	25,000	3,000	3,000	25,000
Travel and accommodation	3,000	3,000	3,500	3,500	3,000	4,000
Marketing-related	5,000	4,500	5,500	6,500	6,000	6,000
Postage, etc	3,000	4,000	4,000	2,500	2,500	3,000
Telephone	1,500	1,600	1,600	1,500	1,500	1,500
Others	6,000	7,000	6,000	6,000	6,000	6,000
TOTAL	89,500	91,100	113,600	91,000	90,000	113,500
EXCESS OF RECEIPTS OVER PAYMENTS	(9,000)	20,400	9,900	26,000	28,000	9,500

7 Take a snapshot with the balance sheet

The balance sheet lists all the assets and liabilities of the business at a particular point in time, usually the financial year end. In effect, it provides an overview of what the business owns and how it is funded. Figure 13.2 summarises the contents of the balance sheet.

Assets

These are either owned by the business (e.g. money, property, equipment) or owed to the business (e.g. payment for client work that is completed or being undertaken). **Fixed assets** such as equipment are kept in the business to be used over a number of years, whereas **current assets** are converted to cash within a year or less (e.g. fees and commissions).

Liabilities

This is anything the business owes to another person and expects to pay off at some point in the future. **Current liabilities** are amounts owed which are due within the year and include:

- Debts that are owed to creditors from whom supplies have been received for which payment has not yet been made: this would include potential commission clawback.
- Outstanding tax.
- Dividends that have been approved but not yet paid.
- Accruals, which are expenses incurred to achieve sales which have not been invoiced and paid (e.g. marketing services or hotel bills).
- Overdrafts, which in theory are repayable on demand.

Long term liabilities are amounts due to be paid after more than one year (e.g. pre-agreed payments for the purchase of another business, mortgages, etc).

Equity is the shareholders' investment in the business. This comes from two sources: new capital invested into the business and retained profits.

When reviewing your balance sheet or that of a potential acquisition, you need to take particular account of the following:

- In practice, advice business balance sheets may present a false picture, because the ability to track anticipated commissions and fees and manage commission clawback is poor: this often means that the simpler cash basis accounting method is used, as opposed to the accruals method that accounts for these.
- Growth in assets does not automatically mean growth in profit: this means that funding has to be found, and it may be derived from debt if the owners are not prepared to provide more capital.

8 Use management information to tell you what is going on

Many advice businesses have a wealth of information, but do not have the resources to draw out what is really useful to them. In addition, there is a myth that you need huge amounts of data to monitor your business; this is not the case. You need to concentrate on what is important and only look at the detail if you suspect a problem. As a result, many firms use the **dashboard** approach that deals with the headlines, with the option of getting into greater detail if concerns arise.

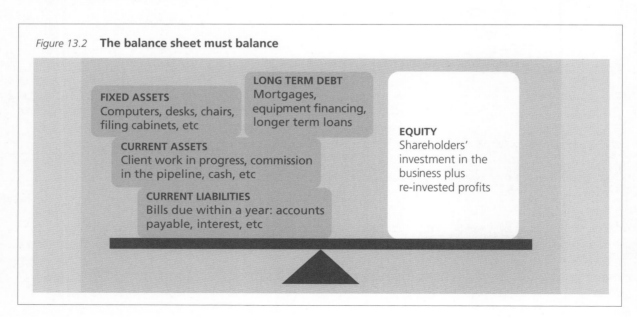

Figure 13.2 **The balance sheet must balance**

FIXED ASSETS
Computers, desks, chairs, filing cabinets, etc

LONG TERM DEBT
Mortgages, equipment financing, longer term loans

CURRENT ASSETS
Client work in progress, commission in the pipeline, cash, etc

CURRENT LIABILITIES
Bills due within a year: accounts payable, interest, etc

EQUITY
Shareholders' investment in the business plus re-invested profits

8.1 How to approach management information

To make sure your management information process works well, you should:

- Identify the data that is going to be useful and tell you something.
- Work out who will produce it and how frequently you need to see it.
- Link it to the data collection exercise for the RMAR returns.
- Set clear targets for all data, so you can monitor progress.
- Always look for the trends and compare over time or against industry benchmarks if they exist.
- Make sure you have a specific point in your management meeting when the data will be discussed.
- Make sure actions are documented and followed up: this is particularly important to provide evidence to the FSA of how well the business is being run, including TCF monitoring and management.
- Share as much of this information as possible with your staff.

To test the effectiveness of your management information process, answer the following questions:

- Do you have a set of data that is informative and which you act on?
- Do you have data that are wider than sales figures and top line financial information?
- Do you involve your senior team in reviewing the data?
- Are the data reviewed on a regular basis (e.g. weekly or monthly)?
- Are the data collated properly and clearly presented?
- Do your staff see the data and, where relevant, discuss them with you?
- Can you drill down into the really important areas if you need to?
- Does your management information pick up the key TCF measures?

These are set out in **Template 2.3 in Part 4** of the website.

If you have answered "Yes" to most of the questions, your data and, more importantly, the use of it is in good shape. If you are not in this position, you are in the majority but should recognise that this may not be as large a task as it may seem.

8.2 Monitor the dashboard

Table 13.4 is the recommended dashboard data set that you should use in your business. It will pick up virtually all the TCF management information, which means that you do not have to maintain the latter as a separate task. As you can see, there are just six categories and 22 lines of data, of which 13 are monitored monthly.

If you tabulate this data to show year to date, you will have a good picture of the main operating areas of the business. In addition, the monthly meeting that reviews this data should call for short reports from those responsible for the main business functions, so that, where necessary, you have context and detail to go with the numbers.

Table 13.5 is an example of the type of data that appears on the dashboard.

As the example shows, most of the data can be contained within the Table, although splits on providers and advisers, plus the client survey and KPI performance, will need to be tabulated separately (shown as 'below' in Table 13.5). If the data is contained within a spreadsheet, it is easy to display some of the trends graphically to concentrate on the really important areas. Provided that you are satisfied with the trends and what the data tells you, there should be no reason to get into any additional detail. As always, good back office software will produce this information for you and has the capability to dig deeper if necessary.

There are three areas where you should pay particular attention, which are often missed:

- Management of debt and its link to cash flow.
- The relationship between expenses and capital adequacy calculations.
- The proportion of recurring income that is fund-based.

Table 13.4 **Dashboard: actual, budget, year to date**

CATEGORY	DATA	SPLIT	FREQUENCY
FINANCIAL HEADLINES	Total revenue Adviser payments Overheads Gross profit Exceptional costs or income Capital reserves	Totals only	Monthly
KEY FINANCIALS	Cash Aged debtors Creditors Notified clawback	 Providers/clients Product/adviser	Cash weekly and remainder monthly
REVENUE	Commission/Revenue: • Initial • Recurring • Fund-based • Fees	Total and by adviser	Monthly
PRODUCTS/FUNDS	Transactions Persistency Provider use Execution only	Product/fund type Adviser Provider	Quarterly
CLIENTS	New clients Annual service delivery Client survey results	Adviser	Quarterly
COMPLIANCE	KPI performance Complaints	Adviser	Quarterly

Table 13.5 **Dashboard: actual, budget, year to date: April**

CATEGORY	DATA	ACTUAL (APRIL)	BUDGET (APRIL)	ACTUAL YTD	BUDGET YTD
FINANCIAL HEADLINES (£)	Total revenue	95,000	100,000	376,000	380,000
	Adviser payments	58,000	61,000	248,000	250,000
	Overheads	26,000	27,000	88,000	85,000
	Gross profit	37,000	39,000	128,000	125,000
	Exceptional costs or income	0	2,000+	5,000-	0
	Capital reserves	na	na	52,000	50,000
KEY FINANCIALS	Cash	15,000	16,000	51,000	55,000
	Aged debtors (number)	5	7	7	8
	Creditors (number)	3	3	3	4
	Notified clawback	6,500	3,000	15,000	12,000
REVENUE	Commission:				
	• Initial	74,000	77,000	275,000	275,000
	• Renewal	6,000	6,000	26,000	30,000
	• Fund-based	13,000	15,000	63,000	65,000
	• Fees	2,000	2,000	12,000	10,000
	NB: Adviser split below				
PRODUCTS/FUNDS	Transactions	25	30	92	100
	Persistency	97%	98%	97%	98%
	Provider	Below	Below	Below	Below
	Execution only	1	5	15	
CLIENTS	New clients	3	7	16	25
	Annual service delivery	92%	100%	90%	99%
	Client survey results	Below	Below	Below	Below
COMPLIANCE	KPI performance	Below	Below	Below	Below
	Complaints	1	0	2	0

CASE STUDY

If it moves, measure it!

Sandra Macgregor was the business manager for Black Advisory Group, which had ten offices and over 100 staff, including 50 advisers, across the country. She had been asked by the directors to overhaul the management information, particularly as their monitoring of the business KPIs was not considered strong enough.

Sandra was thorough and prided herself in doing the job properly and professionally. She knew that the back office system could produce a lot of data along with the financial control software which they used. In addition, there were reports from the compliance agency that had useful information which helped give a picture of what was going on.

The directors were busy, and Sandra received no more detail. At the next senior management meeting, the participants were presented with a folder almost two inches thick, marked 'October management information'. Sandra announced, "Here is your MI pack. You have got everything in here; I didn't know we had so much useful information around the place!"

The debate on management information ran for over an hour as Sandra answered questions, dug into the document and used her calculator to come up with answers, or more questions. Jo Haynes, who was chairing the meeting, called for a tea break: "This is making my head ache! If you think about it, we have been looking at this for over an hour and have not made any decisions or clear observations. I don't think that is meant to be the outcome of a discussion on management information — we've got information overload!"

After the meeting, Sandra thought about this. Her initial reaction was to blame herself for producing such a large and unwieldy pack of data but, as Jo said to her, "This is partly the directors' fault, because we gave you no clue as to what we wanted, and I am not sure we know the answer to that question anyway."

Sandra decided to sort this out and to make sure the directors ended up with MI that would be useful to them. At the next meeting, she ran a short 30 minute session and started by heading up a flip chart with: 'What data do you want, why do you want it and what will you do with it?' There was a good measure of agreement about what was important and also the frequency with which the data should be produced.

Sandra now had a clear brief, and produced one side of A4 for the next meeting, with the key data lines shown by month, year to date and, if the information was available, comparison to previous year. As with the first meeting, the discussion ran for an hour. At the end, Jo had noted six actions to take, and the senior team agreed that this had given them a good overview of how the business was doing. Sandra said, "As you know, we have a lot more data, so if we need to get behind any of this detail, we can."

CASE STUDY KEY POINT

It is very tempting to draw together a lot of data and present it month in, month out, to the senior team. The problem is that this may not be what is really useful, so the team ends up paying lip service to it and hoping that it also covers the data that is needed. It is rare that you won't have the data that is needed to monitor your business effectively. It is well worth taking a few minutes to think about what would be really useful and apply the one side of A4 test. At headline level, that should give you enough data; if you spot adverse trends, you can then get into the detail.

Debt management

If you have frequent issues with debtors, or the problem never seems to be in control because the list of aged debtors just gets longer, you should:

- Make sure that clients agree payments and payment terms in advance of your undertaking any work.
- Review your invoicing procedures.
- Make sure your invoices are clear in terms of what they are for and when payment is expected.
- Review the timescales and controls for issue of invoices, statements and chasing letters.

Expenses and capital adequacy

Capital adequacy calculations are based on overheads, and the FSA proposed that all advice businesses be required to hold 25% of this in reserve. This is subject to a £20,000 minimum. This means that if overheads rise, the capital reserve must increase in line with them. There may be very good reasons for increasing expenses of management, but the impact on capital should be carefully managed. Confirmation of these proposals is expected by the RDR deadline.

Fund-based recurring income

It is surprising how many advisers failed to take account of how reductions in stock market value influenced this source of income in 2008/09. While it is sound to build up recurring income in the long term to support the sale value of the business, it is essential to regularly monitor how it changes every month as markets move. Managing this through the dashboard ensures that reality prevails, and that budgets for the following year can be based on the most up to date forecasts of this category of income.

9 Chapter summary

This chapter has dealt with the disciplines of financial management, which many advisers allow to slip when the market is buoyant. During the 2008/09 recession, many advice businesses were caught out by the rapid change in trading conditions, partly due to the speed of developments but also due to a lack of rigour in their approach to financial control.

You cannot directly influence changes in the market, but you have direct control over the way you run your business. This chapter and the one that follows will equip you with the techniques and approaches to manage financial risk and use financial data to analyse what is really happening in your business and any that you may consider acquiring.

The management skills you have developed as a result of this chapter mean that you can:

- Recognise and manage financial risk.
- Develop effective and realistic budgets.
- Use financial accounts to proactively manage and develop your business.
- Construct a robust cash flow account and forecast.
- Use the dashboard to monitor the progress of your business and identify problems in their early stages.

Chapter 14

Valuing advice businesses

By the end of this chapter, your business will benefit from:

✔ A valuation of the business and possible acquisitions.
✔ Maximising value by ensuring that clients associate with the business as well as the adviser.
✔ Using financial data to improve your business and investigate the worth of others.
✔ Concentration on the drivers of value to enhance your business and investigate others.

Whether you are buying or selling, the value drivers are the same. Clearly, your perspective will be different, and the weighting you apply to individual drivers will vary. You should use the value drivers as follows:

- As a guide to prepare your business for sale.
- As a set of criteria to evaluate any business you might acquire or merge with.

Much of what we will deal with in this chapter does not confront you every day. This implies that it is less familiar and that when issues of business value, acquisition, merger and succession planning arise you should take a measured approach. Indeed, that is very important, because decisions on these issues are critical to the long term development of your business and, in some cases, may benefit from external specialist support.

When considering potential opportunities, you should take nothing at face value and consider propositions from a variety of perspectives. There is no substitute for careful analysis and rigorous due diligence. In addition, it is essential to remember that a business is only worth what a buyer is prepared to pay for it. This means that you should concentrate on what makes the business attractive to buyers, as opposed to assuming that the value will automatically be close to what the multipliers suggest.

1 Look at the market trends

If you took a snap shot of the advice market ten years ago, it would be much more fragmented than it is now and dominated by a huge number of small businesses. Compared to many other sectors, the market is still populated by relatively small firms, but it has consolidated rapidly since the mid-1990s. The level of business accounted for by the advice market has increased in absolute and relative terms, with shares of the life, pensions and investment markets sustained at well over 65% year after year. In addition, the number of advisers has remained around the 20,000 level on average throughout this period, which means that the number of independent businesses will be far lower than ten years ago.

Consolidation in the advice market tends to run in waves instigated by providers (as was the case in the late 1990s), difficult market conditions (2002 and 2008/09) or regulatory change (Retail Distribution Review (RDR), 2008–12). The likely outcome of the implementation of the RDR will be to speed up consolidation towards the deadline when the major changes will be made. These include:

- Increased capital adequacy requirements for IFAs.
- Adviser charges completely independent of product charges for all advisory business.
- A higher examination and professional competence threshold for all advisers.
- A more rigorous implementation of 'whole of market' to encompass platforms, wraps and discretionary management.

- Abolition of commission (except for protection products).
- Abolition of factoring (indemnity commission) by product providers.

As a result, many firms may leave the market up to the RDR deadline, which could have a depressant affect on values. However, there is a scarcity of good quality medium-sized firms, which could have the opposite effect, particularly after the deadline.

Whatever the driver, you have to develop your business in the knowledge that at some point you may be approached to sell it, or you may wish to sell it.

In this chapter, we will deal with:

- Business value: buying and selling.
- Raising the value of clients by strengthening the brand.
- The factors that directly influence value.
- The 'rule of thumb' ratios and multipliers.
- Analysing the accounts: to get your business in shape and look at others in detail.

2 Buying or selling: what underpins business value?

This section is important in the following cases:

- Considering potential acquisitions.
- Preparing and valuing your own business for sale.
- Structuring the due diligence process.

Before we look at the detail, you have to remember that business value is mainly determined by:

- Strength of revenue stream, which implies a bias to recurring revenue.
- Strength of relationships, especially those between advisers and clients and professional introducers, because they tend to be networked.
- Retention of key people: clients, advisers and other specialists.

Figure 14.1 summarises the main factors that influence value, the detail of which will be covered in the following section.

On the left hand side, the power lies with the adviser, and any purchaser will be very concerned that, should the advisers leave, the value-sustaining relationships will leave as well. If you are intending to sell your business and it is located on the left, you have to move across to the right. The clients and introducers must be clear that they are dealing with the business and not one individual. You also need to assess the position of any business that you might consider acquiring. Incidentally, if it is on the left, don't automatically walk away if you believe that you can shift it

to the right after you have acquired it.

As Figure 14.1 shows, firms that are forced to sell out before the RDR deadline could be disadvantaged if the principals, who are likely to hold the key client relationships, leave the business. In addition, if business and risk management are poor then the value will be further depressed. However, for firms which have a sustainable operating model post RDR there is expected to be an uplift in value as the advice market becomes characterised by businesses that are financially stronger, more effective at client management and operate with defined processes.

In such cases it is expected that profit and client relationships will be very sustainable, increasing the attraction of the sector and raising its value. An additional factor that influences value is the balance between the business brand and the 'brand' of the individual advisers. If the advisers control all the key relationships with clients and introducers the value of the business will be diminished. This is because potential acquirers will fear that the loss of advisers will substantially reduce the value of the firm they have purchased.

You can mitigate this by:

- Delivering some client services through other staff in addition to the adviser.
- Promoting the business and the full set of client benefits it provides to existing and new clients: they need to perceive that they cannot get such a good service anywhere else, so that if their adviser leaves they will stay.
- Making sure you have such an attractive business that it retains key people: that may involve equity participation, but it also includes good staff relations, career paths, training and professional development.

If you can achieve this, your business will be far more attractive to potential buyers and secure a higher value. As a buyer, you would be more confident that the business would be sustained as a complete operation, with retention of the key clients and advisers and support of the infrastructure.

2.1 Valuation: where to concentrate for buyers and sellers

Table 14.1 summarises the main drivers of value and the issues of particular importance.

As the Table shows, there is a wide range of factors that influence the value of advice businesses. There are a number of techniques that you can use to help make a judgement, and these will be covered in the next sections.

In most cases, the factors related to finance, risk, advisers and clients tend to have a greater weighting, although compatibility between the two businesses will be significant.

The **financials** should be readily available in the accounts,

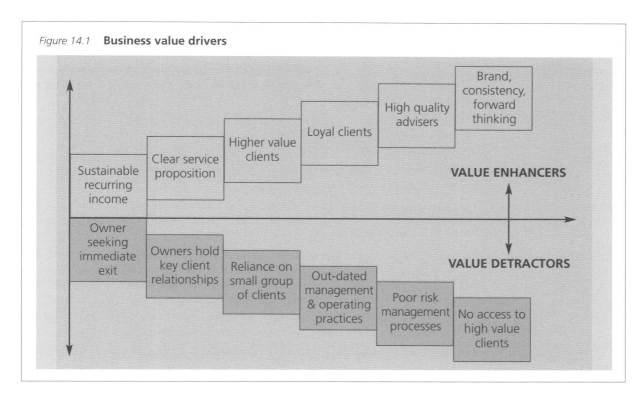

Figure 14.1 **Business value drivers**

and you need to consider the issues raised in Sections 3 and 4 of this chapter to get under the skin of what is going on. You should do this as a matter of course for your own business to manage it effectively and prepare it for sale. Always use other businesses and industry benchmarks as a guide to help assess the position. In addition, if you are acquiring, you need to consider how easily you can deal with any problems that you identify. You may use them to depress the price that you pay, in the knowledge that you have proven processes that can yield a better performance post-acquisition. Remember, anyone buying your business will be adopting the same approach.

The **quality of management** is hard to assess. You cannot base this on numbers, and although it appears third on the list, you cannot make a judgement until you have reviewed all the other criteria. The weighting for this will be lower if you are acquiring a business and the management is not part of the deal. However, if you are expecting the existing management to join you (or you to join a business that is acquiring yours), this becomes much more important. The best way to create the right impression is to deal with all the other factors well in advance of any potential negotiations. However, you have to recognise that the chemistry between management teams is significant and often has to be worked on after the deal.

It is obvious that the due diligence process will concentrate on areas of **risk and compliance**, because it is such a significant issue in the advice market. If you have doubts about the position of your own business, you should engage external specialists to review where you stand and recommend any changes. Negative issues around risk and compliance can depress the price and result in buyers insisting that the current owners retain responsibility for the advice given to clients prior to the deal.

Evidence of the approach to **Treating Customers Fairly** is useful for assessing the way the business is managed, as well as revealing potential shortcomings. You would expect that well run businesses would have major TCF and RDR related issues, such as service, pricing, investment, training and management information, in good shape. If this is not the case, it raises questions about responsiveness to change and the behaviours of the advisers and staff. If you are preparing to sell and you have doubts about this, you should use the external risk consultants referred to above to review your position and recommend any changes. If you are buying, you could use the same experts to support this critical area of due diligence.

Advisers are obviously very important. Buyers will want to retain the high producers and will be concerned if contracts are not up to date or if the model is self-employed. If the business is very fragmented and people ignore the corporate standards, there will be a concern about loyalty and how receptive advisers will be to a new regime. The compliance record of advisers is critical, as well as the range of specialisation and qualifications. Finally, the age profile of the adviser base is significant, because at the very least there has to be enough time to transfer clients to new advisers if necessary.

In many respects, similar issues arise with the **client base**, which is where the balance between brand strength and adviser relationships is important. Client data needs to be in excellent shape to demonstrate the number and value of clients and which advisers look after them. Any buyer or seller needs to assess the loyalty of the key clients and what may happen if their adviser leaves.

If you are acquiring a business or **client bank**, you need to think about the types of client and your familiarity with them. At the extreme, if you normally deal with

Table 14.1

CRITERIA	COMMENT
FINANCIALS: REVENUE AND PROFIT GROWTH	Profit is more important than revenue. and the benchmark is 15%−20% (operating profit against revenue) for the employed model and around 10% for the self-employed model.
	The benchmark rate of growth should be measured against the market and similar businesses. For example, prior to the 2008/09 recession, turnover for advice businesses was increasing at around 10% pa year on year.
	In addition, a strong balance sheet is important, plus a set of clear management accounts for the previous five years.
FINANCIALS: RECURRING REVENUE	The percentage of income accounted for by recurring income is important, and generally the higher, the better. The typical level is 25%, with self-employed models being lower and employed models higher, often at 50% or above.
	The mix of recurring income is also important, with fund-based commissions increasingly dominating. From the acquisition perspective, some will favour fund-based revenue as it fits well with a long term value model, while others will favour traditional renewals as their value is more predictable, although they are declining in importance.
	Revenues arising from funds under the direct management of the business (e.g. in-house OEICS) will be valued much higher than other recurring revenues.
QUALITY OF MANAGEMENT, BUSINESS AND FINANCIAL PLANNING	This is very important if any deal involves retention of the management. Breadth of experience and complementary skills are important, along with business and professional connections. There should be a clear business plan and evidence that good practice planning and monitoring techniques are in place.
	If the business is being acquired and the normal approach of the buyer is to retain the management team, then a track record of growth and sound financial and risk management is significant.
RISK MANAGEMENT AND COMPLIANCE REGIME	The business should have a clean compliance record and clear, well documented processes and audit trails. It is essential to provide evidence of good practice and outcomes and a positive compliance and TCF culture.
	The wider risk management issues, such as the process for managing and investing client monies, risk management plan, disaster recovery planning, IT back up, etc, are all important.
ADVISERS	As indicated above, the split between employed and self-employed advisers is important, and how this is valued depends on the business model of the acquiring/to be acquired business. Clearly, length of association, production record, compliance record, qualifications, specialisation and client numbers will all be significant.
	In addition, the overall mix of advisers by age, experience, skills, etc will be important, along with the position of those who hold equity stakes.
CLIENT BASE	Client data needs to be up to date, accurate and accessible. Clients should be segmented by value and the key clients identified along with a plan to retain them, depending on the nature of the deal. The value of a client base is determined by its financial value, not its size.
SOURCES OF BUSINESS	Generally, these should be diverse and not heavily dependent on adviser or principal relationships, particularly if principals are leaving the business or, in the self-employed model, where the risk of loss of advisers is greater.
INFRASTRUCTURE AND IT CAPABILITY	The importance of this depends on the extent to which the back office capability is an essential part of the new firm after the deal. If the business is run as a freestanding unit, then this will be important; if it is to be integrated into another business, then only the specialist capability will count. This is most likely to reside in key back office staff, but could include software and related knowledge.
BRAND AND REPUTATION	This is difficult to value, and will be partly reflected by the strength of the client base and the robustness of the business sources. However, an obvious, strong local presence is useful and may favour retaining the brand name after the deal.

personal clients and you acquire corporate clients to achieve diversification, they could test your skills if you are not familiar with the corporate market. In those circumstances, you may become over-dependent on the advisers who join you, because they will be aware of how important they are in servicing and retaining those clients. Regardless of the buyer or seller perspective, any service agreements and commitments with clients must be clearly understood. If you are selling, you will want to be sure that your clients will be looked after properly; if you are buying, you need to know the level of work and servicing that you are committing to.

Sources of business may provide diversification in any acquisition, but will need expertise to sustain them, particularly professional introducers or specific marketing activity (e.g. seminars). If you are buying and are attracted by a particular method of client acquisition, you must be confident that the new business can continue with it. If referrals and recommendation are important, then the loyalty of the existing clients to the new company will be significant.

IT and infrastructure, including all the business processes, are very important if they are to be retained. The same applies to the **back office team**, which often contains very skilled and specialist individuals who can be key people and an important part of any acquisition or sale. If the entire business, including the infrastructure, is to be acquired, then compatibility between back office software is a real bonus. If that is not the case, you have to take into account the costs of streamlining onto one system and one set of processes. Indeed, many mergers fail after the event because this issue is not given due recognition and the necessary changes are not made.

Finally, **brand and reputation** must be considered and are often accounted for under 'goodwill'. The majority of adviser brands have little value, which is unfortunate, given that in many cases principals devote a lot of time to building their business and its brand. However, unless there is strong recognition in the target market outside the existing client base, there is little value. The 'goodwill' of the business tends to reside in the relationship between the advisers and the clients, and the consistency of contact and service delivery as managed by the business. You should not expect to receive or pay very much for 'goodwill'.

2.2 When to use the ratios and multipliers

It is tempting to answer "Never" to this, because, as is often stated, the value of a business is determined by the market and particularly the worth of the business to a potential acquirer.

This means that you should only use the traditional multipliers as an extremely rough guide and starting point. When the market is relatively stable, the typical multipliers are:

- Recurring income: 3 × recurring income raised up to 6 if the business has funds under direct management.
- Turnover: 1 × turnover, more typically used if there is little recurring income.
- Profit: between 5 and 7 × operating profit.

The basis for this is partly historical but is also linked to surveys that indicate average profit at 14% and recurring revenues at 33% of turnover. This implies that these multiples will alter as profit changes. For example, if profits fell to 5%, the profit multiplier would need to rise to 20. Clearly, this is stretching the rules of thumb too far and simply demonstrates the care with which these ratios should be used.

Table 14.2 shows the wide variations in value attached to this approach.

As you can see, all three businesses have the same turnover at £1.5m, but different levels of profit and recurring income. The application of the multipliers gives a consistent result for business 1, a very wide range for business 2, which is probably undervalued, and an even wider range for business 3, which is probably overvalued.

It is for this reason that you should use these indicators with care. Obviously, if you are selling, you may use them in initial conversations if they drive up your value, but you should dismiss them if you are acquiring, unless they drive down the value.

Table 14.2

	VALUE OF BUSINESS 1	VALUE OF BUSINESS 2	VALUE OF BUSINESS 3
TURNOVER (£M)	1.5 × 1 = **1.5m**	1.5 × 1 = **1.5m**	1.5 × 1 = **1.5m**
RECURRING INCOME (£K)	500 × 3 = **1.5m**	100 × 3 = **300**	750 × 3 = **2.25m**
PROFIT (£K)	300 × 5 = **1.5m**	150 × 5 = **750**	225 × 5 = **1.13m**

CASE STUDY

Higher or lower?

Roberta and Aaron Brown run a successful 15 adviser business in the Midlands. Aaron tends to concentrate on clients and external relationships, while Roberta has a smaller client base and runs the day to day operations and management of the business.

From time to time, they are approached by advisers who want to sell or merge, and their discussion about the opportunity tends to run along predictable lines. Such an event is about to occur, as Aaron returns from the local AIFA meeting full of enthusiasm and excitement.

"You know I have been talking for ages to the partners at Copper Group about buying their business. Well, Jack Maxwell, the senior partner, wants to retire and that probably means they will have to sell the business!" said Aaron. "Here's a great chance to double in size and pick up a really good business; they have really built their turnover in the past five years — an impressive rate of growth," he added.

Roberta tended to be the more realistic of the two, but she did not want to dent her husband's spirit: "If this is serious, let's have a preliminary meeting with them and look at the books; there is no harm in that." "Jack reckons that four times their recurring income would work, as he says that's the going rate for good businesses — at a guess, that would put them around £2m, because I think he said they had about £500,000 in fees, renewals and fund-based. We could just about afford that, with some help from the bank," said Aaron.

Roberta could tell that, as far as Aaron was concerned, the deal was done and he was already thinking about a 40 person practice with a turnover towards £4m and rising.

The initial meeting with Jack and his partners from Copper was friendly, and Jack repeated that they needed to be in the "region of four times recurring" to have a serious conversation. They agreed to meet again and talk through the operations of the business, client bank, staff and IT to see if there was potential in getting into detailed negotiations.

"I am not sure Copper is as good as Jack suggests," said Roberta. "I know their senior administrator quite well, and it seems obvious to me that they have not invested in the back office; it sounds a bit of a muddle." "We'll soon lick that into shape," said Aaron. "You are good at sorting out problems." Roberta interrupted him: "That is not the point. If it is in a muddle, then they are asking too much. We need to look at this really carefully."

Before the next meeting, Roberta sent Jack a detailed agenda, including back office operations, software, adviser contracts, client profile and data, staff structure, plus a request to look at the accounts.

Jack was late for the meeting and, when he arrived, said, "I had a problem getting some of this stuff together, but this file should give you all you need." The file was as muddled as the back office had been described as being, but Roberta decided to work through the agenda with Jack and his co-founder Gordon to get under the skin of the business.

It became clear that the processes that had been set up 15 years ago were just about working, while their software was obsolete with no further upgrades available. "It never worked properly," said Gordon. "We rely on good old paper; you know where you are with that, provided you can find the file!" he joked. The same issues applied to the adviser contracts, which were inflexible and did not encourage a commercial and entrepreneurial approach.

As the meeting went on, Roberta could see that Aaron was becoming depressed. Later that evening, after returning from client meetings, he said, "I am not sure that four times recurring is good value for that business — even if we paid two or three times, there is a huge amount of work to bring it up to date, plus they have four key advisers due to retire in three years, as well as the exit of Jack, who is the key business producer." Roberta and Aaron went through the financial information that Jack had provided with their accountant, and decided they would offer the equivalent of two times recurring income. "I know the benchmark is three times, so if that were a starting point, then it just comes down and down when you look behind the scenes — two is the absolute tops," said Roberta.

The offer was made and politely rejected. The two businesses parted on amicable terms and went their own ways. Three months later, the 2008 recession really started to bite and Copper's recurring income fell sharply, as much of it was fund-based. In addition, much of the new investment business

stopped and it became clear that if they sold now they would receive a much smaller sum. In fact, Jack had to postpone retirement and work very hard with his partners to see the business through the recession. "If only I had been a bit more realistic about value, I could have been out of this a couple of years ago. That was a lesson I wish I didn't have to learn," said Jack.

CASE STUDY KEY POINT

It is important to be realistic and scientific about business value. This applies to buyers and sellers, and means analysing the financial position and operating practices of the business in detail. The compliance record is also critical, along with the mix of previous business if the agreement involves your taking on liability for past advice. Finally, pay scant attention to the traditional multipliers; these are used by enthusiastic sellers as an opening gambit to drive up the value of their business.

CASE STUDY

Scarlet Independent Financial Advisers: Profit and loss account

We introduced Scarlet in Chapter 13. They are a mature business, and in the past three years turnover has increased by 45%, with recurring income accounting for around 30% of the turnover. There are three directors who also give advice, four advisers (one recruited toward the end of 2011), two para-planners and five administrators.

On the surface (Table 14.3) the headline numbers look quite good, but we will analyse this data in much greater detail to see what is really going on. There is a full profit and loss account for Scarlet as an appendix to this chapter.

Superficial analysis suggests impressive growth of income and rising profit. Turnover is up by 21% year on year, and gross profit has increased by 23% in 2010 over 2009.

However, if we analyse the data graphically, the picture will look different.

As Figure 14.2 shows, headline income has increased by 21% year on year, but overheads are up by 29% in 2010 and 22% in 2012. This means that operating profit virtually stood still between 2013 and 2011 — far less impressive than the headline turnover increase.

If we 'common size' the data and express all the components of the profit and loss account as a percentage of income, we produce another picture (see Figure 14.3). We can immediately spot the rise in percentage of income accounted for by overheads and the consequent fall in percentage accounted for by operating profit.

Table 14.3 **Profit and loss account**

	2013	2012	2011
INCOME	1,380,000	1,140,000	940,000
DIRECT EXPENSES	565,000	475,000	350,000
GROSS PROFIT	815,000	665,000	590,000
TOTAL OVERHEAD	625,250	480,650	394,300
OPERATING PROFIT	189,750	184,350	195,700
INTEREST RECEIVABLE	4,500	4,300	2,750
OPERATING PROFIT BEFORE TAX	194,250	188,650	198,450
TAX ON PROFIT	38,850	37,730	39,690
PROFIT FOR THE FINANCIAL YEAR	155,400	150,920	158,760

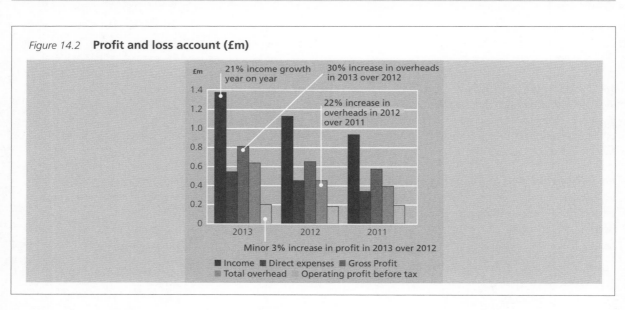

Figure 14.2 **Profit and loss account (£m)**

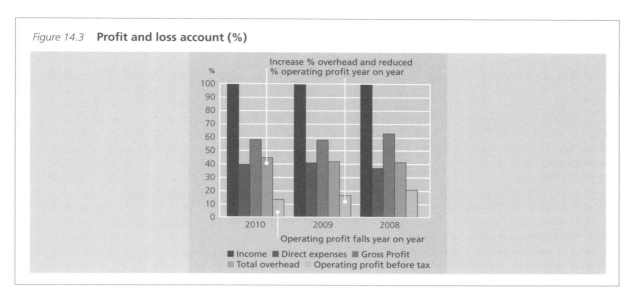

Figure 14.3 **Profit and loss account (%)**

3 Analyse the profit and loss account

A far better way to estimate business value is to analyse the financial data and seek clear answers to the questions this will pose. As with the drivers of value, you should apply this to your businesses as rigorously as you would to a potential acquisition.

The profit and loss account can be very revealing, and we will use the Scarlet Independent Financial Advisers case study to explain how this works.

This instantly raises the question, "Why have we seriously underperformed in terms of profit when turnover has been increasing so strongly year on year, and what should we do about it?"

In many businesses in many markets, the second part of the question is answered first. You must avoid this, because it means actions can be taken with little or no analysis.

The immediate reaction is to cut costs. Overheads have increased by a faster rate than income, so many firms would act to bring this back into line. This would bring the operating profit back to more respectable levels and the owners will be better rewarded.

But you have to get into the detail of why costs have increased and what action should follow, which may not mean cutting costs in the manner described above. You also need to look at income and the split between initial and recurring incomes to gain a different perspective.

3.1 Ask the difficult questions

Cost review

Analysis of the full profit and loss account for Scarlet Advisers in the appendix will show:

- A jump in salaries for support staff from £95,000 to £165,000.
- An increase in business acquisition costs:
  - Marketing up from £20,000 to £45,000.
  - Travel up from £14,000 to £40,000.
  - Entertaining up from £10,000 to £25,000.
  - Telephone up from £10,500 to £17,500.

It should also be noted that adviser remuneration is up from £140,000 to £225,000, although this is partly accounted for by the recruitment of an additional adviser toward the end of 2011.

Income review

As indicated above, the top line income has increased by 21% year on year, but the mix between initial and recurring has changed.

As Table 14.4 shows, the percentage of turnover accounted for by initial income has fallen, with recurring commissions and fees accounting for 35% of turnover in 2011. From a business value perspective, this appears impressive, because high recurring revenues tend to increase value.

However, you need to understand how much of the recurring income is fund-based and what effect stock market changes will have on the total. For example, if Scarlet's recurring income is mainly fund-based and the market rose by 25% in 2013, then only £94,000 of the total £125,000 increase would have been from the efforts of the business.

It is possible that the 35% of income that is earned before the year starts masks a less impressive performance for initial income, mainly linked to brand new clients. It is true that the recurring income requires service support, but an increase of only £75,000 in initial income appears lacklustre. You would need to ask the following:

Table 14.4

	2013		2012		2011	
	£m	% OF TOTAL	£m	% OF TOTAL	£m	% OF TOTAL
Initial income	0.9	65%	0.825	72%	0.75	80%
Recurring commissions plus fees	0.48	35%	0.315	28%	0.19	20%
Recurring commissions excluding fees	0.4	29%	0.275	24%	0.175	19%
Total income	**1.38**		**1.14**		**0.94**	

- Is this happening because there is a genuinely high level of servicing making a large claim on resources, thereby reducing advisers' ability to deal with brand new business and clients, which drives initial income?
- Is there a specific policy of keeping initial charges low to enable the build up of much higher recurring incomes?

To gain a clear understanding of this, you need to consider:

- The productivity of the advisers.
- The relative profitability of different client groups.
- How the support team spend their time.
- The components and cost of delivery of the service proposition.
- The charging structure for initial and ongoing service.

In terms of Scarlet's position, it is clear that a straightforward cost-cutting exercise may not be the answer. The more detailed analysis of the reasons for poor profitability suggests that the problem could be partly related to cost management but also linked to productivity, client values and the service proposition.

CASE STUDY

More haste, less speed

David Trathallan was head of the advice division of a large provincial accountancy practice. The practice had 15 offices across the south-west, and David had four advisers and seven support staff.

The advice division had been very profitable in the 1990s when it was set up, but the position had become less favourable as income had reduced on pensions business and operating costs had increased. As Frederick James, the senior partner, said to David, "Gone are the good old days when this was a bit of a cash cow for the partners; we have to work at this division just as much as all the others." David agreed and started to think about how they could increase their revenue.

David and the other advisers came up with the idea of a 'super-service' for high value clients. This would be proactively marketed in conjunction with the partners to a small number of key clients. They were very enthusiastic, and although they thought the service would be expensive to deliver, it was launched and supported with high value marketing materials and hospitality.

One year after the introduction of the service, there were 45 clients on the list, all receiving frequent contact and a dedicated, 'high touch' service, as David put it. David was pleased with progress, and expected to continue to attract new clients in the second year.

However, at the quarterly review meeting, Frederick had some tough questions. "We have got all these extra clients and the turnover is up, but not much, and our profits are down; something is not right!" David recognised the trends, but expected that client value would continue to rise and that the super-service would be profitable in the longer term. There was quite a heated discussion and David was instructed, in the nicest possible way, to investigate the potential for cost-cutting and to report at the

next monthly management meeting.

David was the largest producer and was always pressed for time. He had to trust his judgement, and he was slightly annoyed that it had been called into question. As he said to his wife, "I have got enough to do. I am sure this will come right, it just needs a bit of time".

As soon as he was able, David sat down with Charlotte Smith, his administration manager, to go through what was going on. In some ways, Charlotte was closer to the business than David, who spent a lot of time with clients and on business development. Charlotte said, "There are two parts to this issue: the clients are not as high value as we planned for, and the level of service is too costly — in effect, we are losing money on these clients, which is why the turnover is up, but Frederick's expression is depressed, because profit is falling!"

David very quickly realised that not only had they not costed the service properly, but they had two members of the support team working on a client group that was losing money. "We need to get to grips with this problem. I am not sure it is just about cutting costs — how will we provide the service if we do that?" he asked.

The plan that emerged was to redeploy one of the staff, because, given the current client numbers, one person could handle the service delivery. In addition, they decided to work much more closely with the partners to make sure their targeting was absolutely right. They had enough information about the clients to be far more rigorous. Finally, they worked out how they would approach clients who were unprofitable, either to increase their fee or recommend a lower level of service. David knew he would need to think very carefully about this, given the importance of the clients to other parts of the practice.

CASE STUDY KEY POINT

An initial review of the headline financial information can suggest a particular problem and related solution. You should always get into the detail and simply ask why the problem has occurred. Keep asking why until you know you have got to the root cause of the issue. It is only then that you can start to put things right, and it won't always be about simply cutting costs.

CASE STUDY

Scarlet Independent Financial Advisers Limited: Balance sheet

Table 14.5 **Balance sheet**

	2013	2012	2011
FIXED ASSETS			
Computer equipment	145,000	135,000	120,000
Office equipment	65,000	50,000	45,000
Depreciation	130,000	125,000	110,000
TOTAL NET FIXED ASSETS	80,000	60,000	55,000
CURRENT ASSETS			
Stocks (work in progress)	25,000	22,500	24,000
Trade Debtors	225,000	220,000	190,000
Other Debtors	12,000	3,500	4,500
Pre-payments and accrued income	35,000	25,000	22,000
Cash at bank	250,000	175,000	140,000
TOTAL CURRENT NET ASSETS	547,000	446,000	380,500
TOTAL ASSETS	627,000	506,000	435,500
CREDITORS (amounts falling due within one year):			
Bank loans and overdrafts	12,500	9,000	7,500
Trade creditors	40,000	35,000	32,500
Tax	85,000	77,500	62,500
Other creditors	35,000	33,000	26,000
Accruals and deferred income	45,000	42,500	38,000
TOTAL CREDITORS	217,500	197,000	166,500
NET CURRENT ASSETS	409,500	309,000	269,000
CAPITAL & RESERVES			
Equity shareholder funds	284,500	184,000	144,000
Long term debt	125,000	125,000	125,000
TOTAL CAPITAL & RESERVES	409,500	309,000	269,000

If you look at the large numbers and trends, they will tell you:

- There is a large pipeline of revenue and unpaid fees.
- The business is relatively sound financially, with cash in the bank.

- The capital and reserves line has been steadily growing, although it is supported by a mortgage of £125,000.

Should you accept this at face value?

4 Analyse the balance sheet

The second stage of financial analysis is to look in detail at the balance sheet. You need to recognise that this provides a snapshot at a given time, so potential buyers of your business will be as sceptical and questioning as you should be of a business you are thinking of acquiring. We will use Scarlet Ltd to show how this works.

4.1 Get under the skin

If you are considering acquisition or preparing your business for sale, analysis of the balance sheet is essential. In most cases, principals will want to present a successful business, so you need to adopt an enquiring and sceptical approach and recognise that possible buyers of your business will adopt the same stance.

The best analysis of this data will be based on industry benchmarks, other similar businesses and past trends.

Flexibility and working capital

First, you need to consider the liquidity of the business. You should look at the difference between current assets and current liabilities, which is known as working capital. You would expect the current assets to exceed the liabilities, which is the amount required to finance the day to day trading operations of the business.

$$\text{The working capital ratio} = \frac{\text{Current assets}}{\text{Current liabilities}}$$

$$\text{In the case of Scarlet, this ratio} = \frac{547,000}{217,500} = 2.5$$

This means that Scarlet has £2.50 in assets for every £1 liability: a healthy position. If the ratio falls below 1:1, there is a serious problem, because as time passes there will be insufficient assets to cover the short term commitments of the business. The business is effectively using money faster than it is generating it, which means that you must look closely at the cash position over time, including any cyclical factors.

This problem can occur when assets have been growing and are not funded properly. For example, when the markets are positive, it is tempting for firms to fund growth by increasing debt. It is not uncommon for advice businesses to use short term debt to fund longer term growth, on the assumption that they can increase the debt or roll it over into a longer time period.

However, if trading becomes difficult and there is little recurring income, the ability of the business to service or repay the debt will be limited. This means that when short term payments are required, such as the monthly payroll, the line of credit has been used.

The golden rule is to match the funding to the life of the asset. Long term assets should be funded by long term loans or equity, while short term assets can be funded through these plus current liabilities. Short term loans should only be used to smooth the short term mismatch between income and expenditure. As a seller, you need to have this correctly structured; as a buyer, you need to understand the detail of any loans, guarantees, restrictions and repayment conditions.

One of the major influences over this ratio is debt, which is normally affected by the speed of payments, including facilitated adviser charges, from providers and fund managers and the payment of fees by clients. The latter may reveal problems with the invoicing process, which means that if you are acquiring the business and have a more effective collection process, you will have an opportunity to enhance the value of your acquisition.

Management of debt

The second important measure is the debt to equity ratio.

$$\text{In the case of Scarlet, this it} = \frac{217,500}{284,500} = 0.76$$

This means that Scarlet has £0.76 worth of debt for each £1 of equity capital. Clearly, if the ratio rises above 1, remedial action is required, because the safety margin is deteriorating.

However, you need to pay particular attention to the following aspects of debt, including overdrafts:

- The specifics of any loan agreements, including terms and interest rates.
- Who is guaranteeing the debt and how that might be affected by an acquisition.

You should never use debt to fund losses, and should only borrow to acquire assets that will increase the productivity, growth and profitability of the business. If you are anticipating additional investment in the business, you should strongly consider retention of profits as opposed to making a call on the shareholders. In advice businesses, not everyone shares the same personal financial circumstances, which means the practicalities of this are often complicated and, depending on structure, can strain the partnership.

Finally, you should look at leases and rental agreements and understand the terms, including responsibility for dilapidations, particularly if you are acquiring a business and expect to vacate their premises. You should note that rates are payable on empty properties.

5 Chapter summary

This chapter has dealt with the major methods of valuing advice businesses, which work from the perspectives of buyers and sellers. Principals will often ask how to maximise the value of their business. The simple answer is to run it effectively using as much good business practice as possible. Such an approach will reflect the main value drivers, thereby increasing the attractiveness of the business to potential purchasers.

The financial statements are an excellent source of information, and should be scrutinised at least annually by you and your management team for any possible acquisition.

The management skills you have developed as a result of this chapter mean that you can:

- Recognise the main drivers of business value as being revenue, clients and people.
- Apply the value drivers to your business and to evaluate possible acquisitions.
- Manage your business to maximise sale value.
- Analyse financial accounts to quantify the strengths and weaknesses of an advice business.
- Break down financial data to understand what is really going on behind the headlines.

Appendix

Table 14.6 **Full profit and loss account for Scarlet Independent Financial Advisers Limited**

	2013	2012	2011
INCOME			
Initial commissions	£900,000	£825,000	£750,000
Recurring commissions	£400,000	£275,000	£175,000
Fees	£80,000	£40,000	£15,000
TOTAL INCOME	£1,380,000	£1,140,000	£940,000
DIRECT EXPENSES			
Adviser remuneration	£225,000	£180,000	£140,000
Directors' remuneration	£240,000	£220,000	£180,000
Directors' pension contributions	£100,000	£75,000	£30,000
TOTAL DIRECT EXPENSE	£565,000	£475,000	£350,000
% OF INCOME	**41**	**42**	**37**
GROSS PROFIT	£815,000	£665,000	£590,000
% OF INCOME	**59**	**58**	**63**
Wages and salaries	£165,000	£110,000	£95,000
Pensions	£5,000	£4,000	£3,500
Rent, rates, insurances	£85,000	£70,000	£60,000
Employers' NICs	£75,600	£61,200	£49,800
Postage, etc	£35,000	£17,000	£14,000
Travel and accommodation	£40,000	£23,000	£14,000
Advertising and marketing	£45,000	£35,000	£20,000
Entertaining	£25,000	£12,500	£10,000
Subscriptions	£5,000	£4,500	£3,500
Audit and accountancy	£25,000	£23,500	£22,500
Telephone	£17,500	£12,000	£10,500
Legal and professional fees	£9,500	£23,000	£7,500
Motor	£9,000	£9,000	£7,000
IT maintenance	£15,000	£12,500	£10,000
Heat, light and power	£5,500	£5,250	£5,000
Repairs, etc	£7,500	£6,000	£8,000
Equipment rental	£11,000	£9,500	£9,500
Training and recruitment	£23,000	£18,000	£9,500
Compensation	£150	£5,500	£15,000
Bank interest and charges	£1,500	£1,200	£2,500
Depreciation	£20,000	£18,000	£17,500
TOTAL OVERHEAD	£625,250	£480,650	£394,300
% OF INCOME	**45**	**42**	**42**
OPERATING PROFIT	£189,750	£184,350	£195,700
% OF INCOME	**14**	**16**	**21**

Chapter 15

Buying and selling advice businesses

By the end of this chapter, your business will benefit from:

✔ Deciding on organic growth or acquisition.
✔ Factoring in the personal ambitions of the principals.
✔ Management of the acquisition process.
✔ Dealing with due diligence.
✔ Identification of relevant sources of funds.
✔ Management of debt and equity.
✔ Considered sale and succession plan.
✔ Choosing the right legal structure.

Advice businesses adopt different positions when it comes to buying and selling. Some are very clear that acquiring other businesses, client banks or teams of advisers are central to their growth plans; others will take the opposite approach. The same applies with selling, because some businesses will be preparing to be sold from day one, whereas others will not think about it seriously until long after the succession plans should have been implemented.

There are many reasons for this, but one of the key ones is personal attitudes and ambitions. This will affect all the decisions that you take, but is likely to have a greater impact when it comes to buying and selling. This is not surprising, because these major decisions directly affect the future of the business, its people and its clients. However, you have to try to set the emotional and personal perspective to one side and deal with these issues in the context of what is right for the business.

1 Growing your business: policy, desire and availability of capital

Your approach to growth will be dominated by two factors:

• Attitude and policy toward organic growth or amalgamations: a mix of subjective views and deliberate policy.
• Access to funds: internal or external.

The significance of these is summarised in Figure 15.1 below.

You can see that your desire to grow will be constrained by availability of funds. However, you will also see that lack of funds should not prevent growth, although it may well be at a slower pace.

Proactive organic growth can be achieved by minimising some of the funding costs of growth. That means increasing adviser numbers using the self-employed model and buying books of business as opposed to whole businesses. You can also support growth through complete streamlining of your processes and financing purchase deals by using recurring income from the business books that have been acquired. So your rate of profit may be less (a likely consequence of adopting the self-employed model), but your dependence on external capital will be far lower. Finally, you have to adopt a very clear policy with regard to profit and the significance of building up capital through retained earnings to fund your growth. The only other internal route is to increase the capital contribution of the shareholders.

Proactive acquisition demonstrates a serious and planned strategy to substantially grow the business. If you adopt this approach, you should develop a detailed plan of action and engage external consultants to help identify potential targets, run the acquisition process and undertake due diligence. You will need to establish a funding policy and sources in advance, publicise your strategy and specifically devote a percentage of senior management time to the exercise.

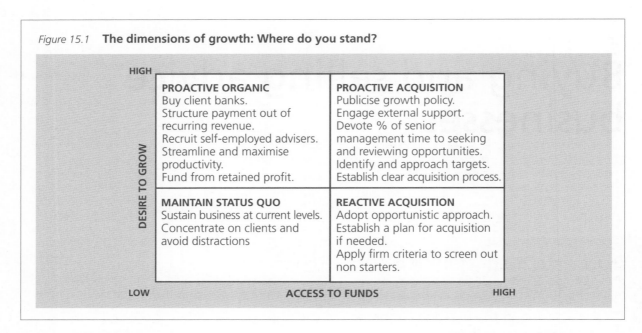

Figure 15.1 **The dimensions of growth: Where do you stand?**

HIGH

DESIRE TO GROW

PROACTIVE ORGANIC
Buy client banks.
Structure payment out of recurring revenue.
Recruit self-employed advisers.
Streamline and maximise productivity.
Fund from retained profit.

PROACTIVE ACQUISITION
Publicise growth policy.
Engage external support.
Devote % of senior management time to seeking and reviewing opportunities.
Identify and approach targets.
Establish clear acquisition process.

MAINTAIN STATUS QUO
Sustain business at current levels.
Concentrate on clients and avoid distractions

REACTIVE ACQUISITION
Adopt opportunistic approach.
Establish a plan for acquisition if needed.
Apply firm criteria to screen out non starters.

LOW   ACCESS TO FUNDS   HIGH

Reactive acquisition is often summarised as 'we never say never'. This is where the enthusiasm for amalgamation is low but, quite reasonably, you would be prepared to have an initial conversation rather than never entertain the idea of acquiring. In this case, you need to screen out non-starters as early as possible so that time is not wasted. Principals often get drawn into lengthy conversations or pre-negotiations that end up going nowhere. Sometimes the parties can only decide this after they have talked in detail, but many principals often reflect that the potential of a deal was highly unlikely from outset.

Maintaining the status quo will be right for some businesses. If the funding does not exist, the adoption of a conservative approach to acquisition is perfectly appropriate. This is particularly the case if the business is in good shape and is looking to sell out within a five year period. In those circumstances, entering into acquisitions and the associated funding may be quite wrong in the context of preparing the business for sale.

1.1 Is there an optimum size for the business?

The answer to this question is "Yes", but it depends on the business model, the range of clients, the mix of business and service levels. In broad terms, businesses with fewer than five people and a turnover as low as £250,000 can be cost-efficient and profitable, particularly if they operate in personal markets. To achieve the same degree of efficiency in corporate markets, you typically need at least ten people and a turnover in excess of £1m.

To identify optimum size, you need to think about:

- The effectiveness of your IT and how efficiently it is used.
- How much activity you want to outsource, and how efficiently you can manage it.

- Which parts of core activity you are willing to outsource (e.g. investment management, research, report writing, etc).
- How much time you have to undertake non-client facing activities (e.g. cultivating press relations takes a lot of time with no directly measurable return).
- Your personal desires and motivations, and those you have for the business.
- The profitability and value of the business.

Correct decisions on these issues will lead you toward the optimum size for your business. This is a mix of personal preference, delegation and clarity about what you really need under your direct control and what can be outsourced.

2 Work out your stance to growth

Because this is so fundamental, it is realistic to take two sets of criteria: your personal attitude to growth and the more specific business issues.

2.1 Where do you stand personally?

To test your own position on the question of organic growth or acquisition, answer the following questions:

- Are you happy with growing the business rapidly?
- Do you want to diversify the business?
- Are you comfortable to share management and ownership with more and different people?
- Can you devote less time to your clients?
- Are you happy to take external funding?
- Do you enjoy managing as opposed to advising?
- Do you have a clear vision for a larger business?
- Are you happy to take risks, sometimes with your own personal finances?

• Do you have experience of acquisitions?

Template 3.1 in Part 4 of the website lays this out as a formal questionnaire.

It is clear that, if you answered "Yes" to most of these questions, you are predisposed toward acquisitions. The more important point is that the issues raised in the questions are those which you have to think about if you are to acquire or be acquired. Incidentally, notice that we rarely use the term 'merger', because in practice this does not happen; one party will always be dominant.

2.2 Think about the relative merits of the two approaches

In addition to these important subjective issues, you should also consider the more objective advantages and disadvantages of organic growth or acquisition. These are summarised in Table 15.1.

As you can see, a very different management style will be needed in both cases, and a clear recognition that, if you decide to embark on the acquisition route, you will have far less time to devote to your clients.

Table 15.1

	ORGANIC	ACQUISITION
PACE OF GROWTH	Likely to be slower, and perception will be 'controlled growth'.	Could be rapid and will have some unexpected outcomes.
FUNDING	Requires retention of profit, but no/limited long term external debt.	Requires careful management of external debt, and ability of the business to service loans.
OWNERSHIP AND CONTROL	Little change.	Likely to be diluted: a smaller share of a larger business.
MANAGEMENT STYLE	Strength in running and refining an existing operation.	Strength in seeking new opportunities and integrating businesses.
CULTURE	Likely to be preserved (regardless of whether it is 'good' or 'bad').	Will change continuously, and the challenge will be to gain commitment of people to the new and evolving business.
CHANGE MANAGEMENT	Little pressure.	Important to devote time to this (see Chapter 24).

CASE STUDY

A one dimensional conversation

Phillipa Green from Green and Partners and Charles Peterson of Gold & Grey Financial Advisers were locked in negotiations to merge their businesses. Phillipa was in her early 50s and was looking to retire within five years, and Charles , who was ten years younger, wanted to grow the new business and sell it in the same time period.

They were determined that the financials of the new business would stack up and give them their exit as planned. "We need to build up the recurring income even further and keep a healthy initial income to demonstrate growth and support cash flow," said Phillipa. "Absolutely right," stated Charles , "and we need to go through the costs in great detail to see what we can cut so we look really good when the time comes!"

They looked at the current client charging structures, and decided that they would introduce a new tariff of charges across the new business at the earliest opportunity. They also planned to cut 10% of the combined staff of 23 and lose two advisers who had persistently underperformed. "We ought to think about moving to a single office and closing one; that would take out a chunk of costs, although it might alienate the staff involved," said Phillipa. Charles was less certain, because he feared the disruption, but as the two businesses had the same back office software, there was merit in complete integration of the two administration set-ups.

The day arrived when the deal was announced to all the advisers and staff. Phillipa and Charles made the announcement to their own staff in their own offices, and then Charles travelled to Phillipa's firm to meet his new colleagues. "We don't know much about Gold & Grey," said one of Phillipa's administrators. "They always seemed so different to us."

Phillipa and Charles then travelled to Gold & Grey, stopping at the Fox Inn for a celebratory lunch and to talk about their planned lives after exit.

Two months later, Phillipa and Charles decided that they needed to get on with the integration and organised a planning meeting for their senior staff. They decided to use an external facilitator to run the meeting, because they wanted to take part and move their agenda forward.

Lawrence Evans, the business consultant from Royal Blue Investment Group, was hard pressed to make the session work and draw out a plan. Both sets of people sat on opposite sides of the table, and it rapidly became clear that they had never met before. Only Phillipa and Charles were the common denominators. As Phillipa's administrator had remarked, the businesses were very different in the ways they worked, their client base, approach to service and charging, and their underlying values. It was obvious that none of these differences had been thought about when the two principals were working out the finances, and little real thought as to how the businesses would really work together and integrate.

At the end of the session, Lawrence said to Phillipa, "This is like two different businesses facing in different directions. Didn't you think about these wider issues when you were talking about the merger to see how this would really work — or not?"

There was no response.

CASE STUDY KEY POINT

It is clear that the financial position of two merging businesses must be analysed in great detail and that the new business should be viable with strong potential. It is not uncommon for merger discussions to get no further than the money, and, when the businesses actually come together, there is a mountain to climb to secure acceptance from the staff and make the new business work as a single entity. This is much harder if they are in separate locations and many of the working practices are different. You must look at all aspects of the business when in merger talks and not let the financials take over completely.

3 If you are buying, use a structured approach

If you have gone past the initial stages of shaping the deal and applying the value criteria and decide to move ahead, there are some important issues to consider. There are three categories:

* Confirmation of what you are purchasing.
* Final valuation and method of payment.
* The timing and process for amalgamating the businesses.

3.1 Be clear about what you are buying

As the case study showed, it is too easy to devote negotiation and planning to the financial issues and exclude other factors. At some point before you agree to go ahead and undertake due diligence, you have to step back and make sure you have asked the broader questions shown in Table 15.2 below.

Finally, you must take expert tax and legal advice throughout the process. This will add to the expense of the deal, but this is not the place to cut corners.

3.2 Be clear about method of payment

You are bound to have dealt with this in principle in the initial stages of the process. However, there is a point at which this should be confirmed in writing so that both parties are clear about what is to happen.

First, you need to agree on the basis of the valuation and then the method and timing of payment. There are no fixed answers, because these arrangements have to reflect the financial position of the two businesses and, in most instances, their principals.

The following examples cover most cases.

Example 1: Full integration of the businesses with the principals remaining with the new business

If the principals of the acquired business are all joining the new enlarged company, a large proportion of the payment for their business will be in equity. They should have standard contracts for their ongoing roles as directors and advisers. The equity share will incentivise them to integrate their business and work hard to grow the new company, and the adviser contract should play a similar role with regard to client retention.

Table 15.2 **Business purchase overview**

THE DEAL	• Am I buying the entire company or leaving some parts behind? • Can we structure the deal to leave liabilities behind? • Have we taken advice and understood the tax implications for all parties if this deal proceeds? • What are the risks that would negate the financial benefits of this deal? • Is the due diligence process capable of identifying all potential risks?
INFRASTRUCTURE	• What capabilities does the acquisition bring that my business does not have? • Can I manage across multiple sites if the business we are acquiring is to remain in its current location? • What are the genuine economies of scale that I am completely confident I can secure? • Am I clear about the IT infrastructure and how compatible it is with mine? • Does the firm have processes that we could benefit from, and vice versa?
PEOPLE AND MANAGEMENT	• Am I certain that the fit will work and we won't end up with two cultures that will destroy what is good about both businesses? • What commitments will I be taking on with regard to the advisers, the staff and the clients? • If key people are to leave within two or three years, what incentive is there for them to maximise their contribution? • Have we decided who does what in the new management team? • What is my plan for retaining key people? • If people are to be made redundant, will the responsibility lie with the existing owner and will this happen before the deal, or does it have to take place afterwards?
CLIENTS	• What is my plan for retaining the key clients? • What else could I do with the money? • What is the opportunity cost? • Do I have the time and capacity to make sure the key clients are fully integrated into my business? • Am I confident that the value that exists in the client base is sustainable? • What is the age profile of these clients? • If I cannot deal with the lower value clients, will I lose them, and what is the recurring income that they account for?

There may be a cash component to the payment, which is not likely to exceed 30% of the agreed value.

Example 2: Acquired business runs as free-standing unit with principals remaining

In cases where the principals are continuing to run their business as a free-standing operation within the parent company, the arrangements will differ. Payment will be in two parts, with a mix of cash and equity as an initial payment when the deal is struck (typically with the bias to equity), up to 50% of the agreed value. The remaining payment will be linked to the performance of the business over the following three years as an incentive to make the acquisition successful and ensure the parent pays no more or less for the stream of profit it has acquired. This payment is typically equity.

Example 3: Principals retire or leave the business

In circumstances where the principals of the acquired business are leaving, the arrangements should be different. They will typically include up to 50% of the value in cash as the deal is struck, with remainder paid over three years, ideally from the recurring income of the acquired clients.

3.3 Plan the integration

The financial arrangements should be dealt with as described above. The other dimension relates to how the businesses will come together.

It is essential that you think through the following list and use the project management techniques set out in Chapter 19 to implement the changes. It is very important to be clear about the eventual outcome and to concentrate on the tasks that are required to achieve it.

IT (hardware and software): This is one of the most challenging issues, but economies of scale are often associated with it. You should avoid running two systems with different software and processes, as this will inevitably raise the cost base. At the very least, you should migrate the key clients to the chosen system and start to work on streamlining the processes.

Premises: The full benefits of amalgamation will be derived if all the staff are located in one office. You can achieve efficiencies, but more importantly move everyone to a single culture and method of working. This will not happen if you have split sites. If you have not considered the importance of this, it is necessary to cost out a move to new premises that will hold everyone and take account of the management time involved in such a project. This should not be a deal breaker, but if it is a consequence of the deal, you must take it into account.

There may be geographic reasons for the business to be located on more than one site. If this is the case, think about the management issues and how you will bring people together as one business as opposed to two very separate parts.

People issues: Your aim must be a single set of contracts and terms and conditions, and you should take external advice on how to achieve this. If differences persist, they will prevent true amalgamation and create jealousies and other personnel issues until resolved. You need to think about the practicalities and cost of making these changes and proactively deal with them, recognising your TUPE responsibilities related to acquired staff.

Communication: You need to use the tools in Chapter 8 on marketing communications to prepare a plan to tell the staff and the clients. Take time over this, because for many this will be their first impressions of the new company. Staff can often tell if changes are likely, so you have to assume there will be a degree of uncertainty. The extent of the time and trouble you take over the initial communication and one to one follow ups will be reflected in how people respond.

Brand: This is an important part of client communications, because the majority of people will want to keep their adviser and the service they have become used to. If you plan to make changes, think carefully about how you will tell people. They won't be very interested in the new company for its own sake; as you would expect, they will be asking, "What does this mean for me?" Key clients should be spoken to personally, ideally before they hear about the changes from another source.

4 Due diligence

This process will cover many of the issues discussed in the previous sections. It is a critical part of the process for transferring ownership, particularly in the advice market, where the liability for incorrect advice can remain with individuals until death.

You should engage specialists to undertake this process if you are acquiring, and make sure you are well prepared if you are selling. Issues raised at this stage could have a direct bearing on the final price, so a buyer will be meticulous in searching for reasons to pay less, whereas a seller should use the process to prove the strength and robustness of the business.

We will structure the range of issues that can arise under due diligence as shown in Table 15.3 by using the drivers of value from Chapter 14.

A good due diligence report will:

- Identify any major areas for concern.
- Provide a realistic assessment of the past track record.
- Provide a realistic assessment of the future prospects.
- Identify areas for negotiation and possible deal breakers.

- Provide guidance on how best to achieve integration
  to maximise the value of the new business.

Table 15.3

CRITERIA	DUE DILIGENCE
FINANCIALS: REVENUE AND PROFIT GROWTH	• What are the long term trends for the key financial indicators? • Are any costs out of line with benchmarks? • Are revenues dependent on key advisers and clients? • What is the value of debt and how long is it outstanding? • What are the conditions and guarantees related to debt? • What is the cash flow and overdraft position over time? • How effective are the financial control and management processes? • What leases and rental agreements are in place, and what are the terms and conditions and guarantees (including premises)? • How effective is the invoicing process?
FINANCIALS: RECURRING REVENUE	• What is the mix between initial and recurring revenue? • What is the structure of recurring revenue? • What is the commitment to ongoing servicing implied by recurring revenue?
QUALITY OF MANAGEMENT, BUSINESS AND FINANCIAL PLANNING	• What are the experience and qualifications of the managers (that are remaining with the business)? • What are their reward structures and other terms and conditions? • What are the obligations regarding redundancy, early retirement, etc?
RISK MANAGEMENT AND COMPLIANCE REGIME	• What is the track record on FSA visits? • What issues were raised and what has been done? • What is the complaints record and are any complaints ongoing? • Are the outgoing principals taking responsibility for past advice? • Has the business sold a high proportion of products or funds regarded as medium or high risk? • Have external compliance consultants raised issues and what has been done? • Is there a process for compliant file management?
ADVISERS	• What are the experience and qualifications of the advisers? • What are the contractual obligations to advisers? • Do any advisers dominate the revenue stream? • How strong is their regulatory record? • Is their T & C up to date?
CLIENT BASE	• Are client records up to date? • Are clients segmented by value? • Are there any clients who dominate the revenue stream? • For fee-based clients, what is their payment record? • What is the service commitment to clients?
SOURCES OF BUSINESS	• What commitments exist to reward recommendations? • Are there any commitments to sponsorships, and what is their value and legal standing?
INFRASTRUCTURE, IT CAPABILITY AND STAFF	• How up to date and effective is the hardware configuration? • When was the hardware last upgraded? • What version of software is running and when was it last upgraded? • Are all essential records held on the main back office software, and are they up to date? • What is the range and quality of client data? • What are the terms and conditions of any outsourcing contracts? • What are the experience and qualifications of the staff? • What are the contractual obligations to staff?
BRAND AND REPUTATION	• Are there are any trademarks in place? • Does anyone else hold any rights over the brand name? • Have there been any legal or regulatory issues that have a negative influence on the brand?

5 Advisers

In the majority of cases, you should appoint external advisers (as a buyer or seller) to support you through the negotiation process and due diligence. For larger amalgamations, business consultants can support the integration process, including the necessary project management.

For buyers, professional advisers include brokers, who will search for potential acquisitions, while both buyers and sellers will need the support of accountants, lawyers and other specialists such as compliance, tax and property consultants.

6 How to fund growth

You need to consider the scale of funding that is required, the likely time period and the appropriate mix of debt and equity before approaching the various external sources of funds. In summary, you can either keep control of your business and borrow funds, or sell all or part of your stake but gain access to a much larger source of finance.

6.1 Where to raise finance

If you wish to retain full control, you should approach banks for a long term loan. At the other extreme, you can raise large sums by selling equity to venture capitalists, product providers or business angels, but clearly you lose control, partially or completely. Table 15.4 summarises the main differences between these.

In broad terms, there is a trade off between the scale of involvement and the funds raised. That is why you have to be very clear about how you intend to use the funds, because in many cases the financing of ambitious growth plans will involve some loss of control. Of course, selling a stake in your business to gain access to capital provides you with a return on the risks and hard work you have undertaken so far. You may well decide that in the long term a smaller stake in a larger business is what you desire; you have to be clear about this, because it will take you away from your clients and into business development and management.

Mezzanine finance, referred to in the Table, is provided by the corporate or business banking arms of commercial banks and some specialists. It is a long term loan with a higher rate of interest attached than a typical bank loan and, for the lender, carries a higher degree of risk.

The benefits of this type of finance are:

* You retain control.
* You do not have to give up equity, although some arrangements may involve turning the debt to equity

if the business performs particularly well.
* Avoidance of the greater pressures attached to the involvement of venture capitalists and business angels.
* It is cheaper than equity finance.

6.2 You must manage debt and equity

As we saw in Chapter 14, it is essential that you fund long term assets with long term loans (debt) or equity. You need to manage the debt to equity ratio with care, because the two types of finance carry different obligations.

Table 15.4 shows that **equity investors** expect a higher return because they are directly sharing the risk with you. Their aim is capital growth and to move on when they can realise their target return. **Providers of debt** wish to minimise risk, and to receive a defined return (interest) and a guarantee that their money is safe and will be repaid at a specific point.

Your policy on the mix of debt and equity will be determined by the following:

* The degree of risk attached to your plan: the greater the risk, the more you should use equity finance.
* The ability of your business to service the interest on loans: these payments have to be made regardless of business performance.

7 Selling your business

Advice businesses are sold for many reasons, but two stand out:

* As part of succession planning when the owners wish to retire.
* For owners to realise all or some of their business value and continue to work.

The options to sell include the following:

* Sell to a third party.
* Sell to the existing management team.
* Retain an ownership and income interest, with the latter related to managing a small number of key clients, business development or acting as chairman.
* Retain an ownership interest and relinquish all day to day responsibilities.

The first of these, selling to a third party, is often used for succession planning, but is also the main route for those who wish to continue to work in the business but extract some of the capital value. The remaining three typically feature as part of succession planning.

Each of these requires the business to be prepared for sale in the way described above. If you are seeking retirement,

Table 15.4 **Sources of finance**

	BANK	PRODUCT PROVIDER	VENTURE CAPITAL	BUSINESS ANGELS
SIZE OF STAKE	None	Can be up to 100%	Will typically require 20% or more	Wide range
ROLE	Lender	Owner	Investor	Investor — but may want to play a specific role
CONTROL	No change	Passes to new owner, and you will be subject to large firm processes and controls	No change	No change — but some like a high degree of involvement
BOARD REPRESENTATION	None	Yes	Yes	Most likely
TYPE OF FUNDING	Loan	Mix of shares and cash to purchase, followed by capital injection to fund growth	Equity stake	Equity stake
REQUIRED RETURN	% above base rate, determined by perceived degree of risk	Internal rate of return established by parent	Target ROR on investment will often be 30%+	Likely to be less than 20%, but personal objectives likely to play a part
SECURITY	Assets and/or personal guarantees	Not applicable	Strong business plan and management team	Belief in the current business owners
EXIT	Predetermined term	None unless business strategy changes	Typically no more than seven years and often less — can involve trade sale or (less likely) pubic offering	Typically four years
ADDITIONAL COMMENT	May be involved in mezzanine finance (see section 6.2)	Rarely provide capital injections: involvement is ownership. Your business can often be integrated with other similar acquisitions or sold to another parent if the strategy changes	VCs often raise finance from others; significant due diligence involved and deals typically take six months	Likely to have personal knowledge of the business and its sector — tend to prefer start-ups

the last thing you want to happen is to retain an interest and find that you have to return to work because you have not developed the business and people to cope without you.

7.1 Selling to third parties

Adopt this approach if you and the other owners wish to continue to grow the business and take out some of the capital value. Also use this route for succession planning if the management team cannot raise the funds to acquire the business.

If you are selling to a third party, you need to recognise that you will probably have to remain with the business for up to three years after it is sold. This will maximise the value to yourself and the buyer through the careful transition of the clients and key staff.

Indeed, if you are the main adviser, it may have been difficult to institutionalise the clients, so you may have to remain with the business for a time if you are to secure best value.

7.2 Selling to the existing management team

This is a popular means of extracting value and sustaining the business, and is very dependent on the development of the management team and its ability to fund the buy-out. In practice, there is often a general understanding between the principal and the potential purchasers, but in many cases the key dates and likely sums involved are discussed very late in the process.

You will know that it is not easy to name a retirement date for many personal and financial reasons. But that is what you have to do at least three years before you intend to retire. This gives the potential buyers time to arrange funding and, if needed, to secure the appropriate management training to take on a larger role. In the conversation at three years to retirement, you need to talk about the likely sum involved and agree the formula for setting it.

These discussions and subsequent arrangements have to be fair to all parties. That is why an independent valuation can be very useful and why, if you cannot be specific, you may want to give a range of dates and values, so that people have some clarity. There are many advice businesses that have suffered because the principal will not name the date and price of retirement. The problem is exacerbated if key staff leave, thereby reducing the value of the business and making it more difficult to survive without the principal.

A related approach is for partners to agree how they will arrange their joint succession plan. Ideally, they will agree that any partner who leaves will sell his part of the business to the others. This should include dates and formulae for agreeing the value, as with the management buy-out.

This works well if there is a reasonable age spread and the opportunity for others in the business to acquire a share as the founding partners retire. The business should be revalued annually so that everyone knows the position and can manage their personal circumstances appropriately.

In all these cases, a deal that enables the sale to be funded over three to five years will be much easier to transact. In reality, that is what you should plan for when establishing the succession plan.

7.3 Keep a proportion of ownership and income with or without day to day responsibilities

An alternative to a sell-out is to retain all or part of your ownership and take on a different role. This is often a consultancy type role related to strategy, business development or maintaining relationships with key clients. In some cases, former principals return to full time advising and the main reason they joined the profession many years before.

There are some important rules to consider if you plan to adopt this approach:

- Provide those who will manage the business on a day to day basis with the opportunity to buy all or part of the business: if they do not have a share of ownership, you will be very exposed if they leave.
- Make sure you stick to your new role: there is no going back.
- Work out a transition to the new role: on a personal level, recognise that this may not be easy, so make the change over a period of time.

For many principals, this is an effective way to move toward full retirement. It enables the gradual development of a different work/life balance, and means that responsibilities can be transferred in an orderly manner. This is particularly important with clients.

8 Don't postpone succession planning

You need to develop your succession plan many years in advance of your planned departure. This is because you must structure the business in a particular way to maximise value, provide time for existing managers to arrange their finances (if a buy-out is one of the options) and secure the position of the employees.

In many respects, running and building the business as described in this book is the foundation of an effective succession plan. As shown in Chapter 14, you have to 'institutionalise' your client relationships and secure your main staff, as these hold the key to business value, potential attraction to buyers and the realisation of your succession plan.

An aspect of succession management that is sometimes missed relates to agreements and protection. You should make sure that shareholder and partnership agreements are in place and that you have adequate shareholder and partner insurance. This applies as much to husband and wife partnerships as all others.

Succession planning is not only about financial arrangements; it is also about people. You have to develop people so that they can move into key management roles and take over your clients. Both of these can take some time, and you should allow at least three years for the careful transfer of clients from you to another adviser.

CASE STUDY

Will he ever retire?

Alun Philips, the owner of Cream Financial Consultants, was chairing the regular monthly management meeting. They were dealing with compliance and administrative issues and, in passing, he said, "I am getting too old for all this detail! I liked advising and, while this is important and we have to make sure it is right, I don't enjoy it."

His 'number two', Lynton Okumwe, had tactfully raised the issue of retirement with Alun in the past, and the subject was usually changed to clients or rugby and cricket. In fact, Alun's wife, Margaret, confided in Lynton that Alun did not want to give up and was "dreading the day he had to retire".

The difficulty was that Alun was 65 years old and had intimated that, "When the time is right, Lynton and the others will have first option to buy the business." This was deliberately vague on Alun's part, not because he wanted to make things difficult for Lynton, but because he really did not want to retire. Naming the day was just too final and a step too far.

Alun was no fool. He knew he had to deal with this, and decided to give it some serious thought when he was next on holiday. He wrestled with the problem: the business had been the centre of his life for over 35 years. How could it possibly survive without him? "He was the business, and the business was him," as one of his long-standing

clients said. At that point, a thought struck him. "I think I can unravel this. I have to put the business first. It will outlast me, and I am proud of what I have achieved. I don't want it to disappear – I owe that to the clients and the staff," he thought to himself.

On returning from holiday, Alun had a meeting with Lynton and told him what he had decided. "I will fix a date for two years time and give further thought to how I will actually retire," he said. Lynton and Alun knew that three others would be interested in buying a share, and they decided to obtain an external valuation to give them a starting point.

Alun thought quite hard about what life would be like in retirement, and decided that he would retain 30 top clients and work with them, passing the rest to Lynton over the two year period. He also decided to retain a 20% stake in the business, and take on the role of chairman as Lynton had suggested.

While this was not ideal, because Lynton and the others would have liked longer to arrange their financial affairs, the succession plan worked. At Alun's 'non-retirement' party, Lynton said, "This is a good arrangement; we can take a long term view for running the business, and Alun can continue to make a valuable contribution and deal with some key clients – it works for everyone!"

CASE STUDY KEY POINT

This scenario is not unusual, and neither is the 'happy ending'. The hard part for principals in this position is to name the day and work out what they will do afterwards. The issue for those waiting to take over is the lack of certainty, and frustration that they cannot move the business and their careers ahead in the way they would like. You need to avoid placing your key people in this position and yourself under increasing pressure to take an inevitable decision. The way into this is to put the business first, and that will usually lead you to the right answer.

Table 15.5 **Business structures**

	SOLE TRADER	PARTNERSHIP	LIMITED LIABILITY PARTNERSHIP	LIMITED COMPANY
OPERATION	Simple to set up and run, but owner is personally liable for debts and losses. There is some initial bureaucracy at start-up, and it may be costly to outsource.	Simple to set up and run, but partners personally liable for debts and losses. Partnership agreement required outlining terms between partners.	Simple to set up and run: liability is with the LLP up to the value of its assets. Carries same reporting requirements and operational onus as a limited company.	More complex, but owners have limited personal liability for debts and losses unless they engage in fraudulent activity. A PLC (public limited company) is listed on the stock exchange, and must have at least £50,000 of shares issued and at least 25% of the value must be paid for.
MANAGEMENT	Simple: owner takes all the decisions, which may be critical in the early days if funds are limited. However, there is no one to share ideas and problems.	More complex decision taking, but more people to share the issues and run the business.	More complex decision taking, but more people to share the issues and run the business.	Likely to employ professional managers, or principals devote some of their time to management activities.
SPECIFIC LEGAL ISSUES	Owner bears full legal consequences for any problems.	Partnership agreement essential to cover capital, profit share, salaries and decision taking. Responsibility is held jointly, which means that if a partner makes a mistake or goes bankrupt, the liability is shared.	Business is an entity in its own right: partnership agreement essential to cover capital, profit share, salaries and decision taking. Responsibility is held jointly, which means that if a partner makes a mistake, gives poor advice or goes bankrupt, the liability is shared.	Business is an entity in its own right, but directors are legally responsible for many issues.
ACCESS TO FUNDS	No access to outside funds: often involves borrowing from friends or family.	Access to external funds via partners and greater pool of initial resources.	Access to a wide range of external funds, but may still involve personal guarantees of the directors.	Access to full range of funds, but could involve personal guarantees of the directors.
TAX AND FINANCE	Reported on personal tax return: no need to have accounts audited or file financial information.	Reported on personal tax returns.	Business is separate entity: full accounts must be audited and filed for public access.	Business is separate entity, and some benefits deductible as business expense, notably pensions. In most cases, full accounts must be audited and filed for public access. Note that small indirectly regulated companies do not require an audit.
VALUE GROWTH	Limited by the scale and capacity of the business.	Larger scale and capacity should enable longer term value growth.	Larger scale and capacity should enable longer term value growth.	Significant potential.
BUSINESS CONTINUITY	Trading stops if owner is ill, and business dies with the owner.	Trading continues if one partner ill (although in practice a long illness can have a major impact), and business is dissolved when a partner dies. If a partner leaves, those remaining will have to buy his share.	Trading continues if one partner ill (although in practice a long illness can have a major impact). If a partner leaves, those remaining will have to buy his share.	Fewer issues with illness and holiday cover. The business survives death of founders and principals.

9.2 What you should do at start-up

When you set out the business plan for a new advice business, you need to think about the scale and scope of the operation and, in particular, how much funding will be required and where it will come from.

That will go a long way to deciding the legal structure. You should avoid any arrangements where your liability is unlimited. This is particularly important in a market where complaints are encouraged by the media, and retrospective reviews and legislation can increase the potential for the payment of compensation. There are many advice businesses that are partnerships without limited liability: if you are in this position, you should investigate a transfer to limited liability partnership (LLP) status at the earliest opportunity.

9.3 Think about some fundamental issues

At start-up, you must consider the following:

- Safeguarding personal assets.
- Protecting the position of your family in the event of illness or death.
- Minimising tax liabilities.
- Obtaining adequate finance to establish and grow the business through its early stages.

Trading as a limited company can help manage these issues, although there may be some drawbacks and additional costs. If you are unsure at the outset, you should start as a sole trader or partnership, particularly as tax legislation makes incorporation far less onerous than disincorporation. Any change in status has to be made in the light of:

- The individual's personal tax position.
- The prevailing and expected rates of personal and corporation tax (particularly related to small businesses).
- The treatment of any losses in the initial years of an unincorporated business.

9.4 You cannot avoid the bureaucracy

If you are setting up an incorporated business, you have to deal with the following:

- Memorandum of association:
  - Name of company.
  - Country of location.
  - Share capital.
- Articles of association, which are regulations governing the company: appointment of directors, share issue, etc.

When the registrar has accepted the documents and company name, a certificate of incorporation will be issued, which brings the company into existence.

Although it is possible to revert to an unincorporated business, there are usually substantial tax problems. This means that you need to consider incorporation with care, and remember that it provides for:

- Limited liability.
- Tax advantages.
- Wider access to finance.
- Larger contributions into pension schemes.

If you set up an **unincorporated** business, you will not have the advantages and administration outlined above, but start-up will be cheaper and your financial affairs will remain private. You should also note that many of the tax advantages from incorporation for small business were removed from April 2007, when the 0% corporation tax rate for small companies was abolished.

10 Chapter summary

This chapter is about major business decisions which do not arise very often, but are critical and very time consuming when they do. They range from the broad strategy of whether or not buying or selling is the correct course through to the detail of due diligence and negotiation.

As with many of the other specialist activities, you do not have to do all the work yourself. However, you do need to take responsibility for it and make sure that any outsourcing or senior management activity is of the highest quality. You can usually survive a series of poor marketing campaigns or even a poor recruitment decision, but failing to undertake succession planning or choosing the wrong business to amalgamate with can be far more damaging.

The management skills you have developed as a result of this chapter mean that you can:

- Decide if organic growth or acquisition is right for your business.
- Deal with your personal ambitions in the context of taking the right decision for the business.
- Manage the acquisition process.
- Deal with due diligence and use it to benefit your negotiating position.
- Evaluate relevant sources of funds.
- Manage debt and equity.
- Sell your business.
- Develop an effective succession plan.
- Choose the right legal structure and review it at the appropriate time.

Part 5: How to make your business more efficient

Using effective processes, IT and project control to manage your business

5

"Efficiency is doing things right; effectiveness is doing the right things."

Peter F Drucker

"Everything should be made as simple as possible, but no simpler."

Albert Einstein

Introduction: Efficiency cuts costs and improves service

When you have completed this Part, you will be able to:

✔ Review current business processes and information technology (IT) use.
✔ Identify opportunities for improvement.
✔ Design new and more efficient processes.
✔ Specify your IT requirements.
✔ Acquire the right IT for your business.
✔ Identify the relative benefits and costs of outsourcing.
✔ Select external suppliers.
✔ Set up projects for work outside 'business as usual'.
✔ Implement a method of continuous process improvement.

Ten years ago, processes and efficiency were rarely mentioned in the strategic plans of advice businesses. Right now, the opposite is the case, and firms that expect to grow will often deal with IT and process improvement before they recruit or acquire.

This Part is about the efficiency of your business, and covers what is often referred to as the 'back office', although this inevitably reaches out into wider areas. The processes that support the operation of advice businesses are generally uncomplicated, which means they can be cost effective at relatively low volumes of activity. This differs from manufactured goods, which need long production runs to secure economies of scale, and is one of the reasons why there are many efficient and profitable small- and medium-sized advice businesses.

To help you gain the advantages of effective operations, this Part will cover:

• The main business processes.
• Information technology.
• Outsourcing.
• Project management.

A majority of the examples are based on the processes and service related to personal clients. You will be able to adapt them for corporate clients, because the same principles and approach apply to both groups. Many of these principles and applications apply to all businesses, regardless of size.

How effective are your operations?

The Table that follows asks Ten Killer Questions about operations. These questions also summarise what is 'good' in cost effective and service-supporting operations in advice businesses.

For each question, give your business an objective score (1 is poor, and 10 is excellent) and ask others what they think. Use **Template 1.1 in Part 5 – How to Make Your Business More Efficient** on the website to circulate the questions.

If you have scored around 50%, you are close to the market average. A good score would be around 70%. After undertaking this exercise, many businesses find they particularly struggle with:

• Data management responsibilities: advisers often fail to collect or update data, and administrators sometimes adopt their own ways of entering data onto the back office software.
• Coverage of work: this is often because processes are not mapped out or there is lack of cross-training. Mapping the main processes is a very useful discipline, even if you have only two or three people in the business.
• Inclusion of advice and investments: for many businesses, the term 'process' only relates to the

CONTROL AND GROWTH: Ten killer questions

Score: 1 = poor, and 10 = excellent

To what extent:

1. Is the business efficient and well organised?

2. Do new joiners comment positively on the clarity of your processes?

3. Are processes closely linked to your main back office software?

4. Do you have clear processes which everybody sticks to?

5. Does everybody carry out their responsibilities for data gathering and data management?

6. Can others pick up 90% of the work of colleagues when they are away?

7. Does everyone share responsibility for making processes work well?

8. Do you include advice and investments as well as new business and commission accounting when you think 'process'?

9. Does one person have the responsibility for developing and maintaining effective operations?

10. Do you genuinely look for better ways of doing things and then implement them?

back office, and there are as many approaches to the advice and investment process as there are advisers. Failure to achieve a degree of consistency on these issues inhibits the extent to which the back office can maximise efficiency, and could place the business at TCF or compliance risk.

Many principals will readily admit that they are distant from back office processes. This is a fact of life in many cases because principals are often the main revenue producers and have the overall responsibility of running the business. There may not be enough time to get into the detail of how the back office works; also, this may not be the best use of principal's time. In these circumstances, they will often perceive that their back office works well when it does not, and will often 'fire fight' when a crisis occurs. To deal with this common circumstance, you have to delegate operations and pay as much attention to recruiting support staff and

operations managers or team leaders as you would for advisers. We will cover recruitment and support staff job descriptions in Part 6.

Finally, the benefits of sustaining effective processes are:

- Efficient, timely and accurate client service.
- Teamworking across the business, and particularly between administrators and advisers.
- Happier staff.
- Less wasted time.
- Lower costs.
- Best use of IT.
- Higher profit.
- Higher business value, making it easier to sell.

EFFECTIVE PROCESSES save time and money, and give you service that will be delivered consistently. Clients' service expectations will be met; they will stay with you and recommend you to others.

Chapter 16

The main business processes and Treating Customers Fairly

By the end of this chapter, your business will benefit from:

✔   Processes that are designed to enhance client service.
✔   Processes that encompass all major activities in the business.
✔   Processes that support Treating Customers Fairly (TCF).
✔   Well defined processes that use resources effectively.

All activity in the business must be designed to give clients the best advice, investment and service outcomes. To achieve this, you need to link operations management to service delivery and Treating Customers Fairly to make sure your business is organised as effectively as possible. The main processes should be directly linked to the customer journey, as shown in Figure 16.1.

The four stages are not equal in size, but provide a logical and manageable way to design, review and update the processes in an advice business. You should keep this as straightforward as possible and not over-engineer what can often be a common sense approach. That is not to underestimate the amount of work that can be involved or the attention to detail which is essential for effective process design and management.

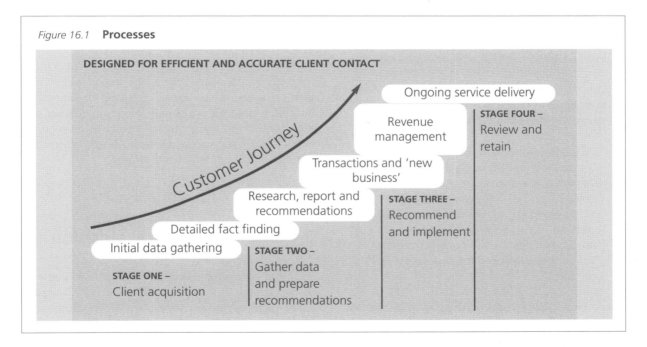

Figure 16.1 **Processes**

Stage One: Client acquisition

- Initial data gathering

Stage Two: Gather data and prepare recommendations

- Detailed fact find.
- Research, report and recommendations.

Stage Three: Recommend and implement

- Transactions and new business.
- Revenue management.

Stage Four: Review and retain

- Ongoing service delivery.

We will look at each of these stages in greater detail in this chapter.

1 Process encompasses everything you do

We should emphasise that processes mean much more than simply the work undertaken by the back office and the administration team, which many advice businesses fail to notice. There is often a lack of understanding between advisers and support staff, and a lack of recognition by advisers that their role in effective operation is just as critical as the support team. It is only when the processes are 'joined up' and everyone takes and shares responsibility that the competitive benefits of effective operations are realised.

To assess where your business currently stands, answer the following process assessment questions (set out as a questionnaire in **Template 1.2 in Part 5** of the website):

- Do you have a process manual?
- Is it used and regularly updated?
- Can you give an overview of your processes to new joiners?
- Would everyone in the business share the same overview?
- Are people's jobs organised around processes?
- Do you have an efficient and proactive process manager?

If you have answered positively to most of these questions, your processes are in good shape and you are in the top 10% of advice businesses. Most have a sound back office, but will be constrained by lack of time or capacity to seek and make improvements. In addition, many suffer from advisers operating in different ways, which prevents the support team from streamlining their activities.

2 Setting service standards

You need to decide on the timeliness and quality of the outputs of the processes we are going to describe. Service **standards** should be distinguished from service **content**.

Service content covers all the actions that you will take for a client, as listed in the service proposition. This is clearly stated in service agreements or in service brochures, and will vary in line with how much the client is paying for service. This is covered in detail in Part 2.

Service standards should be constant regardless of service content. To do otherwise would be extremely confusing for support staff and would overcomplicate service delivery. Service standards normally cover the following:

- Speed of answering the telephone.
- Time lapse for returning calls, e-mails, etc.
- Time lapse between asking for information and chasing.
- When to write to clients to give progress reports between main stages.
- Time between initial meeting and issue of report and recommendations.
- Time between report and recommendations and second meeting.
- Accuracy of communications.
- Quality of written and spoken English.

Businesses will differ on the standards which they set, and judgement needs to be made between when you think clients would want you to respond and what you can actually achieve given workloads and resources. Client needs should dominate your standards, and it is always very useful to ask them about this in a client survey.

For most advice businesses, there is no need to publish these standards — unless you are competing for corporate business, where these will be more important. However, you should publish and monitor these internally, because the extent to which you achieve standards will be another factor that influences your overall brand delivery.

3 Stage one: client acquisition

You might think this is so obvious that it does not need a process, but this stage is often forgotten or badly managed, which means that the beginning of client relationships can be ad hoc and inconsistent. Figure 16.2 provides a generic overview of the main actions that are required from the point at which a client is introduced to the business through to the first meeting. This is one way of running this process; you may have different preferences about the component parts and responsibilities. In this example, the processes owned by the support team are in the white boxes, while the advisers' are in the blue boxes.

Figure 16.2 **Client acquisition process**

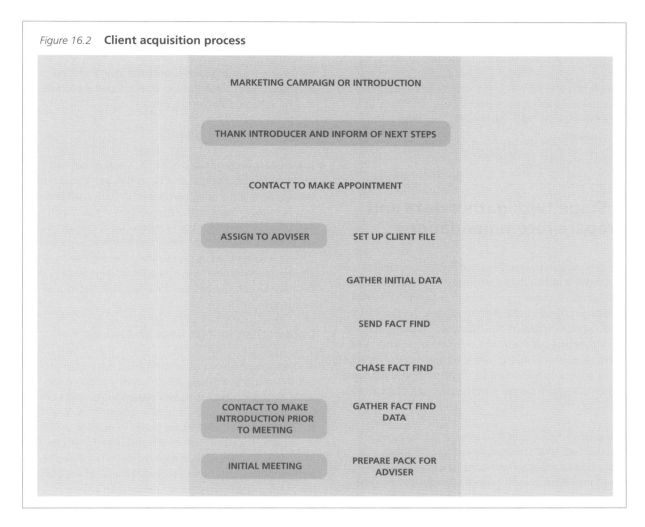

Marketing campaign or introduction

This process will normally begin with a client enquiry resulting from a marketing campaign, introduction or recommendation. You need to ensure that those who introduce or recommend clients are thanked and, with introducers, you should make clear what next steps you will be taking with their client.

Client contact to make an appointment

The aim of this contact is to identify what the client requires and which adviser will be most appropriate. For example, if the need is for a top-up to an ISA, then one of the junior advisers delivering your transactional service will be best suited. Alternatively, if the enquiry is about complex pension issues, then a more senior adviser with pension qualifications will be appropriate.

You need to decide who will make the initial contact to understand what is needed and gather basic personal details. Some advisers adopt a proactive approach at this stage to screen clients and inform them of charges and any minimum amounts that may be payable. If you decide to adopt this approach, it is often best if an adviser makes the call to be certain that both the decision and the guidance to the client are correct.

Set up the client file, gather data and prepare pack for adviser

You should ensure that client files are structured correctly and set up in the same way. There will be basic personal information (name, address, e-mail address, telephone number, etc) that can be gathered initially as the appointment is being made, followed by a letter that confirms the appointment containing a short fact find to support the adviser in the initial meeting. You need to judge how much information to gather at this stage, and at which point to chase if the material has not been returned.

The adviser pack should be prepared (see below) and issued to advisers at least two days before the meeting to make sure that the initial face to face contact is as successful as possible.

Finally, the adviser should call the client to make personal contact and introduce themselves prior to the meeting.

Supporting materials for this stage include:

- A form (or ideally fields on client screen) to capture initial data.
- A fact find — you may decide to send a short version and gather the rest of the information in the first meeting.
- A pack for the adviser, including all the regulatory

documents plus a pre-populated fact find, relevant service or corporate brochures and a risk questionnaire (unless you ask the client to complete it online).

Template 3.3 in Part 5 on the website lists these steps, with an additional column for responsibilities, which you should complete after you have checked that the steps are right for your business.

4 Stage two: gather data and prepare recommendations

This process covers everything that happens in the first meeting and before the second one. You will see that this example is based on a clear split between the adviser, who concentrates on client meetings, and the support team, who undertake all the analysis and report writing. In many businesses, the advisers undertake quite a lot of the technical work concerning the report and recommendations. This is often a combination of a desire to provide a bespoke client service from start to finish and the lack of back office resources.

You need to decide who does what, and to recognise that most advisers' strengths lie with client contact. Administrative tasks are an inappropriate and expensive use of their time. We will cover accountabilities and job descriptions in Part 6, on people.

Figure 16.3 deals with the adviser's responsibilities for the initial meeting. The initial meeting is the start of the advice process, and advisers have many different ways of conducting this meeting. However, the generic process outlined in Figure 16.3 contains all the important activities, starting with regulatory requirements.

Regulatory requirements

This is often a very formal part of the meeting, but it is extremely important because it clears the way for the rest of the process and the potential product or fund arrangements that will follow. Some advisers send some of this material in advance, while others prefer to talk clients through it at the meeting. The key outcome is that clients are aware of the major issues and points covered in the documents, and are encouraged to read them. You should also discuss the structure of your charges and the alternative methods of payment.

Data gathering: fact finds and risk profile

At this stage, the pre-populated fact find can be completed and the investment risk profiling analysis introduced (or reviewed if the client has already completed it). There are wide-ranging views on the different approaches to risk profiling, and it is clear that this needs to be done; most importantly, the client must be made aware of the role of risk in the development and implementation of their plan. It is often claimed that the educational benefits of risk profiling are of far greater value than the results themselves.

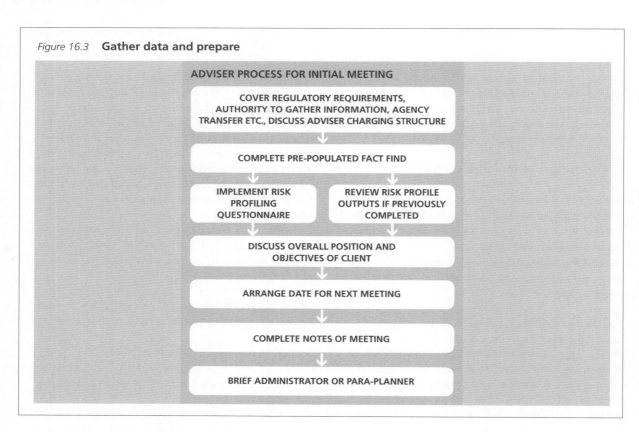

Figure 16.3 **Gather data and prepare**

Overall position and objective of clients

Much of this emerges and is discussed at the fact finding stage. The level of detail surrounding the current position and objectives depends on the complexity of the client's finances and the particular task that is required. An increasing number of advisers spend a lot of time at this stage getting behind the financial issues to understand what the client is trying to achieve. This lifestyle approach provides a very broad context within which the financial plan can be prepared, and, for many clients, this gives them the opportunity to discuss issues they have avoided in the past. It is a matter of judgement as to how useful this route will be, and a lot depends on the skills of the adviser, as well as the requirements of the client.

Next steps: dates and notes

Many advisers arrange the date for the next meeting at this point, and make any additional notes that are required for the client file.

Briefing the support team

The extent of briefing depends on the split of work between the adviser and the support team. In this generic model, we are assuming a clear split, with the adviser concentrating on client contact and the administrators and para-planners doing most of the analysis and report writing. Whatever you decide about the split, you need a process and the inevitable form or checklist to make sure that the support team receives clear guidance. A few quick words while rushing between meetings are not sufficient, particularly as what happens in the initial meeting needs to dovetail with the back office processes.

For experienced advisers, there is nothing new here, but there are some clear benefits from detailing how this works.

Benefits from mapping the initial meeting process:

- Advisers share between themselves the different ways they conduct the first meeting.
- Potential to identify a best practice approach.
- Opportunity to streamline without removing 'individuality'.
- Confirms how the handover to the support team takes place.
- Helps others in the business to understand what advisers do.

The next phase of gathering data and preparing recommendations passes to the support team (see Figure 16.4).

Template 3.4 in Part 5 of the website lists the steps for the initial meeting, including a column for specific responsibilities.

As you will know, there is a lot of work and technical expertise deployed at this stage, particularly with clients who have complex financial circumstances. There is even more detail that could be added, particularly relating to gathering information about existing products and funds (and the interim progress reports to the client, if necessary).

Receive brief from adviser and analyse position

As stated above, the brief needs to be clear and the fact find correctly completed to enable the support team to undertake the analysis of the client's current position. With

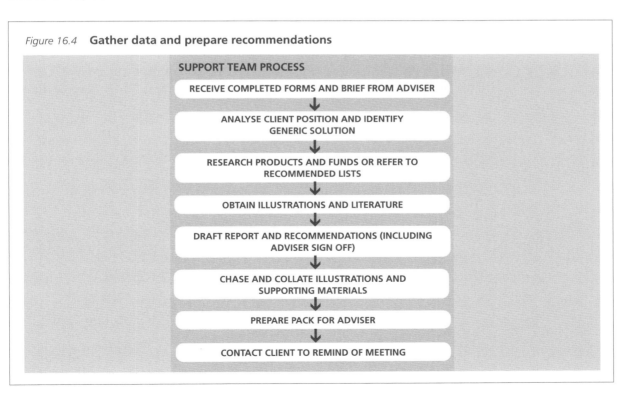

Figure 16.4 **Gather data and prepare recommendations**

SUPPORT TEAM PROCESS

RECEIVE COMPLETED FORMS AND BRIEF FROM ADVISER
↓
ANALYSE CLIENT POSITION AND IDENTIFY GENERIC SOLUTION
↓
RESEARCH PRODUCTS AND FUNDS OR REFER TO RECOMMENDED LISTS
↓
OBTAIN ILLUSTRATIONS AND LITERATURE
↓
DRAFT REPORT AND RECOMMENDATIONS (INCLUDING ADVISER SIGN OFF)
↓
CHASE AND COLLATE ILLUSTRATIONS AND SUPPORTING MATERIALS
↓
PREPARE PACK FOR ADVISER
↓
CONTACT CLIENT TO REMIND OF MEETING

transactional clients, the analysis and generic solution can be very straightforward, while in more complex cases this will require a high level of technical expertise and the use of bespoke software. This is especially so with the lifestyle approach, which typically involves lifetime cashflow analysis and the development of different scenarios to support the final plan.

Research products and funds, and obtain relevant information

There is a wide range of software and external services available to support this research activity. Many firms use online services or outsource research to make this stage as efficient as possible. This is also the stage that is supported by in-house processes related to best advice lists, investment policy and preferred fund choices. External technical advice services are important here to help with complex cases that arise infrequently.

Obtaining illustrations and literature is a key part of this stage, with a majority of what is required being available online.

Adviser pack and preparation for second meeting

As with the first meeting, an adviser pack should be prepared and checked and be ready for the adviser two days before the meeting. In addition, the client should be called to reconfirm the appointment. At this stage, some advisers prefer to send the recommendations ahead of the meeting; their decision depends on the client and how familiar they are with the financial planning process.

Managing client expectations on time scales is important at this stage, particularly if the date arranged for the second meeting has to be altered. This is why some advice businesses set the date during this stage, as opposed to doing so towards the end of the initial meeting. You should be guided by past experience and what works best for your business. The main consideration is to establish and agree a process, and then for everyone to stick to it.

The supporting materials for this stage include:

- Regulatory documents (e.g. CIDD, money laundering, terms of business, service and price agreement etc).
- Pre-populated fact find.
- Risk profiling questionnaire.
- Briefing checklist (adviser to support team).
- Report and recommendations template.

If you can standardise these, it will make the work of the support team much more straightforward and also make the adviser process more consistent without removing the individual approach.

Template 3.5 in Part 5 of the website lists these steps, with an additional column for responsibilities.

CASE STUDY

Advice process – guidelines or prescription?

Nisha Malhoutra is responsible for compliance at Maroon Insurance Services, which has 15 advisers and ten support staff. The business has been operating for 23 years, and is well established in its locality. It has always been a 'general practitioner' (GP) but has moved with the times, and some of the advisers have developed more specialist knowledge. Eric Hammond, one of the founding partners, says, "We have moved from knowing a little about a lot to knowing a lot about a lot."

As part of implementing adviser charging, Maroon is reviewing the advice process and the different ways in which the advisers operate. Nisha Malhoutra has spoken to all the advisers and has drawn up several flip charts to describe the different ways they work, particularly in the initial and second meetings at the start of the relationship. She also asked them what they offered for ongoing service and how they dealt with payment for this.

Eric Hammond invited the advisers to a workshop, which had two main objectives: to identify good practice that worked well, and to decide how they should streamline what they do. As Eric said, "Right now, we do lots of good things with clients, but these are often very different, even with the same types of client. If we had a visit from the FSA, I am not sure that we could explain these differences in treatment."

Eric knew that this would be a lively meeting, because it was getting to the heart of how the advisers worked and what had stood them in good stead for many years. Alan Walters, who had been a successful adviser for 20 years, said, "Surely if we document what we are going to do for the client and what we will charge, that will be sufficient; they know what they will get and how much it will cost." Angela Little was not so sure: "Despite that, it is only half the job. We could still end up doing different things, and in particular offering wide variations in

ongoing service; how can we expect our support staff to cope with that?"

Nisha said that the support team had bent their processes to suit individual advisers, and that they effectively had as many processes for certain tasks as they had advisers. They had different fact finds and risk profiling processes, and presented the information back to the administrators in many different ways. "Sorting out workload and cover, especially holidays, is really difficult, because no one can easily pick up someone else's work."

Eric knew that he should not seek detailed solutions in this meeting, but that the problem had to be faced head-on and that everyone had to be involved in finding the answer. There was broad agreement that the current situation was not the best way to operate, but genuinely different views prevailed as to how the business should move forward.

Alan said, "We all recognise that it is good business practice if we are consistent; it is better for clients, and I can see that it will help the support team. Why don't we ask three or four advisers to work out a process for these initial meetings, and pilot it for a month to see how it works?"

Eric thought this was a positive outcome and, despite not getting as far as he wanted, he recognised that this was complex. It was better to take this in stages and gain the support and confidence of the advisers, rather than try to move more quickly but potentially fail.

As is often the case, the pilot with the small team worked and, with some changes, it was adopted across all the advisers. As Angela said, "This has given us a good track to run on, and in practice I don't think we were ever quite as far apart as we thought." At this stage, Maroon moved on to sorting out the next tricky issue: ongoing service.

CASE STUDY KEY POINT

Many advice businesses have held meetings like this, because they have recognised that greater consistency is better for clients, works well for the back office and reduces business risk. There is often much common ground and the use of a pilot can work well to 'prove the case' to those who need to be re-assured that a new way of working will be right for them.

5 Stage three: recommend and implement

This stage concentrates on the second client meeting and the administration processes that follow. As with the previous stage, this example is based on a clear distinction between the responsibilities of the adviser and the support team. The adviser responsibilities are summarised in Figure 16.5.

Review report and recommendations

For some clients, the review of the *report and recommendations* can be a lengthy process. This depends on the complexity of the plan and the extent to which the client is interested in the detail. As many advisers will testify, some clients will ask, "Can you tell me what to do and what to sign?" In any event, advisers have to be completely satisfied that clients understand the *suitability of the recommendations* and how they fit in with their circumstances and *risk profile*. An increasing number of advisers request that clients sign to confirm that they understand the recommendations and the associated detail.

Secure client agreement

As indicated above, this is part of the report review and moves the meeting into the implementation stage. It is important that service recommendations are confirmed at this stage, because, for many clients, the level of ongoing service is just as important as the product or fund recommendations.

These steps are set out in **Template 3.6 in Part 5** of the website with an additional column for responsibilities.

Brief support team and next steps

The final part of this stage is to brief the support team on the next actions. The clarity of this brief should be at the same high standard as that which followed the initial meeting, so that implementation can move forward. It is also necessary to contact the client to confirm next actions, particularly if there are a number of things that need to happen.

The benefits of outlining this process are the same as the initial meeting: it aids understanding, and enables advisers to discuss best practice and to achieve the consistency required to deliver the brand in a unified manner. It also allows administrators to operate streamlined processes.

The process for the support team is summarised in Figure 16.6.

Receive forms and brief from adviser, and update client file

Provided that all the additional information has been collected, the client file can be updated and the service level indicated. This will enable the appropriate level of service and contact to take place, and ensure that the annual review (if appropriate) is signalled well in advance.

If the client is not proceeding, then an invoice should be issued for the work undertaken to date. This will be easier (and is more likely to be paid) if you have minimum charges clearly shown in the terms of business and cover this in the initial meeting.

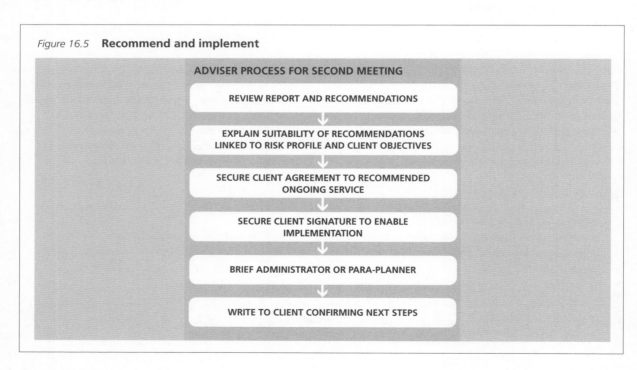

Figure 16.5 **Recommend and implement**

ADVISER PROCESS FOR SECOND MEETING

REVIEW REPORT AND RECOMMENDATIONS

EXPLAIN SUITABILITY OF RECOMMENDATIONS LINKED TO RISK PROFILE AND CLIENT OBJECTIVES

SECURE CLIENT AGREEMENT TO RECOMMENDED ONGOING SERVICE

SECURE CLIENT SIGNATURE TO ENABLE IMPLEMENTATION

BRIEF ADMINISTRATOR OR PARA-PLANNER

WRITE TO CLIENT CONFIRMING NEXT STEPS

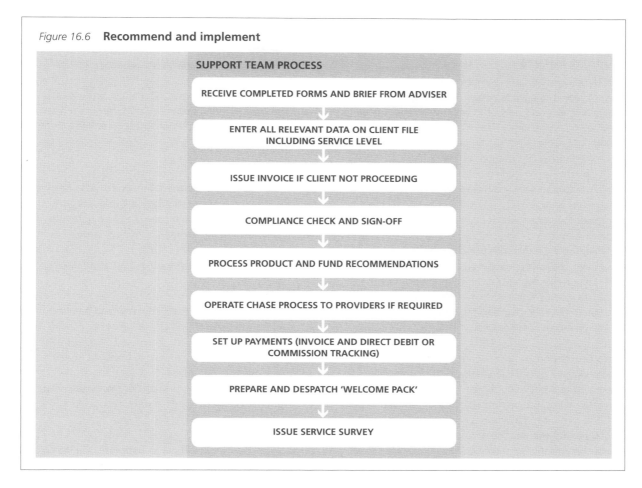

Figure 16.6 **Recommend and implement**

SUPPORT TEAM PROCESS

RECEIVE COMPLETED FORMS AND BRIEF FROM ADVISER

ENTER ALL RELEVANT DATA ON CLIENT FILE INCLUDING SERVICE LEVEL

ISSUE INVOICE IF CLIENT NOT PROCEEDING

COMPLIANCE CHECK AND SIGN-OFF

PROCESS PRODUCT AND FUND RECOMMENDATIONS

OPERATE CHASE PROCESS TO PROVIDERS IF REQUIRED

SET UP PAYMENTS (INVOICE AND DIRECT DEBIT OR COMMISSION TRACKING)

PREPARE AND DESPATCH 'WELCOME PACK'

ISSUE SERVICE SURVEY

Compliance check and recommendation processing

The compliance check must take place before anything is implemented, in case changes are needed. Most processing takes place online, either direct with providers or through portals and platforms.

Payment process

The method of payment will have been agreed with the client at the recommendation stage. This should be set up for revenue tracking or invoicing, depending on the way the client agrees to pay for the service.

'Welcome pack' and service survey

'Welcome pack' is a generic term to denote the need to send all the relevant documents to clients with a covering letter to thank them for their business, inform them that a service survey will be following, and remind them of the next steps in their service agreement (which may well be the annual valuation and meeting in 12 months' time).

The supporting materials for this stage are:

- Report and recommendations.
- Product and fund application forms.
- Product and fund supporting literature and KFDs.
- Service agreement.
- Compliance checklist.
- 'Welcome letter'.
- Service survey.

As with the previous stages, you will find these steps listed in **Template 3.7 in Part 5** of the website with an additional column for responsibilities.

FOCUS POINT

Client survey

Client surveys can provide a very useful perspective on the quality of advice and service. To work well, surveys need to be:

- Short (up to 20 questions or statements).
- Objective – no leading questions.
- Easy to complete – offering clear tick box choices works well.
- Easy to return – either online or with reply-paid envelope.
- Sent to a random selection of clients who have been dealt with over the past 12 months – ask the compliance manager to make this selection.
- Supported with a short covering letter from the principal, which explains the purpose of the survey and emphasises confidentiality.

In practice, response rates vary but can normally be increased if you offer £1 to charity for each completed questionnaire. Ideally, you should aim for at least 100 responses, which will be statistically robust enough to base conclusions on. Most businesses send out between 300 and 500 to achieve this rate of response. An alternative approach is to send the survey at the end of stage three (recommendation and implementation). This provides you with a regular overview of client perceptions, as well as building up a comprehensive set of data.

It is important that you do not include the survey with any sales or lead-generating material; it must be seen for what it is, a genuine desire to find out what clients think of the service they receive.

You need to think about the ease with which you can collate the results. For example, tick box answers work well, because they can easily be recorded into a spreadsheet which, once it is set up, can be used in 12 or 18 months' time if you repeat the exercise.

The benefits of running service surveys are listed below.

- At the business level, you can track client responses on a regular basis and detect any emerging patterns.
- At the adviser level, you can use the responses in advisers' personal development and T & C activities.
- Client retention – clients like to be asked for their views about the business.
- TCF – this is an important part of the management information requirement to support ongoing TCF management.

A typical client survey is laid out in **Template 5 in Part 5** on the website. You will see that it conforms to the guidelines listed above. It has been used with many advice businesses, so you can be confident that it will work.

6 Stage four: review and retain

This stage deals with the active clients for whom the business has agreed to provide ongoing service. Part 2 (on service) contained examples of this, with the main differences being frequency of face to face meetings and management of investments. The process outlined in Figure 16.7 reflects this approach, with the adviser's responsibilities in the white boxes and those of the support team in the blue boxes.

This stage is driven by the service level from the previous stage, which generates the monthly review lists and starts the process.

Prepare monthly review list and valuations

The *monthly review lists* should be prepared well in advance of the anniversary dates to give the advisers time to decide what action to take and, if necessary, to contact the client. The lists should indicate the agreed service level, and, in cases where valuation is part of the agreement, this should be prepared. At this stage, automation of the process is vital, particularly for the preparation of valuations, for which a wide range of online services exist.

Review client file and decide on action

The advisers have a key role, which is to *review the client file* and valuation, and decide on one of three approaches:

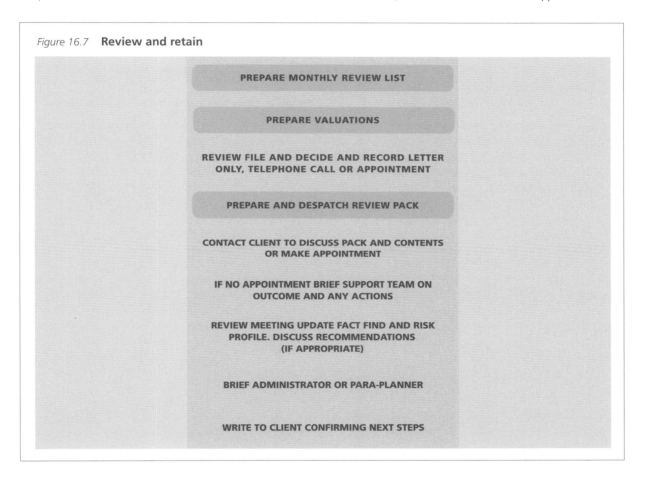

Figure 16.7 **Review and retain**

PREPARE MONTHLY REVIEW LIST

PREPARE VALUATIONS

REVIEW FILE AND DECIDE AND RECORD LETTER ONLY, TELEPHONE CALL OR APPOINTMENT

PREPARE AND DESPATCH REVIEW PACK

CONTACT CLIENT TO DISCUSS PACK AND CONTENTS OR MAKE APPOINTMENT

IF NO APPOINTMENT BRIEF SUPPORT TEAM ON OUTCOME AND ANY ACTIONS

REVIEW MEETING UPDATE FACT FIND AND RISK PROFILE. DISCUSS RECOMMENDATIONS (IF APPROPRIATE)

BRIEF ADMINISTRATOR OR PARA-PLANNER

WRITE TO CLIENT CONFIRMING NEXT STEPS

- To issue the review pack with a covering letter asking the client to call if they wish to discuss their circumstances.
- To issue the pack and follow up with a telephone call to talk through the contents.
- To issue the pack and make contact with the aim of securing a face to face meeting.

It is essential that the adviser *records the decision* and outcome, because this is an essential part of the management information for ongoing service delivery required for TCF monitoring.

The adviser must decide which of the routes to follow. The decision will be based on:

- The service level that the client is paying for.
- The complexity of the client's financial circumstances.
- When the client was last contacted and seen face to face.
- The length of time before an important life stage change (e.g. retirement) or product maturity.

Only the adviser who deals with the client can make this judgement, although if service has been correctly set up and the client is paying (either by direct debit or through the product or funds), then the meeting or telephone call should automatically take place.

Despatch review pack and make contact

For clients that are being seen face to face or telephoned, a *review pack* will be required. This normally includes the valuation, and often a letter outlining any changes that are recommended. If a *review meeting* is to be held, the changes and actions may be more significant and the implementation process initiated from stage three.

The materials required for this stage include:

- A pre-populated fact find.
- A valuation template.
- Covering letter templates.

Template 3.8 in Part 5 of the website is set out for you to complete for your business.

CASE STUDY

"So that's what TCF is about!"

Nisha Malhoutra, the compliance manager at Maroon Insurance Services, has been asked to 'run the TCF process' and, despite her best attempts over several years, she has failed to capture the attention of the senior partners and advisers. They all state their support for TCF, but nothing has changed and the business would not fare well if telephoned or visited by the FSA team that reviews TCF.

Nisha was aware of the range of TCF support offered by product providers, and asked her account manager from Royal Blue Investment Group if they could help. They recommended re-running a formal gap analysis to benchmark where Maroon stood in terms of TCF, which involved two surveys: one for the staff and another for clients.

To her surprise, Eric Hammond agreed to run the surveys, and he accepted that a properly designed survey would give them a good indication of what clients thought of the service from Maroon. He checked with the PI insurers that the survey was not constructed in a way that would invite complaints, and it was sent to 300 clients who had dealt with Maroon in the previous 12 months. Maroon offered a charity donation for each completed survey, and 123 were returned.

The staff survey was completed by everybody. It was split into two, with the first part covering the same areas as the client survey and the second dealing with the internal processes designed to support service.

All of the results were analysed and formed the basis for a workshop involving a wide cross section of advisers and support staff. A business consultant from Royal Blue ran the workshop to enable everyone to participate fully and to keep the conversation on track.

There was a fair degree of overlap in the survey findings. In general, the client responses were very favourable. Lawrence Evans from Royal Blue said, "It is nearly always the case that client surveys give good results, but let's make sure we pick up anything that is not quite at the highest standard." There were three specific areas: timeliness of ongoing service, clarity of the cost of advice, and being kept up to date with the value of investments and other changes.

The internal survey, which typically gave the business lower scores, mirrored these findings. As Eric said, "This tells us what we have known for ages: we are not good at ongoing service, our processes for supporting it are not robust, and the advisers tend to do their own thing." As Nisha said, "For the most part, we do a good job; we have virtually no complaints about service, although we do rush around behind the scenes far too often for my liking."

The debate continued to the point where Lawrence asked the group to identify the priority issues that the TCF surveys had raised, and which Maroon would need to do something about. The combined view was unanimous: service and pricing needed to be sorted out. To Nisha's relief, Eric said, "Now I understand what TCF is really about and how it links with RDR: sorting out a clear service and pricing proposition and delivering it to our clients consistently."

Everyone recognised that this was a major task, but the TCF log-jam had been broken, and the business moved on to working out what their service proposition would be and how they would make sure the processes supported its delivery.

CASE STUDY KEY POINT

Many advice businesses have identified service, pricing and supporting processes as the most important things they need to deal with following the initial start-up of TCF. This shows the link between TCF, service and advice and back office processes. If you get the processes right, you are likely to get the outputs right.

7 Use TCF techniques to review and improve business processes

This section is about using the best practice techniques from TCF to support process improvement. The issues that arise when using this approach are often very similar to those revealed by a 'strengths and weaknesses' analysis. Advice businesses often observe that their back offices are inefficient and need updating. This inefficiency is characterised by:

- Different advisers and administrators operating according to their own methods.
- No process for showing new joiners what to do.
- Re-keying of data into different software packages.
- Lack of use of IT and online services.
- Struggling to meet client service deadlines.
- Reworking of analyses and persistent inaccuracies.

If your business suffers from these problems, it is not alone. Many businesses in financial services experience these issues to differing degrees, and there will often be some inefficiency that you may live with because the cost and disruption of solving it is so great.

However, there is a point when a full review is required, and in recent years this has been triggered by the implementation of TCF and the need to formally design service arising from RDR. This is because TCF and RDR have led many advice businesses to review their service proposition and the way it is delivered. Inevitably, process issues have come to the fore.

The TCF process contains many examples and applications of good business practice. It is not the purpose of this section to deal with TCF implementation, but to take some of its tools and techniques and apply them to process review and redesign.

7.1 Linking service and Treating Customers Fairly

The most effective TCF plans are based on the journey experienced by the client. This is because they concentrate on the outcomes of service delivery and the processes that support them. For example, a client survey that covers the main elements of service – from the initial meeting through to advice, recommendations and ongoing service – will provide a clear indication of whether or not the processes are set up correctly and are being delivered properly. An example client survey is contained in **Template 5 in Part 5** of the website. Indeed, you should not forget the role of people, because it is a combination of effective processes and well trained, competent people that will provide the best outcomes. We will return to people in Part 6.

7.2 How to improve processes

The objective is to make a material improvement in the efficiency of the process that is failing. A good process manager can often step back and identify the problems and the solutions, but will need to work with the people involved to make the change. You should work with those involved, because they will be able to identify all the issues, the best way of working and whether or not a revised approach will bring benefits. Harnessing this knowledge and experience is very useful, as well as achieving staff acceptance.

Figure 16.8 summarises the method of reviewing and improving processes. You should be clear about what the desired outcome of the process in question is. For example, if you ask people to define the outcome of the new business application process, you may get a range of answers:

- To get paid as quickly as possible.
- To deliver service within an agreed time scale.
- To make sure the product and fund data held on the software is as accurate as possible.
- To achieve the monthly target and the associated bonus.

All of these are important and sometimes it is not possible to identify one single outcome. A question that is often posed is. "What does 'good' look like?" It is a clumsy expression, but it helps us to concentrate on achieving the best outcome. For the new business process, that may be:

- Completing a key stage in the client service process in an accurate and timely manner.

The result of this would be:

- Client satisfaction.
- Contribution to business targets and adviser remuneration.

The reason for making this process as effective as possible then becomes much clearer: deliver effective service and this makes us and our clients happier. The review should concentrate on the outcome, with incentives for all those involved of some clear client and personal benefits. The latter is very important, because it is a further way of gaining co-operation and support when changes are being made.

Working through the six steps makes sure that everyone is involved and that the various ways of achieving the end point are reviewed. It is nearly always the case that a 'best practice' approach will emerge, and human nature ensures that all the possible barriers will be unearthed and discussed.

Mapping the new process should be undertaken by the person charged with the review. This should always be presented as a draft and brought to a meeting of all those involved. That way, any remaining issues and possible improvements can be accounted for.

If the process is complex and you cannot achieve full acceptance, it is perfectly reasonable to pilot the new process for a time period. At least one month (and often three months) works well. As long as you take regular feedback on how the pilot is working, you can usually make

Figure 16.8 **Six steps to process improvement**

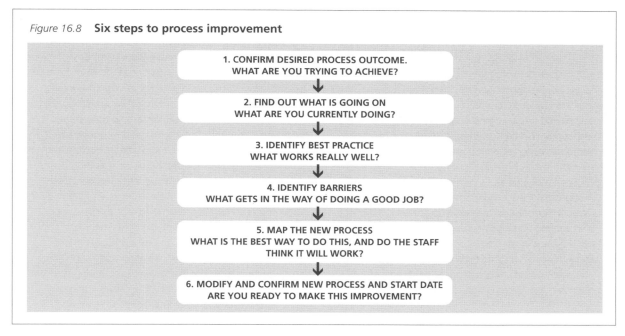

any further changes if needed and secure the support of any remaining doubters.

If you have several processes that require improvement, you will need to prioritise the order of review. In practice, processes often overlap or are interdependent, but you have to work out where to start and, if necessary, break the current set of behaviours and actions. It is never advisable to make more than one change at a time, particularly if software change or development is involved.

The following questions help deal with the complexity of process change prioritisation:

- Is there a compliance risk and how significant is it?
- How important is the process?
- Is this a low cost change?
- Is there an obvious revenue benefit from making the change?
- Is this easy to fix?
- How much will it disrupt the day to day business?
- Do we have to get this process right before we can deal with others?

Examples are included as to how to set this up in **Templates 3.1 and 3.2 in Part 5** on the website.

7.3 Keep improving

The phrase 'a culture of continuous improvement' is heard many more times than it is successful. You would not argue against the intention, but securing it in practice is difficult. There are some businesses that encourage people to speak out when processes need updating, but in many instances, if life is busy and the process has not completely failed, people struggle on. They make do with an inadequate process that works, even when they know there are better ways of achieving the same result. Inertia and time pressure are the greatest enemies of process review and redesign. The danger is that time passes quickly and processes can become out of date or unproductive with nobody noticing or taking responsibility for instigating change.

You have to break this cycle, and an annual process audit is one method. This does not mean that all changes have to wait until the meeting. However, it is the one point in the year — ideally not one of the business peaks — when the administrators and advisers (or a sample of each, depending on the size of the business) meet to review business efficiency. The reason for involving many of the staff is because they know what works and what does not, and they have to be involved in any improvement project.

CASE STUDY

"How should we look after clients' money?"

As Maroon Insurance Services continued their work on TCF implementation and service design, they arrived at the complex issue of finding the best approach for investing clients' money. Nisha Malhoutra observed that there were "several different methods being used, and that this made the audit trail difficult to manage." Eric Hammond, the principal, was worried that advisers were taking investment decisions independently of each other, and that one could be advising clients to move into a particular fund or sector while another was doing the opposite. "The problem is that we don't really know what is happening, and that makes me nervous — we are running a risk at the moment."

The debate between the advisers and para-planners was as lively and polarised as the debate on service. During the latter, they had agreed to use the same approach to risk profiling, which was an important first step in dealing with investment.

Some of the advisers who worked mainly on investment products and funds felt that their experience was sufficient to make sound decisions. Others, who were less experienced, wanted some guidance — and ideally something more formal than just talking to their investment colleagues. The debate moved on to compare the merits of an in-house investment committee with formal responsibilities and meetings, and then to consider outsourcing the complete exercise to an external investment business. Eric observed that this would allow the advisers to concentrate on financial advice and planning, with experts to handle the investments and carry the risk and responsibility attached to it. Angela Little counter-argued, "This will take the flair out of those with a feel for these things, and make us no more than process managers!"

To provide some structure to the meeting, Eric introduced the six steps to process improvement, which quickly focused on the third and fourth steps — best practice and the barriers to achieving it. The advisers decided that, in principle, they wanted all client investments to be managed 'proactively'. In practice, this meant using packaged products and solutions for lower value clients who could not afford a more complex and interventionist approach. They also wanted to continue with external fund managers and the discretionary service for high value clients, particularly when stocks and shares were part of the portfolio. The middle ground, which contained a large proportion of active clients, was more contentious, and the business decided to investigate a range of wrap and platform solutions.

Eric closed the meeting by concluding that, "The overall framework that we want to use is in place; we now need to look at the process for the three approaches to make sure they will give us the desired outcome."

CASE STUDY KEY POINT

In practice, many advice firms have a range of approaches to managing investments, which is likely to increase business risk and give clients an inconsistent service. Many principals are convinced that individual advisers cannot be expert financial planners and keep up with the investment markets; it is impossible to do both properly. Use of the six steps to process improvement helps manage the debate, and, as in this case, firms typically spend a lot of time analysing the different approaches. If this is done thoroughly, there is usually a high degree of acceptance, which makes implementation relatively straightforward. As is often the case with contentious issues, taking time to review current practice and deciding on the route ahead is well worth it to gain support and make sure the new process works.

FOCUS POINT

Annual process audit

Before the meeting:

- Inform everyone that the meeting is taking place and who is being invited. Ask them to think about any processes that are not working, and to make sure that they tell the representative for their area who is attending the meeting.
- Also, make it clear that this meeting is not about identifying problems that do not exist, nor is it about solutions — these come later.
- Appoint a facilitator who is fast at writing clearly on flip charts, and who can watch the time and run the meeting.

Agenda for the meeting:

- The purpose of the meeting: to identify any processes that are not working correctly and to identify why.
- Rank the review and potential redesign of the nominated processes in priority order.
- Take the important ones and estimate how much work it will involve to make changes.

Style of meeting:

- Try to avoid solutions — they have to come later; this meeting is simply interested in finding out if anything needs to change. Committees rarely develop good solutions.

- Avoid judgement, especially reasons why making a proposed change might be difficult. That is for the person charged with reviewing the process to identify and deal with. This is important, because if the meeting concentrates on the reasons why something cannot be changed, nothing will happen apart from the participants leaving in a negative frame of mind, feeling that their time has been wasted.

After the meeting:

- The facilitator writes up the notes and circulates them to everyone in the business.
- The senior team decides which processes to review and redesign, and who will lead the review. These decisions must be taken in the context of cost and other work that is going on in the business (see Chapter 19 on project management).
- The senior team receives a progress report and reviews the recommendations before they are implemented.

8 Chapter summary

The management skills you have developed as a result of this chapter mean that you can:

- Design client-friendly processes.
- Ensure that processes build in the principles of TCF.
- Develop a set of service standards that are right for the clients and the business.
- Save resources through effective process design and implementation.
- Operate a process of continuous improvement.

This completes the description of the four stages of process delivery that are linked to the customer journey. You may decide on different stages and sequencing, depending on the service that you design for your clients. The important thing is to make sure that your processes are coherent and correctly understood by everybody in the business. This aids understanding between advisers and support staff, and enables you to obtain economies of scale at a relatively small size without compromising client service.

Chapter 17

Making information technology work for you

By the end of this chapter, your business will benefit from:

✔ Effective use of software.
✔ Well specified software requirements.
✔ The right software to satisfy the needs of the business.
✔ Software that links directly with business processes.
✔ An information technology (IT) security policy.

The term 'information technology' (IT) relates to the hardware and software that the business uses to support its operations and provide excellent service and advice. The role of IT should always be supportive, and you and the others in the business should be clear about what it needs to do. This is particularly important when software is being acquired for the first time or replaced.

Clearly, there is a very close link between IT and processes, and any assessment of process effectiveness is also an assessment of IT. More specifically, answer the following questions to review your current position on IT:

● Do you feel in control of your IT?
● Do you use all the functionality that is beneficial to your business?
● Are you up to date with IT developments for advice businesses?
● Do your staff replace outdated working methods when better IT solutions are available to them?
● Is there a positive attitude to your main back office software?
● Is there an IT 'champion' in the business?
● Do you make sure that staff are fully trained on new software?

You can work through these as a questionnaire in **Template 1.3 in Part 5** – How to Make Your Business More Efficient on the website.

If you have answered "No" to most of these, you will be close to the market benchmark. This is a tough part of your business to keep on top of, because it takes time and requires a degree of technical knowledge. It is another area where specialist input is critical, as is the case with compliance or para-planning. That does not mean you have

to employ someone full time, but if you do not have the expertise in-house then you have to outsource. Outsourcing will be covered in Chapter 18, but for our current purposes, we should recognise that support for IT is normally split into two:

● Acquiring and managing hardware.
● Implementing and managing software.

The first of these is nearly always outsourced though a service contract, while the second is often the responsibility of an employee either full or part time. The best solution for you depends on costs and the size of the business. There is no doubt that such individuals become key people, and you should try to plan for this if possible.

1 Work out your software requirements

For a majority of advice businesses, the generic software requirement is the same regardless of size. Indeed, the widespread use and availability of low cost software is a source of economy of scale for small and large businesses. If you have more than 500 clients, you should use dedicated back office software, and if much of your work for them involves investment then you should select analysis tools from the wide range that are available. Businesses that start out with Excel spreadsheets rapidly reach their limits and make the transfer to software designed specifically for advice businesses.

The main software requirements for advice businesses are to:

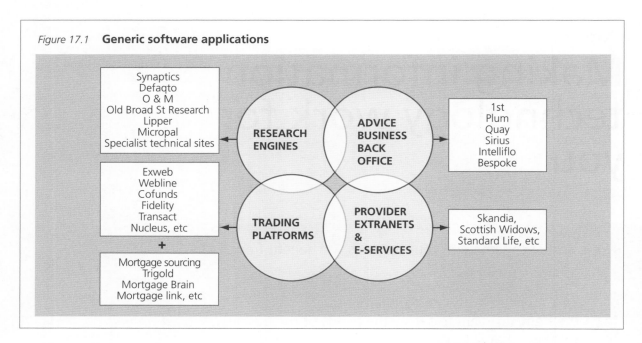

Figure 17.1 **Generic software applications**

- Manage internal processes.
- Make product/fund applications and transactions, and deal directly with providers and fund managers.
- Manage clients and service delivery, and provide clients with information.
- Communicate with clients and prospects through the internet.
- Research products, funds and technical issues.
- Obtain client data direct from providers.
- Gain access to financial advice and planning tools.
- Produce management information.

The chart in Figure 17.1 summarises the typical software mix for an advice business.

Over recent years, many applications have extended their functionality, which is why the circles overlap in the middle of the chart. The development of platforms and wraps has introduced additional capability and complexity, adding to the pressure for advisers to be very clear about what they need their software to do.

The number of instances where advisers have effective software that they have designed themselves is rapidly reducing. Unless you or your partners have the necessary skills, time and enthusiasm, don't design your own software. Also, think very carefully before you engage a specialist consultant to design it for you. You will become completely dependent upon them and, as with software designed in-house, its capability will eventually fall behind the off-the-shelf systems. Indeed, you will never achieve the degree of integration with external systems that is needed to support a modern advice business. You are strongly advised to devote your time to what you are best at: financial planning and advice. Leave software design to the recognised suppliers.

2 Get the best from your existing IT

Many advice businesses claim that their IT is insufficient for their needs and that it fails to provide the range of functionality that competitors seem to have. This leads them to a conclusion that they should replace their back office software, which can often turn out to be an expensive and unnecessary mistake.

This situation occurs when:

- There has been insufficient training at the installation stage.
- Insufficient time has been invested to work with the software and set it up in line with business needs.
- There is no single person who has overall responsibility for managing the software, the implementation programme, updates and version changes.
- Installation was not carried out through a prioritised plan over a period of time (often between 18 and 24 months).
- New joiners are not trained properly.
- Multiple work rounds or spreadsheets are being used alongside the software.
- A general view has developed that the software is not capable of supporting the business.

You may recognise some of these circumstances, because there are very few advice businesses that have really got the best out of their back office software.

If you are faced with this situation, you should implement a comprehensive review of what functionality is required before taking any decisions about changing the current software. This is because most modern back office software has a wide range of functionality and can satisfy over 90% of what typical advice businesses require.

2.1 Specifying requirements

If you have decided to change, or simply consider that you are not fully using your current software, you have to begin with a specification of requirements. This is not a technical IT document, but a set of business requirements to fulfil the needs of the advisers and support staff.

There are three issues to address to ensure good specification development:

- What do you want it to do? (e.g. profile clients by product and fund holdings, age and service level)
- Why do you want it to do it? (e.g. to improve service and relevance of client contact)
- Which process will it be supporting? (e.g. service delivery, and product and fund reviews)

You should develop the specifications under the following headings, which are the main process stages from Chapter 16. This will provide a sound structure and make sure nothing major is missed.

- Client acquisition.
- Gathering data and preparing recommendations.
- Recommending and implementing.
- Reviewing and retaining.

You can conduct this work yourself, ask one of your senior administrators or use a consultant. This is a time-consuming process and is summarised in Table 17.1.

How to conduct the process:

- Ask all staff to complete a pro-forma based on the three questions above (use **Templates 2.1 and 2.2 from Part 5** on the website).
- Interview all (or a good representation of) staff to ensure that you understand the responses.
- Draft an initial specification from the large amount of information that has been gathered.
- Circulate to the senior team and ask them to confer with their staff.
- Take feedback and redraft the specification.

An example of a final draft related to client data capture is laid out in Table 17.1.

This approach will enable you to develop a full specification of what you need the software to do. You will find that two lists will emerge: one that is essential, and another that is nice to have.

2.2 Does the existing IT match up?

At this stage, you need to investigate thoroughly what your current software can do, or what it could do if you upgraded to the current version. Clearly the vendor can tell you, or you can use their website and also talk to other advisers who have the same software. Attending user groups can be very useful as a means of networking and comparing notes. Ideally, someone else in the business who has a direct

Table 17.1 **FUNCTION: Client data   WHAT, WHY AND PROCESS**

FUNCTION:	WHAT, WHY AND PROCESS
FUNCTION: Segment clients	**WHAT:** segment clients by value, product, fund, age. **WHY:** to enable service delivery and marketing contact. **PROCESS:** ongoing service delivery.
FUNCTION: Capture basic data	**WHAT:** capture basic client data (address, d.o.b, etc). **WHY:** to enable efficient contact. **PROCESS:** initial data gathering and service delivery.
FUNCTION: Product and fund holding	**WHAT:** capture all products and funds held by client. **WHY:** to give opportunity to identify them to recommend change. **PROCESS:** ongoing service and marketing contact.
FUNCTION: Annual review	**WHAT:** segment clients by value, product, fund, age. **WHY:** to enable service delivery and marketing contact. **PROCESS:** ongoing service delivery.
FUNCTION: Segment clients	**WHAT:** capture outcome of annual review. **WHY:** to deliver service and provide TCF management information and evidence. **PROCESS:** ongoing service.
FUNCTION: Flag annual review	**WHAT:** flag one month before review due. **WHY:** to give time to prepare review pack. **PROCESS:** ongoing service.

interest in getting the best out of the software should be asked to do this work, and it should be set up as a project with clear outcomes and deadlines. This will be covered in Chapter 19.

You can then carry out an IT 'gap analysis', which identifies any gap between what you want the software do to (hence the need for a detailed specification) and what it can do. You will be highly likely to find that the gap is far less than you expect and the cost of closing it far less than identifying and acquiring replacement software and all the data transfer work that is involved in making the change.

To close the gap, you need to:

- Make sure you have the up to date version of the software and that it has the functionality you require.
- Prioritise functions for full implementation.

- Identify sources of expertise to deploy the functionality – this may be an expert in the business, the vendor or another consultant.
- Establish how the relevant staff will be trained to use the functionality.
- Run the training course, and be sure to include any back up or additional ongoing training that is needed and schedule it into diaries – it is important to avoid previous mistakes.
- Move on to the next prioritised function and repeat the exercise.

You should not be concerned if this takes some time (at least 12 months), because it is best to consolidate at each stage before moving on. Make sure you allow enough time for training and understanding in the context of all the other work that has to be done.

Make sure you allow enough time for training and understanding in the context of all the other work that has to be done.

CASE STUDY

"This software is useless!"

In the process of designing a new service proposition, Maroon Insurance Services had to think about their software and if it was doing what they required. Nisha Malhoutra was running the service design project and, in the meeting to develop the specification of service outputs (they had decided on a three tier ongoing service model), the support team were asked if the software could do what was needed.

Alison Turner was the senior administrator and she knew a lot about the software and what it was capable of. However, before she could speak, Angela Little interjected: "The software is useless; it can't give me a list of clients in the Associated Investment Group high equity fund, I cannot make the valuations work and the report template is in the wrong font." Eric Hammond reminded the meeting that "we acquired that software as a client database – it doesn't do what you are looking for."

Alison exercised great self-control, because she knew that Eric and Angela were wrong. When the software was introduced, several people missed the training and nobody took the data disciplines seriously. As a result, the data was of poor quality and varied by client, which meant that many of the functions could not be used. Alison explained, "If you have the right data entered correctly at the start and then keep it up to date, the software will do all that you need: it will segment and profile, we can link it to providers for valuations and we can even do our commission management on it." Nisha added, "It sounds as if we would be wasting our money if we changed this for something else; we need to get our act together!"

Alison was asked to check the software functionality against the requirements of the service proposition and, as expected, with an upgrade the software would be able to meet their needs. However, as part of implementing the new service, Eric realised that he would need to be firm about the corporate standards for data collection and updating. From the beginning of the year, advisers would need to collect the appropriate data from all new and existing clients and pass it to Alison's team for entry to the system. It would take two years for all the main clients to be covered, but at that point Eric was confident that the software would do the job.

CASE STUDY KEY POINT

Advice businesses should never change their back office software without a thorough review of its capability against clearly stated requirements. The experience of Maroon is typical, and can only be avoided with good compulsory training and well managed data collection and updating disciplines.

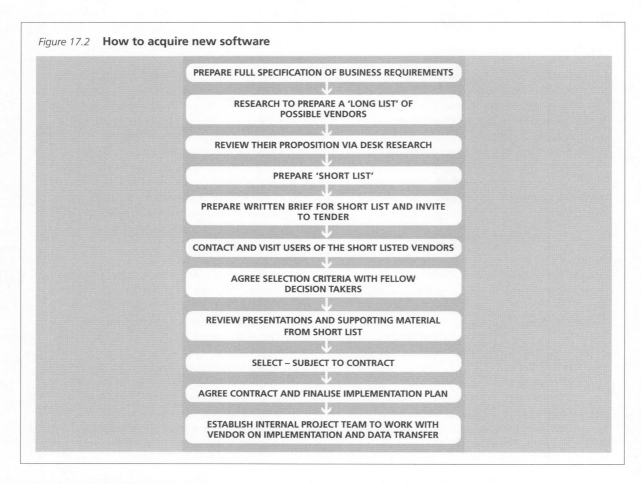

Figure 17.2 **How to acquire new software**

PREPARE FULL SPECIFICATION OF BUSINESS REQUIREMENTS

RESEARCH TO PREPARE A 'LONG LIST' OF POSSIBLE VENDORS

REVIEW THEIR PROPOSITION VIA DESK RESEARCH

PREPARE 'SHORT LIST'

PREPARE WRITTEN BRIEF FOR SHORT LIST AND INVITE TO TENDER

CONTACT AND VISIT USERS OF THE SHORT LISTED VENDORS

AGREE SELECTION CRITERIA WITH FELLOW DECISION TAKERS

REVIEW PRESENTATIONS AND SUPPORTING MATERIAL FROM SHORT LIST

SELECT – SUBJECT TO CONTRACT

AGREE CONTRACT AND FINALISE IMPLEMENTATION PLAN

ESTABLISH INTERNAL PROJECT TEAM TO WORK WITH VENDOR ON IMPLEMENTATION AND DATA TRANSFER

3 How to acquire the right software

There are times when businesses do need to acquire new software. This can be to replace an existing solution that is no longer adequate (e.g. the back office software) or to bring in brand new functionality (e.g. platforms or bespoke planning capability). Whichever is the case, the acquisition process should follow the same route. This is summarised in Figure 17.2.

To maximise the effectiveness of this process, there are some good practice actions that are needed when acquiring new software:

- Make sure the specification of business requirements is thorough and clearly documented: it will be the core part of the written brief and invitation to tender.
- The long list would typically include between four and six possible suppliers. If you exceed this, it will become unwieldy and difficult to make comparisons.
- Use the long list process as a piece of desk research to review the proposition and learn quickly what is available and what can and can't be done. You may review your business requirements at this stage, but be very careful not to add in the 'nice to haves', because there will be plenty of these on offer.
- You will now be in a position to draw up a short list of no more than three possible suppliers.
- The written brief is essential, because it is a disciplined

approach that helps make sure you have got your requirements clearly specified and explained, and it makes it clear to the vendor what you want to achieve (the headings for the brief are summarised opposite).

- Visiting existing users is extremely important, and a list of questions to ask them follows in section 3.3.
- Agreement of selection criteria before the vendors present to you is vital, because, as well as providing you with information, it is a sales pitch. In this situation, it is too easy to take a subjective view, and ideally you and your fellow decision-takers should independently rate each vendor and then begin the discussion about suitability.
- Following selection, contract negotiations should cover initial costs, ongoing charges, licences, training costs, help line charges, update service and break points.
- You should ask all potential vendors to provide you with an implementation plan and timetable as part of their pitch to you. This will help you set up the project team to work with the vendor to prioritise implementation and enable it to run as smoothly as possible.

In addition, you need the vendors to review your current hardware and state clearly if it is capable of running their software and handling potential upgrades. They should also tell you what hardware specification is required in order that you can obtain the cost of making changes if necessary. It is easy to forget this, and it can add several thousand pounds to the final cost.

If you acquire scanning software, you also need to take into account:

- The amount of filing space you will save.
- The savings in time for administration staff, although this will be offset in part by scanning.
- The file structure you will adopt to set up your scanning capability: this is extremely important, as it is difficult to change.
- The longer term storage capacity of your hardware and the cost of upgrading.
- The pace at which you will scan client files: typically starting with the clients as they are seen, which means your most important clients will be on the system within two years.

3.1 Writing the brief

As summarised above, the written brief is very important. The headings should be:

- Name of business, principals, contact details, etc.
- Context to include:
  – History and origins.
  – Business size (turnover, advisers, support staff).
  – Client profile.
  – Service proposition.
  – Three year business objectives.
- Current software to include the full suite as well as that to be replaced/acquired.
- Current hardware specification.
- Business requirements categorised by:
  – Client acquisition.
  – Gathering data and preparing recommendations.
  – Recommending and implementing.
  – Reviewing and retaining.
- Selection criteria that you will use (see following section).
- Timetable for process:
  – List of current users supplied.
  – Written responses.
  – Presentations.
  – Contracts finalised.
  – Implementation started.

This will take some time to prepare, but you should remember that it is performing the same function for you as a report and recommendations perform for a client. It is the foundation on which your future IT plan is based (particularly if it relates to back office software), and its purpose is to avoid an expensive mistake.

3.2 How to select a software supplier

This is important, because it provides the decision-takers with an objective checklist to help them make their decision. We would always like to think that we would never fall for a great sales pitch, but we have to minimise that risk.

For main back office software, your selection criteria should include:

- Size and scale of vendor: will they be around in the future and can they fund ongoing development?
- Functionality compared against your business specification: will it do what you want?
- Technical requirements: is your current hardware up to the job or should you upgrade, and at what cost?
- Ease of use: will the advisers and administrators be able to use this properly without excessive training and refresher courses?
- Back up services: how secure is the data?
- Training and support: how much back up is available and what does it cost?
- Data transfer: will this be easy and low cost, and has the vendor transferred data from your current software to theirs for other advice businesses?
- Implementation timetable: how long will it be before you are up and running?
- Costs: how much to set up and what are the ongoing charges?

These questions are likely to lead to others, but they cover the major areas that you will need to be satisfied about. These are all reasonable questions, and you should note the responses so that you can make an accurate comparison after the presentations. Work through the questionnaire set out in **Template 2.3 in Part 5** of the website to record your conclusions.

3.3 Talk to existing users

Existing users are an invaluable source of information and guidance. Vendors should be able to give you a list of users, although this is unlikely to include those who have experienced major problems. You should certainly try to find users through your normal networking channels, as well as those who have successfully implemented the software.

Questions for existing software users:

- What do you use the software for?
- For the parts of functionality that you do not use, can you explain why?
- Did you have to upgrade your hardware?
- What is the current hardware specification and does that adequately support the software?
- What was your experience of the implementation process, particularly data transfer?
- How good is the service (e.g. response to general queries, technical help lines, etc)?

- How good is the training and what does it cost?
- How are the overall costs working out in practice?
- Did you have a dedicated team or person to manage your account and implementation process?
- Did you have a dedicated person or team internally to work with the vendor on implementation to a clear timetable?
- What has surprised you positively about this software, and what has disappointed you?
- What should I be particularly careful about if I select this vendor?

These questions are listed as a questionnaire in **Template 2.4 in Part 5** of the website.

Most advice businesses recognise the complexity and nature of this decision and will be willing to share their experience. There are very few 'independent IT advisers' who can help, so co-operation in this area is especially useful.

FOCUS POINT

Wrap – source of simplicity or complexity?

The decision to move to wrap (that is, all client data and fund holdings consolidated on a single software platform, with capability to trade in a wide range of funds under a variety of tax wrappers) is a major one. It has significant implications for the business, the advisers and the clients.

Table 17.2 sums up the main issues that you should consider from a client perspective.

As the Table shows, there is no clear cut solution, because what you decide also depends on business issues (see opposite) and the make-up of your client bank.

Some of the issues that came up on the client table reappear here. The most important point is that a move to wrap is far-reaching, with implications for the pattern of revenue as well as service delivery and adviser expertise. Clearly, any business considering a move to wrap should recognise that this will be successful if the business is truly capable of making major changes and if there is a clear plan for implementation.

The range of issues will include:

— Moving to a recurring income and adviser charging structure: firms will need sufficient capital resource to support this.
— Reducing or redeploying staff as technology replaces manual intervention.
— Reducing and managing the client bank to focus on higher value clients, and offering different levels of service for different clients.
— Ensuring compatibility with other back office software.
— Compliance implications.
— Making sure that investment advice expertise is sufficient and that all other processes and software link effectively with the wrap software.

Table 17.3 considers the same issues from the perspective of the business.

Any review or move to wrap involves a series of steps that you should adhere to. These include:

• Review of wrap financial position.
• Detailed analysis of terms and conditions and charges.
• Review of the full range of funds and asset classes available.
• Analysis of functionality and support services.

You should review these in the context of your service proposition and detailed content and the benefits that you will provide to your clients. It is essential that all your software, including wrap, supports this.

Ideally review up to six possible wrap providers using the above criteria and then cut your potential list to two. Following that you should undertake site visits to users as well as the provider — it is extremely helpful if you meet the people that work with the wrap on a daily basis.

The FSA clearly expect this degree of analysis to be undertaken and that you should keep fully up to date with how the wrap market changes to make sure your decision remains correct for your clients as time passes. Be certain to document all of this to demonstrate to the regulator that you have adopted a rigorous approach.

All of the good practice actions in Sections 3 to 3.3 of this chapter must be applied as part of the wrap decision — this is a key software change and effective due diligence must be undertaken.

When you are scrutinising possible providers, you must ask the following questions:

• What is your financial backing and security?
• Who receives any fund management rebate and how much is it?
• What are the charges and how do these alter as total funds under wrap increase?
• How will assets be moved onto and off the wrap, and what support is provided?
• What training support is given to staff?
• What is the expected impact on workloads at implementation and in the future?
• Does the wrap software interface with existing back office software and the website?
• What support tools will be available? For example, risk profiling, portfolio construction and asset allocation.

Finally, there are an increasing number of tools and support services that will enable you to make detailed comparisons between providers, including charges. It is important to use these to support your due diligence and ongoing review process.

You could use **Template 2.5 in Part 5** of the website to fill in the answers to the questions above.

Table 17.2 **Client perspective**

ADVANTAGES	DISADVANTAGES
HOLISTIC PORTFOLIO MANAGEMENT Easier to 'actively' manage investment if in one place. Access to wide range of funds. Funds can be traded more quickly, so not out of the market so long.	Clients already expect this – so they will resist paying an extra charge explicitly for this service. Many wraps cannot include legacy products. Issues with in specie transfers (up to December 2012).
FINANCIAL Potential transparency of payment for advice and fund charges. Adviser remuneration and charges can be agreed as part of service proposition. Lower transaction costs (e.g. discounted initial charges and switching costs).	In practice, charges can be complex and lack transparency – particularly if they are 'bundled'. Advice, wrap and fund charges can result in uncompetitive total expense ratio (TER).
CONVENIENCE Less paperwork (e.g. money laundering, tax information, etc). Ability to view and obtain consolidated and up to date valuations in one place.	Effectively locked into wrap provider. Potential costs and tax implications of moving off wrap or changing wrap provider.

Table 17.3 **Advice business**

ADVANTAGES	DISADVANTAGES
FINANCIAL Facilitates the move from commission to adviser charging. Supports move to recurring income. Remuneration on all assets under management rather than products – supports increased business value.	Financial strain of switching from commission to adviser charging. Fluctuating recurring income (service fees) if entirely fund-based.
CONVENIENCE Less administration freeing up time for advice. Easier process for: • Valuations. • New business. • Illustrations. • Fund switches. Easier compliance audit trail and potentially lower PI costs. Client self-serve for certain information	Management of legacy business. Transfer of existing clients to new wrap can be complex. Insufficient clients on wrap will fail to secure economies of scale. Difficult to switch wrap provider (e.g. logistics, client communication, etc). FSA stance is for businesses to use wrap for clients where appropriate, with clear implications that this will not be suitable for ALL clients.
CLIENT RELATIONSHIP Consolidated client reporting. Opportunity to build a closer client relationship based on whole portfolio.	Concern that all client data is with an external wrap provider.
INVESTMENT MANAGEMENT Portfolio design. Standard asset allocation models. Straightforward trading. Direct link to fund research. Access to investment management tools.	Essential that advisers have the required investment skills and knowledge to provide a compliant service. Need for investment qualifications. May need to hire investment specialist.

4 Make sure you manage your IT with great care

The need to ensure effective management of IT is one of the reasons why many advice businesses have one person dedicated (either full or part time) to their IT operations. IT management splits into two main areas:

- Security and risk management.
- Rules and disciplines.

The first of these covers legal and regulatory obligations, while the second deals with additional rules and behaviours that are specific to your business.

4.1 Making sure IT is secure

Much of what is required relates to good business practice as well as specific disciplines required by law. Of particular significance are the requirements of the FSA and the Data Protection Act.

Rules for managing your IT legally and compliantly (which are also good business practice) include the following:

- Full password protection for all computers and particularly laptops that may be used outside the office.
- Effective firewalls and file scanning to prevent virus entry and to protect clients by preventing those viruses that have got through from getting out again.
- Clear and effective policies for dealing with virus detection and management.
- Full and automatic offsite data back up, either to the internet or media that will be held in an alternative safe location.
- Recovery of IT services in disaster situations, part of the disaster recovery plan.
- Clear policies on data ownership (particularly client data) and what happens when an individual (particularly an adviser) leaves the business.
- Management and use of client data in the context of the permissions they have given.
- Prevention of access to client data by unauthorised parties.

In addition, you will need to make, publicise and enforce internal rules that support the requirements listed above.

Internal disciplines:

- Access control to manage who can view and alter data.
- Internet use and abuse.
- Use of internet services for personal or alternative business use.
- Protocols for data entry (e.g. what data is required for a new client and how it should be entered).
- Management of software acquisition and updates, particularly who is allowed to sanction these.
- Permissions and rules related to taking data off site (usually by laptop or downloads to disc, memory sticks or personal computers).
- Policy for data use in marketing campaigns.

To assess the effectiveness of your IT management policies, answer the following questions, which are also set out in **Template 1.4 in Part 5** of the website:

- Are your rules and legal requirements clear, published and explained to all new joiners and repeated to everyone if there is a breach?
- Has everyone in the business signed to confirm they have read and understood the rules?
- Do you deal with breaches when they occur, and also raise this issue within the personal appraisal and/or T & C process?
- Are you confident that your data back up is foolproof?
- Does everyone stick to the data entry and data management disciplines?
- Do you have one person who is responsible for developing, maintaining and updating the rules?
- Are your password controls effective, and are you confident that you have taken all reasonable steps to ensure your data does not fall into the wrong hands?

The extent to which advice businesses conform to the standards required by the regulator has increased over the past few years. The main danger is that, as small businesses, informal methods of working take place. This is not particularly harmful in many instances, but it can lead to significant problems and fines if it is IT- and/or data-related.

5 Chapter summary

The management skills you have developed as a result of this chapter mean that you can:

- Ensure that software is used effectively.
- Make sure the business has the right software for its requirements.
- Ensure that people understand what the software can do and how they should use it.
- Specify what the business requires from its main back office software.
- Prepare selection criteria and manage the selection process.
- Select a software provider.
- Implement a compliant software security policy.

One of the greatest problems that advice businesses face is the selection and use of software that is right for the business. It is difficult to keep up to date and to be certain that your choice is correct. As with so many management processes, the software specification and selection process is designed to reduce the risk of making the wrong decision. It cannot guarantee success, but it will make sure that you do the right things in the correct order to maximise the chance of achieving the right solution.

The final point is to emphasise that software is not used properly for several reasons. These include lack of training, poor understanding of what the software can do, and lack of management of the processes and disciplines designed to maintain data quality and software effectiveness. It is important to make sure these are in place before you make changes to your back office software or develop work-arounds alongside it.

Chapter 18

When to outsource

By the end of this chapter, your business will benefit from:

✔ Well managed outsourcing arrangements.
✔ Outsourcing that is cost effective and does the job better than could be done in-house.
✔ A culture of benchmarking outsourced and internal solutions against each other.

Outsourcing is the practice of buying in services that you could probably do for yourself, but for which you do not have the skills, expertise, time, or resources. Importantly, outsourcing is one of the ways in which small and medium-sized advice businesses (up to 25 advisers or £5m turnover) can gain access to economies of scale, thereby reducing operating costs. This is why the market continues to be dominated by a large number of relatively small businesses.

The decision about this depends on how effectively you are managing the business at its current size. For example, start-ups may only outsource compliance services and retain everything else due to cost pressures. However, as the business grows, this should be reviewed, because there will be certain functions that can be outsourced to save money and time, which may not have been the case in the early days.

1 Outsourcing opportunities

The best examples of outsourcing are networks and related support services, but the concept also includes the following:

Advice support:

- Investment management.
- Product and fund research.
- Technical support.
- Compliance support.

Business operations support:

- IT support and equipment.
- Company cars.
- Lead generation.
- Website development and management.
- Newsletter and marketing materials.

CASE STUDY

The great debate: is investment management too important to outsource?

Eric Hammond was attending the local AIFA meeting and met with his ex-colleague, Graeme Rider, who was enthusing about his outsourcing arrangement with Racing Green Investment Managers.

"They do everything for us: asset allocation, fund selection, client communication and so on. It has taken a weight off my mind in terms of compliance and risk, and we attract lower fund charges for all our clients as the total funds under management increase." Graeme was clearly pleased with his decision, and was actively promoting his approach to others.

Eric had recently been through the same debate with his colleagues at Maroon, and they had come to a different view. They recognised the importance of consistency, audit trails and tight disciplines over asset allocation and funds, but had decided this was too important to leave to an external supplier. The total expense ratio (TER) was not very different in the end, although in some cases Eric was able to secure good discounts from investment houses which matched those available through wraps or Racing Green.

Eric asked Graeme, "What do your clients think when you tell them that one of the core parts of the service is run by another firm? Don't they look to you to do the whole job and make sure you have the expertise to do it properly?" Graeme acknowledged that they had thought long and hard about that issue. "You are right, it is a core requirement and it is why many of our clients come to us, but I just don't think we have the time or expertise to manage money properly and be really diligent about it — we are good planners and advisers, we are not fund managers."

The debate continued for some time, and it became clear that neither Eric nor Graeme were right or wrong. They both had the same objective, which was to ensure that they had effective investment management processes that met the needs of their clients. They agreed that their core offering was advice and service, and that investment management should be outsourced if the in-house regime could not meet the necessary standards.

CASE STUDY KEY POINT

The debate between Eric and Graeme is very typical and is often as passionate as the commissions versus fees debate. There is no single correct answer, because all advice businesses and their clients are different. The important issue is to set clear requirements and standards for investment management, and then work out if an in-house or outsourced solution is the answer. The two must be compared, but as long as they can do the job in a compliant and low risk manner, they are both equally valid.

Table 18.1 **Outsourcing decision**

THE FUNCTION TO BE OUTSOURCED	TESTS FOR SPECIFIC OUTSOURCING OPPORTUNITIES
• Is it core or peripheral? • Is it a source of competitive advantage? • Do we have the expertise in-house? • Are we confident we can manage it if we outsource?	• Will it cost less to outsource? • Will it reduce business risk? • Is there an opportunity to learn from the outsourcer and bring the activity in-house in the future? • Will the quality of the outputs be better than the in-house solution? • Can we use the time released by outsourcing more productively?

Table 18.2 **Compliance services**

FUNCTION	CONSIDERED VIEW
• Is it core or peripheral?	It is an essential service, but is not a core output of the business.
• Is it a source of competitive advantage?	Not directly, although compliance failure could place the business at risk.
• Do we have the expertise in-house?	No – we cannot keep up with all the changes, and we do not have time to undertake all the checks and other activities.
• Are we confident we can manage it if we outsource?	Yes – we know what is involved from managing with our current in-house solution.
• Will it cost less to outsource?	Yes – we will make our compliance officer redundant, which will save more than the external supplier costs.
• Will it reduce business risk?	Yes – provided we select the right provider.
• Is there an opportunity to learn from the outsourcer and bring the activity in-house in the future?	Yes – and we would intend to consider bringing this back in-house in 24 months.
• Will the quality of the outputs be better than the in-house solution?	Yes – because the supplier will be more up-to-date than we are.
• Can we use the time released more productively by outsourcing?	Yes – the salary saved will enable us to hire a para-planner.

2 When outsourcing makes sense

Each opportunity for outsourcing has to be treated on its merits. This means that outsourcing may be a good solution for one particular activity but a non-starter for another. In addition, what may be right to outsource for one advice business may be the opposite for another. Table 18.1 summarises the main questions that you need to ask to decide whether or not to outsource a specific activity.

As the Table shows, the questions need to be split into two groups which should help make the right decision. Firstly, you should think about the function itself and how important it is. Incidentally, it does not follow that if the function is a core activity it should not be outsourced. For example, investment management is a core activity for most advice businesses, and is often considered to be a source of competitive advantage, because it is of such importance to clients. However, as the case study shows, there are circumstances where it is right to outsource, in the knowledge that this key activity will be dealt with correctly and with less risk.

Secondly, you should ask questions that are specific to the outsourcing opportunity you are considering.

Table 18.2 provides an example of how these questions can help you make an outsourcing decision. It uses compliance

services as an example. If you adopt this approach, a member of the senior team should complete the table prior to discussion at a senior management meeting. Use **Template 3.9 in Part 5 – How to Make Your Business More Efficient** on the website to do this.

As you can see, this is relatively straightforward and enables the key issues to be considered in a logical order. Often the decision is easy, but the implementation is more complex.

3 How to select an outsource supplier

We can deal with this in the same way that we considered software provider selection in Chapter 17. Figure 18.1 is based on that process, and you will see there is very little difference.

The activity to be outsourced will determine how many possible providers you look at and the extent to which you speak with their existing clients. Investment management and compliance services should be as thorough as the list suggests, whereas product selection software or technical services might be more straightforward.

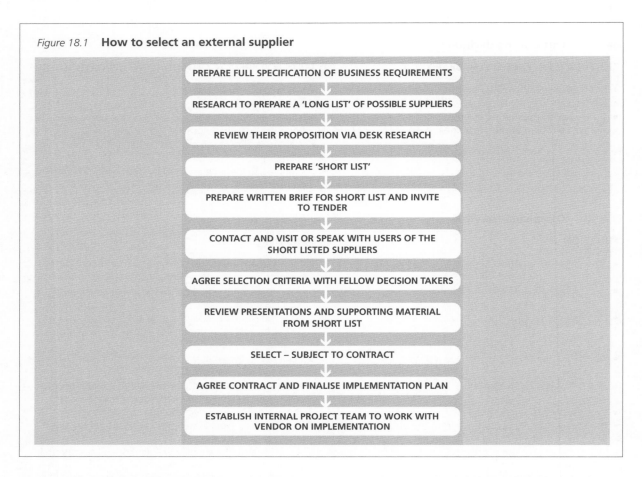

Figure 18.1 **How to select an external supplier**

This process can be used with any external services, even those such as networks which are relatively complicated.

4 Should you use networks and business service providers?

Networks and business services have changed with the market over the past 20 years. The initial purpose of networks was to support advice businesses in compliance practice and management, and to use their buying power to achieve increased remuneration from product providers. As time has passed, a wider range of services has been provided and the relationships with providers have developed. Some networks have evolved into service providers from whom advice businesses can buy as much or as little as they require. This has taken outsourcing to a new level, and there is considerable competition in this part of the market.

The advantages of network membership include the following:

- Access to specialist services, particularly compliance.
- Opportunity to attend training and business development sessions.
- Dedicated business development support.
- More concentrated attention from providers.
- Enhanced commission (likely to stop when the RDR is implemented).
- Access to different business models (e.g. restricted or whole of market).
- Preferential terms for professional indemnity cover.
- Coverage of capital adequacy requirements.
- Opportunity to sell the business or client base to another member.
- Networking with other members.

The disadvantages are:

- Loss of some freedom to act – you have to follow the rules and processes of the network.
- Some constraints if you terminate your membership.
- Less individual attention from providers.
- Bureaucracy and decision-taking processes may be slow.
- The costs may outweigh the commission enhancement up to the RDR deadline.

Network services should always be reviewed at regular intervals (for example, every three to five years). This is because the level and range of service from your network may change and your business requirements may alter. This is particularly the case if you joined a network to help start up the business. It will be inevitable that your needs will alter, and you may need to switch networks or at least review the service range that you purchase.

5 Chapter summary

The management skills you have developed as a result of this chapter mean that you can:

- Specify what you need from an outsourced supplier.
- Select and manage an outsource supplier.
- Compare outsourced and in-house solutions.
- Evaluate the value of network or business services for your business.

Outsourcing has been increasingly used in the advice market since the introduction of networks. The range and availability of services has increased along with competition between suppliers. This brings benefits to advice businesses in terms of lower costs and better services, but they can only be realised if suppliers are selected with care and then managed as effectively as any in-house department or individual.

Chapter 19

How to design and manage projects

By the end of this chapter, your business will benefit from:

✔ Effective project management.
✔ Prioritisation of major pieces of work.
✔ The most effective use of development time and money.
✔ Effective implementation of change.

You need some practical project management skills to help get things done. A majority of advice businesses do not have a suite of large and interlocking projects to manage, but they still need to implement change as efficiently as possible. In some cases, this is more acute than in very large firms where dedicated resources exist to support project management. In small businesses, there is no spare capacity and no case to employ full time project managers.

1 The difference between projects and 'business as usual'

It is important to consider what constitutes a project and what can be dealt with as part of 'business as usual'. Projects are tasks or activities that require work that is additional to normal day to day activities. For example, you may decide to recruit a further three advisers over an 18 month period. That is a very important task and is clearly critical to the longer term development of the business. However, you are likely to undertake this as part of business as usual using skills that you have developed, possibly with some external support. You do not have to set up a specific project to undertake this.

By contrast, the implementation of new back office software will certainly be a project, because it is not a day to day activity and will require great attention to detail and time management. Clearly, it is critical to the business and a relatively high risk project in terms of costs and operational capability. It is also the type of work that may require a specific portion of time from two or three of your best and most expert people. That implies cost, either in overtime payments or buying in temporary resources to cover some of the work they may have normally undertaken.

The chart in Figure 19.1 summarises the difference between 'business as usual' and formal project management.

As the chart shows, the business as usual changes are straightforward and often low cost and low impact. Projects tend to be the opposite.

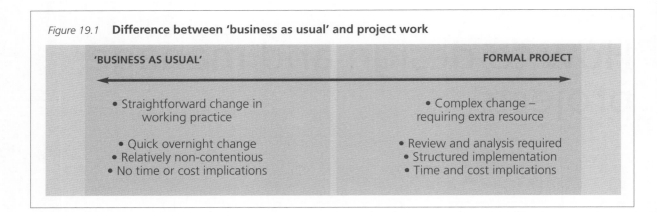

Figure 19.1 **Difference between 'business as usual' and project work**

'BUSINESS AS USUAL'   FORMAL PROJECT

- Straightforward change in
  working practice
                                                      - Complex change –
                                                        requiring extra resource

- Quick overnight change   - Review and analysis required
- Relatively non-contentious   - Structured implementation
- No time or cost implications   - Time and cost implications

2 The way to design a project

There are three dimensions to projects that have to be balanced and managed. These are:

- Outcome.
- Cost.
- Time.

The outcome is the final result in terms of what has to be achieved and the standards that are required. The cost includes expenditure on materials, external expertise and any other 'paid for' item as well as time. Time is the specified time period from start to finish, with nothing left to be completed at a later date.

Figure 19.2 demonstrates the balance and what happens if one of the three dimensions changes.

It is often the case that costs have to be cut when a project is in progress. If you were running a project to extend your offices, you may have reason to reduce the cost but would still want the work to be completed by a certain date. That could imply a lower specification to the building or smaller size. The same issues often arise with large scale IT projects that have to be 'de-scoped' to come in on time and within a reduced budget.

Project planners never intentionally set out to make such changes, but it is important to recognise that if the project is not planned correctly unforeseen circumstances may force the initial balance to be altered.

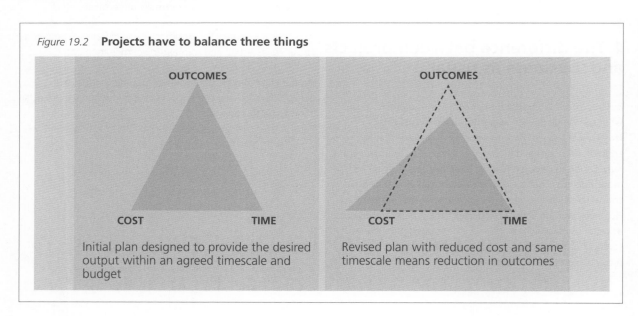

Figure 19.2 **Projects have to balance three things**

Initial plan designed to provide the desired output within an agreed timescale and budget

Revised plan with reduced cost and same timescale means reduction in outcomes

3 How to deal with the detail

The detail of projects should be dealt with in a specific sequence, as follows:

- Set a clear and time-scaled objective.
- Identify what has to be undertaken at high level.
- Undertake the work and monitor progress.
- Review the final outcome and experience of the project team.

This is summarised in Figure 19.3, with investment management outsourcing as an example.

The objective should be precise and measurable, so that you know if the project has achieved the desired outcome. It helps if you define the objective starting with the word 'to'. The actions are not the solution: they are what need to be done to achieve the objective. It is the job of the team (even if it is a team of one or two) to work out what to do under each of the headings. The controls are the frequency of communicating progress within the team and to senior management. The aim is not necessarily to check up on people, but to identify if there are problems and put them right as early as possible.

The template set out in Table 19.1, which includes two examples, is a good way to set up a project in a workshop with the project team. The same framework is set out in **Template 4.1 in Part 5** of the website. As the table shows, the plan does not have the solutions, but it does cover what steps need to be taken to get to them. The projects have very clear objectives and time scales, and give those responsible a good degree of autonomy to complete the work.

The benefits of this process are as follows:

- All parties can see exactly what has to be done.
- The project team has a very clear brief and can take part in setting up the project.
- The reporting (which can be just one side of A4) is established at outset.
- Setting out the individual tasks provides opportunity to estimate how long the work will take: this is very important, because there is no point in trying to move too quickly, as the project will fail.
- If you have more than one large project running concurrently, you can review any overlaps or issues with resources, particularly if you have somebody working on both projects.

Finally, the project review can be a short meeting that essentially answers the following questions:

- What went well?
- Why?
- What went badly?
- Why?
- What would we do differently next time?

Collate the answers to these questions as set out in **Template 4.2 in Part 5** of the website.

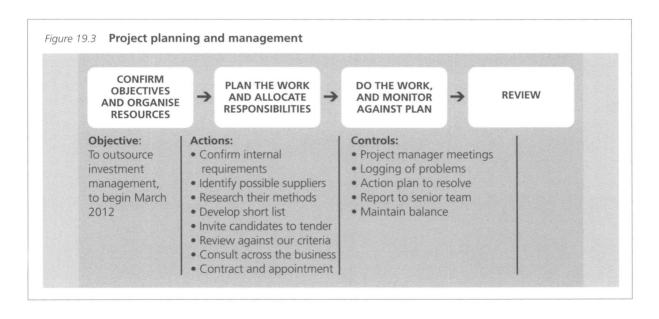

Figure 19.3   **Project planning and management**

CONFIRM OBJECTIVES AND ORGANISE RESOURCES	PLAN THE WORK AND ALLOCATE RESPONSIBILITIES	DO THE WORK, AND MONITOR AGAINST PLAN	REVIEW
Objective: To outsource investment management, to begin March 2012	**Actions:** • Confirm internal requirements • Identify possible suppliers • Research their methods • Develop short list • Invite candidates to tender • Review against our criteria • Consult across the business • Contract and appointment	**Controls:** • Project manager meetings • Logging of problems • Action plan to resolve • Report to senior team • Maintain balance	

Table 19.1

NAME	OBJECTIVE	MAIN ACTIONS	RESPONSIBILITY
TCF MANAGEMENT INFORMATION	To develop a robust set of management information for TCF monitoring by December 2011	• Identify what is required against client outcomes. • Review current collection of data. • Develop reporting template. • Gather from all sources. • Confirm data suppliers and co-ordinator. • Decide frequency of review. • Confirm process for review and communication of any trends, changes and outcomes. • Deadline December 2011.	ANDREW AND NIKKI REPORT PROGRESS TO SENIOR TEAM EACH WEEK
PEOPLE	To review and refine the performance management process by March 2012	• Identify good practice approach from Investors in People. • Review processes specific to performance management. • Map process specific to the business. • Design pro-forma. • Consult with others in the business. • Train those who will be appraising in the performance management process. • Seek feedback and prepare to make changes after the next round of appraisals. • Deadline March 2012.	JOANNE AND RAJ REPORT PROGRESS TO SENIOR TEAM EACH WEEK

THE AIM is not necessarily to check up on people, but to identify if there are problems and put them right as early as possible.

CASE STUDY

Project design meeting

5/45

Nisha Malhoutra and Alison Turner at Maroon Insurance Services were responsible for the project to design and implement a new service proposition. Eric Hammond recognised that this was a large piece of work and told them to make sure that they set up the project as carefully as possible. "This is much more than business as usual, so when you get started we will use overtime or temps to cover some of your work."

Nisha had the task of making sure the project objective was clear. She spoke to several key people with regard to the type of outcome they were looking for and the preferred deadline. She agreed that the objective was to "design and commence pilot implementation of a new tiered service proposition by January 2011."

She then spent two hours with Alison, working through all the things they needed to do to complete the work. They asked one adviser and a para-planner to join them, and they all wrote as many actions as they could think of on post-it notes. This seemed a bit like a party game, but it produced a lot of ideas with a fair degree of overlap. They grouped these together and then worked out the best sequence for completing the work. This also enabled them to work out who else they would need to involve. They realised there was quite a lot of expertise that they could draw on.

The plan and timescale were taken to the next senior management meeting for approval. It was one of the largest pieces of work that Maroon had undertaken, and they wanted to set it up properly. The plan was approved and the project started, although it proved impossible to find a temp to cover Nisha's work, which meant that one of her colleagues had to take more responsibility.

CASE STUDY KEY POINT

The project plan is like the foundations for a building. If it is done well, the rest of the project is successful; if it is not, then a lot of reworking is inevitable, which adds to time and cost, with an inevitable reduction in quality.

4 Chapter summary

The management skills you have developed as a result of this chapter mean that you can:

- Specify project objectives and requirements.
- Develop a detailed project plan.
- Estimate the level of resources needed for individual projects.
- Prioritise between projects.
- Manage projects.
- Use projects to make sure changes happen.

Project management is a particular capability that is essential for advice businesses. This is because there is ongoing change in the market, which often requires implementation within the business. Businesses do not have people with a lot of spare time, which means that any work that exceeds 'business as usual' must be carefully planned. We can draw a parallel with your clients and the need to map out how they will achieve their goals: the use of good project management disciplines will provide the same benefits for your business.

Part 6: How to recruit, develop and retain the best people

How do you provide fulfilling jobs and gain commitment from your people?

"Tell me and I'll forget; show me and I may remember; involve me and I'll understand."

Chinese proverb

"If you think you're too small to have an impact, try going to bed with a mosquito in the room."

Anita Roddick

Introduction: Implement robust people processes to gain commitment and loyalty

When you have completed this Part, you will be able to:

✔ Design jobs to support the operation and development of the business.
✔ Allocate management roles and responsibilities.
✔ Manage the performance of all the people in the business.
✔ Ensure that personal training plans meet the needs of the business as well as individuals.
✔ Design reward structures for advisers and staff.
✔ Implement profit-related bonus schemes.
✔ Reduce the risks related to recruitment.
✔ Design and manage the recruitment process.
✔ Use appropriate selection techniques.
✔ Communicate effectively within the business.
✔ Manage change through dialogue and understanding.

This Part is about people, and it applies to senior managers and business owners as much as employees. The aim is straightforward: to recruit, retain and develop people who are effective in their job, receptive to change and committed to your business. As you will know, this is a tall order, because people are different from other business assets. They are unpredictable and prone to leave you for a competitor, and often have commitments that dilute their loyalty to you and sometimes their ability to do the job.

Your aim should be to minimise the risks around these issues by using 'people processes' that are straightforward and effective. There will be plenty of checklists and templates to help you achieve this.

We will cover:

• Job descriptions, including management responsibilities.
• Performance management.
• Reward structures.
• Recruitment.
• Communications and change management.

Joining up the people processes

You have to operate clear processes to help get the best out of people and minimise the risk to your business if things go wrong. The key people processes that help with this are:

• Job descriptions: clear objectives and responsibilities for each job.
• Performance management: managing performance against the job description, developing people and rewarding them.
• Reward structure: ensuring that the way you reward people creates the outcomes and behaviours that are right for your business.
• Recruitment: recruiting against the job description and well defined selection criteria.
• Communications and change management: avoiding the vacuum of silence, and working with people to make changes happen and help the business to develop.

The links between these people processes are summarised in Figure 6.i.

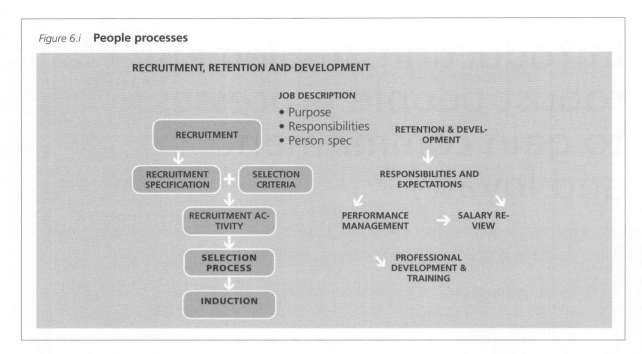

Figure 6.i **People processes**

The job description is at the centre of the process. It provides the basis for all the people-related activities that follow under:

- Recruitment and selection.
- Retention and development.

Without a clear job description, none of the other activities can be undertaken properly, which means the business will find it difficult to recruit, retain and effectively manage the performance of people.

The benefits of having well defined people processes are:

- People know what is expected of them and how they are performing.
- Setting pay scales, salary increases and bonuses can be undertaken against objective and clear criteria.
- Recruitment can be undertaken with a good degree of objectivity.
- Development and training can be linked to business needs as well as individual career development.
- Managing people becomes a professional task as opposed to an emotional challenge.

People and processes are essential for excellent service

The relationship between people, business processes and IT has a direct influence on client service. This is summarised in Figure 5.1 (Chapter 5) and further in the chapters on service proposition (Part 2).

The figure concentrates on the main people question: have you got the right people in the right jobs doing the right

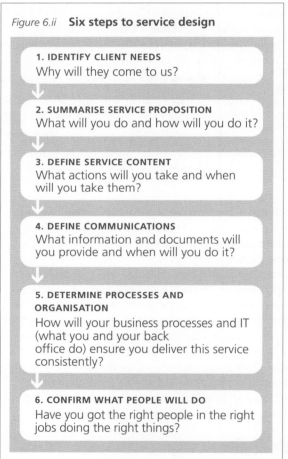

Figure 6.ii **Six steps to service design**

1. IDENTIFY CLIENT NEEDS
Why will they come to us?

2. SUMMARISE SERVICE PROPOSITION
What will you do and how will you do it?

3. DEFINE SERVICE CONTENT
What actions will you take and when will you take them?

4. DEFINE COMMUNICATIONS
What information and documents will you provide and when will you do it?

5. DETERMINE PROCESSES AND ORGANISATION
How will your business processes and IT (what you and your back office do) ensure you deliver this service consistently?

6. CONFIRM WHAT PEOPLE WILL DO
Have you got the right people in the right jobs doing the right things?

things? Clearly, the management and development of people is extremely important, because if you fail to run the people processes effectively, service delivery and advice quality will suffer. You should also remember that people are central to brand delivery. You will recall that brand is 'every part of the business that touches the customer', so if people are in the front line, you have to be sure that they are the best you can get and work as effectively as possible.

Linking your people plan to the business strategy

The direction and scale of your business and the target clients will help decide your people plan. If you think about the following questions, you will be able to work out what type of people you need, and how many of them.

- What are the main needs of your target market?
- What is the service proposition?
- How will the client bank change over the next three to five years?
- How many clients can be supported by an adviser?
- How many advisers do you need, and which knowledge mix will be required?
- What type of support roles will be needed and in what number?
- What additional roles will be needed (e.g. specialist managers)?

Thinking about this (which we did in section 1.3 on strategy) will help you decide on the numbers and mix of people, and the skills and capabilities they must possess. Work through these issues using **Template 1.2 from Part 6 – How to Recruit, Develop and Retain the Best People** on the website.

How effective are your people processes?

The table asks Ten Killer Questions about people processes. These questions also summarise what 'good' looks like for the recruitment, development and management of people.

For each question, give your business an objective score (1 is poor, and 10 is excellent) and ask others what they think. Use **Template 1.1 from Part 6** of the website to distribute the questions.

This is quite difficult to benchmark, because there is a wide variation between advice businesses. Fewer than 20% of advice businesses would achieve 80% or above. Most would be around 50%, but with a different mix of responses.

Quite often, businesses have the processes in place but do not use them. As a result, good practice falls into disrepute, with each situation being dealt with on an ad hoc basis instead of as part of a consistently applied policy.

Despite the fact that most advice businesses cannot justify a full time personnel specialist, you have to avoid an inconsistent and fire-fighting approach. One of the principals must be accountable for effective people management, using external specialists where necessary.

Use external support where it makes sense

Many advice businesses have been accredited by Investors in People (IIP). This is a very good way to introduce effective processes into the business and monitor progress.

You can use the IIP standard to assess whether or not your business meets the IIP benchmarks and to identify what you need to do if you fall short. The assessment is undertaken by a trained IIP assessor and, once you have passed, the award is for an indefinite period, subject to reviews which will be no more than three years apart.

You can check your current position by using the free online IIP business support tool or requesting an information pack from iipuk@tso.co.uk.

In addition, there are many organisations that can provide you with a complete human resources service (or parts of it), or consultancy related to specific issues. Advice businesses often use these services to support contract design, and disciplinary and dismissal procedures.

PEOPLE: Ten killer questions

Score: 1 = poor, and 10 = excellent

To what extent:

1. Do you have an up to date set of descriptions for all jobs?
2. Do people know what they are accountable for?
3. Do you set clear objectives when you review performance?
4. Does your performance review process run regularly (e.g. formal meetings at least once a year)?
5. Has each member of staff got a personal training and development plan?
6. Do you have a good track record in recruiting people?
7. Are your disciplinary processes clear and effective?
8. Is your remuneration structure up to date and clear, carrying no anomalies?
9. Do staff complement you on internal communications?
10. Are all your people really motivated, and do they work as a team?

Chapter 20

The importance of job descriptions

By the end of this chapter, your business will benefit from:

✔ Clarity in what people do.
✔ Clear accountabilities for performance review.
✔ Pathways for career progression.
✔ Clarity of management roles and responsibilities.
✔ Analysis of the potential contribution of a practice manager.

Job descriptions are at the centre of all people processes and policies. You have to get them right, because people processes are just as important as IT and the operation of the back office for maximising efficiency and client service.

Table 20.1 outlines the benefits of job descriptions You should review your current job descriptions, if you have them, and decide how they measure up. Use **Template 1.6 in Part 6** of the website for your evaluation.

Table 20.1   **Benefits of job descriptions**

BENEFIT	WHICH MEANS...
• Clear brief for staff	• What you want them to do
• Clear basis for performance measurement	• How effective they are
• Part of the criteria for selection	• Getting the right people
• Sound basis for deciding on reward	• Setting the right pay scales and incentives
• Essential part of the disciplinary process	• Setting objectives and measuring performance
• Description of the rungs on the career ladder	• Providing a clear career development path

1 Job description on one side of paper

Making sure that you can describe jobs on a single sheet has the following benefits:

- You concentrate on what is important.
- You have to think hard about the objective of the job.
- There is less room for misinterpretation.
- It avoids bureaucracy.
- It provides a straightforward agenda for the performance review meeting.
- It is a clear brief for recruitment agencies.

The template has four sections:

- Reporting lines.
- Purpose of job: one single objective.
- Main responsibilities: ideally not more than ten, based on actions and outputs.
- Person specification: skills, experience and knowledge.

Table 20.2 provides an example for an adviser.

You may have a different specification for your advisers, but you can see how the template works with very specific objectives and responsibilities to avoid any confusion.

Template 2.1 in Part 6 of the website provides an outline that you can adjust across different roles.

Table 20.2 **Adviser**

REPORTS TO:	Sales director or equivalent.
PURPOSE OF JOB:	To acquire new clients, and maintain and develop existing relationships with profitable clients and key introducers.
MAIN RESPONSIBILITIES:	• Generate revenue to agreed targets. • Deliver financial plans and service to clients to a professional standard. • Implement a client review process – with agreed frequency of contact. • Maintain an agreed number of professional introducers. • Support the plans to market the business and its services, and acquire new clients. • Delegate and communicate clearly with technical and client support. • Operate within the compliance and corporate standards of the business. • Undertake appropriate professional development and training. • Report on key measures on a regular basis.
PERSON SPECIFICATION:	• Interpersonal skills to develop and maintain client trust and inspire confidence. • Articulate – able to communicate effectively in verbal and written form. • Solutions-orientated – imaginative. • Commercially orientated. • Motivated, ambitious and hard-working. • Minimum professional qualification – QCA Level 4. • Comprehensive understanding of key areas of financial planning and generic solutions. • Minimum five years experience.

CASE STUDY

Round pegs and square holes

Emily Rose is the principal of Rose Associates, which has been operating for five years. The business has grown quickly and, as occurs frequently, the structure and jobs have fallen behind. "We need to sort out these job descriptions; we have people who are doing very different things from their official list of responsibilities – and we have some gaps that need to be filled." Emily was speaking to her co-director, Chris South, who had overall responsibility for personnel.

Chris responded, "You are absolutely right. I need some time to sort this out; what about if we spend half a day on this, put in some concentrated effort and get this back on track?" Emily agreed, and two weeks later they met, with a list of existing job descriptions and a blank flip chart.

Chris suggested that, for the first part of the meeting, they ignore the current job descriptions. "Let's think about what the business needs now and for the next three to five years, and ignore what was right when we started up." Emily responded, "That's all very well, but we have to fit our people into these jobs, so we are going to have to bend the descriptions accordingly."

This issue was hotly debated for half an hour, with Chris taking a strong line that the jobs had to come first and that they should then see what the implications were for the people. He said, "We need to start with the needs of the business, and then deal with the people. The chances are that over 80% of the skills we need already exist, so this should not give us an insurmountable problem."

Emily reluctantly agreed, and they got started, using a straightforward set of headings: purpose of job, reporting, responsibilities and skills. Chris suggested that they begin by listing the types of job they needed and then test this with the following questions: "What is the purpose of this job?", "What do we want it to achieve?", and "Why is it justified?" As they did this, they gave some thought to the number of people they might need in the

particular jobs and what the organisation structure should look like.

Emily suggested they split the four main jobs (adviser, technical support, administrator and office manager) between them and list the responsibilities for each one. "We need to think about what we actually want them to do, so we can be clear what they are responsible for. We should also think about delegating some of the work we do, if possible." This took some time, but they eventually shared their work and came to an agreement on the responsibilities quite quickly.

The final part, on person specification, was split into qualifications, skills/knowledge and experience. They worked through this together, and tried to think outside their immediate sector, especially for the office management role. When they had finished, their meeting had over-run and they both had to leave for client meetings. "Maybe that is a good thing – just to put some space between our views of what the business needs and what our people can currently cover", reflected Chris.

They managed to reconvene five days later, and both Chris and Emily had given quite a lot of thought to who fitted in where. Chris suggested that they take each job and the most likely jobholders, and rate their current position against the needs of the job. They immediately regretted not having carried out formal performance reviews in the past, because their discussion was more subjective than they would have liked. "Once we have got this sorted out, we must make sure that these reviews take place", said Emily. "That way, we can also update these descriptions if we need to."

As Chris suggested, most people fitted into jobs, while others would need training and development. It was also clear that nobody could take on the technical support role, and that this would require recruitment. "At least we have a clear brief for the agency now that this description is in place", said Chris.

CASE STUDY KEY POINT

The process that was adopted here is the right one. Job descriptions do become dated, and their revision has to be based on business requirements. Sometimes this means that people have to be made redundant, but the more typical outcome is for retraining and development. The way to avoid this situation is to run regular performance reviews, help people rate and benchmark their own performance, and update the descriptions as time passes.

2 Take account of different job characteristics and career structure

If you have not reviewed the jobs in your business for some time, you should take a broad overview before you get into the detail. As the chart in the introduction reminds us, jobs must be designed to ensure that processes and their outputs work as effectively as possible. For example, if your three year business plan is based on developing clients who have complex financial affairs, it follows that your people plan is likely to include para-planners. Alternatively, if you were planning to grow the mortgage team, then the staff requirement should reflect that.

2.1 The difference between strategic and operational jobs

The chart in Figure 20.1 shows how the content and style of jobs differs between those who lead and develop the business and those who operate the processes on a day to day basis.

You will need to reflect these differences in your overall job structure. When you design jobs, it is important to consider where they sit on the spectrum between strategic and operational. This should provide clear distinction between jobs and give you a good framework for recruitment.

Figure 20.1 **Job characteristics**

DIRECTORS: STRATEGIC	STAFF: OPERATIONAL
• Business generation	• Business servicing
• Consultancy with clients	• Service contact with clients
• 'Top level' (as opposed to day to day) operations management	• Day to day operations
• Direction and development of business	• Efficient process management
• Staff policies	• Development of 'juniors'
• Delegation	• Control of 'upward delegation'
BEHAVIOURS	**BEHAVIOURS**
Create – delegate – lead – motivate – define – lead change	Operate within parameters – support – prioritise – suggest change

Figure 20.2 **Advice businesses: job structure**

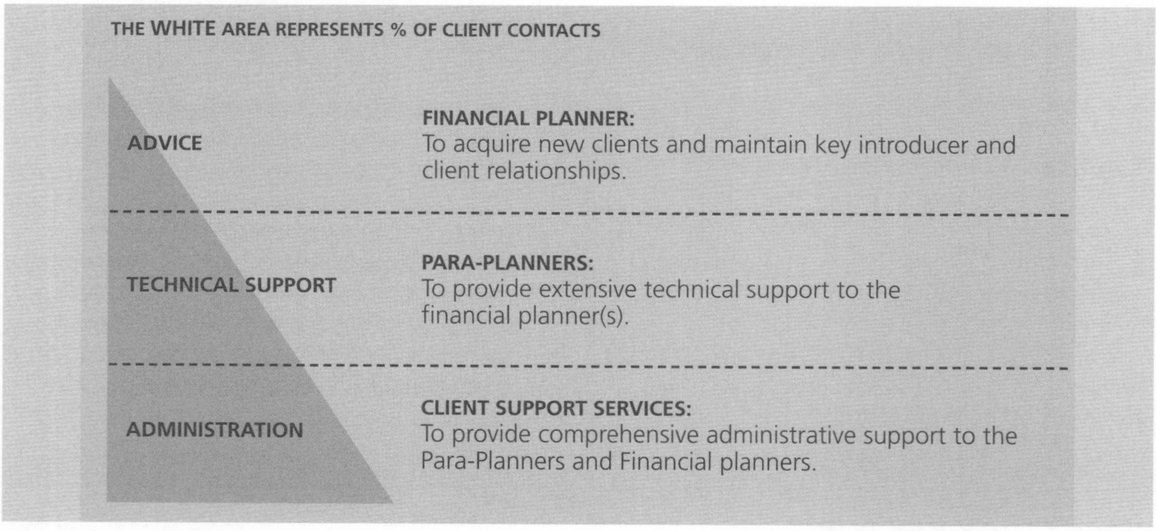

THE WHITE AREA REPRESENTS % OF CLIENT CONTACTS

ADVICE

FINANCIAL PLANNER:
To acquire new clients and maintain key introducer and client relationships.

TECHNICAL SUPPORT

PARA-PLANNERS:
To provide extensive technical support to the financial planner(s).

ADMINISTRATION

CLIENT SUPPORT SERVICES:
To provide comprehensive administrative support to the Para-Planners and Financial planners.

2.2 The importance of career and job structure

This dimension is the more familiar one, which tends to form the typical career structure in many advice businesses, and is summarised in Figure 20.2.

As the chart shows, there is a clear framework, which places delivery of advice through the financial planner at the top, with every other role in support. That is why the percentage of client contact time is maximised for the adviser, which should maximise income for the business. Those occupying the planner roles will tend to have the more strategic responsibilities, while those in support will be more operational. However, larger businesses will also have professional managers, either in a 'practice manager' role or as a technical expert who also takes on team-leading responsibilities. Marketing or IT managers are examples of this.

Detailed examples of job descriptions for these roles are given in **Templates 3.1–3.4 in Part 6** of the website.

The chart in Figure 20.3 plots these jobs across the two dimensions of strategic content and client contact.

You can use this framework to help you to decide exactly what you want people to do. If you are reviewing the jobs in the business, you have to set aside the current jobholders and their existing jobs and work back from service delivery to the jobs that you need to support it.

3 What should managers do?

In the majority of smaller advice businesses, the management roles tend to be shared in a relatively ad hoc manner across the principals. As businesses grow, this should become more formal, particularly if specialist managers are employed. However, few businesses have gone through the process of listing all the management tasks that need to be undertaken and then distributing them around the senior team.

The management tasks can be split between developing the business and running the business. These tasks include those listed in Table 20.3.

It does not always follow that the principals carry responsibility for all these tasks, which means that delegation is extremely important. This is particularly necessary, because running the business means providing a supportive framework to enable the main task of advice delivery, which is often a key responsibility of the senior team.

The chart in Figure 20.4 provides greater detail for the business development tasks.

Figure 20.3 **Job matrix**

DEVELOPING THE BUSINESS	RUNNING THE BUSINESS
• Strategy • Marketing • Introducer development • Provider liaison	• Financial management • People • IT • General management • Compliance

---

Table 20.3 **Management tasks**

DEVELOPING THE BUSINESS	RUNNING THE BUSINESS
• Strategy • Marketing • Introducer development • Provider liaison	• Financial management • People • IT • General management • Compliance

Figure 20.4 **Generic management tasks: developing the business**

STRATEGY
- Market monitoring
- Setting direction
- Reviewing strategy
- Staff communication

MARKETING
- Marketing plan
- Campaign design and management
- Advertising
- Mailings
- Preparing articles and liaising with press
- Hospitality (typically lunches and dinners)
- Follow up to the above
- Management of client database

INTRODUCERS
- Developing introducers
- Maintaining introducers
- Other networking

PROVIDER LIAISON
- Meeting sales consultants
- Provider training
- Obtaining information
- Dealing with escalated problems

The application of this will vary across different businesses and, in many cases, the amount of marketing and introducer activity will be relatively low. However, if these are significant, they can grow into jobs in their own right, along with the key tasks shown in Figure 20.5 that deal with the day to day running of the business.

As with the development tasks, these can grow into individual roles or be partly encompassed in the generic practice manager role. In addition, some of this work can be outsourced, especially compliance and IT, as detailed in Part 5 on making your business more efficient.

3.1 Should I hire a practice manager or operations manager?

This is a frequent question when the management team is feeling under pressure and recognises that it does not have the time or skills to manage the business effectively.

To decide whether or not you need a practice manager, you should ask yourself the following questions:

- Which management responsibilities am I truly prepared to delegate?
- Can I truly step back from some of the bigger issues and let someone else take the decisions?
- How much additional revenue will we generate from the time made available by hiring a practice manager?
- What are the specific skills and contributions that I am expecting?
- What are the specific measures of success?
- How much am I prepared to pay?

These tend to be expensive roles, which means that you have to be completely certain that this is the right thing

to do. **Template 1.9 in Part 6** of the website sets these questions out for you to work through. If the questions raise any doubts, then it may be that you need a good 'operations' manager as opposed to somebody who operates at the managing director level. Indeed, in most cases, attempts to hire an MD have failed, either because the right candidate was never identified or because the firm had not worked out what it really needed.

The evidence for this need is that a gap often exists between the principals and the rest of the team. The advisers are typically managed by one of the principals, but the administrators are often not well managed and have no clear reporting lines.

In these circumstances the role of operations manager can bring the following benefits:

- The job is 'hands on' and not strategic, which means a real day to day contribution.
- The reporting lines and structure of the administration and support teams will improve.
- The management of all the non-advisory staff will be taken care of.
- Special projects can be resourced and more effectively managed.
- The right person will provide a different perspective in senior management meetings.

Both practice and operations managers are not easy people to find. Common mistakes that you must avoid include:

- Hiring someone who has 'large company' experience: this could be useful, but the culture gap is immense.
- Assuming that a 'general manager' from outside the industry will automatically bring fresh and creative ideas: they might, but the learning curve is very steep.
- Not being absolutely clear about what you want them

Figure 20.5 **Generic management tasks: running the business**

GENERAL MANAGEMENT
- Management meetings
- Staff benefit management (PHI, pension scheme, etc)
- TCF monitoring and management
- Employment contracts
- Health and safety
- Premises management
- Company secretary tasks
- Ad hoc management tasks
- Management of outsourced relationships

PEOPLE
- Monthly staff meetings
- Staff appraisals
- Delegation and communication (day to day)
- Staff training (more on the job as opposed to formal courses)
- Recruitment process (from job design through to interviews, etc)

FINANCIAL MANAGEMENT
- Budget design
- Cost management
- Financial reporting and forecasting

COMPLIANCE
- T & C process
- Checking files
- FSA returns and reports
- Quarterly review meetings
- Complaints log
- Money laundering process
- PI cover, etc

IT
- Website design and maintenance
- Software management
- Hardware management
- Data protection
- Back/front office software

to do and testing their views on this at selection stage: this is new territory for you and for them, so you have to develop a crystal clear job description (think of it as their brief for the next two years).

- Pitching the salary too low and not getting the breadth of experience that is probably needed.
- Not fully testing their skills to manage people and come into a key role that is bound to create some disruption and suspicion, even if it is handled very well.
- Expecting them to sort out the issues the existing principals disagree on.

A job description for the practice management role is given in **Template 3.4 in Part 6** of the website.

FOCUS POINT

Management roles: Who does what?

The purpose of this focus point is to outline a process for allocating roles and responsibilities across the management team.

Before the meeting:

Ask all those who hold management responsibilities to list everything they do. Collate the responses under clear headings and circulate before the meeting.

Meeting process:

Explain that the objectives are to:

- Identify all the management tasks that have to be done.
- Allocate the tasks across the management team, thinking about potential delegation and outsourcing for some of the tasks.
- Identify any changes to sales objectives or reward packages that may be required.

Review the collated lists and ask the following questions:

- Are there any management responsibilities that are missing?
- Which responsibilities could be candidates for delegation or outsourcing?

Work through the tasks and identify who has the skills, capability and desire to take on the various groups of tasks (e.g. marketing, IT, compliance, etc). Avoid splitting individual tasks between people unless there is a very strong reason.

This part of the meeting should ask the following questions:

- Do those who are allocated tasks have the skills required or do they need training and development?
- Are there any individuals who are also advisers, for whom an adjustment to sales objectives should be made to account for their management workload?
- Should any individuals have their reward package adjusted to reflect a change in their mix of work between advice and management?
- Is there a case to employ a practice manager (e.g. at MD level) or operations manager (e.g. at senior management level)?
- Is there a case to employ specialist managers?
- Is there a case to outsource any of this work?

Make sure that all the tasks have been covered.

After the meeting:

Write up the outcomes, with clear allocation of tasks to individuals, plus those which will be delegated or outsourced.

At the next senior management meeting, confirm the outcomes and establish:

- Next steps for any outsourcing.
- Communication to individuals outside immediate team who will be picking up responsibilities.
- Communication to staff.

Six months after implementation:

Review progress and be prepared to make adjustments if necessary.

4 Chapter summary

The management skills you have developed as a result of this chapter mean that you can:

- Link your people plan to the business strategy.
- Design job descriptions in a time-efficient manner.
- Distinguish between different types of job and how they should be rewarded.
- Identify and allocate the full range of management accountabilities.
- Decide whether or not you need a practice or operations manager.

This chapter has dealt with the detail of designing job descriptions that support all the other people processes. They provide the foundation for everything you do to recruit, develop, reward and retain people, which means you have devote time to their preparation and ongoing maintenance.

Chapter 21

How to manage performance

By the end of this chapter, your business will benefit from:

- ✔ Clarity of process for reviewing performance of staff.
- ✔ Time-efficient management of performance review meetings.
- ✔ Training to support the business as well as the individual.
- ✔ Structured training plans.

Reviewing performance is a crucial part of your people management process. You need to set up objective methods and criteria that will support the review of rewards, professional development and training, and any disciplinary processes that may be required.

We are not specifically covering T & C methods in this chapter, although there is overlap because the objective is the same. We will introduce processes that are straightforward, easy to implement and time-efficient.

1 Why performance management is important

We readily understand that people management can be emotive and subjective. That is why you have to operate very clear and widely understood processes in order that you can be fair to employees and also the business. Under modern human relations legislation, there is no room for rapid hire and fire methods, even if circumstances appear to justify such action.

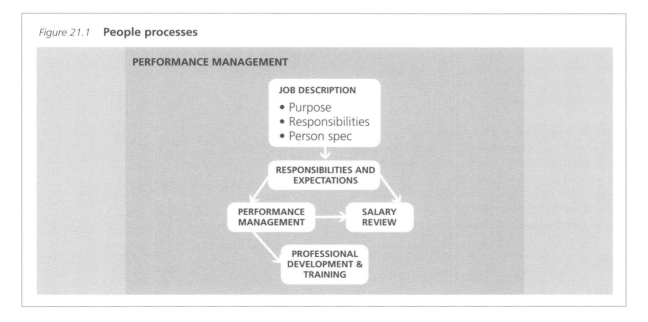

Figure 21.1 **People processes**

The chart in Figure 21.1 shows the link between the job description, performance management, rewards and professional development.

As the chart shows, performance management is the driver for:

- Salary reviews.
- Professional development and training.
- Periodic review that the job description is still applicable.

Given the importance of performance management, you should set this up and operate it effectively. That means simple processes and avoidance of bureaucracy. Answer the following questions to review the current position in your business.

- Do you have a clear process in place?
- Does the process run regularly at least once a year?
- Does everybody understand its purpose?
- Have the appraisers been trained?
- Do you use clear review criteria based on the responsibilities of the job?
- Do you normally arrange for people to be appraised by their immediate manager or team leader?
- Do you produce a written report or summary?
- Does somebody review all the reviews to identify trends?
- Is the review used as a basis for setting objectives for the next time period and any increases in pay or bonus?
- Do you encourage staff to benchmark and assess their own performance?

The benchmark for this is similar to the killer questions in the introduction to this Part. You can work through these questions formally using **Template 1.5 in Part 6** of the website. Most businesses would say "Yes" to half of these, but the mix of responses would differ. Importantly, when running performance management, your aim must be to avoid bureaucracy and make sure that meetings and outcomes are taken seriously.

In small businesses with fewer than ten people, a case is sometimes made that performance management processes are not necessary because they are often replaced by ongoing informal feedback. However, there is little evidence to support this, because it is just as easy for individuals in smaller operations to be completely unaware of how well they are doing as their counterparts in larger businesses.

2 Performance management on one side of paper

The aim of the Template example that follows is to provide:

- An agenda for the review meeting.
- A convenient way to record the outcome.

This is based on the main responsibilities of the job, plus any special projects that were undertaken during the review period. The Template also records career ambitions and any training needs, plus specific objectives for the following review period.

The review is based on three levels of performance:

- White (W): performing to the standard expected.
- Red (R): below standard.
- Green (G): above standard.

The example in Table 21.1 shows how this works. **Template 2.2 in Part 6** of the website provides a blank proforma for you to use to create review documents.

2.1 The significance of performance review meetings

You should always position these meetings positively, with the aim of giving and receiving constructive feedback on performance. Because these meetings naturally take place between people who work together, they need an agenda and process to provide a degree of detachment from the normal day to day relationships. If you have not run these types of meeting before, they will feel artificial and somewhat 'process driven'. However, as they become part of day to day activity they will seem more natural and work in the way that many other operational meetings work.

Table 21.1   **Performance review**

NAME:	Michael Jennings	PERFORMANCE
JOB:	Client service administrator	6/19
DATE OF REVIEW:	12/08/10	
REVIEWER:	Mary Moorhouse	
RESPONSIBILITIES:	• Manage the administration workflow.	W
	• Develop, consistently implement and review processes.	W
	• Receive and implement requests from planners and para-planners.	W
	• Register and utilise appropriate extranets/websites and other forms of e-business.	R
	• Maintain up to date client files and data.	W
	• Obtain illustrations, valuations and other information, etc.	W
	• Process and track applications.	W
	• Diary management — for client reviews and planner meetings.	G
	• Prepare annual review listings by month.	W
	• Prepare and issue annual review data (fact find, etc) to clients.	W
	• Commission monitoring and invoice preparation.	W
	• Liaise with clients and providers.	W
	• Operate within the compliance and corporate standards of the business.	G
	• Undertake appropriate professional development and training.	W
	• Report on key measures on a regular basis.	W
SPECIAL PROJECTS:	Data cleaning exercise — three months (Jan–March).	G
OBJECTIVES FROM LAST TIME:	• Keep close track of work flow.	W
	• Prepare review lists on the right dates.	W
	• Review invoicing process.	R
COMMENTS:	Good overall, apart from not getting the invoice review sorted — but time pressure noted. Needs to keep working on use of internet. Well done on contribution to data clean-up, an essential project for the business.	
CAREER AMBITIONS:	Move to para-planner	
DEVELOPMENT NEEDS:	CII Diploma	
OBJECTIVES NEXT PERIOD:	Take and pass two CII papers	

FOCUS POINT

Agenda for the performance review meeting

PERFORMANCE REVIEW

Purpose of meeting:

To review the performance of X over the past 6/12 months, to identify any problems and, particularly, any opportunities for development.

Before the meeting:

Prior to the meeting, both people should review the job description, consider the performance levels and think about any particular issues they wish to raise. The 'upward' feedback to the manager should be taken as seriously as the other agenda points.

Agenda:

- To confirm that the job description is still relevant.
- To work through the responsibilities and agree on performance level.
- To ensure that special projects and objectives set last time are reviewed and a performance level agreed.
- To discuss and confirm career ambitions.
- To confirm objectives for the next 6/12 months.
- To confirm any training and development needs.
- To discuss anything that the person being appraised would like the manager to do differently.

After the meeting:

After the meeting, the person who was appraised should complete the form and send it to the manager for final sign-off.

Typically, these meetings should be no more than one hour, but it is important that they remain top priority and are not cancelled or postponed: it sends the wrong message to the person who is being appraised.

A copy of the form should be sent to the manager with responsibility for people to review for trends and issues that are common across the business.

2.2 Managing your own performance

Managing people is clearly different from managing all the other functions of your business, and we have to accept that some of us may be good managers and others relatively poor. To overcome this, it is important to adopt good practice and to use it consistently.

The core of effective people management lies in the word 'trust'. It is just as important for your staff as it is for clients. The chart in Figure 21.2 provides a framework.

You need to make your own judgement about the issues raised above, although in some businesses people do ask colleagues for open feedback. This is very good practice, but you and your colleagues have to be completely comfortable to do it. At the very least, think about the questions and form a view as to how well the people processes run and are managed in your business. Use **Template 1.8 in Part 6** of the website to create a formal questionnaire. . If there are gaps, work on them through your own personal development plan; it is really hard for us to achieve perfection, but most of us can make improvements.

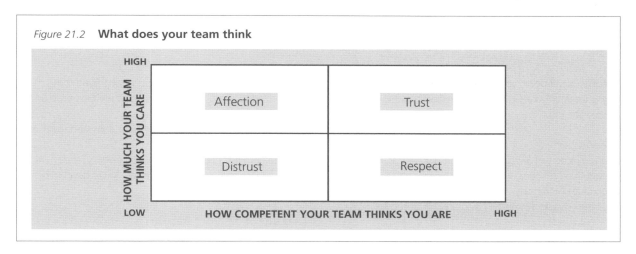

Figure 21.2 **What does your team think**

As you can see, this is based on the types of question that your people will ask from time to time: "Does he care?", "Is he competent?" You can only second guess where you may be on the chart, but you must be aware of the framework. The way that people see you directly affects all the policies and practices covered in this Part. Those whom you are trying to recruit will form a view of you just as much as those you work with on a daily basis.

Where you stand in this chart will be tested more under a period of change than at any other time. This is because your people will look to you to lead the business (and implicitly them) through the change. In Chapter 9, we reviewed a case study on self-awareness; the issues raised there should be re-considered in this context. At the very least, if you think about the effect you have on other people, it is likely your approach to people and change management will be enhanced.

Answer the following questions to assess your current capability:

- Do you make sure that all the people processes are up to date and work properly?
- Are you a proactive communicator?
- Do you communicate regularly with the staff?
- Do you apply your people processes consistently?
- Are your people loyal and hard working?
- Where are you on the spectrum between dictatorship and laissez-faire?
- Do you have a good record for recruiting and retaining people?
- Do you make difficult announcements and decisions, or delegate them to others?

3 The importance of professional development

You need to think about the overall approach to professional development that will be right for each individual and also benefit the business. Figure 21.3 summarises the generic approaches.

As the chart in Figure 21.3 shows, you need to combine the needs of the business with where the individual currently fits.

Those in the top left hand quadrant, who are capable but in the wrong job, should have a development plan designed to help them move to a role where they can perform more effectively. Those in the top right quadrant are your key people, and you need to lock them in with bonus and profit share schemes or, in certain cases, an equity stake in the business.

People in the bottom right, who are suited to the job but performing badly, need on the job training, mentoring and, possibly, some additional skills. Those in the bottom left should be encouraged to move to another business. Larger firms will use out-placement services to make this as positive as possible, but it is not always possible or appropriate with smaller businesses.

The person specifications in the job descriptions should contain the standards that are required for each job. That does not mean that people who are new to a job should have all the skills and knowledge that are required, because they will often need to fill a training gap as they develop

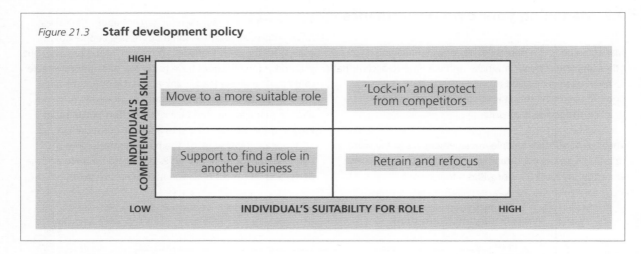

Figure 21.3   **Staff development policy**

into the role. Indeed, you can set any training or experience that is required as an initial objective and condition of being offered the job.

This approach means that the training and development that is agreed will always benefit the business as well as the individual. In practice, most businesses pay for their staff training and offer one-off bonuses for examination success. The latter should always be celebrated in staff meetings.

3.1 Alternatives to face to face tuition

The term 'professional development' normally implies standard face to face training courses. While that is often what is required, there are many other ways that people can gain knowledge and skills. These include:

- Shadowing or working with somebody who already has the skills.
- Swapping jobs (or parts of jobs) for a time period.
- Interviewing colleagues to find out what they do and how they work.
- Observing others doing the job (e.g. observing a fellow adviser).
- Role plays, particularly for those with client contact.
- Online tutorials and courses, and computer-based learning.

4 Structured training

While a majority of training should be at the individual job level, there is sometimes a case for a more structured business-wide approach. This can be beneficial in the following circumstances:

- There are several people who need the same training or development.
- The regulator has set specific standards to be achieved (as is the case with the Retail Distribution Review and adviser qualifications).
- Access is possible to external courses or providers

if you have sufficient numbers (recognising that providers often provide training at their expense or at a subsidised charge).
- The business wishes to implement consistent policies and procedures.
- Training has not been managed centrally, and there is evidence that many people have similar development requirements.

In the case of the final bullet point, you should take stock of the position and undertake a training needs analysis. The process is very straightforward:

- Ensure that the person specification is up to date.
- Ask everyone to complete a checklist against the specification for their job to show what experience they have and which qualifications they hold.
- Ask individuals to rank their current capability against their job description.
- Draw the information together on a matrix to provide for a 'gap analysis' between what is required and where people actually stand.

With this information, you can identify what can be done collectively and where individual plans will be required. The areas that typically emerge are:

- IT skills, including understanding of main operating software.
- Regulatory standards (e.g. money laundering, data protection, etc).
- Generic product or financial planning knowledge.
- Office skills (answering the phone, managing enquiries, etc).
- Technical product areas that the advisers in the business have tended not to deal with

Finally, you should prioritise what should be done and when. Again, the needs of the business should dictate this, along with availability of courses.

5 Chapter summary

The management skills you have developed as a result of this chapter mean that you can:

- Run objective and effective performance review sessions.
- Use the outputs of the sessions to set reward and bonus.
- Work with colleagues to identify their training needs.
- Decide on the balance between training at the individual and company level.

In this chapter, we have covered the development and operation of an efficient performance management process. This will help you make an objective assessment for salary reviews and bonuses, as well as give clear feedback to your staff on their contribution. Finally, this process provides the basis for training plans at the individual and business level.

6/23

Chapter 22

How to design an effective reward structure

By the end of this chapter, your business will benefit from:

✔ A fair and clear reward structure.
✔ Staff remunerated correctly for their role and contribution.
✔ Rewards benchmarked against the market.
✔ A reward structure that supports the objectives of the business.
✔ Analysis of potential for profit-related reward.

To understand the importance of achieving the right reward structure, consider the main problems that exist in many advice businesses:

- Lack of overall reward policy: that is, principles and practice.
- Inconsistent remuneration for people in the same jobs: too many ad hoc cases built up over time.
- Arbitrary approaches to pay reviews and bonus payments: people in the same jobs end up with very different levels and structures of reward.
- No clear split between the reward for owners as employees and as owners: no clarity of the reward for doing the job and taking the risk attached to business ownership.
- Adviser rewards heavily linked to sales.

1 Pay attention to how reward is structured

Your reward structure must be tightly linked to your business plan. Quite simply, this is because the way in which you pay people will determine what they do. Reward structures are based on the following elements:

- Basic salary: for carrying out the core requirements of the job.

- Incentives: performance-related. Typical examples are commission related to sales, administration service standards, project completion, etc.
- Employee benefits (EB): pension schemes, health care, etc.
- Perks: cars are the main example.
- Profit-related: either as an incentive or equity participation.

The terms 'bonus' and 'incentive' are often interchanged, which can be confusing. An incentive is directly related to a predetermined outcome as described above, whereas a bonus is a one-off discretionary payment for something outstanding either at individual, team or business level.

The mix between these elements will vary between jobs. However, it is important that all jobs in the business have a reward structure that includes each element if possible. This means that if you introduce profit share, everyone should take part: this is covered in detail in section 8 of this chapter. The typical mix is summarised in Figure 22.1.

The support staff package is dominated by basic salary and benefits; the advisers have 50% of their remuneration 'at risk', while the adviser-owners have 60% at risk. Generally, the potential for high rewards is associated with higher degrees of risk, with the ultimate reward for the owners being the realisable value of the business.

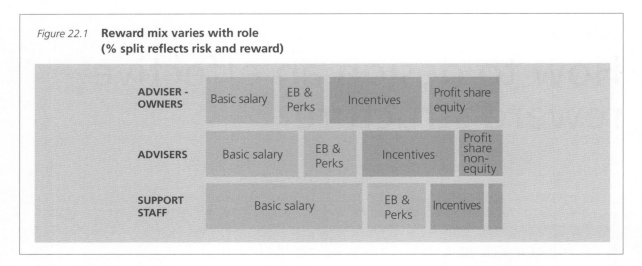

Figure 22.1 **Reward mix varies with role (% split reflects risk and reward)**

2 The link between reward and Treating Customers Fairly (TCF)

The TCF initiative requires firms to think very carefully about their reward structure. The characteristics of a TCF-friendly reward structure are:

- Low emphasis on achievement of sales targets alone.
- High emphasis on client satisfaction and service.
- Performance management that concentrates on securing the best outcome for the client and development for the individual.
- Rewards for adherence to robust and compliant business practices.
- Recognition of sharing good practice with colleagues.

In addition, you should design your performance management processes to identify how people can perform more effectively in their jobs and what training and professional development they require. There is a strong emphasis on people being properly trained for the jobs they do. Use **Template 1.7 in Part 6** of the website to evaluate your reward structure against TCF guidelines.

From an adviser perspective, the RDR is enhancing a move away from commission-only reward that is directly related to sales. That is why you would be wise to formalise your ongoing service proposition and reward advisers for service delivery as well as brand new business. This can be achieved by including any recurring revenues in the reward package for advisers to ensure that the service which the client has paid for is provided.

In addition, you should include the achievement of good practice key performance indicators (KPIs) in your reward structure. These can include:

- Achievement of ongoing service delivery targets: making sure that regular client reviews are carried out.
- Attainment of compliance standards.
- Advocating and supporting TCF best practices.
- Sticking to important corporate standards (e.g. new business processes, use of common fact find, data management, etc).

This will provide you with a reward structure that is more broadly based than in the past, requiring advisers and staff to achieve more than sales targets that exceed the previous year. That is not to reduce the importance of securing income and rewarding good performance, but you should include additional factors in the overall reward framework.

3 Link rewards to strategy and principles

It is important that the principles of the reward structure reflect the values, principles and direction of the business. We can use the firms Bronze and Gold from section 2.1 on marketing to demonstrate this.

You will recall that these businesses occupy different parts of the market. The headline service proposition for Gold is:

"We provide financial consultancy for business and private clients with complex affairs. We work with other professionals to create and manage a comprehensive and evolving plan."

The proposition for Bronze is:

"We provide straightforward financial advice to make sure you have the right products for your future needs."

If we start with the market positioning and objective statements for both firms, we can see how the remuneration policy will differ in Table 22.1.

As you would expect, the pattern is very different and, given the variation between propositions and target markets, the type of adviser who will be attracted will also be different. In addition, the balance between basic salary, sales incentives, employee benefits and any profit-related arrangements will also vary.

Table 22.1

	GOLD	BRONZE
WHAT WE DO	Expert financial and tax planning to enable the long term management of investments through a detailed plan that is regularly reviewed.	Streamlined advice in one meeting to make sure that people have the right policies for their needs.
WHO WE DO IT FOR	Private clients with over £500,000.	Families and working people between the ages of 30 and 50.
BUSINESS OBJECTIVE	To increase turnover from £2m to £2.5m, and raise the proportion of income that is recurring from 45% to 60% over the next two years.	To increase turnover from £1m to £2m by taking full advantage of our high street position over the next two years.
MARKETING OBJECTIVE	To acquire an additional 25 high value clients and continue to sell our premier service to existing clients.	To sell products to an additional 2,000 people (at £500 initial charge).
ADVISER REWARD STRUCTURE: MAIN DRIVERS		
CLIENT ACQUISITION	Low	High
CLIENT RETENTION	High	Medium
NEW BUSINESS	Low	High
ONGOING SERVICE DELIVERY	High	Low
UPSELL INTO HIGHER SERVICE LEVELS	High	Low
TECHNICAL EXAMINATION SUCCESS	High	Low
SUSTAINING EXTERNAL BUSINESS SOURCES	High (introducers)	High (support for external events)
COMPLIANCE KPIS	High	High
PROFIT SHARE	High	Low
TEAM BONUS	Low	High

4 You get what you pay for

If your advisers are paid solely by commission on sales, you will get high levels of sales. However, you will also get:

- A wide variety of clients that are not in the target market.
- Low persistency.
- Non-compliance.
- Complaints.
- High adviser turnover.
- No ongoing client servicing.

This may seem exaggerated, but it directly reflects the UK experience of the 1960s, when unfettered commission-only remuneration was introduced for the first time.

However, if you have people in a sales role and only pay a basic salary, you will get the opposite of the 1960s experience, including a low level of sales. In essence, you should make sure that you have the right reward structures for your business. This should make an important contribution to recruiting and retaining the advisers and support staff that are necessary for day to day operations and longer term growth.

5 How to structure adviser remuneration

You will be familiar with the split between employed and self-employed advisers. In some cases, the latter adopt self-employed status for personal taxation reasons and for all other purposes operate and behave like their employed counterparts. In other cases, they are effectively businesses within the business and operate with a great deal of autonomy, using the business to provide essential administration and compliance services.

There is a rough rule that has been applied for many years, which is that advisers, regardless of status, would normally expect to receive rewards equivalent to two-thirds of the income they secure for the business. There will be variations around this, but this split normally achieves the right balance between adviser income and business costs and profitability.

5.1 What is the typical self-employed reward structure?

The typical reward model for self-employed advisers has two

components, although some businesses only use the second one. These are:

- Fixed charge to cover compliance and regulator costs and, in some cases, basic administration costs.
- Variable sum based on percentage of income.

The fixed sum or 'desk charge' has the following benefits for the business:

- Costs are covered regardless of income.
- Financial risk of recruiting is reduced: avoids losses on poor producers.
- Cash flow is improved.
- Changes in external charges (e.g. FSA fees) can be automatically covered if this is built into the fixed charge contract.

The benefits for advisers are:

- There is clarity about what will be received in return for the charge.
- Such charges will normally be associated with higher starting and finishing percentages of the income received, thereby benefiting high income producers.

The starting point for the variable sum will depend on the amount of support that the business is providing. This can range from everything advisers would expect in the employed model through to virtually nothing above desk and essential compliance services.

The typical models are summarised in Figure 22.2.

The ranges that currently prevail in the market are shown opposite. If the business is providing high levels of adviser support, the range will run from 50% to around 70%. The extra percentage only applies to additional tranches of business as shown by the stepped changes. Low levels of support are typically associated with higher starting and finishing points.

Levels of support can include the following:

- Lead generation.
- Secretarial and para-planning services.
- Marketing activity (e.g. newsletters).
- Access to research tools and external services.
- Regular technical training.
- New business and ongoing servicing support.

In the self-employed model, support will not include cars, telephones, pension contributions and so on. Those are typically the responsibility of the adviser.

5.2 The optimum mix of support and reward

The structure that you adopt depends on:

- The level of support that you will provide.
- The certainty that you can deliver it consistently.
- Your financial model.
- The need for certainty of coverage of fixed costs to avoid loss on low-producing advisers.

You will need to judge this based on financial management and business risk and the expected income production of the advisers. If your experience is of low productivity advisers, then you should include the desk charge to make sure you cover your costs. For high-producing advisers, the desk charge is largely irrelevant. However, in both cases you have to scale the income bands to retain approximately one-third of the income for the business. At the same time, you need to be sure that the model is sufficiently attractive to recruit and retain advisers.

Tiered bands: 70% to 80%

The following examples in Tables 22.2 and 22.3 are based on the tiered bands from 70% up to 80%. The first Table

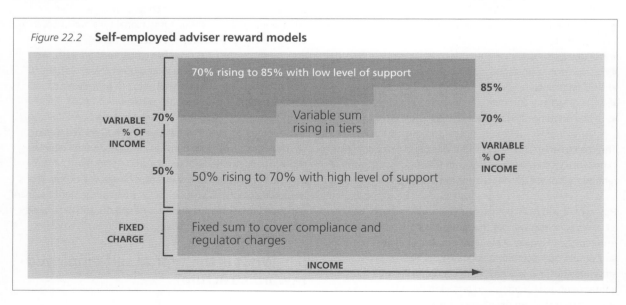

Figure 22.2 **Self-employed adviser reward models**

Table 22.2

DESK CHARGE INCLUDED	DESK CHARGE	70% TO £100,000 INCOME	INCOME SPLIT FROM £100,000 TOTAL	75% FROM £100,000 TO £150,000	INCOME SPLIT FROM £150,000 TOTAL	80% FROM £150,000 TO £200,000	INCOME SPLIT FROM £200,000 TOTAL
Adviser (£k)		70	70−12 = 58	37.5	107.5−12 = 95.5	40	147.5−12 = 135.5 (68%)
Business (£k)	12	30	42	12.5	54.5	10	64.5 (32%)

Table 22.3

DESK CHARGE EXCLUDED	DESK CHARGE	70% TO £100,000 INCOME	INCOME SPLIT FROM £100,000 TOTAL	75% FROM £100,000 TO £150,000	INCOME SPLIT FROM £150,000 TOTAL	80% FROM £150,000 TO £200,000	INCOME SPLIT FROM £200,000 TOTAL
Adviser (£k)	0	70	70	37.5	107.5	40	147.5 (74%)
Business (£k)	0	30	30	12.5	42.5	10	52.5 (26%)

includes a desk charge of £1,000 per month, and you will see that an adviser producing a total income of £200,000 will receive £135,500 (68% of the total). In the second Table, the desk charge is removed and the adviser income rises to £147,500 (74% of the total).

Table 22.2 works well if most advisers are likely to produce around £100k income. The business will cover its costs and the adviser will receive almost 60% of income.

Table 22.3 works well if the advisers are self-sufficient and produce up to £200,000 because the business more than covers its costs and the advisers receive almost 75% of the total income. In this scenario, the support levels provided by the business would be relatively low to justify the total percentage received by the advisers.

Tiered bands: 50% to 80% and lower break points

Table 22.4 and Table 22.5 are based on lower tiered bands from 50% to 80% with different income break points. Once again, the first Table includes the desk charge.

This type of structure is normally associated with high levels of support and, with the desk charge, only works for advisers when production exceeds £125,000. For those who are very capable of producing income but less self-sufficient, particularly in lead generation, it has to be accepted that income will be lower but the job will be made easier.

Removal of the desk charge in Table 22.5 is a better proposition for advisers, but still retains more for the business than the structure in Table 22.2 and Table 22.3.

To summarise, the route that you adopt depends on the balance between:

- Adviser income potential.
- Level of support for advisers.
- Cost of generating leads for advisers.
- Cash flow pressures that require desk charges to be included.

Table 22.4

DESK CHARGE INCLUDED	DESK CHARGE	70% TO £100,000 INCOME	INCOME SPLIT FROM £100,000 TOTAL	75% FROM £100,000 TO £150,000	INCOME SPLIT FROM £150,000 TOTAL	80% FROM £150,000 TO £200,000	INCOME SPLIT FROM £200,000 TOTAL
Adviser (£k)		37.5	37.5−12 = 25.5	30	67.5−12 = 55.5	60	127.5−12 = 115.5 (58%)
Business (£k)	12	37.5	49.5	20	69.5	15	84.5 (42%)

Table 22.5

DESK CHARGE EXCLUDED	DESK CHARGE	70% TO £100,000 INCOME	INCOME SPLIT FROM £100,000 TOTAL	75% FROM £100,000 TO £150,000	INCOME SPLIT FROM £150,000 TOTAL	80% FROM £150,000 TO £200,000	INCOME SPLIT FROM £200,000 TOTAL
Adviser (£k)	0	37.5	37.5	30	67.5	60	127.5 (64%)
Business (£k)	0	37.5	37.5	20	57.5	15	72.5 (36%)

As you would expect, principals of self-employed business models spend a lot of time working out which model will work for them and their advisers. In practice, the greatest problem is setting the balance too far in favour of advisers. This is not about depressing adviser remuneration; it is about generating sufficient revenue for the business to enable it to operate and maintain profitability. In many instances, profitability for this model tends to settle in the 5%–10% band of gross turnover, compared to employed models which are in the 15%–20% band.

6 What is the typical employed adviser remuneration structure?

The starting point for remuneration for employed advisers is the two-thirds rule of thumb referred to above. However, in this case the reward package is likely to be very different from the self-employed model.

There are variations, but the typical package can include many of the elements summarised in the introduction to this section:

- Basic salary.
- Income related incentive; and/or
- Car or car allowance.
- Pension contributions.
- Other perks and employee benefits.
- Profit-related incentives.
- Full office support.

You should manage the relationship between the fixed and variable elements in exactly the same way as for self-employed advisers. You need to decide the balance between basic salary and incentives, and how key performance indicators (KPIs) related to quality will be included.

For advisers, these KPIs are often based on:

- Compliance record.
- Complaints record.
- Attendance at training events.
- Data management and collection.
- Persistency.
- Referrals and recommendations.
- Carrying out client reviews.

In most cases, firms set a minimum standard to be achieved before incentives are paid. This tends to be more effective than applying penalties if the KPIs are not met. Provided that you monitor these KPIs, you can identify any issues and put them right long before they become a remuneration problem.

The average income generated for the business by an employed adviser would be in the region of £150,000, recognising wide variations across the market. The remuneration for this would be around £50,000, made up of the following:

- Basic salary: £20,000.
- Car and pension: £5,000.
- Production incentives: £25,000.

A typical incentive structure that would support this is:

- £0–£50,000: 0%.
- £50,000–£100,000: 20%.
- £100,000–£150,000: 30%.

In this example, the £25,000 incentive is made up from:

- 20% of £50,000 (£10,000).
- 30% of £50,000 (approx £16,000).

If cars and pensions are not provided, the basic salary may be increased to £25,000 or the incentive structure altered to deliver the same £50,000 total reward for the adviser.

7 What is the typical remuneration structure for support staff?

You should design the reward structure for support staff in the context of the arrangements for advisers. If there is the potential for incentive payments, then you should reflect this throughout the business. As with advisers, the package for support staff is typically made up of a combination of elements:

- Basic salary.
- Pension contributions.
- Incentives.

Basic salary ranges tend to be as follows:

- Junior administrators: up to £12,000.
- Senior administrators: up to £25,000.
- Junior para planners: up to £15,000.
- Established para planner: up to £35,000.
- Office or practice managers: up to £50,000.

These will vary across the country and by specific job descriptions. In addition, experience and qualifications will have a direct affect on salary rates. Recruitment agencies and websites, plus the jobs section of the trade press, will provide you with an up to date picture of market rates, on which you need to overlay the local labour market conditions.

8 Manageable profit-related rewards

Profit-related schemes have become increasingly common, particularly in light of TCF implementation and the pressure to move away from rewards that are closely linked to sales.

When you design a scheme, you need to make sure it is straightforward, easy to understand and consistent across the business.

As with all incentive schemes, you have to start with the sum that you are prepared to commit to and any thresholds that must be reached to trigger payment. For example, if a firm with a turnover of £1m has a profit target of £100,000, it may decide to pay a profit incentive provided that this is achieved. The next stage is to set a budget for the 'incentive pot' – which might be £15,000 – which should be included in the overall reward budget. It is essential to set the incentive payments as a percentage of salaries, which means you can budget exactly how much to set aside if the profit target is achieved. Typically, tiered rates are used, with 2% of salary for juniors, 3% for middle range and 4% for senior managers.

In Table 22.6 profit incentive payments for the following staff structure would be:

- Six advisers at 4%.
- One administration manager at 3%.
- One para-planner at 3%.
- Four junior support staff at 2%.

In this case, the total payment is just under 15% of profit. However, as indicated above, it is important to budget this as an expected cost in the annual budgeting process.

In most cases, these schemes are kept very simple with the single percentage rates as shown above with payment made if profit reaches or exceeds the target. Simple schemes have the following advantages:

- The 'target' can be published at the beginning of the year.
- It is easy for people to understand how much they might receive.
- Progress can be tracked through the year – a good incentive.
- The potential cost to the business is predictable and not open-ended.
- Everyone takes part.
- The outcome is set objectively by the rules; there are no subjective judgements.

In addition, as with adviser remuneration, you can couple incentives with a set of thresholds that must be achieved. For example, this could include:

- No major issues arising from the forthcoming FSA visit on TCF progress.
- No more than one complaint upheld.
- Completion of a major project.

This list should not be lengthy (possibly only one very important item to get real concentration), and it should be measurable and achievable. In essence, you should base it

Table 22.6

STAFF	SALARY (£K)	PAYMENT RATE (%)	INDIVIDUAL INCENTIVE PAYMENT (%)	TOTAL PAYMENT (£)
Advisers × 6	50	4	2,000	12,000
Administration manager	30	3	900	900
Para-planner	23	3	690	690
Support staff × 4	14	2	280	1,120
Total cost				14,710

on important developments for the business, as opposed to major and difficult hurdles.

There is an obvious drawback to this type of incentive, which is related to non-payment if the target is not reached. Despite all the logical arguments related to this, it is human nature to be disappointed if there is no payment. It is even worse if the reason for missing the target is outside the control of the individual or the firm. This is a challenge, because incentive schemes are meant to be positive incentives and not the cause of dissatisfaction.

Despite the simplicity referred to above, the payment rates can be tiered. Using the preceding example, the structure may be adjusted as follows:

- Profit target remains £100,000.
- Profit between 80% and 100% of target paid at 0.8% of the on-target rate.
- Profit between 101% and 120% of target is paid at the full target rate.
- If profit exceeds 120% of target payment is 1.2 times the target rate.

This greatly increases the chances of a payment, and also means that a really strong performance receives greater recognition. The additional cost of the extra payment if £120,000 profit is reached is just under £3,000, which is easily manageable from the additional profit. If you make the tiers more pronounced – say, 0.5% up to 1.5% – the incentive is greater and the additional cost is 35% of the extra £20,000 profit.

Table 22.7 summarises how this works.

The chart in Figure 22.3 compares the three ranges, and clearly shows the variations in incentive payment.

As the chart shows, the flat percentage pays nothing up to 'on target' and does not alter if performance exceeds target. The degree of variation increases as the incentive range widens. However, note that payment does not increase above 120% of profit target for any of the schemes, because incentive payments are based on salary which ensures that the cost to the business is being capped.

Table 22.7

STAFF	SALARY (£K)	ON TARGET RATE (% AND £)	RANGE 0.8%–1.2% (£)	RANGE 0.5%1.5% (£)
Advisers × 6	50	4 = 2,000	1,600 – 2,400	1,000 – 3,000
Administration manager	30	3 = 900	720 – 1,080	450 – 1,350
Para-planner	23	3 = 690	552 – 828	345 – 1,035
Support staff × 4	14	2 = 280	224 – 336	140 – 420
Total cost		14,710	11,768 – 17,652	7,355 – 22,065

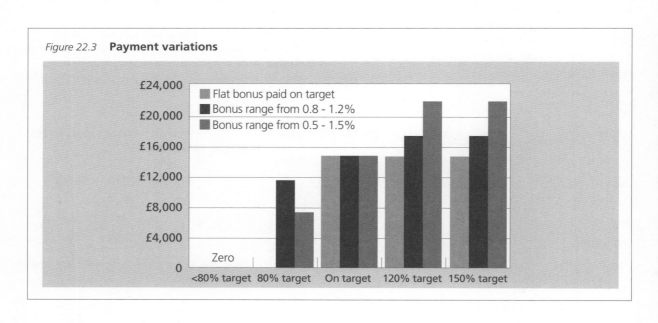

Figure 22.3 **Payment variations**

CASE STUDY

The bonus bone of contention

The directors of Emerald Financial were discussing the possibility of introducing a profit incentive scheme. Scott Jones was in favour and said, "We have always believed that the staff should share in the success of the business and, for those we want to keep, profit share is a good way to achieve that."

Derek Ford was not convinced. "If we have a really good year, mainly through our sales efforts, the staff could get large payments without actually putting in the same effort – and what about Sally, who never really pulls her weight? Will she get the same as the others? I don't mind this in principle, but it is fraught with problems – we don't want a blank cheque!"

Scott admitted that these issues also concerned him – it seemed fair in a broad sense to share some of the profit, but potentially unfair when individual circumstances were taken into account. "I understand your reservations, but I think we need to see if we can work around them, with the proviso that any scheme is straightforward – if we have to over-complicate it, then we should forget it." Scott did not really mean the last point, because he was still mindful of the last meeting when staff bonuses and incentives were agreed, and remembered that it was even more unfair and arbitrary than a properly thought-out profit-related scheme could be.

"Let's deal with the issues one by one and see how we could make this work," suggested Scott. He split them into three groups:

- The level of the incentive and the profit target that triggered payment.
- How to avoid the open-ended cheque.
- What should be done about poor performers?

Derek said, "Last week, when I was talking to Alison Black at Topaz Retirement Planning, she told me about their scheme: they started with a budget for incentives and bonuses, and worked backwards to set the targets and percentages that would be paid; that's how they capped the total payment. If you think about it, our profit has been around £150,000–£175,000 for the last four or five years, and our target this year is the same – we could simply say that we pay a profit-related incentive above £160,000, and we could set the budget at £16,000, but include that in our cost budgets. So we don't cut the profit by £16,000 as soon as we hit £160,000 – that would be self-defeating!"

Scott agreed with this approach, and said he would work out what the percentages could look like on that basis. He reminded Derek, "We have a performance review process that should pick up the poor performers – we could easily set KPIs in that process that have to be met if someone is going to get the payment." Derek liked this idea: "That will give us more rigour in the review process and make the goalposts very clear."

Scott and Derek decided to go ahead along the lines they had discussed, and made it clear to the staff that they believed such a scheme was right, but they would review it at the end of the year to see if adjustments were needed. They were very open and, as Scott said, "This is new for all of us, and we will need to make sure it is fair to everyone, including the business, so we will review how it works next year and change it if need be."

As it turned out, the scheme worked well, mainly because they had set the percentages in line with the budget. However, they did move to paying 0.75% if profit was 90% of the target, up to 1.25% if it was 110%. As Derek commented, "We cannot break the maximum if profit is over 110%, because we fixed the percentage payments on the salary levels, not the profit total. That works well as a cap, but also gives the staff more if we make more!"

CASE STUDY KEY POINT

It is important to work out how you will deal with poor performers. For anyone on disciplinary, it is straightforward, as you would not pay an incentive. For those who are between this and on-target performance, you need to have the KPIs in place, and then your decision on whether to pay or not becomes clear. That should also avoid negative reaction from your good performers, who will often ask why a poor performer gets the same incentive or bonus payment as them, when they have contributed more.

Finally, if you are introducing this for the first time, be very clear with staff that you will review it, ask them for their views and potentially make changes. That is fair to them and to you.

9 Chapter summary

The management skills you have developed as a result of this chapter mean that you can:

- Link rewards directly to business objectives.
- Design reward structures that work for employees and the business.
- Embody TCF principles in the reward structure.
- Design reward structures for self-employed advisers that enable the business to make a profit.
- Identify key performance indicators to be used in the reward structure to encourage good behaviours.
- Construct a straightforward profit incentive scheme that secures commitment and high performance.

In this chapter, we have analysed the complex area of reward. As you will have seen, there are many pressures on the reward policy, from how much people believe they are worth through to the views of the regulator and benchmarks from the wider market. You should set your policy to support your business objectives, and make sure you are consistent across the business and treat staff fairly.

Chapter 23
How to recruit effectively

By the end of this chapter, your business will benefit from:

✔ A reduction of recruitment risks.
✔ Clear recruitment specifications.
✔ Cost effective recruitment plans.
✔ Rigorous selection criteria and processes.
✔ Motivating and informative induction processes.

This chapter will cover the practical issues that you need to deal with to enable effective recruitment. This normally relates to new people, but can also include recruiting people already in the business into a new role. Both cases require clear and objective processes.

The chart in Figure 23.1 summarises the process that will be covered in this chapter.

You should base your process on the job description, the recruitment specification and your selection criteria. If these are in place, you will increase the chances of successful recruiting.

1 Reducing recruitment risk

Recruiting new people to your business is relatively high risk. This is because:

- There is a shortage of well trained and effective people, advisers and support staff.
- Adviser sales performance cannot really be proven until six months after they have joined you.
- Some advice businesses have poor recruitment processes.
- Processes to identify potential recruits are unreliable

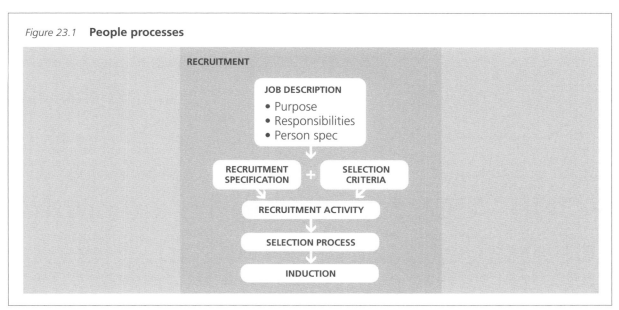

Figure 23.1 **People processes**

RECRUITMENT

JOB DESCRIPTION
- Purpose
- Responsibilities
- Person spec

RECRUITMENT SPECIFICATION + **SELECTION CRITERIA**

RECRUITMENT ACTIVITY

SELECTION PROCESS

INDUCTION

and experience varies (e.g. agencies, networking, specialist websites, etc).

- The impact of bringing new people into small teams cannot be understood until at least three months has passed.

This means that your aim has to be to minimise the risks around recruiting. It is not a perfect science, and it is impossible to design a process that is foolproof. However, you can implement good practice methods that increase the chance of securing the right people and, as time passes, of having them making the contribution you are expecting.

To review the effectiveness of your current recruitment process, you need to answer the following questions.

- Are your job descriptions up to date?
- Do you always decide on selection criteria before you interview people?
- Do you formally describe the personal capabilities that you require, along with the formal job requirements?
- If you use recruitment agencies, do you provide them with a written brief?
- Do you network locally to keep up with the movement of people between firms?
- For key roles, do you use additional selection methods alongside formal interviews?
- Do you typically involve more than one person in the selection process?
- Think of the last five people you recruited — have all or most of them stayed with you successfully?

You can work through these questions using **Template 1.3 in Part 6** of the website.

If you have answered "Yes" to half of these, you are in line with most advice businesses. It is likely that the mix of positive responses will be different, as there is no pattern across the market. For example, some advice businesses have a good experience with agencies, whereas others cannot make the relationship work. Or, more frustratingly, what seems to work well — be it agencies or networking — suddenly lets you down for no apparent reason.

This reinforces the fact that you cannot get this right all the time, which means that the good practice implied by the questions needs to be adopted.

YOUR AIM has to be to minimise the risks around recruiting. It is not a perfect science.

CASE STUDY

"Why do we lose so many advisers?"

Ben Walters and Sue Hart have run Ruby Financial Advisers for 15 years. They operate the self-employed model, and currently have 12 advisers, six of whom have been with them for several years. At one time, there were 23 advisers, although, in the past week, three of the current 12 have been given contractual notice to leave because their production is poor. In fact, at less than £40,000 in all cases, the business is making a loss on each one, which, as Sue says, "is not sustainable, but once again calls into question the way we recruit people."

Ben said, "If we are honest, we are not careful enough when we recruit, because we know the cost to the business of poor producers is quite low, especially compared to the employed model. However, I hate to think of the time and money we have wasted over the years — recruitment seems to be a continuing treadmill."

Samantha Reading, their administration manager, asked them how they went about recruiting advisers. "Do you have an organised approach, or do you base your judgement on experience?" she asked. Samantha knew the answer, because for years Ben and Sue had been making these same observations and repeating the same process. Samantha was respected by Ben and Sue, so she was always able to speak her mind. "Do you recall the last time we tried to deal with this? You asked me to sit in on some interviews — and we all disagreed on who to hire. We should try to be better organised throughout this entire process, from what we send the agencies through to the way we decide on candidates."

Ben admitted that the current process, where the initial interview was with Ben or Sue and the second was with both of them, was not sufficiently thorough. "We are too soft and give people a chance when we know they are unlikely to make it — then we have all the problems that follow. We must sharpen up our act. We should not recruit and give in to the pressure of maintaining revenue if we are doubtful about a particular candidate."

Sue agreed, and they both decided to find a course on successful recruiting. In fact, all three attended the course, because they were advised to have somebody who was slightly independent of the decision to take part in the selection process. "What we learned on this course, in addition to some good techniques, was that we needed to be as objective as possible," observed Sue. As Samantha said, "The techniques we are planning to use will give us a better all-round picture of the candidates and should increase our chances of getting the right people."

CASE STUDY KEY POINT

Many advice businesses use one or two interviews and experience as the main method of selection. They rely upon experience, which is good, but this needs to be backed up or challenged by objective processes and techniques. As a rule of thumb, the greater the variety that is built into the recruitment process, the wider the perspective of the candidate and the better the selection decision.

2 How to draw up a recruitment specification

This section is about the clarity of the job you need filled and the type of person you are looking for. You should prepare a written brief, even if the job is to be advertised and filled internally.

The benefits of a written brief are:

- Agreement within the business on the job and person required.
- Clear communication to external recruitment agencies.
- Clarity for candidates.
- Basis for selection criteria.

The written brief should include:

- Job title.
- Reporting lines and position on organisation chart (which should be attached).
- Why the job is available.
- Brief profile of the firm.
- Person specification.

- Attached job description.
- Pay and conditions.
- Desired starting date.

An example is laid out in Table 23.1 and there is a blank pro forma at **Template 2.3 in Part 6** of the website.

As the example shows, you can summarise what is required in a few words. Clearly you should tailor the content of this to the nature of the job and likely applicants. The section on profile of the firm would be different if you were recruiting an adviser, and you might attach a high level summary of your corporate plan. In addition, it can be useful to show which requirements are essential and which are desirable.

It is important that all those in the firm who have an interest in recruiting for this role agree the specification. It is exactly the same approach as the IT specification we looked at in Chapter 15. You need to be clear about what you want the person to do, and deal with any disagreements or misunderstandings before the recruitment process starts.

Table 23.1 **Client services administrator**

REPORTING LINES	Reports to senior administrator and is one of a team of five.
WHY THE JOB IS AVAILABLE	Business expansion and the need for more capacity in the client servicing team.
PROFILE OF STONE INVESTMENTS	Stone Investments is based in Clevedon near Bristol, and advises around 500 clients on their investments and retirement planning. The firm was set up in 1988, and employs six financial advisers, one para-planner and six administrators. The offices are purpose built, and there is good access to all local transport links.
PERSON SPECIFICATION	**PERSONAL QUALITIES** The personal qualities are very important and are taken from the attached job description: • Interpersonal skills — team working and communicating with clients by telephone and e-mail. • Proactive and willing to continue to develop career and capabilities. • Enthusiastic. • Highly organised, methodical, disciplined, meticulous. • Able to prioritise. • Computer literate (Word, Excel, back office). • Excellent keyboard skills. **QUALIFICATIONS** GCSE English and Mathematics, plus five other passes. Ideally, we would like the jobholder to have, or be working towards, the QCA Level 3. **PREVIOUS EXPERIENCE** Previous experience in financial services or a client service role would be an advantage, but for this role we are willing to train if you have no direct experience but the right personal qualities.
PAY AND CONDITIONS	Salary: starting at £14,000 pa plus profit-related bonus, and pension scheme after 12 months service. 37 hour week with flexitime available. 25 days paid holiday per year.
DESIRED START DATE	21 November 2011
ATTACHMENTS	Client service administrator: job description Website address: www.stone-ifa.com

3 Developing selection criteria

You need to prepare an objective set of criteria that you will use to decide who is appointed before the selection process begins. This should be agreed with all those involved in the final decision, and should form the agenda for the selection meeting when all the candidates have been seen. This tends to be an activity which is done badly in advice businesses, because decision takers use their intuition or experience, which is subjective, as opposed to supporting their views with objective analysis. Both approaches are important, and you should combine them.

Selection criteria include:

- The responsibilities listed in the job description.
- The personal qualities listed in the recruitment specification.
- Your overall conclusion on suitability.

You should list these on a template, make notes against them during the interview and give an independent score when the candidate has left. You should then work through this when the selection panel meets after all the candidates have been seen.

An example for the client services administrator is set out in Table 23.2.

Table 23.2 **Client services administrator NAME OF APPLICANT: ANDREW CORRY**

CRITERIA	NOTES	SCORE
RESPONSIBILITIES		**1 = POOR** **5 = EXCELLENT**
1. Manage the administration workflow.	Has worked at British Investment	1 & 2 =3
2. Develop, consistently implement and review processes.	Group (BIG) in customer services, deals with clients remotely, and	3 = 1
3. Receive and implement requests from planners and para-planners.	understands prioritisation and	4 = 2
4. Register and utilise appropriate extranets/websites and other forms of e-business.	managing the workflow.	5 – 8 = 4
5. Maintain up to date client files and data.	No technical knowledge, so needs	
6. Obtain illustrations, valuations and other information, etc, and process and track applications.	generic product training.	9 = 2
7. Diary management – for client reviews and planner meetings.	Strong on TCF and the need to process and discipline.	10 = 1 11 = 4
8. Prepare annual review listings by month.		12 = 5
9. Prepare and issue annual review data (fact find, etc) to clients.	Being part of BIG, he understands the importance of corporate	13 = 4 14 = 5
10. Commission monitoring and invoice preparation.	standards and process – and reporting.	
11. Liaise with clients and providers.		
12. Operate within the compliance and corporate standards of the business.	Has broad experience of an administration role and seems	
13. Undertake appropriate professional development and training.	to want to progress.	
14. Report on key measures on a regular basis.		
PERSON SPECIFICATION: PERSONAL QUALITIES		
1. Interpersonal skills – team working and communicating with clients by telephone and e-mail.	Works in a team at BIG, and seems to get on well with people.	1 = 4 2 = 4
2. Proactive and willing to continue to develop career and capabilities.	Clearly wants to progress and	3 = 5 4 = 4
3. Enthusiastic.	seems well organised – especially	5 & 6 = 4
4. Highly organised, methodical, disciplined, meticulous, able to prioritise.	for this interview.	
5. Computer literate (Word, Excel, back office).	Claims good keyboard skills (not	
6. Excellent keyboard skills.	tested, but current job would require these).	
QUALIFICATIONS		
GCSE English and Mathematics, plus five other passes. CII Certificate.	Has GCSE and A levels, no CII.	
PREVIOUS EXPERIENCE		
Previous experience in financial services or a client service role.	Yes, with BIG, three years from school.	
CONCLUSION		
Seems to have the right experience and broad knowledge; personable and will get on with people and clients – but we will need to train on products and funds, otherwise he won't be able to support the para planner.		

This will give you a good overview of the qualities of the candidate. It will be invaluable if you are expecting to interview more than three people and if your decision meeting is delayed for a few days after the final interview.

You must keep clear notes of all the interviews and other selection methods to a standard that would bear external scrutiny. In essence, treat these in exactly the same way as you would a fact find and other client notes. This is because:

- You may need to go to a second choice candidate if your first choice declines the offer.
- You may receive another application from the same person at some point in the future.
- The notes will support the first set of KPIs for the successful candidate when they join you.
- You will need the notes to defend your position should an unsuccessful applicant claim that you discriminated against them.

A blank pro forma version is supplied as **Template 2.4 in Part 6** of the website.

4 Designing the recruitment plan

Because it is difficult to find and recruit the right people, you need to make a concerted and structured effort to recruit effectively. For example, if your business plan involves recruiting five advisers over a two year period, you will need to do more than advertise in the trade press or call one of the recruitment agencies.

In many ways, this is exactly the same challenge as marketing a new product or service, which means you can use the marketing techniques that you developed in Part 3. It is also important to consider the full range of sources of candidates, which include:

- Trade press advertising.
- Recruitment agencies.
- Local networking.
- Public relations.
- Own website.
- Local employment agencies and press.

You can support each of the above using public relations, although that depends on the numbers that you wish to recruit.

Table 23.3 summarises the relative merits of the different approaches.

You need to select the right method for the task. Taking two extremes, if you need five advisers, you may use agencies and trade press (supported by PR if you are recruiting over a long period), but if you need a school leaver in an administration role, you would advertise in local press or use a local employment agency.

4.1 Planning a recruitment campaign

If you intend to recruit several people, you need to plan the activity to increase the chances of success. A slightly modified marketing campaign planning template can be used here, as shown in Table 23.4.

Table 23.3

	FOR	AGAINST	WHEN TO USE
TRADE PRESS ADVERTISING	• Wide coverage. • Obvious place to look for people in the market. • Should attract a lot of interest. • Good selection of titles to use. • Can be linked to PR.	• Attracts many unsuitable candidates. • Not suitable for admin jobs. • Covers entire country not just your locality.	• If you need several people. • Good for the 'national' market: advisers and para planners. • If you have a rolling recruitment programme. • If you are recruiting in different parts of the country.
RECRUITMENT AGENCIES	• Specialist knowledge. • Obvious source of candidates. • Can screen potential applicants.	• Relatively expensive (up to 20% of salary). • May send unsuitable candidates. • Wide variations in market knowledge.	• If the job is very specific. • If you need direct 'head-hunting' contact. • When you have to search nationally.
LOCAL NETWORKING	• Often considered the best method. • You gain knowledge of people long before they apply to you. • Provides opportunity to approach directly. • Enables you to make it known you are recruiting.	• Time consuming. • Limits the recruitment pool.	• If you want to recruit locally — applies to senior administration posts. • If you wish to ensure you are 'on the radar' if people are looking to move.
PUBLIC RELATIONS	• When you need to recruit nationally. • When you need to recruit a lot of people. • If you consider that image is important to attract people.	• Time consuming. • Needs to fit with your marketing plan.	• If profile and image are required to support the recruitment plan. • If you need to recruit a lot of people in a short time period.
OWN WEBSITE. LINKEDIN	• You directly control the message and the environment within which it is read. • If you use PR and messaging to attract attention.	• Could attract many unsuitable candidates. • Covers entire country, not just your locality. • Needs continuous updating.	• All the time if you have a website and presence on Linkedin, but never rely on it as the main source of contact.
LOCAL EMPLOYMENT AGENCIES AND PRESS	• Low cost. • Good if your candidates live locally.	• Only works for specific roles — and not for advisers.	• If you need administration staff. • If temporary staff are needed.

Table 23.4 **Proposed campaign plan**

WHAT ARE YOU TRYING TO ACHIEVE?	WHAT IS THE ACTIVITY ABOUT?	WHO ARE WE TRYING TO INFLUENCE?	WHAT DO WE WANT THEM TO KNOW?	HOW WILL WE COMMUNICATE? WHEN WILL THIS HAPPEN?	WHO WILL DO THE WORK AND WHAT WILL IT COST?
(Objective)	(Proposition)	(Target)	(Key messages)	(Method and timing)	(Resources and budget)
Recruit five advisers between 1/1/10 and 1/6/11	Recruiting five advisers to provide a net increase of three (covering two retirements).	**GROUP 1:** Three experienced advisers with specialist knowledge (pensions knowledge is essential in one) and at least some high value clients.	We are professional and operate to high ethical standards. Our training is recognised as superb. We have a clear business direction with supporting growth plans.	**TRADE PRESS** PR to support profile with press releases on: • Opening of new office. • Our 'recruitment drive'. • Comment on major industry developments.	Throughout 2010–11 (Alan).
		GROUP 2: Two graduate trainees.			Brief agreed by 1/12/09.
				AGENCIES Very specific written brief for the three experienced roles.	Agencies contacted and briefed face to face, 31/12/09 (Brian).
				LOCAL NETWORKING Continue to attend local AIFA and IFP meetings and provider seminars.	Ongoing (Mary and Alan).

This provides you with an organised plan that aims to reduce the risks around recruitment and deliver a shortlist of suitable candidates. As with all marketing activity, this is time consuming, but as we saw in Part 3 on marketing, if you get the foundations right, the plan is more likely to achieve its objective. Use **Template 2.5 in Part 6** of the website to work through your own plan.

5 How to develop the selection process

The process for selecting candidates depends on the job and the scale of the negative impact if you recruit the wrong person. This means that for a junior administration role you may use an interview supported with aptitude tests. For an adviser, you may use the above plus role play and psychometric tests.

The methods available to support selection include:

- Formal interviews with key decision takers.
- Informal meetings with potential colleagues.
- Role plays to simulate certain characteristics of the job.
- 'In-tray' exercises, typically pieces of work to complete (e.g. preparing recommendations for a fictitious client).
- Psychometric tests, typically to identify personality trends.

5.1 How to get the best out of formal interviews

We are all familiar with formal interviews, and for practically all jobs they are an important part of the recruitment process. You should plan and formally conduct these, because if they turn into a general discussion you can be certain that important issues will be missed. In addition, you should recognise that the interviewee is assessing you, the firm and the job as much as you are assessing the candidate. You need to adopt a consistent approach for all candidates, and this structure helps achieve that.

5.2 Allowing candidates to talk to their potential colleagues

You have to judge how appropriate this is, and how formal you want the process to be. In many cases, these meetings are a straightforward ten minute session with other members of the team that gives the firm and candidates a broader perspective. They are often unstructured, although you should make the ground rules clear with your team beforehand. It is best if they take place before the formal interview so that you can take feedback from team members and explore further if necessary.

The benefits of informal colleague meetings are:

- Other members of the team feel part of the process.
- It normally places candidates at ease and gives them a practical and wider perspective of the firm.
- Colleague opinions can be factored into the decision process.
- Candidates obtain a better feel for the firm, which contrasts with the formal parts of the process.

There are disadvantages which you need to manage in advance if you intend to use this technique, including the following:

- Team members may prefer a different candidate from the one selected.
- A poor briefing can make this an unproductive experience, and a poor impression will be conveyed to candidates.

On balance, these informal meetings contribute positively to the process, and provide an impression of openness and confidence that the firm is happy to give candidates access to a broader range of people. If you think this would not work for your business, you should ask yourself why that would be the case.

FOCUS POINT

Interview plan

This interview plan is generic: it provides a structure and questions that can be adapted to specific jobs.

FORMAL INTRODUCTION

Introductions, the role that joint interviewers will play, expected length of interview, what happens next and when final decision is expected.

CONTEXT

Why have you applied for this job? What attracts you to it? Have you applied for other jobs recently, and what is their status?

How does this job fit with your career? Does it take you in the direction you desire, or does it mark a change?

Why are you thinking of leaving your existing job? What did you particularly like/dislike about it? If it did not work out, what could you or the firm have done differently?

PERSONALITY

What are your strengths and weaknesses? What have you done about these? How do you think they will influence your contribution to this job?

What do your subordinates/managers/peers say about you? What feedback did you get at your last performance review? What aspects of your strengths/weaknesses are you currently working on?

What do you look for in a manager? What really irritates you (give examples)? Are you a single minded person who is self-motivating and self-sufficient, or a team player who thrives on the support of others?

What is the greatest challenge/success you have experienced in a work context? What did you do and how did it turn out, and would you have done anything different?

What is your greatest disappointment in a work/career context? How did you feel, and what would you do to avoid a similar situation in the future?

How did you prepare for this interview?

JOB SPECIFIC

Questions related directly to the responsibilities on the job specification, probing any gaps.

What development would you need if you got this job? Would you need support for this or can you do it alone?

If you got this job, what would be the greatest challenge it would present you with? How would you deal with that?

What is your current salary, etc? In your view, how do the terms and conditions for this job match your current circumstances? What notice period and/or other restrictions do you have?

CANDIDATE QUESTIONS

Ensure you leave plenty of time for this section.

CLOSE

Summary of next steps, and check if the candidate needs any more information at this stage.

5.3 The role of role plays

These are exactly as the term suggests: they attempt to simulate certain conditions of the job. You will be familiar with these techniques through T & C and sales training, and they do have a role to play in the recruitment process. If you decide to use this technique, you should set it up properly, as follows:

- Brief the candidates in advance that you intend to do this and that they will be given time to prepare.
- Decide on the scenario and the broad content.
- Be clear about what you are trying to assess and shape the content accordingly.
- Practice the role play with a colleague to make sure it works.
- Provide the candidate with feedback at an appropriate point in the overall decision process.

These techniques are widely used across the business world, but far less extensively with advisers. Advice businesses that use role plays normally use them for adviser recruitment and particularly if they do not know the candidate. Anecdotal evidence suggests that these work extremely well, and candidates who use their skills to sell themselves in the formal interview sometimes reveal weaknesses in the role play. There is little doubt that this will provide you with a different perspective and give you an insight into how potential advisers will deal with your clients.

5.4 The use of 'in-tray' exercises

These exercises present candidates with a practical piece of work. This can range from several tasks through to a single case study. In all cases, they aim to assess how well a candidate actually carries out a key part of the job, as opposed to telling you how they would do it.

These exercises will differ by job. For example, administration jobs may include a typical in-tray that needs prioritising and dealing with. If candidates have to know a particular piece of software, then you can include that as part of the process. You could base adviser exercises on a client case study requiring a report and recommendations. This can be very flexible, so you may set aside two hours, provide a fact find and other data and ask for a verbal report, or you may wish to test written communication and request that it is typed into your company template.

The advantages are similar to role plays, because you are assessing the actual capability of the individual as opposed to talking about it.

THESE EXERCISES aim to assess how well a candidate actually carries out a key part of the job, as opposed to telling you how they would do it

CASE STUDY

In-tray: important process or side show?

Emily Rose and Chris South have completed their review of job descriptions and are thinking about their recruitment process. They have a technical support person to recruit, and don't want to rely solely on the formal interview.

Emily said, "For this type of job, where we want proven ability to use some of the research software and draft recommendations, we could set up an exercise to see how people react." Chris was slightly wary, and asked, "Do we tell them in advance? What if they interview well and mess up the exercise? And do you think they will actually do it?"

Emily thought that candidates should be told in advance and was not worried about how they fared. "The reason for doing this is to give us as much information as possible to make our decision — if some of that conflicts, we will have to deal with it at the time."

Chris set up the brief, which included:

- A completed fact find.
- Written notes from the adviser, with generic guidance on the recommendations.
- The Rose Associates report and recommendations template.

The candidates were told in advance when invited for interview and were informed that the exercise could take up to an hour. One candidate dropped out, citing the exercise as "a bit of an insult". Emily reckoned that this was a good contribution to the selection process. "That tells us something negative about the person and their desire for the job, if they cannot take the opportunity to demonstrate their expertise," she noted.

Emily and Chris ran the exercise, and one of the three candidates produced a far superior answer to the others. His interpersonal skills were not as good as one other candidate, but they offered him the job, because, in this instance, they were comfortable that he could work well with colleagues and, over time, could gain the confidence needed to deal with clients when necessary.

As Emily said, "At the end of this process, I feel confident that we know much more about the person we appointed than used to be the case, and we were able to balance up the pluses and minuses much better than if we were just going on interview."

CASE STUDY KEY POINT

Using a range of selection techniques will provide you with more information — which will always lead to a better informed and better quality decision

5.5 When to use psychometric tests

These are specialist tools that are designed to supplement the decision taking process. You should never use them as the main driver of the decision, but they will normally raise issues (positive and negative) that can be discussed at interview.

It is strongly recommended that you use a trained person to administer and analyse psychometric tests. Many recruitment agencies will have such people, or you can go to specialists whom they can recommend. If you have not used these techniques before, it is reasonable to undertake the exercise yourself. It will give you a clear indication of how the process works, as well as feedback that you may not have received before. Most importantly, it will give you confidence in the process and make it clear how you can use it effectively.

These will be most cost effective when used with senior roles and advisers, particularly if the specialist can provide you with benchmarks as well as a specific report on the candidate in question.

6 Deciding which selection techniques to use

It is often clear which techniques you should use, but your selection should be based on whether or not they will aid your final recruitment decision. You could use all of the techniques with senior roles, because they provide different dimensions and perspectives. The wider the range of information you have, the better your final choice. It is recognised that this is time consuming and costly, but you should set it in the context of the difficulty of finding and recruiting the right people.

The order in which you apply these techniques is not too important, except that the formal interview must come last. This is because all of the information you have gathered in the preceding stages can be fed into your questions and issues to be raised. If you are using specialists to run the psychometric tests, these are usually done first and often at their offices.

You should provide feedback on all the assessment methods at the end of the process. You could do this at the end of the formal interview or, for the successful candidate, at a full debrief when they join you. After all, it is highly likely that the process will have revealed development opportunities, and you may want to set these as the first batch of objectives to cover in the initial six months.

If you are using assessment methods in addition to the formal interview, you should tell candidates when you invite them to the selection process. There is little preparation they can do for some of the techniques, but managing expectations is very important. Some businesses provide a list of methods with a short description of each, which helps

candidates prepare and acts as a checklist for the business.

Finally, when you have completed a recruitment exercise, you should review how each method worked and consider what changes you might make next time you use them.

7 The importance of induction processes

The approach to this varies across the market. If you recall the last time you joined a new organisation, you will remember how long it took to know how everything worked and what everyone did. It is not just the formal processes but the day to day workings and relationships that are important.

The formality of your induction programme will depend on the size of your business and how many people you employ. Assess the effectiveness of your arrangements by answering the following questions:

- Do you have a formal, written down induction programme?
- Do you formally set up meetings for new joiners with staff they will be working with?
- Is there a manual that tells people how the main processes work?
- Do you have a clear and up to date list of all the things a new joiner should know by the end of their first week?
- Do you take them through the relevant parts of the business plan, including your approach to TCF and their responsibilities to adhere to corporate and compliance standards?
- Is there an organised approach to training new joiners on essential software and other procedures relevant to their job?
- Do you make sure that somebody looks after new joiners in their first week (e.g. particularly at lunch breaks)?
- Does somebody meet with the joiner at the end of their first week to talk through their experiences and in particular identify any problems?
- After a month, do you ask them if there is anything that could have been done differently in their first few weeks?

You can make this as formal as appropriate, but it is important that all of this is done. Use **Template 1.4 in Part 6** of the website to create a formal checklist. Clearly, you would tailor the induction to the job and type of person, including their experience. Many firms have low levels of recruitment, which means the induction process can become outdated or be forgotten. Hence, it is important that you prepare it well when new joiners are expected; their first impressions of your business are as important as your clients' first impressions of you.

A typical induction programme would include the following:

- Meeting with principals and line manager if appropriate.
- Meetings with colleagues with whom the joiner will be working.
- Explanation of relevant parts of business plan and TCF plan, and how they relate to the jobholder.
- Coverage of legal and regulatory rules around health and safety, absence management, money laundering, etc.
- Clear explanation of corporate standards (e.g. risk management, service levels, performance management, T & C processes, pricing policy, etc) that the joiner will be expected to respect and take part in.
- Overview, and as much detail as required, of main processes that joiner will be working with.
- Agreeing the objectives for the first three months.

8 Chapter summary

The management skills you have developed as a result of this chapter mean that you can:

- Reduce the risks associated with recruitment.
- Design a clear recruitment specification.
- Develop selection criteria that are relevant to the job.
- Apply selection criteria in the recruitment process.
- Decide on specific selection techniques which are relevant to the job.
- Manage the selection process in an objective manner.
- Design and implement an effective induction process.

This chapter is designed to remove as much of the risk from the recruitment process as possible. As we have seen, it is difficult to achieve perfect results all the time, but the costs associated with recruitment are such that we need to maximise our chances. You need to apply the processes and good practice included in this chapter to gain the best outcome for your business and potential employees.

Chapter 24
How to manage communication and change

By the end of this chapter, your business will benefit from:

✔ Clear communications within the business.
✔ Less speculation and more fact.
✔ Staff who are confident in knowing what is going on and where the business is going.
✔ Low staff turnover.
✔ Change management that recognises the concerns and potential of individuals.

Effective communication is an important management task, because it is central to motivating and retaining people. You will have spent time and money on recruiting and developing staff, so keeping them informed and involved with progress and change in the business is essential.

1 Make your internal communication effective

Most businesses find the challenge of achieving effective communication elusive. It is very hard to get right, partly because staff are all different. Clearly they hold different jobs, but their personalities and levels of commitment to the business will also vary. This means that pitching the quantity and level of communication is difficult — along with when to gather people together or simply e-mail them. There are no right answers, and what works well for one business can fail in another.

You also need to consider the context within which you are communicating.

You cannot read the minds of your staff, so you need to create the conditions that are appropriate to communication. You also need to choose the right medium for your communication; Table 24.1 provides a guide as to how you might achieve this.

As the Table shows, there is a variety of methods of communicating and creating the right feeling. You may only

take 30 minutes to present the annual business plan, but if it is set up as an important and positive event, people will recognise it as such. However, there are other day to day matters that you can deal with by e-mail. You would not e-mail the business plan to everybody and hope that they read it, but you would e-mail procedural changes and follow up in a team meeting.

1.1 What internal communications tools are available?

A generic mix of communication tools is:

• Monthly senior management meetings.
• Weekly staff team meetings.
• All major news on intranet or by e-mail.
• Ad hoc gatherings for one-off important events.
• Principal leading major announcements, with local team meeting to back this up if needed.

You have to decide what will work best for your staff and be prepared to make changes. It is worth checking at least once a year if people consider that communication is working and what, if any, changes they would like. If this means that you go back to something they rejected two years ago, it does not matter, as long as it meets the need (and probably reflects some changes in personnel).

There is an important discipline related to communication with staff, which is that every time you make a change that has consequences for staff (ranging from mergers to expense forms) you must think about what you will

Table 24.1

TYPE OF ISSUE	EXAMPLE	WHERE	METHOD
Strategic	Merger Annual business plan	In the office Local hotel	Face to face by principal Face to face by senior team – followed by drinks or meal
People	Senior appointment or departure Junior appointment or departure Examination success	In the office E-mail or intranet and office At the person's desk	Face to face: principal or senior manager Electronically, with team meeting back up Short face to face with champagne or cakes, or small gift for individual
Operational changes	New process for submitting expenses Health and safety policy (e.g. smoking location)	E-mail or intranet In the office	Electronically, with team meeting back up Team meeting

communicate and how and when you will do it. This should be just as important a part of the discussion as the decision itself.

1.2 Getting the best out of meetings

A lot of communication takes place in meetings. To get the best out of these, you should do the following:

- Provide notice of when and where the meeting will be held and who is invited.
- Issue an agenda in advance, with timings for each item.
- Start and finish on time.
- Try as hard as you can to keep the meeting on track and to the point.
- Issue a note of actions (not full minutes unless really necessary, as with investment committee).
- Share responsibility for chairing the meeting and for some of the content.
- Make sure everyone has the opportunity to take part.
- If appropriate (and particularly for regular meetings) have prizes for client service, TCF actions and helping colleagues; these often cost little, but recognition in front of colleagues is a huge boost to morale.
- For senior management meetings, confirm who will brief the rest of the staff (as appropriate) and what they will say.
- Do not change decisions after the meeting.
- Be prepared to cancel the meeting if there is nothing to talk about.

Every so often, you should check that regular meetings are working. Ask the participants if anything needs to change; it is possible that the need for the meeting has gone, or the content is no longer relevant. Inertia can often result from meetings taking place because they always have, so do remember to check.

1.3 Communicating bad news

There will be times when you have to communicate bad

news to one or more of your staff. This typically relates to redundancy or dismissal. With regard to the latter, there can be very different circumstances, ranging from misconduct through to poor performance. Dismissal can be more difficult if the individual has tried to achieve objectives and failed due to lack of capability as opposed to lack of application.

You should prepare meetings like these carefully, and make sure that the location is private and there will be no interruptions. It is essential to take notes and follow the recommended procedures in case there is an appeal in the future. You also need to think about what you are going to say and how you expect the individual to react. This type of meeting is infrequent and unfamiliar, so you do need to plan in advance.

Before the meeting, you should:

- Prepare what you are going to say and think through the possible reactions.
- Prepare an agenda.
- Assemble key information or evidence that may be required.

During the meeting, you should:

- Get to the point quickly, but not too bluntly or insensitively.
- Show empathy and be aware of the individual's personal circumstances.
- Use clear, unambiguous language and plain English.
- Allow individuals to express their feelings and ask questions.
- Note questions which you are unable to answer, and make sure you provide answers as soon as possible.
- Clearly explain the next steps.

You should not:

- Communicate the message without rehearsing exactly what you are going to say.
- Prolong the meeting with small talk.
- Get defensive or angry.

- Criticise the changes you are communicating.
- Say "I know how you feel".
- Imply that bad news is a blessing in disguise.
- Rush through the meeting because you feel uncomfortable.
- Make promises or negotiate 'deals'.
- Ignore the individual's responses or questions.
- Try to answer questions you are unprepared for.

For many advice businesses, these meetings are related to poor performance of advisers. You need to make sure that you have given the adviser the opportunity to perform effectively, and that you have previously agreed production and quality targets. These must be clearly stated and in writing. Dismissal is serious, so you need to give people at least one chance to prove their capability.

There is a clear legal process that must be followed, and you should take advice from your own human resources manager, your external HR support or one of the service providers you can engage to support the process.

2 How to manage change

This is an abstract concept, because the market and the business are constantly changing. Indeed, one of the fundamental characteristics of the financial services sector is change and disruption. In some cases, this will affect your business immediately and directly (e.g. a sudden stock market crash), while in others the time lag will be longer (e.g. changes in the regulatory stance following the credit crisis).

The type of change we are concerned with in this section is that which you instigate in the business and which affects many of your staff directly. Typical examples include:

- Changes in job content and re-allocation of responsibilities.
- Major changes in methods of working, particularly if teams are being re-organised.
- Mergers and acquisitions.
- Redundancies.

Because change of this type occurs infrequently, you need to consider how you will manage the announcement and the period that follows. Ideally, you need to make sure that you move quickly from the present to the new position — from uncertainty to stability.

2.1 The change curve

You are likely to have come across the change curve which is shown in Figure 24.1 — either on a course or through your own experience of change. The various stages on the curve show how individuals react and move through periods of change, some inevitably more slowly than others.

As Figure 24.1 shows, most people go through a sequence of reactions to major change. The speed with which this happens depends on:

- The nature of the change.
- The balance between the negative and positive elements of the change.
- The extent to which the individual is directly affected (e.g. from a minor change in working practice through to loss of job).
- Individual personalities.
- The time period over which the change will be implemented.

It is inevitable that when major changes are announced each person asks, "What does this mean for me?" The greater the change (particularly if it is negative), the longer it is likely to take before the upward slope is reached.

There is nothing that you can do directly to manage the pace at which people move through the curve, but there are actions you can take that will ease the path from the apparent turmoil of the present to the desired stability of the future.

2.2 Managing the transition to the future

For most people, there is a desire for stability. This enables them to feel in control and to plan ahead. When you announce a major change, this creates the opposite effect, which means you have to help people through the uncertainty. There are various things you can do, including:

- Making sure that everyone understands why the change is happening and what the next steps are.
- Giving as much information as possible in a variety of formats.
- Listening with care to comments, concerns and reactions.
- Ensuring that you answer all the questions as soon as you can.
- Remaining sympathetic where appropriate, but repeating why the change is necessary.
- Communicating progress, ideally weekly.
- Giving time for people to absorb the messages and respond to change.

There will be some people who are particularly important in the change process. These are:

- People you want to retain in the business.
- Opinion leaders.

You need to pay attention to everyone in the business, but make sure you know the reactions of your key people. Take them to one side and discuss the issues in detail if that is required. Opinion leaders often include key people, but will also include those who tend to be vocal in their reactions. In essence, you have to win them over, because that will

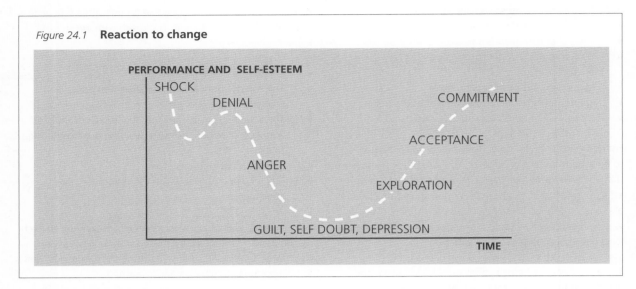

Figure 24.1 **Reaction to change**

gradually tip the balance towards exploration, acceptance and commitment.

In the early days after announcing a major change, you have to be in the office and be prepared to give time to people. It is essential that you pick up the mood and reaction, and tailor your ongoing communications accordingly. As soon as you can, bring the key people and opinion formers into the implementation phase of the change. Of course, it is likely that some of your key people will have been involved in the initial decision, which makes this part easier.

Provide people with a clear picture of the expected outcome. This helps to give direction and makes the opportunities and positive outcomes seem attainable and realistic. For those who will be part of the future, this can quickly remove uncertainty and gain commitment.

In some cases, the outcome is clear, such as re-organisation and changes in responsibilities. However, if two firms are joining together, you may have a general picture of the future in terms of the size and scale of the business, but no detail around how it will be structured. Most people understand that you cannot get to that level of detail at the outset, but you do have to tell them when you expect to have done it. You may not be able to remove uncertainty about jobs, but you can help by telling people when they will know what is going to happen.

Finally, if the change involves a full implementation plan (such as a merger), you need to communicate the timetable and give very regular updates on progress. You must remember that failure to communicate creates a vacuum which will rapidly be filled with rumour, gossip and misunderstanding. You must avoid this at all costs.

If you have a major change to announce and implement, here are some questions that will help you prepare:

- How did you react the last time you were involved in a major change?
- What would have made it easier to adapt and move forward?
- How do you feel about this change?
- How will your key people react, using the change curve for context?
- What is your presentation plan (what you will say, where and when)?
- How quickly can you get to the point?
- What questions will be asked?
- How will you articulate what the future looks like?
- Do you have key dates in the future by which the change will be implemented?
- What is the plan to follow up with key people plus all those directly affected?
- Are you going to be around over the few days following the announcement?
- How frequently will you communicate as the change plan progresses?

CASE STUDY

Communicating major change

The financial services business of Cyan Insurance Brokers is to be acquired by Garnet Investment Services. The directors of Cyan have been seeking a retirement option for the past three years, and those involved with financial services have agreed to sell to Garnet. They have also agreed to transfer to Garnet and stay for at least two years to effect a smooth transition. The general side of the business will be unchanged, and the two directors responsible for it will continue to run it while they also look for a buyer.

At the end of the final long and detailed meeting at which agreement was reached, Edward Forest, the oldest partner from Cyan, said, "Thank goodness that is over; we can tell the staff tomorrow and then I'm off on holiday for a week. I'm exhausted!" His co-partner, Eleanor Chambers, looked shocked. "Hang on, Ted. How long have these people worked for us? This will be a real shock — we cannot treat them like that. We haven't finished the job just yet," she stated.

Bruce Norman from Garnet said, "Edward, I know how you feel; we went through the same thing three years back when we acquired Thomas Muir's business. He wasn't sure how to handle it and we worked out a communications plan with him." Edward looked slightly annoyed. "This sounds very elaborate; there won't be any changes for a while, the general business is not changing and the good people will most likely keep their jobs, so do we have to plan this like some military operation?"

Eleanor suggested that she and Bruce spent two hours working out how to deal with this, while Edward sorted out some final legal points with one of Bruce's colleagues.

Bruce said, "Edward is right, we don't need to go over the top, but we must sort out how we handle this. If we mess up the initial communication, we are on the back foot from the start."

Cyan had 23 staff, split evenly between financial services and general insurance. Bruce suggested that Edward and the director responsible for the general side, Francoise Delaford, make a joint presentation to all the staff the following day at 11 am. "That will give people time to sort their day out, but not too much time for speculation to start — we want to avoid unsettling people."

The plan that emerged was very straightforward, and when Bruce and Eleanor met Edward and Francoise later that evening, they had a clear way forward. Eleanor said, "You need to make a joint presentation, introduce Bruce and be prepared to take questions — in addition, we must all make sure we are around over the next couple of weeks to see how people really feel and keep a close eye on those we don't want to lose."

Bruce said, "The presentation needs to come straight to the point, because that is what people will want to know. Tell them what is going to happen, give them some background and re-assure them that it is a good way forward for Cyan. Invite Bruce to give them an overview of Garnet — and, Francoise, you will need to say something about the general side."

"We need to spend some time thinking about the questions they will ask and how we will answer them — and don't duck the difficult ones, because they are bound to ask them," said Bruce.

Edward agreed that this was the right approach: "I had been so focused on this that I just didn't think about planning how we would tell the staff. I must say, if I had been on the receiving end of a poor communication that involved such a big change, I would have been quite offended — the holiday will have to wait for a couple of weeks!"

CASE STUDY KEY POINT

It is not very often that we have such major changes as this to announce, but anything that affects staff needs to be communicated with care. The practice of working out and writing down the expected questions and answers is a really good way to prepare, and, as always, if there are some things that you don't know, always admit that this is the case and try to give some idea of when you will have the answer. This is particularly important when jobs are involved.

3 Chapter summary

The management skills you have developed as a result of this chapter mean that you can:

- Communicate effectively with your colleagues and staff.
- Operate two-way communications.
- Use a variety of communication methods.
- Select the right communication methods for the circumstances.
- Manage change effectively.

We are all aware that our ability to communicate and manage change is determined in part by our personalities and behaviours. Inevitably, some of us will be good communicators and others less so. However, these management skills are as important as those related to finance, marketing and selling. So we have to work at these just as much as the others and, given our leadership role within the business, if we are not naturally good at communicating, we need to work even harder.

Part 7: Fine tuning your business

Making sure your business is fit and efficient

"We are not retreating – we are advancing in another direction."

Douglas MacArthur

Introduction: Check the condition of your business

When you have completed this Part, you will be able to:

✔ Recognise when the time is right to 'fine-tune' your business.
✔ Follow the quick route toward performance improvement.
✔ Know when to undertake contingency planning.
✔ Take a structured approach to improving business performance.

When businesses are created or brand new strategies are designed, there is an air of excitement, challenge and energy. If you have been involved in a start-up, you will recognise this, as the strength of optimism takes you through all sorts of problems and barriers. However, as the business matures or the hard work of implementing the new plan takes place, there is a return to normality. Clients have to be seen and serviced, difficult staff issues need to be dealt with and the everyday processes of compliance and operations come to the fore.

You can keep your business fresh by the way you manage it, and by ensuring that successes are celebrated and problems quickly and fairly dealt with. This keeps the business moving on and sustains positive behaviours and attitudes. But you will need to do more, and fine tuning the business is an important formal management exercise that you will have to undertake from time to time.

This Part explains how to do this and, through the case studies, applies the process to different circumstances.

For each question, give your business an objective score (1 is poor, and 10 is excellent) and ask others what they think. Use **Template 1.1 from Part 7 — Fine Tuning Your Business** on the website to distribute the questions.

If you have scored over 30%, you will be ahead of the market. If you are in the majority and have scored less, you should not be overly critical of yourself, because time is as much the enemy of continuous fine tuning as it is of strategic planning.

There is nothing in the list that principals argue with, because it is good business practice. Indeed, one of the core elements of the Treating Customers Fairly (TCF) initiative is to adopt good practice techniques and then monitor progress to enable further change.

This Part will show how you can implement a straightforward process to fine tune your business. It is structured and designed to quickly identify and prioritise potential improvements. As you will see, it is more specific than a strength and weaknesses analysis, and is best applied under particular circumstances.

How fit is your business?

The Table that follows asks Ten Killer Questions about business fitness. These questions also summarise what is 'good' for an advice business that is in prime condition.

FINE TUNING: Ten killer questions

Score: 1 = poor, and 10 = excellent

To what extent:

1. Do you regularly review the management information dashboard and take action?

2. Are your staff genuinely encouraged to suggest and implement changes?

3. Do you conduct an annual strengths and weaknesses analysis?

4. Have you invited third parties to review the effectiveness of your business?

5. Do you ask clients to identify potential for improvement?

6. Do you ask and answer the question, "Is there a better way of doing this?"

7. Have you identified improvements by looking at what other businesses do?

8. Are you spending enough time working on your business as opposed to in your business?

9. Are you satisfied that your business is keeping its competitive edge?

10. Do competitors and respected clients compliment you on proactive and consistently efficient service?

Chapter 25
The fine tuning process

By the end of this chapter, your business will benefit from:

✔ A sustained competitive advantage.
✔ Quick reaction to sudden market changes.
✔ Dealing with a perceived crisis in a structured manner.
✔ A positive approach to continuous change.

There are times when you need to improve the performance of your business without a fundamental re-organisation. Think of your business like a new car: it is designed and built to do a particular job and you may not change it for five years or more. However, it has to be serviced and retuned at regular intervals to keep it in perfect running order. The same approach applies to all businesses, and the advice sector is no different. This applies to all trading conditions, and the process can be used to position the business for a period of market growth as much as to deal with a downturn.

1 When to fine tune your business

You should fine tune your business when:

• Your annual business plan review confirms your overall strategy but reveals a number of new weaknesses or threats.
• Your instinct tells you that your business is not as sharp and proactive as it used to be.
• Standards seem to be slipping.
• Clients are leaving unexpectedly.
• There is an upturn in complaints or compliance issues.
• You look enviously at a competitor who seems to do things better than you.

In addition, there are external changes that should trigger fine tuning:

• Sudden change in trading conditions.
• Change in regulations that directly affect the business.

Fine tuning is not a substitute for strategic planning. But it is very useful when your direction and vision are right, but the issues listed above begin to concern you. The 2009-11 recession provides a perfect example, because many businesses reviewed and confirmed their overall strategy and direction but needed to take quick short term action to cope with a difficult market.

Template 1.2 in Part 7 of the website sets out these issues in the form of a questionnaire that you can work through more formally.

2 What to look for under the bonnet

You need to take a structured approach to fine tuning, and the framework for this is set out in Figure 25.1.

Figure 25.1 **Improve performance**

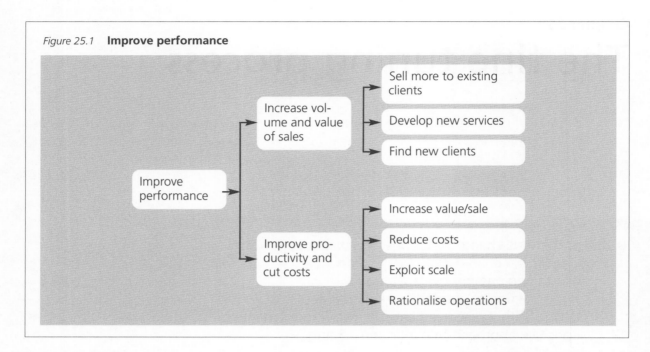

To improve performance, there are two routes to pursue:

- Increase the volume and value of sales.
- Increase productivity and cut costs.

You are recommended to pursue both paths as rigorously as possible, especially if there is a rapid and unexpected downturn in the market. You should adopt the same approach as reviewing financial performance, where you need to ask the detailed questions and challenge all assumptions if problems arise; don't assume that the entire answer will be to cut costs.

The top part of the chart is designed to increase sales volume and value and is about clients and services. You should use the client/service matrix from section 2.1, which looks at new services for existing clients as well as new clients for existing services.

The lower part of the chart is about improving productivity and cutting costs to support an increase in profit. You should ask the range of questions listed for reviewing budgets from Chapter 11 as a starting point.

CASE STUDY

The plan we want to leave on the shelf

Roberta and Aaron Brown heard about how the 2009-11 recession was starting to affect their local competitors, Copper Group. With 15 advisers and 12 support staff, Roberta and Aaron had a relatively high cost base, and although their business was more diversified than Copper, they were starting to see a fall in initial income and a sharper fall in new enquiries for investment-related business.

Aaron said, "We'll have to work harder, try to see more clients and sell our way through this recession." "I am sure that type of approach is part of the answer," said Roberta, "but I think we need to take this seriously and not have a false sense of security from our recurring income. I am going to look at all our costs, and you should look at all our market opportunities."

Roberta spent the next weekend going through all the cost and revenue sources and recasting the cash flow forecast to show a pessimistic scenario and a more positive one. She summarised her conclusions to Aaron: "Did you realise that almost half our recurring income is fund-based? With the markets down by over one-third, we will end up £150,000 short at the end of the year – that's what we made in profit last year!" Aaron was not aware of this trend, and it worried him, because he had no control over when the markets would get back to more reasonable levels and did not like the idea of working for no profit that year. "What do you think we should do to protect ourselves and make some money over our salaries?" he asked.

Roberta said, "You were right that we will have to bolster our sales, but we have to look at costs as well. I think we should look at where we could cut staff costs if it comes to it, and also identify other ways we can increase the revenue so we avoid redundancies. Finally, let's face it, we should think about reducing our drawings if we have to – where would we cut down?"

Roberta's final suggestion was that they looked at all their outsourcing, mainly IT, compliance and marketing services. "This may not be a quick fix, but if this recession runs for a couple of years, it will be worth it. I am also going to look at some of the service suppliers to see if we can secure what we need at a lower cost."

Aaron was talking about these issues to Frank Peters, a sole trader who has been in the business for over 25 years. Frank said, "This is one of the more difficult times we have experienced; I really need to cut my costs and make sure I spend as much time with clients as I can – I need to sustain my income." Aaron suggested that Frank think about using his and Roberta's back office and compliance support, for a fee, to get rid of his overheads and free up some time. To his surprise, Frank called him five days later and agreed: "Let's get this set up. I will ask my wife, who does some of the admin, to see Roberta so we can get this sorted; I don't want to sell out but I think this is worth pursuing."

The final piece of work that Aaron did was to think hard about latent potential in the client bank. "It's no good writing to clients about investments, pound cost averaging and buying in at the bottom, because most of them will not bite the bullet, and for some they probably shouldn't," he told Roberta. "But there are a lot in the 'silver' group that we have not contacted for at least two years. We should work out an approach and then set the advisers up to deliver it," he said. "After all, their incomes are also falling, so I am sure they will be up for a joint effort."

What had started out as a contingency plan had turned into a set of actions that they would take, with redundancy and reducing their drawings as a last resort. Roberta said, "We are going to have to monitor how we do really tightly over the next few months, and keep working with the advisers to find new approaches and keep their morale up. Also, we must talk with the staff to see how we can cut costs and take out waste without compromising service."

CASE STUDY KEY POINT

While you should always run the business as effectively as possible, it is usually the case that – when the market is good and turnover is rising – an increasing amount of slack develops. It is essential that you explore every opportunity to take this out if the market becomes difficult. Preparing a contingency plan for a recession is not much fun, but it is as important as any other activity. If you have the plan, you know what to do if certain trigger points are reached. Such a plan puts you in control; there is nothing worse than suddenly realising you have to make some serious changes and that you have little time to implement them.

3 How to increase sales volume and value

There are three main routes:

- Sell more to existing clients.
- Develop new services.
- Find new clients.

The chart in Figure 25.2 shows the paths to follow.

There are some specific actions that you can take here, although it is very important to concentrate on client groups that are likely to respond and to take full account of the cost of any additional service that you offer.

4 Sell more to existing clients

You should approach this in three parts:

- Offer additional services to new clients.
- Review existing clients more frequently.
- Work even harder on client retention.

arrangements and sorting them out.

- Tax saving: minimum charge to review income tax, holdings of tax savings products and IHT planning.
- Mortgages: free survey of the market to identify if any savings can be made (if nothing right now, add clients to the database for when current arrangements finish).
- Family and income protection: review to rebroker existing arrangements to save money.
- Recession and investments: complete review and rearrangement of portfolio in light of completely changed circumstances.

Clearly, you will have clients for whom this work has been done or additional reviews are not appropriate, but for dormant clients or those who are not seen very often, this approach is cheap to set up and should yield additional business. You can also use these specific services to target new clients, particularly if their current adviser is not paying them enough attention.

4.2 Up the pace of regular reviews

Reviewing existing clients more frequently means exactly what it says. This may not apply to the top group, but you could consider bringing forward the reviews of the lower value groups. For those who might only be reviewed bi-annually, bring the list forward six months or offer a full

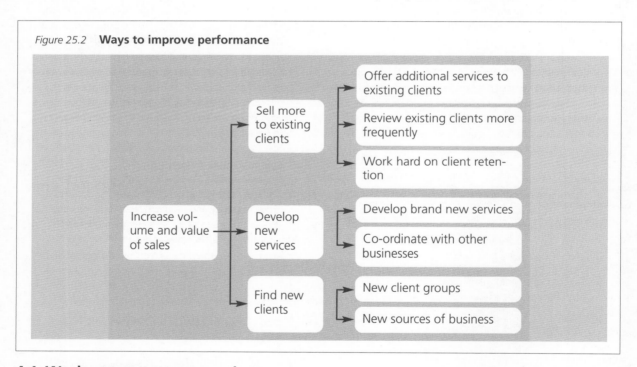

Figure 25.2 **Ways to improve performance**

Increase volume and value of sales →
- Sell more to existing clients →
  - Offer additional services to existing clients
  - Review existing clients more frequently
  - Work hard on client retention
- Develop new services →
  - Develop brand new services
  - Co-ordinate with other businesses
- Find new clients →
  - New client groups
  - New sources of business

4.1 Work out some new services

Offering **additional services** to existing clients does not mean adding extra service components, which will add cost. It means offering a specific piece of work or analysis for which you could charge and expect to transact additional products or funds or secure a new service contract. Examples for review include:

- Pensions: minimum charge for reviewing all existing

financial check up to a segment of dormant clients (ideally selected by value of product holdings to indicate potential).

4.3 Make sure you don't lose anyone valuable

You should always work hard on **client retention** as a matter of course and as discussed in Chapter 9. However, if the market is difficult due to stock market fluctuations or unforeseen economic developments, then additional contact is very important. This is a time when you can really demonstrate personal service by making contact with clients when they will most value it.

Contact needs to be timely and reassuring. Many people become confused during crises and misunderstand the situation. Communications with the following characteristics work well:

- Straightforward and factual: cut through the sensational headlines.
- Very few numbers and no jargon: clarity is key.
- Single side A4 maximum length: a good discipline for the writer and easier for the reader.
- Generic advice if possible: people always want to know what to do.
- Opportunity to contact you.

Advisers often avoid this, because they think it will generate a lot of questions or make people complain. There is little evidence to support this, although it depends on how well the adviser has explained the issues around risk and return in the past. If you communicate regularly with clients and pay particular attention to them when times are difficult, you will reduce the potential for complaints. Calls from anxious clients give you a further opportunity to retain them through empathy and clear explanation.

5 Develop new services

There are two parts to this:

- Develop brand new services.
- Co-ordinate with other businesses.

Development of brand new services is an extension of the new services you might offer existing clients. This goes a step further, and is about new services, possibly for new markets. For example, if you only deal with corporate clients, you could consider introducing personal financial planning for the directors and senior managers. If you run pension schemes but have no service for the workforce, you could work out how that could be delivered at the work place to firms with large numbers of employees.

Alternatively, if you normally concentrate on investments, there may be opportunities to diversify into pensions work. This is, of course, very easy to suggest and more difficult to put into practice, especially if you do not have the experience or qualifications required for these complementary market opportunities.

That is why this is coupled with **co-ordinating with other businesses**, and the networked relationships that you have will determine the extent to which you can offer such diversification in the short term. However, many advisers

use other businesses to undertake work for them, subject to a commercial arrangement. Pension transfers are the best example, but this also applies to mortgages, equity release and investment fund management. There may be opportunities for business alliances that pool the joint capability of both businesses to the benefit of both sets of clients and the firms.

6 The hardest part: find new clients

The approach to **finding new clients** has been covered in detail in Chapter 10 on client acquisition. As the heading suggests, this is the hardest part, particularly if trading conditions are difficult. The reality is that you may not have funds available for client acquisition, and the time it takes to open up new business sources, such as introducers, is too great if the pressures are immediate.

If conditions are better, this is an important route to pursue, and if you have introducers in place, you could review your approach and revisit them with fresh ideas and client opportunities. During a recession, they may well be very receptive, because they could also be suffering from adverse trading conditions. Chapter 10 deals with the detail of developing introducers.

7 Push hard for productivity

You can increase productivity and cut costs by reviewing:

- The productivity of each sale.
- People and process costs and efficiency.
- The effectiveness of resource use.
- Opportunities to rationalise.

These are summarised in Figure 25.3.

8 Push up client productivity

You can do this in three ways:

- Sell more services and products.
- Increase your prices.
- Cut the cost of acquiring business.

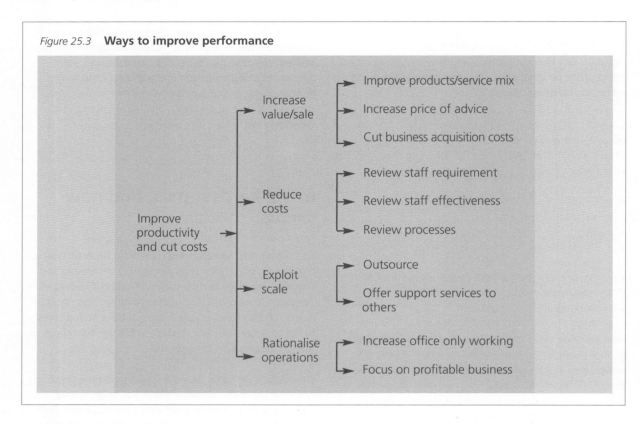

Figure 25.3 **Ways to improve performance**

8.1 Make sure your advisers are really thorough

Many principals complain that advisers do not identify all the advice and planning opportunities with clients, and fail to sell them the right level of service or the full range of products or funds that they need to implement their plan. To **improve the product and service mix**, you should:

- Raise the issue with advisers.
- Provide training in full fact finding.
- Role play and accompany them in client meetings.
- Review fact finds, reports and recommendations before the second client meeting.

8.2 When did you last review your prices?

This does not mean 'take more commission', because with the implementation of the Retail Distribution Review and the operation of Treating Customers Fairly, you need to think about the **price you charge for your advice services**. You should regard any payments from products as a means of helping the client pay for your services; that way, you can think about the price you charge far more constructively.

It is clear that if the market is difficult and clients are experiencing falls in the value of their investments, straightforward price increases may be hard to justify. However, regardless of circumstances, if you think you are not charging enough for some of your services or that some clients are losing you money, you should consider the following:

- Introduce minimum charges: this is much easier to do with new clients, but is perfectly reasonable for specific pieces of work for existing clients.
- Place a minimum charge on initial planning work for all new clients: that will remove the timewasters and make sure you get paid if people don't go ahead.
- Take the opportunity with any new service you offer to put a price on it from outset.
- Deal with specific clients where you are obviously losing money: these will all be one-off conversations, but they are important if you are heading for a loss.

8.3 Are you paying too much for introductions?

As the pressures on profit gradually increase, you should review your introducer **acquisition** costs. There are still instances where these exceed 25%, which is too high unless there are very special reasons. As with increasing the price of advice, you will need to work out how to deal with this, and raising the level of reciprocal business is a positive way to open the discussion.

In addition, if you are able to develop a specific joint campaign, it is reasonable to negotiate a different rate of return, which you could tier to provide an incentive for the introducer to make sure his part of the process works well.

Finally, if you are using an external marketing agency to generate appointments, make sure that your contract is based on payment by results and business written as opposed to the volume of leads. That way, you should get better quality leads and only pay for those that are up to standard.

9 Manage costs tightly

The chapters on making your business more efficient and recruiting and developing people are the source of the actions you can take here. There are three areas for review:

- Staff requirement.
- Staff effectiveness.
- Process efficiency.

9.1 Have you got the right number of people in the right jobs?

You need to review how **effective people are and how many you need** against the total volume of work and the different tasks that are required. Provided that your job descriptions and performance management records are up to date as discussed in Part 6, you can take these decisions fairly easily. Implementation is clearly more difficult, particularly if you have to make people redundant or move them to different jobs. However, if there is a recession, you have to think about how long the reduced workload is likely to last and what effect the loss of colleagues will have on the morale and productivity of those who remain.

9.2 Cut out waste

This is not about a full process review, but there should be a permanent effort to cut waste and make the current **processes more efficient**. You need to work with the staff on this, and explain very clearly that you need their continuing support to reduce unnecessary costs. This works well if you are honest and, particularly in a recession, you should make it clear that much of this is about preserving jobs as well as the business.

It may seem trivial, but prizes for the best ways of saving money or doing things quicker keep this high on the agenda, and if someone discovers a really awful way of doing things differently, don't concentrate on the negative but thank them for pointing it out. This is an activity that really does work better if you recognise positively the contributions that people make.

10 Run at lowest unit cost

This links to the previous Section but takes the actions a further step. You should consider:

- Outsourcing.
- Offering service to other advisers.

We covered **outsourcing** in detail in Chapter 18, and you should identify candidate activities that might save you

money if you pursue this route. Remember that a decision on outsourcing made 12 months ago may be different now in different circumstances. It may take a while to set up outsourced arrangements, but that should not deter you from reviewing this option.

Offering service to other advisers means that you can take up the slack in the back office, avoid losing good people in a recession (whom you will have to hire back when the market improves) and generate revenue. The speed with which you can take advantage of this approach depends on the strength of your networking with other advisers. You need to find out who may benefit from spending more time with their clients and doing less of their own administration.

In addition, selling your expertise to other advice businesses as in section 5 is just as important here.

11 Changing the way you do things

The final opportunity to cut costs is to step back and consider if there is anything fundamental that you can do without or change. This includes:

- Office-only working.
- Concentrating on profitable clients.

If you adopt **office-only working**, you will save a lot of travelling time and tend to deal with higher value clients who have a strong reason to travel to see you. It is recognised that not all clients can do this, but this does provide a good filter for profitable clients.

Advisers will often observe that if they spent time with only the **top 20% of clients**, they would have a more profitable business. If that is the case and you are certain that you will be more productive if you concentrate your attention, work out how some of the lower value clients can be dealt with by another adviser or para planner.

CASE STUDY

Prepare for change

White Personal Financial Planning, run by Roberta and Aaron Brown, had weathered the 2009-11 recession. Business was down around 15% compared to 2008, which had turned out to be flat against 2007. "Looking back over the past couple of years makes you realise how tough this has been," said Aaron. "We have effectively been marking time". Roberta agreed: "I wish we could have kept Brian and Sally, but at least it gave us good reason to part with Emma, who never really pulled her weight."

"I think we need to make sure we are completely ready to get back into growth mode when confidence fully returns, so we can hit the ground running," said Aaron, who was as always optimistic and positive. Roberta suggested that they dig out the 'Fine Tune Your Business' programme that Royal Blue Investment Group had given them, which, as Roberta said, "worked well when we hit the start of the recession, and should help us build our way out — we know our long term goals are right, but let's make sure we are ready to make up for two lost years!"

Roberta set up a half-day 'Prepare for Lift Off' session at the Windmill Inn, to which she invited the three senior advisers and two senior back office staff. "I want to make sure we have a broad perspective on this and that we have a good range of ideas. I might ask Mike Jones, who runs the Windmill, to give us 15 minutes on how he got his lovely country pub through such a difficult market — maybe we could learn something."

Mike agreed to talk through what he had done, and opened the meeting in a positive mood. "I didn't realise at the time how we were changing things and how adaptable we had been. In summary, we faced being one of the ten pubs that was closing every week, taking away everything we had built up. We decided we had to use our building better and take every opportunity to bring in money, however small it looked. We didn't change the type of customer, because we knew they had the money; we just had to get them to spend it." Aaron asked,

"Did you not think to go for a younger crowd and change one of your bars to attract them?"

Mike replied, "We thought long and hard about that, but we reckoned that would dilute our customer base, take us into a part of the market we were less familiar with, and hold us back when times improved; we didn't want to reduce our service and welcome to our core customers." Mike continued, "In essence, we increased the range of services: we had special menus, offers on our accommodation, facilities for business meetings like this, wine tastings and so on. We thought the extra variety would keep our customers interested and bring in a few more people — and set us up for better times."

It was the final point that Roberta picked up on when Mike went back to the bar. "We have followed a similar path, with the extra planning services we offered and the more frequent reviews, seeing the customers more and, like Mike, we stuck to the client base for the same reason: fear of dilution."

After a break, Roberta took the group through the 'fine tuning' charts and asked for thoughts and ideas. "As many as possible — it does not matter how wacky they are, let's use our imagination to see what we can do to get on the front foot."

The ideas that came top of the list were:

- Invite key clients and a friend or relative to an investment recovery seminar with one of the fund managers from Racing Green Fund Managers — the aim was to run this three times in a single day and get 100 people involved.
- Get back to the professional introducers to re-invigorate their capacity to introduce clients.
- Review their charges to coincide with the new 'adviser charge' from RDR.
- Think seriously about offering their investment service to other advisers who wanted to concentrate on planning and were less certain about the robustness of how they looked after clients' money.

"This is a good list," said Aaron. "We couldn't have done this six months ago, but I think we should start planning these and be ready when the time is right."

"I don't want to put a damper on proceedings," said Roberta, "but there must be some things we started 18 months ago that we should keep going — I know they felt negative at the time, but I don't think we should drop them now." Everyone agreed, and they decided to continue to sub-let the offices at the back of their building, stick with the more modest car policy and retain the 'Cost Cutter of the Month' award.

Roberta said, "We have a much better attitude to costs, efficiency and how we deal with clients than before the recession; we mustn't let that slip — it will give us a much stronger business as we move ahead."

In the bar at the end of the meeting, Aaron said, "I know we can't call the bottom of the stock markets or when the economy will really start to pick up, but we must be closer to the upturn and we know the markets will move quite quickly as they look through to the growth part of the cycle."

CASE STUDY KEY POINT

The steps of the fine tuning process can be applied at any time. They work well in recession and they ask the right questions to prepare for growth. Use them to structure your meeting whenever you need to work with your colleagues to generate ideas around cost cutting or new sources of revenue.

12 Chapter summary

The management skills you have developed as a result of this chapter mean that you can:

- Recognise when the business needs to be fine tuned.
- Use a structured approach to fine tuning.
- Make sure that all revenue generating and cost cutting opportunities are identified.
- Use fine tuning to keep the business on track to achieve its strategic objectives.

The greatest challenge is to find the time to undertake fine tuning. One of the best approaches is to bring it into staff and adviser meetings and use it as a process to generate ideas. When business is stable, you could do this twice a year, but an alternative approach would be to use it only when there is a strong reason that will secure the support and interest of others.